Other Kaplan Books for College-Bound Students

College Admissions and Financial Aid

Conquer the Cost of College

Kaplan/*Newsweek* College Catalog

Parent's Guide to College Admissions

Scholarships

The Yale Daily News Guide to Succeeding in College

Test Preparation

SAT & PSAT

SAT Verbal Velocity

SAT Math Mania

SAT II: Biology

SAT II: Chemistry

SAT II: Mathematics

SAT II: Writing

SAT Verbal Workbook

SAT Math Workbook

SAT or ACT? Test Your Best

ACT

KAPLAN

SAT*

ALL ☆ STAR

by the Staff of Kaplan, Inc.

Simon & Schuster

New York · London · Singapore · Sydney · Toronto

Kaplan Publishing
Published by Simon & Schuster
1230 Avenue of the Americas
New York, NY 10020

Contributing Editors: Trent Anderson, Marc Bernstein, Chad Schaedler, and Seppy Basili

Project Editor: Megan Duffy

Cover Design: Cheung Tai

Interior Page Layout: Michael Shevlin

Desktop Publishing Manager: Michael Shevlin

Editorial Coordinator: Deá Alessandro

Executive Editor: Del Franz

Thanks to: Michael Bitz and Darcy Galane

The material in this book is up-to-date at the time of publication. However, the College Entrance Examination Board may have instituted changes in the test after this book was published. Be sure to carefully read the materials you receive when you register for the test.

April 2001

10 9 8 7 6 5 4 3 2 1

Manufactured in the United States of America

Published simultaneously in Canada

ISBN 0-7432-2419-1

The Play Book

Round 5: Scrimmage: Practice Test and Explanations

Round 6: SAT Locker Room

Dear Student:

For more than 60 years, Kaplan has been helping students meet their academic and admissions goals. More than three million students have passed through our doors, and as their evaluations of our courses have repeatedly shown, one thing stands out that sets Kaplan apart from the rest: our teachers.

We have long known that our outstanding teaching staff is Kaplan's most important asset. Throughout the years we have committed ourselves to finding expert, enthusiastic, and engaging teachers for every Kaplan course. That's why we interview only those candidates who scored high on the test they are to teach and from this pool select only the most promising candidates: individuals who are enthusiastic about helping students reach their goals. All prospective teachers complete an intensive Kaplan training, and from ongoing observations, evaluations, and reviews of student feedback, they get even better as they teach.

The knowledge and experience that our teachers have acquired from working with students like you—about standardized tests, study habits, test panic, and more—is something we'd like to share outside of the classroom. We're pleased to incorporate the wisdom, tips, and inspiration of Kaplan's teachers in this test-prep guide so that you may benefit from the best we have to offer. I hope you find their expertise useful in your quest for academic success. If you decide you'd also like to work with our first-rate instructors in person, give us a call at (800) KAP-TEST.

Jonathan Grayer

President and CEO, Kaplan, Inc.

How to Use This Book: The Game Plan

Ideally, you should take a month or more to work through this book, though it's certainly possible to read it in less time. Here's how you should go about training with it:

1. Read through each chapter completely, learning from the example problems and trying the practice problems. In the "SAT Locker Room" section, you'll find a root list and a word teams list, as well as a review of the 100 most important math concepts to know for the SAT.
2. At the beginning of each chapter, there is a Highlights box containing the most important concepts in the chapter. At the end of most chapters, you'll find a Replay list that allows you to check off the concepts as you master them.
3. Read the chapter on stress management to set the stage for your training and testing success.
4. Take the Practice Test under strictly timed conditions.
5. Score your Practice Test. Find out where you need help and then review the appropriate chapters.
6. Reread all the Highlights boxes once more to help review your areas of weakness.
7. Give yourself a day of rest right before the real exam.

Q. Where did Michael Jordan play college basketball, and what was his major?

If you have time, do just two or three chapters a week, and let the material sink in slowly. Don't hesitate to take some time off from your SAT preparation when you need to. Nobody can take this stuff day in and day out for weeks at a time without a break.

Throughout this book you'll also find sports-trivia questions that will stretch your test-taking muscles. The answers start on page 301. Good luck!

How to Use This Book: The Two-Minute Drill

Maybe you have only two or three weeks—or even less time than that. *SAT All*Star* has been designed to work for students in your situation, too. If you go through a chapter or two every day, you can finish this book in a couple of weeks. If you have limited time to prepare for the SAT (fewer than two weeks), we suggest you do the following:

1. If you're feeling totally stressed out, take a slow, deep breath. Read "In the Zone: Stress Management" to maximize your study and testing time.
2. Read the "Rules of the Game" chapter.
3. Read the "Two-Minute Drill" sidebar at the beginning of each chapter. The suggestions in these sidebars can really streamline your study strategy as well as ensure that you cover the vital concepts before Test Day.
4. Take the Practice Test—*under timed conditions*.
5. Review your results, with special attention to the questions you missed.
6. Give yourself the day before the test off.

Scattered throughout the text you'll find "hints"—special points that we feel deserve emphasis and amplification. Pay special attention to these hints, which spotlight some very important test prep information. Sidebars also highlight key concepts and strategies, fun facts, and real-world stories.

What to Do If You're Out of Your League

Q. It's two days before the SAT and I'm clueless. What should I do?

A. First of all, don't panic. If you only have a day or two to prepare for the test, then you don't have time to prepare thoroughly. But that doesn't mean you should just give up. There's still a lot you can do to improve your potential score. First and foremost, you should become familiar with the test. Read the "Rules of the Game" chapter. And if you don't do anything else, take the full-length practice test at the back of this book under reasonably testlike conditions. When you finish the practice test, check your answers and look at the explanations to the questions you didn't get right.

Q. Math is my weak spot. What can I do to get better at math in a big hurry?

A. Review the "SAT Math Scouting Report" chapter, which highlights the 100 key math concepts for the SAT. Then do as many of the sample problems in chapter 12, "Problem Solving," as you have time for. If you don't have time to do the sample problems, just read the sidebars in the math chapters. They contain really helpful facts and tips.

Q. I'm great at Math, but Verbal scares me. How can I improve my Verbal score right away?

A. Go straight to the section called "Decoding Strange Words on the Test" in chapter 3. Much of the SAT Verbal depends on your ability to work with unfamiliar words. It's also a good idea to check out the SAT Word Teams, as well as the SAT Root List. Then do as many of the sample problems in the Verbal chapters as you have time for. If you don't have time to do the sample problems, just read the sidebars in those chapters. These strategies can help boost your score.

Q. I get to use a calculator on the SAT! Does that mean I don't have to worry about learning math?

A. Not exactly. You ARE allowed to bring a calculator to the SAT, but that's actually a mixed blessing. If you don't use your calculator wisely, you could actually end up wasting time or, even worse, generating wrong answers. Make sure to read the "Equipment: Calculators" chapter, particularly the pages on Common Calculator Mistakes, before you take the test. Knowing when and how to use your calculator will help you immeasurably. And remember, your calculator won't think for you!

Q. My parents are upset with me for waiting till the last minute to study, and now I can't concentrate. Help!

A. Take a deep breath! Anxiety and stress are the enemies of all test takers—no matter how much time they have to prepare. Turn to chapter 15 and read through Kaplan's suggestions for managing stress. Do the suggested exercises. And don't forget to think positively!

Q: The SAT is tomorrow. Should I stay up all night studying geometry formulas?

A: The best thing to do right now is to try to stay calm. Read the "Peaking at the Right Time" chapter to find out the best way to survive, and thrive, on Test Day. And get a good night's sleep.

Q: I don't feel confident. Should I just guess?

A: You should always guess if you can do so intelligently. The SAT does have a wrong answer penalty for most question types, but that doesn't mean you should never guess. If you can rule out even ONE answer choice, you should guess, because you have significantly increased your chances of guessing correctly. Also, on questions that appear early in a section, more obvious answers will tend to be correct, so you can guess more confidently on those questions. Finally, always guess on Grid-ins, since there is no wrong answer penalty on that question type.

Q: What's the most important thing I can do to get ready for the SAT quickly?

A. In addition to basic Math and Verbal skills, the SAT mainly tests your ability to take the SAT. Therefore, the most important thing you can do is to familiarize yourself with the directions, the question types, the answer grid, and the overall structure of the test. Make sure you feel comfortable with the logistics—how to get to your test center, how to fill in Grid-ins, how (and when) to use your calculator. Read every question carefully—many mistakes are the result of simply not reading thoroughly.

Q. Who is the youngest Grand Slam singles champion in women's tennis?

Q. So it's a good idea to panic, right? RIGHT?

A. No! No matter how prepared you are for the SAT, stress will hurt your performance, and it's really no fun. Stay confident, and don't cram. So . . . breathe. Stay calm, and remember, it's just a test.

ROUND 1

Pre-Game

1

Rules of the Game

HIGHLIGHTS

- Familiarize yourself with the breakdown of questions
- Learn how the test is timed and scored
- Learn how to use the structure of the SAT to your advantage
- Formulate a plan for attacking the questions

To perform well on the SAT, you need to draw on a set of skills that the College Board does not mention in any of their materials. You need to be a good SAT test taker.

Acquiring this ability, and the confidence it produces, is what this book is about.

There are three simple things you need to master the SAT:

- You need to have a basic understanding of SAT content.
- You need to hone the thinking and testing skills that underlie the SAT.
- You need to know the nature of the SAT.

Two-Minute Drill

If you have just a few weeks to prep for the SAT, don't panic. The first thing you should do is become familiar with the test. This chapter is the place to start.

Content and skills are obviously important. You can't do well without them. But understanding the nature of the SAT, its setup, its structure, and the traps it often sets for you will allow you to gain points on the test that you might not otherwise have earned.

When you sit down to take the test, you should already know what kind of questions you'll find, what the instructions say, how the test will be scored, and how you will be timed.

Q. What major American sport has the most rules?

STRUCTURE OF THE TEST

There are six types of questions on the SAT, three Verbal and three Math. The likely number of questions you'll see of each type is shown below.

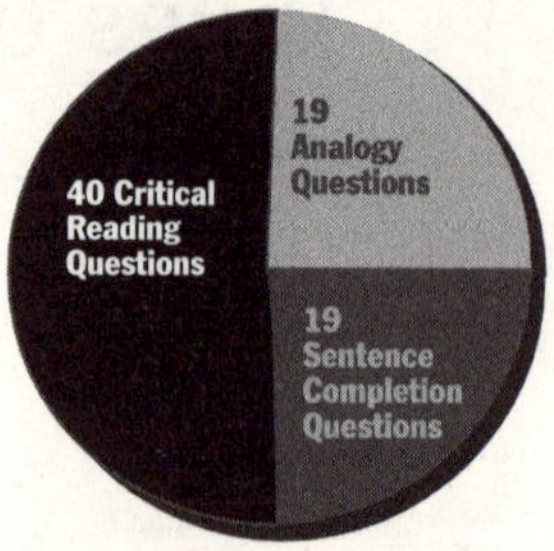

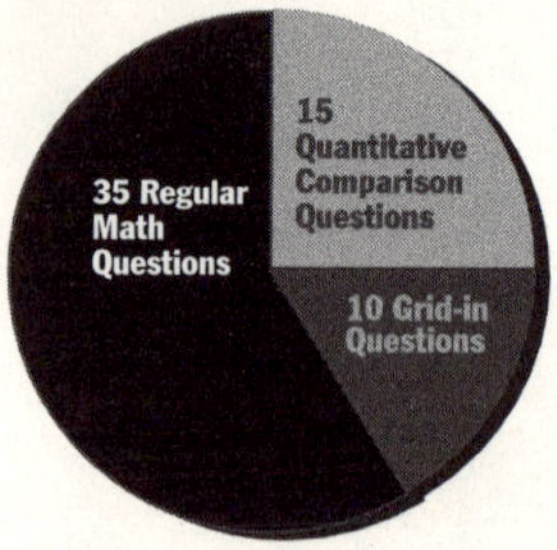

Verbal

On the Verbal section of the SAT you'll find:

- 19 *Analogies*—Analogies test your ability to see relationships between words.
- 19 *Sentence Completions*—These test your ability to see how the parts of a sentence relate. About half will have one word missing from a sentence; the rest will have two words missing. Both types test vocabulary knowledge and reasoning ability.
- *40 Critical Reading questions*, in four separate sets—Critical Reading tests your ability to read and understand a passage. The passages are long (400–850 words), and at least one passage contains two related readings. Some reading questions test your understanding of the content of the passage; others will require you to draw conclusions. Some will also explicitly test vocabulary in context.

Kaplan Rules

Getting familiar with the SAT can get you a higher score on the SAT. Once you know the setup of the test and you've learned what to expect, you'll be more confident about your ability to master every section and question type. Familiarity gives you confidence and confidence gets you points.

Math

On the Math section you'll find:

- 15 *Quantitative Comparisons*—QCs, as they're called, give you two quantities and ask you to compare them. You have to determine if one quantity is larger, if they're equal, or if you don't have enough information to decide. They test your knowledge of math, your ability to apply that knowledge, and your reasoning ability. They're also designed to be done quickly, making them a good source of quick points.
- 35 *Regular Math* questions—These are straightforward multiple-choice math questions, with five answer choices.
- *Ten Grid-ins*—These questions are open-ended, with no answer choices. Instead, you enter your response into a small grid. These questions test the same math concepts as the other types of questions.

SECTION BREAKDOWN

The SAT is divided into seven sections, which can appear in any order:

- Two 30-minute Verbal sections with Analogies, Sentence Completions, and Critical Reading
- One 15-minute Verbal section with Critical Reading
- One 30-minute section with QCs and Grid-ins
- One 30-minute section with Regular Math
- One 15-minute section with Regular Math

There is also one 30-minute Experimental section. This section does not affect your score and is used to try out new questions. It can show up anyplace and it will look like any other Verbal or Math section. Don't try to figure out which section is experimental so you can nap during that period. First of all, you'll lose your momentum in the middle of the test. Second, and more important, you might be wrong.

SCORING

You get one point added to your score for each correct answer on the SAT, and lose a fraction of a point for each wrong answer (except for Grid-ins—but we'll go into that later). If you leave a question blank, you neither gain nor lose points. The totals are added up for all the Verbal and Math questions, and that produces two raw scores.

These numbers aren't your SAT scores. The raw scores are converted into scaled scores, each on a scale of 200 to 800, and these are the scores that are reported to you and the colleges you choose. (The reports include subscores as well, but most colleges focus on the two main scores.)

Did You Know . . .

. . . that a little bit of improvement on the SAT can go a long way? Getting just one extra question right every ten minutes on the SAT translates to 15 more questions right over the entire test. This improvement could boost your scaled score by close to 150 points.

In April of 1995, the College Board adjusted or "recentered" the scoring of the SAT. The average scaled score (on a 200- to 800-point scale) for either Math or Verbal is now 500, for an average combined score of 1,000 points. This is almost 100 points higher than the old combined averages. The test isn't any easier or harder; only the scoring has changed.

Bottom line: If you compared your SAT score with that of someone who took the test before 1995 (someone who got the exact number of questions right as you did), your score would probably be higher. Sounds great, right?

Well, it's not so cut-and-dried. Remember, everyone's score is adjusted, so you'll fall in the same percentile range using this new scale as you would using the old. The percentile is the percentage of SAT takers scoring at or below a given score.

WORKING THE CLOCK

The SAT:

- Is three hours long
- Includes two ten-minute breaks (after Sections 2 and 4)

There are some rules about how you can and cannot allocate this time:

- You are not allowed to jump back and forth between sections.
- You are not allowed to return to earlier sections to change answers.
- You are not allowed to spend more than the allotted time on any section.
- You can move around within a section.
- You can flip through your section at the beginning to see what type of questions you have.

Q. How long does an NBA team have to shoot the ball?

You'll get more familiar with the format and setup of the SAT as you work your way through this book. For now, just remember the basics: The SAT is predictable, there are elements built right into the test that allow you to prep for it, and you need to develop an approach to answering the questions.

USING THE STRUCTURE OF THE SAT TO YOUR ADVANTAGE

The SAT is different from the tests that you're used to taking. On a school test, you probably go through the problems in order. You spend more time on the hard questions than on easy ones, since this is where you get more points. And you often show your work since the teacher tells you that how you approach a problem is as important as getting the answer right.

None of this works on the SAT. You can benefit from moving around within a section, the hard questions are worth the same as the easy ones, and it doesn't matter how you answer the question—only what your answer is.

To succeed in this peculiar context, you need to know some fundamentals about the overall structure of the SAT.

A Different Kind of Test

The SAT is not like the tests you take in school. In school, you might need to get about 85 or 90 percent of the questions right to get a decent score. On the SAT, you sometimes need little more than 75 percent of the questions right to get a 1300—a very solid combined score.

The SAT Is Highly Predictable

Because the format and directions of the SAT remain unchanged from test to test, you can learn the setup in advance. On the day of the test, Analogies, QCs, Grid-ins—or the setup of any other question type or section—shouldn't be new to you.

One of the easiest things you can do to help your performance on the SAT is to understand the directions before taking the test. Since the instructions are always exactly the same, there's no reason to waste your time on the day of the test reading them. Learn them beforehand, as you go through this book, and skip them during the test.

Most SAT Questions Are Arranged by Order of Difficulty

You've probably noticed that not all the questions on the SAT are equally difficult. Except for the Critical Reading problems, the questions are designed to get tougher as you work through a set.

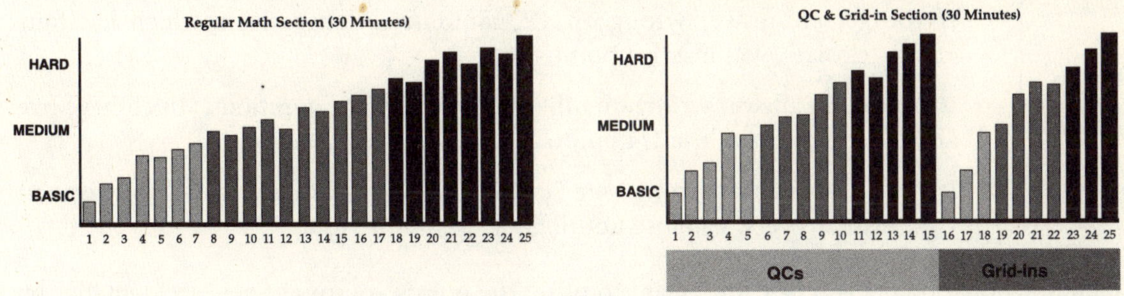

Questions get harder as you move through a section.

Here's how to use this pattern to your advantage. As you work, you should always be aware of where you are in the set. When working on the easy problems, you can generally trust your first impulse—the obvious answer is likely to be right.

As you get to the end of the set, you need to become more suspicious. Now the answers probably won't come easy. If they do, look at the problem again, because the obvious answer is likely to be wrong. Watch out for the answer that just "looks right." It may be a *distractor*—a wrong answer choice meant to entice you.

Q. Who was the last Major League batter to hit .400?

There's No Mandatory Order to the Questions

You're allowed to skip around within each section of the SAT. High scorers know this. They move through the test efficiently. They don't dwell on any one question, even a hard one, until they've tried every question at least once.

When you run into questions that look tough, circle them in your test booklet and skip them for the time being. Go back and try again after you have answered the easier ones if you have time. On a second look, troublesome questions can turn out to be amazingly simple.

If you've started answering a question and get confused, quit and go on to the next question. Persistence may pay off in school, but it usually hurts your SAT score. Don't spend so much time answering one tough question that you use up three or four questions' worth of time. That costs you points, especially if you don't get the hard question right.

Kaplan Rules

DON'T GUESS, unless you can eliminate at least one answer choice.

DON'T SKIP IT, unless you have absolutely no idea.

There's a Guessing Penalty That Can Work in Your Favor

The test makers like to talk about the guessing penalty on the SAT. This is a misnomer. It's really a *wrong answer* penalty. If you guess wrong you get penalized. If you guess right, you're in great shape.

Q. Approximately how many dimples are on a golf ball?

(A) 40

(B) 400

(C) 4,000

The fact is, if you can eliminate one or more answers as definitely wrong, you'll turn the odds in your favor and *actually come out ahead* by guessing.

Here's how the penalty works:

- If you get an answer wrong on a Quantitative Comparison, which has four answer choices, you lose 1/3 point.
- If you get an answer wrong on other multiple-choice questions, which have five answer choices, you lose 1/4 point.
- If you get an answer wrong on a Grid-in math question, for which you write in your own answers, you lose nothing.

The fractional points you lose are meant to offset the points you might get "accidentally" by guessing the correct answer. With practice, however, you'll learn that it's often easy to eliminate several answer choices on some of the problems that you see. By learning the techniques for eliminating wrong answer choices, you can actually turn the guessing "penalty" to your advantage.

The Answer Grid Has No Heart

It sounds simple but it's extremely important: Don't make mistakes filling out your answer grid. When time is short, it's easy to get confused going back and forth between your test book and your grid. If you know the answer, but misgrid, you won't get the points. To avoid mistakes on the answer grid:

Circle Before You Skip

A common cause of major SAT disasters is filling in all of the questions with the right answers—in the wrong spots.

Every time you skip a question, circle it in your test book and make doubly sure that you skip it on the answer grid as well.

Always Circle the Questions You Skip

Put a big circle in your test book around any question numbers you skip. When you go back, these questions will be easy to locate. Also, if you accidentally skip a box on the grid, you can check your grid against your book to see where you went wrong.

Always Circle the Answers You Choose

Circling your answers in the test book makes it easier to check your grid against your book.

Grid Five or More Answers at Once

Don't transfer your answers to the grid after every question. Transfer your answers after every five questions, or at the end of each reading passage. That way, you won't keep breaking your concentration to mark the grid. You'll save time and you'll gain accuracy.

These fundamentals apply to every section of the test. But each question type also has its own structural peculiarities that make them easy to prep for. Some examples: On Grid-ins, the grid cannot accommodate five-digit answers, negatives, or variables. If you get such an answer, you know you've made a mistake and need to redo the problem.

Analogy answer choices are always ordered with the same parts of speech; this helps you determine if you're building an appropriate bridge.

Critical Reading questions with line references, "Little Picture" questions, can often be done quickly and don't require you to read the entire passage. You can do these first in a later reading passage if you're running out of time.

We'll show you lots of these structural elements, and the strategies you can use to take advantage of them, throughout this book.

Transferring Your Answers

You need to be careful at the end of a section when time may be running out. You don't want to have your answers in the test booklet and not be able to transfer them to your answer grid because you have run out of time.

APPROACHING SAT QUESTIONS

Apart from knowing the setup of the SAT, you've got to have a system for attacking the questions. You wouldn't travel around a foreign city without a map and you shouldn't approach the SAT without a plan. Now that you know some basics about how the test is set up, you can approach each section a little more strategically. What follows is the best method for approaching SAT questions systematically.

Think about the Question Before You Look at the Answer

The people who make the test love to put distractors among the answer choices. Distractors are answer choices that look like the right answer, but aren't. If you jump right into the answer choices without thinking first about what you're looking for, you're much more likely to fall for one of these traps.

SAT Myth

Some people believe that the SAT is an absolute predictor of college performance. Not true—despite the fact that female students score about 43 points lower than male students on the SAT, females tend to earn higher grades in both high school and college!

Use Backdoor Strategies If the Answer Doesn't Come to You

There are usually a number of ways to get to the right answer on an SAT question. Most of the questions on the SAT are multiple-choice. That means the answer is right in front of you—you just have to find it. This makes SAT questions open to a lot of ways of finding the answer. If you can't figure out the answer in a straightforward way, try other techniques. We'll talk about specific Kaplan methods such as backsolving, picking numbers, and eliminating weak Analogy bridges in later chapters.

Guess Only When You Can Eliminate One Answer Choice

You already know that the wrong answer "penalty" can work in your favor. Don't simply skip questions that you can't answer. Spend some time with them to see if you can eliminate any of the answer choices. If you can, it pays for you to guess.

Recommended Timing

Section	On Average
Analogies	40 seconds
Sentence Completions	40 seconds
Critical Reading*	75 seconds
Regular Math	70 seconds
QCs	45 seconds
Grid-ins	90 seconds

* Average time for Critical Reading includes time to read the passage. Spend about 30 secs. per question.

Pace Yourself

The SAT gives you a lot of questions in a short period of time. To get through a whole section, you can't spend too much time on any one question. Keep moving through the test at a good speed; if you run into a hard question, circle it in your test booklet, skip it, and come back to it later if you have time.

In the sidebar to the right are recommended average times per question. This doesn't mean that you should spend exactly 40 seconds on every Analogy. It's a guide. Remember, the questions get harder as you move through a problem set. Ideally, you can work through the easy problems at a brisk, steady clip, and use a little more of your time for the harder ones that come at the end of the set.

One caution: Don't completely rush through the easy problems just to save time for the harder ones. These early problems are points in your pocket, and you're better off not getting to the last couple of problems than losing these easy points.

Locate Quick Points If You're Running Out of Time

Some questions can be done quickly; for instance, some reading questions will ask you to identify the meaning of a particular word in the passage. These can be done at the last minute, even if you haven't read the passage. On most Quantitative Comparisons, even the hardest ones, you can quickly eliminate at least one answer, improving your chances of guessing correctly. When you start to run out of time, locate and answer any of the quick points that remain.

Q. Name the French city that annually hosts an endurance auto race.

Because it's a standardized test, you can feel safe in knowing that the structure, contents, and questions on the SAT will be pretty much what you should expect after working your way through this book.

When you take the SAT, you have one clear objective in mind—to score as many points as you can. It's that simple. The rest of this book will help you do it.

ROUND 2

Verbal Skills Workout

2

The Rules: SAT Verbal

HIGHLIGHTS

- Understand the breakdown and setup of the Verbal section
- Tap into existing Verbal skills such as paraphrasing and making inferences

Imagine yourself racing through Le Mans, France. As you approach an intersection, you see a red octagonal sign with the word *arrêtez* on it. Even if you don't speak a word of French, you come to a stop and look down the crossroads before driving on through the city.

If you didn't know the language, you probably took the information given to you—the shape, color, and location of the sign—and related it to what you already know. You may also have noticed, maybe subconsciously, that *arrêtez* sounds something like *arrest*, which means "stop."

The skills you displayed by making this deduction are skills of inference. To do well on the SAT Verbal section, you need to apply these same skills. The SAT does not test spelling or grammar. It does not test your knowledge of English literature or literary terms. It will never ask you to interpret a poem. SAT Verbal questions cover a fairly predictable, fairly limited body of skills and knowledge: vocabulary, verbal reasoning, and reading skills.

Two-Minute Drill

This chapter will help you get a handle on the SAT Verbal section. You should read this chapter even if you have two weeks or fewer to prep.

There are three scored Verbal sections on the SAT. The breakdown of the questions will go something like this:

What Matters

Your score on the Verbal section is based on your ability to do the following:

- Solve analogies by finding two words that are related in the same way as the two words they give you.
- Fill in the blanks in sentences that are missing one or two words.
- Read a passage and answer a bunch of questions about it.

- One 30-minute section with nine Sentence Completions, 13 Analogies, and 13 Critical Reading questions
- One 30-minute section with ten Sentence Completions, six Analogies, and 14 Critical Reading questions
- One 15-minute section with 13 Critical Reading questions

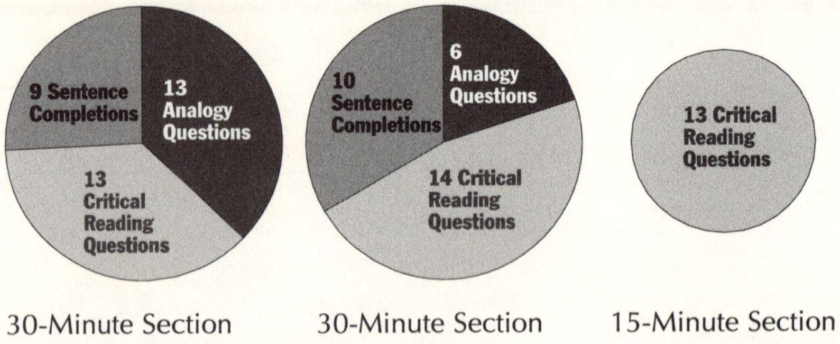

The Sentence Completions and Analogy sets are arranged by order of difficulty. The first few questions in a set are meant to be fairly straightforward and manageable. The middle few questions will be a little harder and the last few are the most difficult. Keep this in mind as you work and move through the early questions a little more quickly to leave yourself more time for the difficult ones. Work through the Sentence Completions and Analogies quickly and efficiently. Make sure you get all the points you can there, and then move on to Reading.

Critical Reading is not arranged by difficulty. Any time you find yourself beginning to spend too much time on a question, you should skip it and return to it later.

HOW TO APPROACH SAT VERBAL

To do well on SAT Verbal, you need to be systematic in your approach to each question type and each of the three Verbal sections. Sentence Completions and Analogies are designed to be done relatively quickly. That means you can earn points fast, so you should do these first. Critical Reading takes a lot longer, so you can't just leave yourself five minutes to do a passage. Remember, you earn just as many points for an easy question as you do for a hard one.

What Doesn't Matter

You don't need to know pronunciation, antonyms, foreign languages, creative writing, spelling, or anything about literature.

Tapping Your Verbal Skills

Although the test materials never explain this, a big key to doing well on the verbal part of the SAT is sharpening your verbal critical thinking skills—skills that you already use every day.

If you get to a movie ten minutes late, do you give up and walk out, deciding you'll never understand what's going on? Probably not. Instead, you use your inference skills—the ability to draw valid conclusions from limited information—to catch up and enjoy the rest of the film.

If you have a sudden urge for a tub of popcorn, do you leave during the climactic scene? More likely, you use your ability to distinguish important concepts from minor details to pick a dull moment to make your move.

When your younger brother asks you what the movie was about, do you take two hours to explain it to him? You probably use your paraphrasing skills—the ability to condense complex ideas into a few words—to give him the highlights in a few minutes before you go back to ignoring him.

Know What to Expect

Doing your best on SAT Verbal comes from knowing what to expect, and knowing that you have the skills to handle it. You use words every day. You make your own ideas clear and you understand and respond to those of others. In all of these cases—talking with friends or talking with teachers, reading a textbook or reading a billboard, listening to lyrics or listening to your SAT proctor's instructions—you take limited information, process it through your own intellect and experience, and make sense of it. If you can learn to make the most of these skills on the test, you'll be well on the road to a great Verbal score.

Q. In what city were the first modern Olympics held? How about the 1996 Olympics?

3

Vocabulary

HIGHLIGHTS

- Practice working with unfamiliar words and familiar words with secondary meanings
- Improve your vocabulary by studying word roots and families
- Find out how to decode strange words

You know how to read. You can explain the relationship between *kitten* and *cat* to a three-year-old. You can finish a friend's sentence when she sneezes in the middle. So what makes the Verbal section such a challenge? Vocabulary. You may have a solid understanding of a Critical Reading passage but then get thrown by one tough vocabulary word. You may know the relationship between the original pair of words in an Analogy, but have a tough time finding the answer because all the choices have words you've never seen before. You may know precisely what kind of word to fill in on a Sentence Completion, and then find that all the answer choices look like they're in a foreign language.

All three Verbal question types—Analogies, Sentence Completions, and Critical Reading—depend upon your ability to work with unfamiliar words. You won't be asked to define words on the SAT. But you'll need to have a sense of their meaning in order to answer the questions.

Two-Minute Drill

If you have only a week or two to prep for the SAT, go straight to the section called "Decoding Strange Words on the Test" and try to master those skills.

TWO TYPES OF HARD WORDS

There are two types of hard SAT words:

- Unfamiliar words
- Familiar words with secondary meanings

Who Cares?

Somewhere in the process of studying for the Verbal section, you may decide that learning the difference between *taciturn* and *tenacious, obdurate,* and *obloquy*, and even *plaudit* and *pusillanimous* is among the silliest things you've ever done. After all, no one on television talks that way.

Your vocabulary says a lot about your ability to express yourself, as well as giving some valuable hints as to how well read you are. Colleges like students with big vocabularies, so humor them. Learn some new words.

The single best way to do well on SAT verbal is to read as much as possible. Read newspapers and magazines to see words in use. Underline the ones you need to look up. If you recognize the words you see on the exam, you'll be on your way to acing the SAT.

Some words are hard because you haven't seen them before. The words *scintilla* or *circumlocution*, for instance, are probably not part of your everyday vocabulary. But they might pop up on your SAT.

Easy words, such as *recognize* or *appreciation*, may also trip you up on the test because they have secondary meanings that you aren't used to. Analogies and Critical Reading in particular will throw you familiar words with unfamiliar meanings.

To get a sense of your vocabulary strength, we've provided a representative list of words you might find on the SAT. Take a couple of minutes to look through it and see how many you know. Write your answer right in the book. Give yourself one point for each word you know. (Answers follow the quiz.)

irritate ____________________

truthful ____________________

conquer ____________________

passionate ____________________

inactive ____________________

eliminate ____________________

benevolent ____________________

elocution ____________________

irk ____________________

pragmatic ____________________

breadth ____________________

rectify ____________________

duplicity ____________________

impartial ____________________

abandon (n.) ____________________

vie ____________________

overt ____________________

august (adj.) ____________________

laud ____________________

voluble ____________________

flag (v.) ____________________

perspicacity ____________________

maladroit ____________________

sonorous ____________________

doleful ____________________

serpentine ____________________

rail (v.) ____________________

quiescence ____________________

idiosyncrasy ____________________

kudos ____________________

Q. What NFL team's *indomitable* defense was nicknamed "The Purple People Eaters"?

Strange Word Origins

Learning the derivation of words can often help you remember the meaning of words. Did you know . . .

- *Jovial* (joyful) comes from the Roman deity Jove, who was known for his pleasant disposition.
- *Sardonic* (characterized by bitter mockery) comes from sardinia, a mythical plant from the island of the same name. Ingestion of the plant caused convulsive laughter followed by death.
- *Maudlin* (overly sentimental) comes from Mary Magdalene, a follower of Christ who is shown weeping in many paintings. *Maudlin* is an alternate pronunciation of Magdalene.

Here are the definitions of the words in the list on the previous page:

irritate	to annoy, bother
truthful	honest, straightforward, trustworthy
conquer	to defeat, overthrow
passionate	emotional, ardent, enthusiastic
inactive	not active, not moving
eliminate	to get rid of
benevolent	generous, kind
elocution	the study and practice of public speaking
irk	to irritate, anger, annoy
pragmatic	practical; moved by facts rather than abstract ideal
breadth	broadness, wideness
rectify	to correct
duplicity	deception, dishonesty, double-dealing
impartial	fair, just, unbiased, unprejudiced
abandon (n.)	total lack of inhibition
vie	to compete, contend
overt	apparent, unconcealed
august (adj.)	dignified, awe-inspiring, venerable
laud	to praise, applaud, honor
voluble	speaking much and easily, talkative; glib
flag (v.)	to droop, lose energy; to signal, to mark
perspicacity	shrewdness, astuteness, keenness of wit
maladroit	clumsy, tactless
sonorous	producing a full, rich sound
doleful	sad, mournful
serpentine	serpentlike; twisting, winding
rail (v.)	to scold with bitter or abusive language
quiescence	inactivity, stillness
idiosyncrasy	peculiarity of temperament, eccentricity
kudos	fame, glory, honor

If you got ten definitions or fewer right, you should probably work on building your vocabulary. The techniques and tools in this chapter will help you improve your vocabulary and make the most out of what you do know about words.

If you got between 10 and 20 right, your vocabulary is average. If you're willing to put in the time, using these techniques and tools can help you do better.

If you got 20 definitions or more right, your vocabulary is in great shape. You can polish it further, but you don't have to. If time is short, learn the strategies in the "Decoding Strange Words" section and concentrate on other aspects of the SAT that you find difficult.

A VOCABULARY-BUILDING PLAN

A great vocabulary can't be built overnight, but you can develop a better SAT vocabulary with a minimum of pain. Here's a plan:

Learn Words Strategically

The best words to learn are words that have appeared often on the SAT. The test makers are not very creative in their choice of words for each test; words that have appeared frequently are likely bets to show up again.

> Q. College basketball's "Lew Alcinder Rule" temporarily *eliminated* what type of scoring play?

The Word Teams list in the "SAT Locker Room" section of this book groups words into common meaning families. For example, *loquacious, verbose,* and *garrulous* all mean "wordy, talkative." *Taciturn, laconic, terse, concise,* and *pithy* all mean "not talkative, not wordy." Instead of learning just one of these words, learn them all together—you get eight words for the price of one definition.

Be strategic. How well you use your time between now and the day of the test is just as important as how much time you spend prepping.

Work with Word Roots

Most SAT words are made up of prefixes and roots that can get you at least partway to a definition. Often, that's all you need to get a right answer.

Use the Root List in the "SAT Locker Room" section to pick up the most valuable SAT roots. Target these words in your vocabulary prep. Learn a few new roots a day, familiarizing yourself with the meaning.

Personalize Your Vocabulary Study

Figure out a study method that works best for you, and stick to it.

- Use flashcards: Write down new words or word groups and run through them whenever you have a few spare minutes. Put one new word or word group on one side of a 3 × 5 index card and a short definition on the back.

- Make a vocabulary notebook: List words in one column and their meaning in another. Test yourself. Cover up the meanings, and see which words you can define from memory. Make a sample sentence using each word in context.

Personalize Your Home Study

- Use flashcards.
- Make a vocabulary notebook.
- Make a vocabulary tape.
- Look for hooks or phrases that will lodge a new word in your mind.

- Make a vocabulary tape: Record unknown words and their definitions. Pause for a moment before you read the definition. This will give you time to define the word in your head when you play the tape back. Quiz yourself. Listen to your tape in your portable cassette player. Play it in the car, on the bus, or whenever you have a few spare moments.
- Think of hooks that lodge a new word in your mind: Create visual images of words.
- Use rhymes and other devices that help you remember the words.

It doesn't matter which techniques you use, as long as you learn words steadily and methodically. Doing so over several months is ideal.

DECODING STRANGE WORDS ON THE TEST

Trying to learn every word that could possibly appear on the SAT is like trying to memorize the license plate number of every car on the freeway. It's not much fun, it'll give you a headache, and you probably won't pull it off.

No matter how much time you spend with flashcards, vocabulary tapes, or word lists, you're bound to face some mystery words on your SAT. No big deal. Just as you can use your basic multiplication skills to find the product of even the largest numbers, you can use what you know about words to focus on likely meanings of tough vocabulary words.

Go with Your Hunches

When you look at an unfamiliar word, your first reaction may be to say, "Don't know it. Gotta skip it." Not so fast. Vocabulary knowledge on the SAT is not an all-or-nothing proposition.

- Some words you know so well you can rattle off a dictionary definition of them.
- Some words you "sort of" know. You understand them when you see them in context, but don't feel confident using them yourself.
- Some words are vaguely familiar. You know you've heard them somewhere before.

If you think you recognize a word, go with your hunch!

Try to Recall Where You've Heard the Word Before

If you can recall a phrase in which the word appears, that may be enough to eliminate some answer choices, or even zero in on the right answer.

EXAMPLE

Between the two villages was a ---- through which passage was difficult and hazardous.

(A) precipice

(B) beachhead

(C) quagmire

(D) market

(E) prairie

To answer this question, it helps to know the word *quagmire*. You may remember *quagmire* from news reports referring to "a foreign policy *quagmire*" or "a *quagmire* of financial indebtedness." If you can remember how *quagmire* was used, you'll have a rough idea of what it means, and you'll see it fits. You may also be reminded of the word *mire*, as in "We got *mired* in the small details and never got to the larger issue." Sounds something like stuck, right? You don't need an exact definition. A *quagmire* is a situation that's difficult to get out of, so (C) is correct. Literally, a *quagmire* is a bog or swamp.

Decide If the Word Has a Positive or Negative "Charge"

Simply knowing that you're dealing with a positive or negative word can earn you points on the SAT. For example, look at the word *cantankerous*. Say it to yourself. Can you guess whether it's positive or negative? Often words that sound harsh have a negative meaning, while smooth-sounding words tend to have positive meanings. If *cantankerous* sounded negative to you, you were right. It means "difficult to handle."

You can also use prefixes and roots to help determine a word's charge. *Mal, de, dis, un, in, im, a,* and *mis* often indicate a negative, while *pro, ben,* and *magn* are often positives.

Not all SAT words sound positive or negative; some sound neutral. But if you can define the charge, you can probably eliminate some answer choices on that basis alone.

EXAMPLE

He seemed at first to be honest and loyal, but before long it was necessary to ---- him for his ---- behavior.

(A) admonish . . steadfast

(B) extol . . conniving

(C) reprimand . . scrupulous

(D) exalt . . insidious

(E) castigate . . perfidious

Q. Which U.S. president famous for his *malapropisms* has a father who played baseball at Yale?

All you need to know to answer this question is that negative words are needed in both blanks. Then you can scan the answer choices for a choice that contains two clearly negative words. Choice (E) is right. *Castigate* means "punish or scold harshly," and *perfidious* means "treacherous."

> Q. Which sport competes in a *velodrome*?

Use Your Foreign Language Skills

Many of the roots you'll encounter in SAT words come from Latin. Spanish, French, and Italian also come from Latin, and have retained much of it in their modern forms. English is also a cousin to German and Greek. That means that if you don't recognize a word, try to remember if you know a similar word in another language.

Look at the word *carnal*. Unfamiliar? What about *carne*, as in *chili con carne*? *Carn* means "meat" or "flesh," which leads you straight to the meaning of *carnal*—pertaining to the flesh. You could decode *carnivorous* ("meat eating") in the same way.

You can almost always figure out something about strange words on the test because SAT words are never all that strange. Chances are that few words on the SAT will be totally new to you, even if your recollection is more subliminal than vivid.

When All Else Fails

Eliminate choices that are clearly wrong and make an educated guess from the remaining choices. A wrong answer won't hurt you much; a right answer will help you a lot.

Don't forget to study the lists in the "SAT Locker Room" section!

REPLAY

Once you've mastered a concept, check it off.

Vocabulary:

- ❑ A vocabulary building plan
- ❑ Decoding strange words

4

Analogies

HIGHLIGHTS

- Become proficient in building bridges
- Study the Kaplan Three-Step Method for Analogies
- Review the nine classic bridges
- Use process of elimination as a backup strategy
- Complete the Analogies Practice Set

Analogies may seem frightening at first because they don't look like anything you've ever done before. But you'll feel better about them as soon as you realize that you speak and think in analogies all the time. Any time you say "my sister is like a slug," you're drawing an analogy between your sister and slugs—perhaps your sister is as gross as a slug. That may not be the kind of relationship that will appear on your SAT, but the way of thinking is the same.

Once you get familiar with the Analogy format, you'll find there's a simple method for mastering this question type. In fact, prepping often gains you more points on Analogies than on any other Verbal question type. With practice, you can even learn to get the Analogy right when you don't know all of the vocabulary words involved.

Two-Minute Drill

If you don't have much time to prep for the SAT, here's the best way to spend your time:

- Learn the Kaplan Three-Step Method for Analogies.
- Do the practice set in this chapter.
- If you miss an answer, review the tips in this chapter.

THE FORMAT

There are 19 Analogies in all on the SAT. You'll probably see one set of 13 and one set of six. Each 30-minute Verbal section contains a set of Analogies. A question looks like this:

EXAMPLE

FLAKE : SNOW ::

(A) storm : hail

(B) drop : rain

(C) field : wheat

(D) stack : hay

(E) cloud : fog

The two words in capital letters are called the *stem words*. The instructions will tell you to choose the pair of words from the five answer choices that is related in the same way as this pair. In this example, the answer above is (B). A flake is a small unit of snow, just as a drop is a small unit of rain.

BUILDING BRIDGES

In every Analogy question, there exists a strong, definite connection between the two stem words. Your task is to identify this relationship, and then to look for a similar relationship among the answer pairs.

What's a strong, definite relationship?

- The words *library* and *book* have a strong, definite connection. A library is defined as a place where books are kept. LIBRARY : BOOK could be a question stem.
- The words *library* and *child* do not have a strong, definite connection. A child may or may not have anything to do with a library. LIBRARY : CHILD would never be a question stem.

The best way to pinpoint the relationship between the stem words is to build a bridge. A bridge is a short sentence that relates the two words. Often, a bridge reads like a definition of one of the two words. For instance: "A *library* is a place where BOOKS are kept."

The ability to find bridges is fundamental to Analogy success. Your bridge needs to capture the strong, definite connection between the words.

KAPLAN'S THREE-STEP METHOD

The Kaplan Method for solving Analogies has three simple steps:

1. Build a bridge between the stem words.
2. Plug in the answer choices.
3. Adjust your bridge, if you need to.

Here's an Analogy stem. We've left out the answer choices because you need to focus first on the stem.

EXAMPLE

LILY : FLOWER ::

1. Build a Bridge

The best bridge here is, "A LILY is, by definition, a type of FLOWER."

2. Plug in the Answer Choices

Here is the complete question.

EXAMPLE

LILY : FLOWER ::

(A) rose : thorn

(B) cocoon : butterfly

(C) brick : building

(D) maple : tree

(E) sky : airplane

Take the bridge you have built and plug in answer choices (A) through (E). If only one pair fits, it's the answer.

HINT: *Be sure to try all five choices.*

Here's how plugging in the answer choices works:

(A) A *rose* is a type of *thorn*? No.

(B) A *cocoon* is a type of *butterfly*? No.

(C) A *brick* is a type of *building*? No.

(D) A *maple* is a type of *tree*? Yes.

(E) A *sky* is a type of *airplane*? No.

We've got four nos and only one yes, so the answer is (D).

What Makes a Strong Bridge?

You might be lured into thinking the words *trumpet* and *jazz* have a strong bridge. They don't.

You can play lots of things on trumpets other than jazz—fanfares, taps, whatever. You can also play jazz on things other than trumpets.

Trumpet and *instrument* do have a strong bridge. A trumpet is, by definition, a type of instrument. This is always true—it's a strong, definite relationship.

3. Adjust Your Bridge If You Need To

If no answer choice seems to fit, your bridge is too specific and you should go back and adjust it. If more than one answer choice fits, your bridge is not specific enough. Look at this example:

EXAMPLE

SNAKE : SLITHER ::
(A) egg : hatch
(B) wolf : howl
(C) rabbit : hop
(D) turtle : snap
(E) tarantula : bite

With a simple bridge, such as "a snake slithers," you'd have a hard time finding the answer. All the answer choices make sense: an *egg hatches*, a *wolf howls*, a *rabbit hops*, a *turtle snaps*, and a *tarantula bites*. Don't worry. Go back to step one and build another bridge, this time making it more specific. Think about what *slither* means.

New bridge: "Slithering is how a snake gets around."

(A) *Hatching* is how an *egg* gets around? No.
(B) *Howling* is how a *wolf* gets around? No.
(C) *Hopping* is how a *rabbit* gets around? Yes.
(D) *Snapping* is how a *turtle* gets around? No.
(E) *Biting* is how a *tarantula* gets around? No.

Four nos and one yes; the answer is (C).

HINT: *If no answer fits, or too many answers fit, build a new bridge and plug in again.*

WHAT PART OF SPEECH IS A STEM WORD?

Occasionally with an Analogy you might have to take a quick peek at the answer choices before you can build a bridge for the stem. The part of speech of a stem word may be ambiguous. When you're not sure whether a stem word is a noun, verb, adjective, or adverb, look at the words directly beneath that stem word. As a rule, the words in a vertical row are all the same part of speech.

For example, you might see this:

VERB : NOUN ::

(A) verb : noun

(B) verb : noun

(C) verb : noun

(D) verb : noun

(E) verb : noun

or this:

ADJECTIVE : NOUN ::

(A) adjective : noun

(B) adjective : noun

(C) adjective : noun

(D) adjective : noun

(E) adjective : noun

Q. In what sport is the term "tack" found?

but you'll *never* see this on an SAT Analogy:

NOUN : NOUN ::

(A) verb : noun

(B) noun : noun

(C) verb : verb

(D) verb : noun

(E) verb : noun

To establish the part of speech of a stem word, you don't usually have to look at more than choice (A).

How would you think through the following example?

EXAMPLE

PINE : DESIRE ::

(A) laugh : sorrow

(B) drink : thirst

(C) watch : interest

(D) listen : awe

(E) starve : hunger

The word *pine* can be a noun, but that's not likely here. You can't build a bridge between a tree with needlelike leaves and *desire*. Try another part of speech. A glance at the answer choices below *pine* (*laugh, drink, watch, listen,* and *starve*) tells you *pine* is being used as a verb.

What about *desire*? It could be a noun or a verb, but the answer choices beneath it (*sorrow, thirst, interest, awe,* and *hunger*) tell you it's used as a noun.

You've probably heard of someone pining away from unrequited love. As a verb, *pine* means "to yearn or suffer from longing." A good bridge would be: "By definition, to pine is to suffer from extreme desire." Plugging in the answer choices, you get:

(A) To *laugh* is to suffer from extreme *sorrow*? No.
(B) To *drink* is to suffer from extreme *thirst*? No.
(C) To *watch* is to suffer from extreme *interest*? No.
(D) To *listen* is to suffer from extreme *awe*? No.
(E) To *starve* is to suffer from extreme *hunger*? Yes.

Once again, four nos and one yes; the answer is (E).

TEST YOUR ANALOGY SMARTS

Try out what you've learned on these Analogies. (Answers on p. 32.)

1. SWEEP : BROOM ::

(A) cut : scissors
(B) soil : cloth
(C) dry : bucket
(D) thread : needle
(E) wash : dish

Ⓐ Ⓑ Ⓒ Ⓓ Ⓔ

2. MAP : ATLAS ::

(A) lock : key
(B) road : highway
(C) recipe : cookbook
(D) concept : encyclopedia
(E) theory : hypothesis

Ⓐ Ⓑ Ⓒ Ⓓ Ⓔ

> Q. What is the bridge between this pair?
> ELDEN : TIGER ::

3. HUNGRY : FAMINE ::

(A) thirsty : rainfall
(B) sick : plague
(C) sated : dinner
(D) dry : flood
(E) sore : injury

Ⓐ Ⓑ Ⓒ Ⓓ Ⓔ

NINE CLASSIC BRIDGES

It's easier to build bridges when you know the types of bridges that have appeared on the SAT in the past. While no one can give you a list of the words that will appear on SAT Analogies, you can learn what types of relationships to expect. The following classic bridges appear over and over again on the SAT. Don't memorize these bridges, or lists of words that fit these bridges. Instead, learn which types of bridges can lead you to the right answer on SAT Analogies and which cannot.

HINT: *Become familiar with the types of bridges that connect stem words on the SAT. They can lead you to the right answer.*

Classic bridges may take different forms, depending on what parts of speech are used. But the underlying concepts are what matter. Here are examples of nine classic types:

Bridge Type #1: Description

In many Analogies, one stem word is a person, place, or thing, and the other word is a characteristic of that person, place, or thing.

Look at these examples:

PAUPER : POOR—A PAUPER is always POOR.

GENIUS : INTELLIGENT—A GENIUS is always INTELLIGENT.

TRAGEDY : SAD—A TRAGEDY is always SAD.

This classic bridge can also describe a person, place, or thing by what it is *not*.

PAUPER : WEALTHY—A PAUPER is never WEALTHY.

GENIUS : STUPID—A GENIUS is never STUPID.

TRAGEDY : HAPPY—A TRAGEDY is never HAPPY.

Here are more types of classic bridges. Fill in each blank with a stem word that will complete the bridge. There is more than one way to fill in each blank. The important thing is to get the right idea. Suggested answers follow.

Bridge Type #2: Characteristic Actions

An INSOMNIAC can't ----.

A GLUTTON likes to ----.

A PROCRASTINATOR tends to ----.

Bridge Type #3: Lack

Something MURKY lacks ----.

A PESSIMIST lacks ----.

A PAUPER lacks ----.

Do It Yourself

One way to see the inner workings of Analogies is to put some together yourself. Make sure you include five answer choices. This exercise will give you a good feel for the structure of SAT Analogies and may help you spot and avoid bad answer choices.

Answers to Analogy Questions on p. 30

1. (A) (A broom is used to sweep.)
2. (C) (An atlas is made up of many maps.)
3. (B) (Many are hungry during a famine.)

Bridge Type #4: Categories

MEASLES is a type of ----.

A MOTORCYCLE is a type of ----.

A POLKA is a type of ----.

Bridge Type #5: Size/Degree

To SPEAK very quietly is to ----.

To LIKE strongly is to ----.

To BRUSH is to ---- lightly.

Bridge Type #6: Causing/Stopping

A REMEDY stops or cures an ----.

An OBSTACLE prevents ----.

Something INCENDIARY causes ----.

Bridge Type #7: Places

A JUDGE works in a ----.

A PLAY is performed on a ----.

BREAD is made in a ----.

Bridge Type #8: Function

GILLS are used for ----.

A PAINTBRUSH is used to ----.

A HELICOPTER is used for ----.

Bridge Type #9: Part/Whole

An ARMY is made up of ----.

A CROWD is made up of many ----.

An arrangement of FLOWERS is a ----.

Suggested Answers to Bridge Types

Your answers may vary from our suggested answers. As long as you've got the basic idea, that's okay.

Characteristic Actions:

An INSOMNIAC can't SLEEP.

A GLUTTON likes to EAT.

A PROCRASTINATOR tends to DELAY.

Lack:

Something MURKY lacks CLARITY.

A PESSIMIST lacks OPTIMISM.

A PAUPER lacks MONEY.

Categories:

MEASLES is a type of ILLNESS.

A MOTORCYCLE is a type of VEHICLE.

A POLKA is a type of DANCE.

Size/Degree:

To SPEAK very quietly is to WHISPER.

To LIKE strongly is to LOVE (or ADORE).

To BRUSH is to TOUCH lightly.

Causing/Stopping:

A REMEDY stops or cures an ILLNESS.

An OBSTACLE prevents PROGRESS (or MOVEMENT).

Something INCENDIARY causes FIRE.

Places:

A JUDGE works in a COURTROOM.

A PLAY is performed on a STAGE (or in a THEATER).

BREAD is made in a BAKERY.

Function:

GILLS are used for BREATHING.

A PAINTBRUSH is used to PAINT.

A HELICOPTER is used for FLYING.

Part/Whole:

An ARMY is made up of SOLDIERS.

A CROWD is made up of many PEOPLE.

An arrangement of FLOWERS is a BOUQUET.

Kaplan Rules

Not all bridges are classic bridges, but there is always a strong and definite relationship between the stem words.

Q. The following is an example of what type of classic bridge?

DOUBLE : HIT ::

HOW TO FILL VOCABULARY GAPS

Sometimes on an SAT Analogy, you simply don't know one of the stem words. When this happens, the basic three-step process won't do much good. You can't even do step one; you can't build a bridge using a word you don't know. You need another plan.

Q. Who is the only athlete to play in both the World Series and the Super Bowl?

The best backup strategy is not to focus on the stem pair. Instead, try looking at the answer pairs and eliminate those that simply can't be right. If you can knock out even one, guessing from the remaining choices is to your advantage. You may be surprised at how far this strategy can take you.

Before you guess, take these three steps to eliminate some answer choices. (And remember, even if you can eliminate only one answer choice, guessing comes out in your favor.)

1. Eliminate answer choices with weak bridges.
2. Eliminate any two answer choices with identical bridges.
3. Eliminate answer choices with bridges that couldn't work with the stem pair no matter what that unknown word means.

Here's how you do it.

Eliminate Answer Choices with Weak Bridges

You learned earlier that a strong, definite relationship always exists between the pair of stem words. The answer pairs, however, don't always have a good bridge—and any choice without a good bridge can't be right. In other words, you can eliminate certain answer choices without looking at the stem at all.

Try this exercise. Here is a list of six answer pairs without any stem pairs—answers without questions. Try to make a bridge for each pair. If no strong bridge is possible, mark the pair with an *X*. (Answers on p. 36.)

1. DOG : HOUSE
2. AQUATIC : WATER
3. NOCTURNAL : ANIMAL
4. INFANTILE : TOY
5. STEAK : POTATOES
6. RAISIN : GRAPE

Kaplan Rules

The following relationships are not SAT-type bridges. If you encounter one, it's wrong.

- synonyms (example: PREDICT : FORETELL)
- antonyms (example: WEALTHY : IMPOVERISHED)
- members of the same category (example: DOG : CAT)

In many cases, this method alone will allow you to eliminate one, two, or even three answer choices.

Eliminate Answer Choices with Identical Bridges

There's another way of eliminating some wrong choices that's so obvious you might not think of it. If two choices have the same bridge, it follows that neither one can be more right than the other. And since they can't both be right, they must both be wrong. For example, look at the following question:

EXAMPLE

LEGERDEMAIN : MAGICIAN ::

(A) baggage : immigrant

(B) justice : pragmatist

(C) sluggishness : racer

(D) diplomacy : diplomat

(E) indifference : fanatic

Don't Fall for Same-Subject Traps

Same-Subject Traps are wrong answer choices that lure you in by providing words that remind you of stem words. The same subject doesn't make it right.

Remember, you're looking for an answer choice that has the same relationship as the stem, not an answer choice that reminds you of the stem.

What if you don't know what *legerdemain* means? (C) seems like a possible answer because this pair of words has a strong bridge: "Sluggishness is the opposite of what you'd expect from a racer." But choice (E) has a very similar bridge: "Indifference is the opposite of what you'd expect from a fanatic."

Since a question can't have two right answers, and both (C) and (E) have the same bridge, both must be wrong. The correct answer is (D).

Eliminate Answer Choices with Bridges That Can't Fit the Stem

What do you do with answer pairs that can't be eliminated by either of the first two methods? The next step is to find bridges for the remaining answers, and then to plug in the stem word pair. It's true that you don't even know what one of the stem words means. But in some cases you'll see that the stem word pair can't fit the answer bridge no matter what that unknown word means. Here's an example:

EXAMPLE

GENUFLECT : KNEE ::

(A) pierce : ear

(B) hold : hand

(C) nod : neck

(D) stub : toe

(E) pick : tooth

You may not know what *genuflect* means. Since you can't work directly with this stem, take a look at the answer choices instead.

Answer pair (A) has a strong bridge: To *pierce* an *ear* is to put a hole in it. Now try plugging *genuflect* and *knee* into this same bridge: To *genuflect* a *knee* is to put a hole in it. Hmmm. Can you really imagine that there exists a verb in the English language that means "to put a hole in a knee"? No way. The concept doesn't even make sense. So GENUFLECT : KNEE and pierce : ear can't possibly have the same bridge. (A) can't be the right answer.

Answers to Weak Bridges Exercise on p. 34

1. A dog may or may not live in a house.—Weak bridge
2. Aquatic means "having to do with water."—Strong bridge
3. Not all animals are nocturnal, or active at night.—Weak bridge
4. You don't have to be infantile, or immature, to play with a toy.—Weak bridge
5. You can eat steak and potatoes, but you don't have to.—Weak bridge
6. A raisin is, by definition, a dried-up grape.—Strong bridge

The same technique can be used to eliminate choice (E). *Picking* your *teeth* is a way of cleaning between them. Is there a comparable way of cleaning between your knees? Not likely.

So you've been able to eliminate two of the answer choices—without knowing what *genuflect* means. Sometimes, of course, this technique demands a bit more intuition. Without knowing for sure, you might just have a feeling that there wouldn't be a word for a very large telephone or for a group of hammers. If you're guessing anyway, go with these hunches. The correct answer is (C).

Putting It Together

Now apply all three answer-eliminating techniques to one question. (Pretend that you don't know the word *scimitar* even if you do.)

EXAMPLE

SCIMITAR : SWORD ::

(A) diamond : ring

(B) greyhound : dog

(C) saddle : horse

(D) lance : shield

(E) forest : tree

(A) A *diamond* may adorn a *ring*, but plenty of rings don't have diamonds, and plenty of diamonds don't have rings. Choice (A) has a weak bridge. Eliminate.

(B) A *greyhound* is a kind of *dog*. Could a *scimitar* be a kind of *sword*? It sounds possible.

(C) A *saddle* is used for riding a *horse*. A *scimitar* is used for *riding* a sword? That can't make sense. Eliminate.

(D) A *lance* and a *shield* are both part of the traditional gear of a knight, but that's all we can say to connect them. Again, a weak bridge. Eliminate.

(E) A *forest* is a group of *trees*. Could a *scimitar* be a group of *swords*? Maybe.

Without knowing a stem word, you've gotten down to two answer choices—(B) and (E). Is there more likely to be a word for a kind of sword or for a group of swords? Take your best guess.

(B) is, in fact, the answer.

A DOUBLE VOCABULARY GAP

What if you don't know either of the stem words? You can still eliminate weak bridges and identical bridges. For example:

EXAMPLE

MANUMISSION : THRALL ::

(A) submission : employee

(B) prediction : artist

(C) promotion : rank

(D) tip : waiter

(E) parole : prisoner

Promotion is the act of raising an employee in rank. A *tip* is a type of gratuity or reward given to a waiter. *Parole* is the act of freeing a prisoner. These are all good bridges, and none of them repeat, so (C), (D), and (E) are all possible answers. But *submission* is not a characteristic of every *employee*, and there's no particular connection between *prediction* and *artist*. So eliminate (A) and (B).

To make your final decision, of course, you still have to guess. But now that you've eliminated answer choices, guessing works in your favor. The answer here happens to be (E), since *manumission* is, by definition, the act of freeing a *thrall*, or slave.

Now test your Analogy skills on the questions in the Analogies Practice Set that starts on the next page.

Q. JAI ALAI : CESTA ::

(A) football : penalty

(B) baseball : glove

(C) referee : flag

(D) soccer : champion

(E) race : car

ANALOGIES PRACTICE SET

1. COPPER : METAL ::

(A) grain : sand
(B) helium : gas
(C) stem : flower
(D) tree : trunk
(E) stone : clay

Ⓐ Ⓑ Ⓒ Ⓓ Ⓔ

2. BROOM : DIRT ::

(A) brush : bristles
(B) fork : plate
(C) rake : leaves
(D) mirror : face
(E) scissors : blades

Ⓐ Ⓑ Ⓒ Ⓓ Ⓔ

3. COWARD : BRAVERY ::

(A) eccentric : conformity
(B) hero : fortitude
(C) prophet : vision
(D) sage : wisdom
(E) comedian : humor

Ⓐ Ⓑ Ⓒ Ⓓ Ⓔ

4. REVERE : ADMIRE ::

(A) cherish : conceive
(B) release : reject
(C) guess : solve
(D) propose : change
(E) despise : disdain

Ⓐ Ⓑ Ⓒ Ⓓ Ⓔ

5. PERPLEXING : CONFUSION ::

(A) appalling : dismay
(B) static : change
(C) unpleasant : chaos
(D) dignified : pride
(E) grave : regret

Ⓐ Ⓑ Ⓒ Ⓓ Ⓔ

6. AMUSING : MIRTH ::

(A) ailing : health
(B) painful : sympathy
(C) optimistic : objectivity
(D) protective : insecurity
(E) terrifying : fear

Ⓐ Ⓑ Ⓒ Ⓓ Ⓔ

7. FOOD : MENU ::

(A) accounting : inventory
(B) index : foreword
(C) silverware : spoon
(D) merchandise : catalog
(E) films : credits

Ⓐ Ⓑ Ⓒ Ⓓ Ⓔ

8. IMPERCEPTIBLE : DETECT ::

(A) fundamental : begin
(B) inconceivable : imagine
(C) rugged : seize
(D) costly : overcharge
(E) immense : notice

Ⓐ Ⓑ Ⓒ Ⓓ Ⓔ

9. PERSEVERE : DOGGED ::

(A) comply : obedient
(B) inspire : pompous
(C) hesitate : reckless
(D) speak : laconic
(E) retard : expeditious

Ⓐ Ⓑ Ⓒ Ⓓ Ⓔ

10. ENTHRALLING : TEDIUM ::

(A) witty : frivolity
(B) insipid : appetite
(C) glaring : illumination
(D) wearisome : redundancy
(E) trite : originality

Ⓐ Ⓑ Ⓒ Ⓓ Ⓔ

Answers and Explanations for Analogies Practice Set

1. (B) (Copper is a kind of metal.)
2. (C) (A broom is used to clear away dirt.)
3. (A) (A coward does not display bravery.)
4. (E) (By definition, to revere is to admire very much.)
5. (A) (Something that is perplexing causes confusion.)
6. (E) (Something that is amusing causes mirth.)
7. (D) (A menu is, by definition, a list of available food.)
8. (B) (If something is imperceptible, you cannot detect it.)
9. (A) (A dogged person is one who perseveres.)
10. (E) (Something that is enthralling lacks tedium.)

REPLAY

Once you've mastered a concept, check it off.

Analogies:

❑ The format

❑ Building bridges

❑ Kaplan's Three-Step Method

❑ Test your analogy smarts

❑ Nine classic bridges

❑ How to fill vocabulary gaps

❑ Analogy practice set

5

Sentence Completions

HIGHLIGHTS

- Master the Kaplan Four-Step Method for Sentence Completions
- Learn to pick up on clues and predict answers
- Practice special techniques for tackling hard or tricky questions
- Complete the Sentence Completions Practice Set

Of all the Verbal question types, Sentence Completions are probably the most student-friendly. Unlike Analogies, they give you some context in which to think about vocabulary words, and unlike Critical Reading, they only require you to pay attention to a single sentence at a time. The 19 Sentence Completions count for about one-fourth of your verbal score.

Two-Minute Drill

If you have only a week or two to prep for the SAT, here's the best way to spend your time:

- Learn the Kaplan Four-Step Method for Sentence Completions.
- Do the practice set. If you miss an answer, skim through the chapter and look at the examples.

THE FORMAT

There are 19 Sentence Completions in all on the SAT. You'll probably see one set of nine and one set of ten. They appear in both 30-minute Verbal Sections. The instructions for Sentence Completions look something like this:

Select the lettered word or set of words that best completes the sentence.

Q. In a ---- conclusion to a Hall of Fame career, Ted Williams hit a home run in his last at bat.

(A) mundane

(B) disappointing

(C) fitting

(D) random

(E) jocular

EXAMPLE

Today's small, portable computers contrast markedly with the earliest electronic computers, which were ----.

(A) effective

(B) invented

(C) useful

(D) destructive

(E) enormous

In the example, the new computers, which are small and portable, are contrasted with old computers. You can infer that the old computers must be the opposite of small and portable, so (E), *enormous*, is right.

KAPLAN'S FOUR-STEP METHOD

Here's the basic method for Sentence Completions:

1. Read the Sentence for Clue Words

Think about the sentence before looking at the answer choices. Figure out what the sentence means, taking special note of clue words.

HINT: *Clue words such as* and, but, such as, *and* although *tell you where a sentence is heading.*

2. Anticipate the Answer

You can see the direction some sentences are headed in from a mile away. Consider these examples:

Kaplan Rules

To solve a Sentence Completion question:

1. Read the sentence for clue words.
2. Anticipate the answer.
3. Compare your prediction with each answer choice, and pick the best match.
4. Read the sentence with your answer choice in the blank or blanks.

"I still want to be your friend . . . ."

"Despite your impressive qualifications . . . ."

"If I ever get my hands on you, you little . . . ."

You could probably finish off these sentences on your own with pretty much the same language that the speaker would use. That's because the tone and structure of a sentence often clue you in to the meaning of the sentence.

On SAT Sentence Completions, you need to fill in missing pieces. Predict the word that goes in the blanks before looking at the answer choices. Do this by using the sentence's clue words (e.g., *despite, although*) and structural clues (construction and punctuation) to determine where the sentence is headed.

You don't have to make an exact prediction. A rough idea of the kind of word you'll need will do. Often enough, it's simple to predict whether the missing word is positive or negative.

3. Compare Your Prediction with Each Answer Choice, and Pick the Best Match

Scan every answer choice before deciding.

4. Read the Sentence with Your Answer Choice in the Blank or Blanks

Keep in mind that only one choice will make sense.

If you've gone through the four steps and more than one choice seems possible, don't get stuck on the sentence. If you can eliminate at least one answer as wrong, guess and move on. If a question really stumps you, skip it and come back when you're done with the section.

Let's take a look at how the four-step method works on some examples.

> **Kaplan Rules**
>
> Timing Tip: Spend no more than 40 seconds per Sentence Completion question. Don't read the sentence five times, plugging in every answer choice. That method takes too much time and makes you vulnerable to traps. Think about the question before you look for the answer.

EXAMPLE

Alligators, who bask in the sun for hours, appear to be ---- creatures, yet they are quite capable of sudden movement.

(A) active

(B) violent

(C) stern

(D) content

(E) sluggish

Read the sentence carefully, looking for clue words. *Yet* is a major clue. It tells you that the sentence switches direction midstream. The word in the blank must be the opposite of *sudden*.

Predict the word that goes in the blank. You can guess that alligators seem like lazy or idle creatures.

Compare your prediction with each answer choice, and pick the best match. (A), *active*, has nothing to do with being lazy or idle. Neither does (B), *violent*. Neither does (C), *stern*. Neither does (D), *content*. But (E), *sluggish*, means inactive or slow moving, so pick (E).

Check your answer by plugging it into the sentence. Let's check: "Alligators, who bask in the sun for hours, appear to be sluggish creatures, yet they are quite capable of sudden movement." Sounds okay. Finally, scan the other choices to make sure this is the best choice. None of the other choices works in the sentence, so (E) is correct.

Get Charged

Look for word charges, the positive or negative connotations that a word may have, to help you make your prediction about what to put in the blanks.

See the Vocabulary chapter for more on word charges.

EXAMPLE

The king's ---- decisions as a diplomat and administrator led to his legendary reputation as a just and ---- ruler.

(A) quick . . capricious

(B) equitable . . wise

(C) immoral . . perceptive

(D) generous . . witty

(E) clever . . uneducated

Read the sentence carefully, looking for clue words. A big clue here is the phrase *led to*. You know that the kind of decisions the king made led to his reputation as a just and ---- ruler. So whatever goes in both blanks must be consistent with *just*.

Predict the word that goes in the blank. Notice that both blanks must be similar in meaning. Because of his ---- decisions, the king is viewed a certain way, as a just and ---- ruler. So if the king's decisions were good, he'd be remembered as a good ruler, and if his decisions were bad, he'd be remembered as a bad ruler. *Just*, which means "fair," is a positive-sounding word; you can predict that both blanks will be similar in meaning, and that both will be positive words. Write a "+" in the blanks or over the columns of answer choices to remind you.

Q. In a ---- example of the ---- of drug use, Ben Johnson was stripped of the 1988 Olympic 100-meter gold medal for steroid use.

(A) noisome . . stupidity

(B) pertinent . . benefits

(C) banal . . usefulness

(D) peerless . . credibility

(E) stark . . pitfalls

Compare your prediction with each answer choice, and pick the best match. One way to do this is to determine which answers are positive and which are negative.

In (A), *quick* and *capricious* aren't similar. (*Capricious* means "erratic or fickle.")

In (B), *equitable* means "fair." *Equitable* and *wise* are similar and they're both positive. When you plug them in, they make sense, so (B)'s right.

In (C), *immoral* and *perceptive* aren't similar at all. *Perceptive* is positive but *immoral* isn't.

In (D), *generous* and *witty* are both positive qualities, but they aren't really similar and they don't make sense in the sentence.

In (E), *clever* and *uneducated* aren't similar. *Clever* is positive but *uneducated* isn't.

Check your answer by plugging it into the sentence. "The king's equitable decisions as a diplomat and administrator led to his legendary reputation as a just and wise ruler." (B) makes sense in the sentence. Finally, a scan of the other choices reveals that none works as well. So (B) is our answer.

EXAMPLE

Charlie Parker was ---- artist, inspiring a generation of modern jazz musicians with his brilliant improvisations and experiments in bebop style.

(A) an arbitrary

(B) a benign

(C) a seminal

(D) an emphatic

(E) a candid

Impulse Answer Buyer

Don't be an "impulse answer buyer." It's hard to know what to buy when you don't know what you're shopping for. The same thing is true of Sentence Completions. You should make a prediction of the answer you're looking for before you go to the answer choices. This way, you won't fall for a distractor. You'll find the answer you want rather than the answer the test maker wants you to find.

Read the sentence carefully, looking for clue words. The big clue is: Whatever goes in the blank must fit with the phrase *inspiring a generation.*

Predict the word that goes in the blank. The sentence tells you Parker inspired a generation of musicians, so you can predict that he was an influential artist.

Compare your prediction with each answer choice, and pick the best match.

(A) *arbitrary:* Too negative—you need a positive word.

(B) *benign: Benign* means "mild or gentle"—again, not what you want.

(C) *seminal:* Most closely matches your prediction—it means "containing the seeds of later development."

(D) *emphatic:* Might sound reasonable at first, but it means "expressive or forceful," which is not the same as "major or important."

(E) *candid: Candid* means "frank or open," which doesn't adequately describe how Parker influenced a generation.

Choice (C), *seminal,* is the answer. Notice that you could have found this answer by elimination, without actually knowing what the word means. Check your answer by plugging it into the sentence. "Charlie Parker was a seminal, or influential, artist inspiring a generation with his brilliant improvisations." Sounds fine.

PICKING UP ON CLUES

To do well on Sentence Completions, you need to see how a sentence fits together. Clue words help you do that. The more clues you get, the clearer the sentence becomes, and the better you can predict what goes in the blanks.

What do we mean by clue words? Take a look at this example:

Get a Clue

Clue words help you get to the right answer. Look for the following types of words:

Contrasts:

- but
- however
- although

Continuations:

- ; (a semicolon)
- also
- and
- because
- due to
- notably

EXAMPLE

Though some have derided it as ----, the search for extraterrestrial intelligence has actually become a respectable scientific endeavor.

Here, *though* is an important clue. *Though* contrasts the way some have derided, belittled, or ridiculed the search for extraterrestrial intelligence with the fact that that search has become respectable. Another clue is *actually*. *Actually* completes the contrast—though some see the search one way, it has actually become respectable.

You know that whatever goes in the blank must complete the contrast implied by the word *though*. So for the blank, you need something that describes the opposite of a *respectable scientific endeavor*. A word such as *useless* or *trivial* would be a good prediction for the blank.

Try using clue words to predict the answers to the questions below. First, look at the sentences without the answer choices and:

- Circle clue words.
- Think of a word or phrase that might go in each blank.
- Write your prediction below each sentence.

1. One striking aspect of Caribbean music is its ---- of many African musical ----, such as call-and-response singing and polyrhythms.

   ______________________________ ______________________________

2. Although Cézanne was inspired by the Impressionists, he ---- their emphasis on the effects of light and ---- an independent approach to painting that emphasized form.

   ______________________________ ______________________________

3. They ---- until there was no recourse but to ---- a desperate, last-minute solution to the problem.

   ______________________________ ______________________________

4. Her normally ---- complexion lost its usual glow when she heard the news of her brother's accident.

   ____

Here are the same questions with their answer choices. Now find the right answer to each question, referring to the predictions you just made. See p. 48 for the answers.

1. One striking aspect of Caribbean music is its ---- of many African musical ----, such as call-and-response singing and polyrhythms.

   (A) recruitment . . groups
   (B) proficiency . . events
   (C) expectation . . ideas
   (D) absorption . . forms
   (E) condescension . . priorities

   Ⓐ Ⓑ Ⓒ Ⓓ Ⓔ

2. Although Cézanne was inspired by the Impressionists, he ---- their emphasis on the effects of light and ---- an independent approach to painting that emphasized form.

   (A) accepted . . developed
   (B) rejected . . evolved
   (C) encouraged . . submerged
   (D dismissed . . aborted
   (E) nurtured . . founded

   Ⓐ Ⓑ Ⓒ Ⓓ Ⓔ

3. They ---- until there was no recourse but to ---- a desperate, last-minute solution to the problem.

   (A) compromised . . try
   (B) delayed . . envision
   (C) procrastinated . . implement
   (D debated . . maintain
   (E) filibustered . . reject

   Ⓐ Ⓑ Ⓒ Ⓓ Ⓔ

4. Her normally ---- complexion lost its usual glow when she heard the news of her brother's accident.

   (A) wan
   (B) pallid
   (C) sallow
   (D) ashen
   (E) sanguine

   Ⓐ Ⓑ Ⓒ Ⓓ Ⓔ

Q. Despite continual advances in race car and track safety, tragedy can still occur. Which NASCAR champion died at the Daytona 500 in 2001?

Answers and Explanations to Picking Up On Clues Exercises

Kaplan Rules

Don't pick tough words just because they're tough—pick them because they work in the sentence.

1. (D) Clue: *aspect*. The only choice that could logically complete a description of Caribbean music is (D): Caribbean music is characterized by its *absorption* of many African musical *forms*.
2. (B) Clue: *Although*. *Although* indicates that Cézanne must have somehow differed from the Impressionists. So he must have (B) *rejected* or (D) *dismissed* their emphasis on the effects of light. For the second blank, there's no reason to say that Cézanne *aborted* an independent approach to painting. Only (B) works for both blanks.
3. (C) Clues: *until, desperate*. For the first blank, you can predict that they must have waited until only a "desperate solution" was possible. (C) and (D) fit this prediction. (C)'s *implement*, or carry out, makes more sense in the second blank.
4. (E) Clue: *usual glow*. If her complexion had a "usual glow" it must have been normally rosy. The only choice that means rosy is (E), *sanguine*.

TACKLING HARD QUESTIONS

The last few Sentence Completions in a set are usually difficult. If you're getting stuck, here are a few special techniques to pull you through:

- Avoid tricky wrong answers.
- Take apart tough sentences.
- Work around tough vocabulary.

Q. Bill Wambsganss completed the only ---- triple play in World Series history.

(A) intelligent

(B) failed

(C) home run

(D) unassisted

(E) reclining

Avoiding Tricky Wrong Answers

Towards the end of a set, watch out for tricky answer choices. Avoid:

- Opposites of the correct answer
- Words that sound right because they're hard
- Two-blankers in which one word fits but the other doesn't

HINT: *Questions go from easiest to hardest—the higher the question number, the harder the question.*

The following example would be the seventh question out of a ten-problem set.

EXAMPLE

Granted that Joyce is extremely ----, it is still difficult to imagine her as a professional comedian.

(A) dull

(B) garrulous

(C) effusive

(D) conservative

(E) witty

A Sentence Like This Might Show up Towards the End of a Set

Read this sentence carefully or you may get tricked. If you read too quickly, you might think, "If Joyce is hard to imagine as a comedian, she's probably extremely dull or conservative. So I'll pick either (A) or (D)." But the sentence is saying something else.

Pick Up the Clues

The key is the clue word *granted*. It's another way of saying *although*. So the sentence means, "Sure Joyce is funny, but she's no professional comedian." Therefore, the word in the blank *must* resemble funny. That means (E), *witty*, is correct.

Don't Pick an Answer Just Because It Sounds Hard

Garrulous means "talkative" and *effusive* means "overly expressive." You might be tempted to pick one of these simply because they sound impressive. But they're put there to trick you. Don't choose them without good reason.

Now let's look at a two-blank sentence. The following example is another seventh question out of a ten-problem set.

Two-Blankers

Two-blank sentences can be easier than one-blankers.

- Try the easier blank first.
- Eliminate all choices that won't work for that blank.

EXAMPLE

When the state government discovered that thermal pollution was killing valuable fish, legislation was passed to ---- the dumping of hot liquid wastes into rivers and to ---- the fish population.

(A) discourage . . decimate

(B) regulate . . quantify

(C) facilitate . . appease

(D) discontinue . . devastate

(E) prohibit . . protect

Look at All the Choices

Check out the first blank first. Legislation was not passed to *facilitate* dumping, so that eliminates choice (C). The other four are all possible.

Now check the second blanks. The legislature wouldn't pass a law to *decimate*, or *quantify*, or *devastate* the fish population, so (A), (B), and (D) are wrong. Only choice (E), *prohibit . . protect*, fits for both blanks. The legislature might well pass a law to *prohibit* dumping hot liquids and to *protect* fish.

HINT: *Don't jump at an answer choice because one blank fits. Check both blanks.*

Taking Apart Tough Sentences

Look at the following example, the seventh question of a nine-problem set.

Weird Words Don't Work

Listen to the part of the sentence around the blank. Rule out funny-sounding answer choices.

If you can rule out even one or two weird-sounding choices, you can profit by making an educated guess.

EXAMPLE

Although this small and selective publishing house is famous for its ---- standards, several of its recent novels have a mainly popular appeal.

(A) proletarian

(B) naturalistic

(C) discriminating

(D) imitative

(E) precarious

What if you were stumped, and had no idea which word to pick? Try this strategy.

The process might go like this:

(A) *Proletarian* standards? Hmmm . . . sounds funny.

(B) *Naturalistic* standards? Not great.

(C) *Discriminating* standards? That's got a familiar ring.

(D) *Imitative* standards? Weird-sounding.

(E) *Precarious* standards? Nope.

(C) sounds best and, as it turns out, is correct. Although the small publishing house has *discriminating*, or picky, standards, several of its recent novels appeal to a general audience.

Now try a complex sentence with two blanks. Remember our rules:

- Try the easier blank first.
- Save time by eliminating all choices that won't work for one blank.

The following example is the fifth question out of a nine-problem set.

EXAMPLE

These latest employment statistics from the present administration are so loosely documented, carelessly explained, and potentially misleading that even the most loyal Senators will ---- the ---- of the presidential appointees who produced them.

(A) perceive . . intelligence

(B) understand . . tenacity

(C) recognize . . incompetence

(D) praise . . rigor

(E) denounce . . loyalty

Q. The Philadelphia 76ers ended their ---- 1972–73 season with an ---- 9-73 record, the worst in history.

(A) truculent . . enervating

(B) anemic . . egregious

(C) querulous . . horrific

(D) timid . . exemplary

(E) tumultous . . outstanding

It's not so easy to see what goes in the first blank, so try the second blank. You need a word to describe presidential appointees who produced the "loosely documented," "carelessly explained," and "misleading" statistics. So it's got to be negative. The only second-word answer choice that's definitely negative is (C), *incompetence*, or inability to perform a task. Now try *recognize* in the first blank. It fits, too. Choice (C) must be correct.

Working Around Tough Vocabulary

The following example is the second question out of a nine-problem set.

EXAMPLE

Despite her ---- of public speaking experience, the student council member was surprisingly cogent, and expressed the concerns of her classmates persuasively.

(A) hope

(B) depth

(C) method

(D) lack

(E) union

Kaplan Rules

If you find a word you don't understand, look in the sentence for its definition.

If you don't know what *cogent* means, work around it.

From the sentence, especially the clue word *and*, you know that cogent goes with "expressed the concerns of her classmates persuasively." So you don't have to worry about what *cogent* means. All you need to know is that the student council member was persuasive despite a ---- of speaking experience. Only (D), *lack*, fits. "Despite her lack of public speaking experience, the student council member expressed the concerns of her classmates persuasively." (By the way, *cogent* means "convincing, believable," roughly the same as "expressing concern persuasively.")

Let's look at this Sentence Completion problem. This time the tough vocabulary is in the answer choices. This example is the sixth question out of nine questions.

A Valuable Resource

To help yourself earn extra points, study the word lists in the "Locker Room" section.

EXAMPLE

Advances in technology occur at such a fast pace that dictionaries have difficulty incorporating the ---- that emerge as names for new inventions.

(A) colloquialisms

(B) euphemisms

(C) compensations

(D) neologisms

(E) clichés

Again, look at the sentence. Whatever goes in the blank has to describe "names for new inventions." If you don't know what the word *colloquialisms* or *euphemisms* means, don't give up. Rule out as many choices as you can, and guess among the remaining ones.

You can eliminate (C) and (E) right off the bat. They don't describe names for new inventions. Now you can make an educated guess. Again, educated guessing will help your score more than guessing blindly or skipping the question.

Or, if you studied your word roots, you might know that *neo-* means "new," so the word *neologisms* might be the best choice for names of new inventions. In fact, it's the right answer. *Neologisms* are newly coined words.

If All Else Fails

If you're really stumped, don't be afraid to guess. Eliminate all answer choices that seem wrong and guess from the remaining choices.

SENTENCE COMPLETIONS PRACTICE SET

1. In the years following World War II, almost all Canadian Inuits ---- their previously nomadic lifestyle; they now live in fixed settlements.

   (A) abandoned
   (B) continued
   (C) fashioned
   (D) preserved
   (E) rebuilt

   Ⓐ Ⓑ Ⓒ Ⓓ Ⓔ

2. A newborn infant's ---- skills are not fully ----, for it cannot discern images more than ten inches from its face.

(A) perceptual . . stimulated
(B) visual . . developed
(C) descriptive . . ripened
(D) olfactory . . shared
(E) average . . familiar

Ⓐ Ⓑ Ⓒ Ⓓ Ⓔ

3. Some geysers erupt regularly while others do so ----.

(A) consistently
(B) copiously
(C) perennially
(D) sporadically
(E) violently

Ⓐ Ⓑ Ⓒ Ⓓ Ⓔ

4. Because of the lead actor's ---- performance, the play received poor reviews from influential theater critics, and was canceled only one week after it opened.

(A) erudite
(B) corporeal
(C) overwrought
(D) fractious
(E) resplendent

Ⓐ Ⓑ Ⓒ Ⓓ Ⓔ

5. Sociologists have found that, paradoxically, many children of unorthodox, creative parents grow up to be rather tame ----.

(A) idealists
(B) conformists
(C) individualists
(D) alarmists
(E) elitists

Ⓐ Ⓑ Ⓒ Ⓓ Ⓔ

6. In Han mortuary art, the ---- and the ---- are combined; one tomb may contain eerie supernatural figures placed next to ordinary likenesses of government administrators at work.

(A) fantastic . . mundane
(B) inventive . . remorseful
(C) illusory . . derivative
(D) enlightened . . conservative
(E) unique . . historical

Ⓐ Ⓑ Ⓒ Ⓓ Ⓔ

Turn to the next page for answers and explanations.

Answers and Explanations to the Sentence Completions Practice Set

1. (A) *Nomadic* means "wandering, transient." If Inuit people now live in fixed settlements, we can predict that they rejected, or *abandoned*, "their previously nomadic lifestyle."
2. (B) If a newborn infant "cannot discern (or perceive) images more than 10 inches from its face," then the infant's ability to see things has not fully evolved. In other words, its visual skills are not fully developed. The word *olfactory*, choice (D), means "relating to sense of smell."
3. (D) The clue words *while others* indicate contrast. If some geysers "erupt regularly," we can predict that others do so irregularly. The best choice is (D), since *sporadically* means "infrequently or irregularly."
4. (C) If the play "received poor reviews" and was canceled because of something about the lead actor's performance, that performance must have been quite bad. The word *overwrought*, choice (C), means "overdone" or "excessively agitated." It is one of two negative words in the answer choices, and the only one that could logically describe a performance.
5. (B) Paradoxically (or contrary to what one would expect), children of creative and unorthodox parents grow up to be something other than creative and unorthodox. We need a word that contrasts with *creative* and *unorthodox* and goes along with *tame*. (B) is the best choice; *conformists* are people who follow established norms and customs without challenging anything or anyone.
6. (A) If "one tomb contains eerie supernatural figures" and "ordinary likenesses of government administrators," it's likely that Han mortuary art combines the unearthly or bizarre with the ordinary or mundane. The best answer is (A). In Han art, the *fantastic* (eerie supernatural figures) and the *mundane* (administrators) are combined.

REPLAY

Once you've mastered a concept, check it off.

Sentence Completions:

❑ The format

❑ Kaplan's Four-Step Method

❑ Picking up on clues

❑ Tackling hard questions

❑ Practice set

6

Critical Reading: The Basics

HIGHLIGHTS

- Practice reading actively
- Apply the Kaplan Five-Step Method for Critical Reading questions
- Review Big Picture, Little Picture, and Vocabulary-in-Context question types

Improving your Critical Reading score means building the skills you have and applying them to the SAT. You don't need outside knowledge to answer the Critical Reading questions. And you don't need an amazing vocabulary, since unfamiliar words will be defined for you.

Doing well on the Critical Reading section isn't really that hard. Take this everyday situation as an example. If you bought a new VCR, as soon as you unpacked it you'd read the instruction manual to figure out how to hook it up and get it working. You probably wouldn't sit down and read the whole book, though. You'd skip the pages that contain step-by-step instructions on how to record programs from the TV until you'd gotten the VCR connected and plugged in. If the manual said, "connect the xygupts to terminal c," you'd probably figure out how to do that, even though you don't know the word *xygupts*.

In setting up your VCR, you'd have demonstrated that you know how to read with a purpose; know how and when to deal with details; and can figure out the meaning of unfamiliar words from context—all skills you'll be using in the Critical Reading section.

Two-Minute Drill

If you have two weeks or fewer to prep for the SAT, here's the best way to spend your time:

- Since Critical Reading makes up half of the Verbal section of the SAT, it's important that you read the whole chapter.
- Pay special attention to the practice questions beginning on pp. 59 and 64.

Critical Reading passages and questions are very predictable, since the test makers use a formula to write them. You'll be given four reading passages, 400 to 850 words each, drawn from the arts, humanities, social sciences, sciences, and fiction. One of these is a "paired passage" consisting of two related excerpts. You'll be asked about the overall tone and content of a passage, the details, and what the passage suggests. You'll also be asked to compare and contrast the related passages.

Q. True or False? Michael Jordan was cut from his high school basketball team.

THE FORMAT

Critical Reading instructions tell you to answer questions based on what is stated or implied in the accompanying passage or passages. As with other question types, you should get familiar enough with the Critical Reading format that you don't waste time reading the directions again on the day of the test.

Each reading passage begins with a brief introduction. Related questions follow the passage. Don't skip the brief introductions. They'll help you focus your reading.

Critical Reading questions have a specific order: The first few questions ask about the beginning of the passage, the last few about the end.

Questions following "paired passages" are generally ordered. The first few questions relate to the first passage, the next few to the second passage, and the final questions ask about the passages as a pair—generally, but not always. You'll learn more about this on p. 66.

Critical Reading questions are not ordered by difficulty. Unlike the other kinds of questions on the SAT, the location of a Critical Reading question tells you nothing about its potential difficulty. So don't get bogged down on a hard Critical Reading question. The next one might be a lot easier.

How NOT to Read

DON'T wait for important information to jump out and hit you in the face. Search for important points.

DON'T read the passage thoroughly. It's a waste of time. Skim the passage to get the drift.

DON'T skim so quickly that you miss the passage's main point.

DON'T get caught up in details.

HOW TO READ A PASSAGE

Some students find Critical Reading passages dull or intimidating. Remember that each passage is written for a purpose: The author wants to make a point, describe a situation, or convince you of his or her ideas. As you're reading, ask yourself, "What's the point of this? What's this all about?" This is active reading, and it's the key to staying focused on the page.

Active reading doesn't mean reading the passage word-for-word. It means reading lightly, but with a focus—in other words, skimming. The questions will help you fill in the details by directing you back to important information in the passage.

Getting hung up on details is a major Critical Reading pitfall. You need to grasp the outline, but you don't need to get all the fine features.

The less time you spend on reading the passages, the more time you'll have to answer the questions—and that's where you score points.

Test Your Critical Reading Smarts

Test your reading skills on the following sample passage, keeping our tips in mind. Remember that active reading will make this difficult passage—and every passage—more doable.

EXAMPLE

In this essay, the author writes about her childhood on a Caribbean island that was an English colony for many years.

When I saw England for the first time, I was a child in school sitting at a desk. The England I was looking at was laid out on a map gently, beautifully, delicately, a very special jewel; it lay on a bed of sky blue, its yellow form mysterious, because though it looked like a leg of mutton*, it could not really look like anything so familiar as a leg of mutton because it was England. England was a special jewel all right, and only special people got to wear it. The people who got to wear England were English people. They wore it well and they wore it everywhere: in jungles, in deserts, on plains, in places where they were not welcome, in places they should not have been. When my teacher had pinned this map up on the blackboard, she said, "This is England"—and she said it with authority, seriousness, and adoration, and we all sat up. We understood then—we were meant to understand then—that England was to be our source of myth and the source from which we got our sense of reality, our sense of what was meaningful, our sense of what was meaningless—and much about our own lives and much about the very idea of us headed that last list.

At the time I was a child sitting at my desk seeing England for the first time, I was already very familiar with the greatness of it. Each morning before I left for school, I ate a breakfast of half a grapefruit, a bowl of oat porridge, bread and butter and a slice of cheese, and a cup of cocoa. The can of cocoa was often left on the table in front of me. It had written on it the name of the company, the year the company was established, and the words "Made in England." Those words, "Made in England," were written on the box the oats came in too. The shoes I wore were made in England; so were my socks and cotton undergarments and the satin ribbons I wore tied at the end of two plaits of my hair. My father, who might have sat next to me at breakfast, was a carpenter and cabinet maker. The shoes he wore to work would have been made in England, as were his khaki shirt and trousers, his underpants and undershirt, his socks and brown felt hat. Felt was not the proper material from which a hat that was expected to provide shade from the hot sun should be made, but my father must have seen and admired a picture of an Englishman wearing such a hat in England. As we sat at breakfast a car might go by. The car, a Hillman or a Zephyr, was made in England. The very conception of the meal itself, breakfast, and its substantial quality and quantity was an idea from England; we somehow knew that in England they began the day with this meal called breakfast and a proper breakfast was a big breakfast.

At the time I saw this map—seeing England for the first time—I did not say to myself, "Ah, so that's what it looks like," because there was no longing in me to put a shape to those three words that ran through every part of my life, no matter how small; for me to have had such a longing would have meant that I lived in a certain atmosphere, an atmosphere in which those three words were felt as a burden. But I did not live in such an atmosphere. My father's brown felt hat would develop a hole in its crown, the lining would separate from the hat itself, and six weeks before he thought that he could not be seen wearing it—he was a very vain man—he would order another hat from England. And my mother taught me to eat my food in the English way: the knife in the right hand, the fork in the left, my elbows held still close to my side. When I had finally mastered it, I overheard her saying to a friend, "Did you see how nicely she can eat?" But I knew then that I enjoyed my food more when I ate it with my bare hands, and I continued to do so when she wasn't looking. And when my teacher showed us the map, she

Kaplan Rules

As you read the passage, ask yourself:

- What's this passage about?
- What's the point of this?
- Why did someone write this?
- What's the author trying to say?
- What are the two or three most important things in this passage?

asked us to study it carefully, because no test we would ever take would be complete without this statement: "Draw a map of England."

I did not know then that the statement "Draw a map of England" was something far worse than a declaration of war. I did not know then that this statement was part of a process that would result in my erasure, not my physical erasure, but my erasure all the same. I did not know then that this statement was meant to make me feel in awe and small whenever I heard the word "England": awe at its existence, small because I was not from it. I did not know very much of anything then—certainly not what a blessing it was that I was unable to draw a map of England correctly.

*the flesh of a sheep

It's important to learn how to read the passage quickly and efficiently. Remember, though, that reading the passage won't earn you points—it's the questions that count.

KAPLAN'S FIVE-STEP METHOD

Here's Kaplan's proven approach to Critical Reading questions:

1. Read the question stem.
2. Locate the material you need.
3. Come up with an idea of the right answer.
4. Scan the answer choices.
5. Select your answer.

1. Read the Question Stem

This is the place to really read carefully. Take a second to make sure you understand what the question is asking.

2. Locate the Material You Need

If you are given a line reference, read the material surrounding the line mentioned. It will clarify exactly what the question is asking.

If you're not given a line reference, scan the text to find the place where the question applies, and quickly reread those few sentences. Keep the main point of the passage in mind.

Critical Reading Is Critical

The 38 to 40 Critical Reading questions count for about half your Verbal score. You need to do well on these questions.

3. Come up with an Idea of the Right Answer

Don't spend time making up a precise answer. You need only a general sense of what you're after, so you can recognize the correct answer quickly when you read the choices.

4. Scan the Answer Choices

Scan the choices, looking for one that fits your idea of the right answer. If you don't find an ideal answer, quickly eliminate wrong choices by checking back to the passage. Rule out choices that are too extreme or go against common sense. And get rid of answers that sound reasonable, but don't make sense in the context of the passage.

5. Select Your Answer

You've eliminated the obvious wrong answers. One of the remaining should fit your ideal. If you're left with more than one contender, consider the passage's main idea, and make an educated guess.

Now try the following Critical Reading practice questions. (Answers on p. 62.)

Having Trouble?

Unlike the other Verbal question types, Critical Reading questions are not ordered by difficulty. If you're having trouble answering a question, the next one might be easier.

1. According to the author, England could not really look like a leg of mutton (lines 4–5) because

   (A) maps generally don't give an accurate impression of what a place looks like
   (B) England was too grand and exotic a place for such a mundane image
   (C) England was an island not very different in appearance from her own island
   (D) the usual metaphor used to describe England was a precious jewel
   (E) mutton was one of the few foods familiar to her that did not come from England

   Ⓐ Ⓑ Ⓒ Ⓓ Ⓔ

2. The author's reference to felt as "not the proper material" (line 27) for her father's hat chiefly serves to emphasize her point about the

   (A) extremity of the local weather
   (B) arrogance of island laborers
   (C) informality of dress on the island
   (D) weakness of local industries
   (E) predominance of English culture

   Ⓐ Ⓑ Ⓒ Ⓓ Ⓔ

3. The word *conception* as used in line 30 means

   (A) beginning
   (B) image
   (C) origination
   (D) notion
   (E) plan

   Ⓐ Ⓑ Ⓒ Ⓓ Ⓔ

4. The word *substantial* in line 31 means

(A) important
(B) abundant
(C) firm
(D) down-to-earth
(E) materialistic

Ⓐ Ⓑ Ⓒ Ⓓ Ⓔ

5. In the third paragraph, the author implies that any longing to put a shape to the words *made in England* would have indicated

(A) a resentment of England's predominance
(B) an unhealthy desire to become English
(C) an inability to understand England's authority
(D) an excessive curiosity about England
(E) an unfamiliarity with English customs

Ⓐ Ⓑ Ⓒ Ⓓ Ⓔ

Q. Name the cancer survivor who came back to win the 2000 Tour de France.

6. The author cites the anecdotes about her father and mother in lines 37–43 primarily to convey their

(A) love for their children
(B) belief in strict discipline
(C) distaste for anything foreign
(D) reverence for England
(E) overemphasis on formal manners

Ⓐ Ⓑ Ⓒ Ⓓ Ⓔ

7. The word *erasure* (line 49) as used by the author most nearly means

(A) total annihilation
(B) physical disappearance
(C) sense of insignificance
(D) enforced censorship
(E) loss of freedom

Ⓐ Ⓑ Ⓒ Ⓓ Ⓔ

8. The main purpose of the passage is to

(A) advocate a change in the way a subject is taught in school
(B) convey the personality of certain figures from the author's childhood
(C) describe an overwhelming influence on the author's early life
(D) analyze the importance of a sense of place to early education
(E) relate a single formative episode in the author's life

Ⓐ Ⓑ Ⓒ Ⓓ Ⓔ

9. For the author, the requirement to "Draw a map of England" (line 46) represented an attempt to

(A) force students to put their studies to practical use
(B) glorify one culture at the expense of another
(C) promote an understanding of world affairs
(D) encourage students to value their own heritage
(E) impart outmoded and inappropriate knowledge

Ⓐ Ⓑ Ⓒ Ⓓ Ⓔ

10. At the end of the passage, the author suggests that her inability "to draw a map of England correctly" indicated a

    (A) heartfelt desire to see the country in person rather than through maps
    (B) serious failure of the education she received
    (C) conscious rejection of the prestige of a foreign power
    (D) harmful preoccupation with local affairs and customs
    (E) beneficial ignorance of her own supposed inferiority

    (A) (B) (C) (D) (E)

Applying the Five-Step Method

Try Kaplan's five-step method on question one from the sample reading passage above.

> **What's *Mutton*?**
>
> When a word is too obscure for the SAT, they'll define it at the bottom of the reading passage.

1. Read the Question Stem

In this case, the question is straightforward: Why couldn't England really look like a leg of mutton? (Notice that *mutton* is defined for you at the end of the passage—you aren't expected to know the meaning of unfamiliar terms.)

2. Locate the Material You Need

You're given a clue: The answer lies somewhere near the fourth or fifth line. But don't read just those lines—read the line or two before and after as well. By doing so, you learn that England was mysterious and special, so it couldn't look like something as familiar (to the author) as a leg of mutton.

3. Come up with an Idea of the Right Answer

After reading those couple of lines, you'd expect the answer to be something like, "England was too special to look like a familiar leg of mutton."

4. Scan the Answer Choices

Choice (B) comes close to the ideal—it should have popped out. But if you weren't sure, you could have quickly eliminated the other choices. Thinking of the main idea would have helped you eliminate (A) and (C). England was precious—like a jewel—but the author doesn't imply that England was usually compared to a jewel (D). And you never learn where mutton comes from (E).

5. Select Your Answer

Choice (B) is the only one that works here. By reading the material surrounding the line reference and putting an answer into your own words, you should have been able to choose (B) with confidence.

> Q. What club was called a "niblick" before golf clubs were numbered?

Now try the five-step method on the remaining questions for the passage.

HINT: *From the questions, you can "fill in" the information you don't get in a quick reading. It's a way of working backwards, to reconstruct the passage.*

BIG PICTURE, LITTLE PICTURE, AND VOCABULARY-IN-CONTEXT QUESTIONS

Most SAT Critical Reading questions fall into three basic types. "Big Picture" questions test your overall understanding of the passage's biggest points. "Little Picture" questions ask about localized bits of information. About 70 percent of Critical Reading questions are "Little Picture." Vocabulary-in-Context questions ask for the meaning of a single word.

In the passage above, question eight is an example of a Big Picture question. Question two is an example of a Little Picture question. Question three is a Vocabulary-in-Context question.

HINT: *Remember to skip around if you need to. You can tackle whichever passages you like in any order you like within the same section. But once you've read through the passage, try all the questions that go with it.*

Big Picture Questions

Big Picture questions test your overall understanding of a passage. They might ask about:

- The main point or purpose of a passage
- The author's attitude or tone
- The logic underlying the author's argument
- How ideas relate to each other

One way to see the Big Picture is to read actively. As you read, ask yourself, "What's this all about? What's the point of this?"

Answers to Critical Reading Questions, pp. 59–61

1. (B)
2. (E)
3. (D)
4. (B)
5. (B)
6. (D)
7. (C)
8. (C)
9. (B)
10. (E)

HINT: *Still stumped after reading the passage? Do the Little Picture questions first. They can help you fill in the Big Picture.*

Turn back to the passage you tried above. What did you get out of the first reading? Something like, "England was a profound influence on the author's early life, but not a completely positive influence"? That would have been enough.

Now look at question eight. It's a Big Picture question, asking for the main point of the passage. Use the five-step method to find your answer.

1. Read the Question Stem

Simple enough: What's the main point of the passage?

2. Locate the Material You Need

In this case, you're asked about the overall point. You should have grasped a sense of that from reading the passage.

3. Get an Idea of the Right Answer

Again, you need just a rough statement. Here, something like this would do: "The purpose is to describe how England was a huge influence, but maybe not a completely positive one, in the author's young life."

4. Scan the Answer Choices

(C) should have popped out. But (D) might have looked good, too, if you focused on the words "sense of place." So put those two aside as contenders. How a subject was taught in school (A), figures in the author's childhood (B), and a single formative episode (E) are too narrow.

5. Select Your Answer

You've crossed off the poor choices, and you're down to two possibilities. Which matches your ideal? (C) comes closer. Look closely at (D) and you'll see that it's too general. Go with the best choice.

Avoid the Farfetched

Don't pick farfetched inferences. SAT inferences tend to be strongly implied in the passage.

Little Picture Questions

More than two-thirds of Critical Reading questions ask about the Little Picture. Little Picture questions usually give you a line reference or refer you to a particular paragraph—a strong clue to where in the passage you'll find your answer.

Little Picture questions might:

- Test whether you understand significant information that's stated in the passage
- Ask you to make inferences or draw conclusions based on a part of the passage
- Ask you to relate parts of the passage to one another

Question two is a Little Picture question. You're asked about the felt hat of the author's father—what does this point emphasize? Applying Kaplan's Step Two, locate the material you'll need. You're given a clue—a line reference—to help you here. Reread that, and the lines before and after it as well.

So why did the father wear a felt hat, which was probably quite hot in the tropical sun? Because it was English. That's what correct choice (E) says. Rereading that bit of the passage should have led you right to that answer. (A) comes close, but doesn't fit the main point of the passage. Even with Little Picture questions, grasping the main point of the passage can help you find the correct answer.

HINT: *Beware of answer choices that provide a reasonable answer to the stem, but don't make sense in the context of the passage.*

Kaplan Rules

Once you find the tested word in the passage, you can treat a Vocabulary-in-Context question like a Sentence Completion.

Pretend the word is a blank in the sentence. Read a line or two around the "blank," if you need to. Then predict a word for the "blank." Check the answer choices for a word that comes close to your prediction.

Vocabulary-in-Context Questions

Vocabulary-in-Context questions ask about an even smaller part of the passage than other Little Picture questions do. They ask about the usage of a single word. These questions do not test your ability to define hard words such as *archipelago* and *garrulous*. They do test your ability to infer the meaning of a word from context.

In fact, the words tested in these questions will probably be familiar to you—they are usually fairly common words with more than one definition. Many of the answer choices will be definitions of the tested word, but only one will work in context. Vocabulary-in-Context questions always have a line reference, and you should always use it!

HINT: *CONTEXT is the most important part of Vocabulary-in-CONTEXT questions.*

Sometimes one of the answer choices will jump out at you. It'll be the most common meaning of the word in question—but it's rarely right! We call this the "obvious" choice. For example, say *curious* is the word being tested. The obvious choice is *inquisitive*. But *curious* also means "odd," and that's more likely to be the answer. Using context to find the answer will help prevent you from falling for this trap. You can use these choices to your advantage, though. If you get stuck on a Vocabulary-in-Context question, you can eliminate the "obvious" choice and guess.

HINT: *If a question has an "obvious" choice, steer clear of it.*

Vocabulary-in-Context Practice

(Answers on p. 66.)

1. Embodied and given life in the social realities of her own period, Jane Austen's satire still has currency in ours.

   In the lines above, *currency* most nearly means
   (A) usualness
   (B) stylishness
   (C) prevalence
   (D) funds
   (E) relevance

   Ⓐ Ⓑ Ⓒ Ⓓ Ⓔ

2. A perpetual doubting and a perpetual questioning of the truth of what we have learned is not the temper of science.

   In the lines above, *temper* most nearly means
   (A) disposition
   (B) nature
   (C) anger
   (D) mood
   (E) mixture

   Ⓐ Ⓑ Ⓒ Ⓓ Ⓔ

3. Captain Wentworth had no fortune. He had been lucky in his profession, but, spending freely what had come freely, had realized nothing.

   Which most nearly captures the meaning of the word *realized* in the sentence above?
   (A) understood
   (B) accomplished
   (C) learned
   (D) accumulated
   (E) fulfilled

   Ⓐ Ⓑ Ⓒ Ⓓ Ⓔ

4. Anyone with more than a superficial knowledge of Shakespeare's plays must necessarily entertain some doubt concerning their true authorship.

In the lines above, *entertain* most nearly means

(A) amuse
(B) harbor
(C) occupy
(D) cherish
(E) engage

Ⓐ Ⓑ Ⓒ Ⓓ Ⓔ

5. Many people who invested in the booming art market of the 1980s were disappointed; few of the works appreciated in value.

In the lines above, *appreciated* most nearly means

(A) admired
(B) applauded
(C) spiraled
(D) increased
(E) acknowledged

Ⓐ Ⓑ Ⓒ Ⓓ Ⓔ

6. Charles de Gaulle's independence of mind can be seen by the fact that he negotiated with Algerian nationalists, although he was pressed by his advisors, French colonists, and the army itself to continue the war.

Which most nearly captures the meaning of the word *pressed* in the sentence above?

(A) squeezed
(B) urged
(C) troubled
(D) required
(E) compelled

Ⓐ Ⓑ Ⓒ Ⓓ Ⓔ

7. Today some would say that those struggles are all over—that all the horizons have been explored—that all the battles have been won—that there is no longer an American frontier. But I trust that no one in this vast assemblage will agree with those sentiments.

In the lines above, *sentiments* most nearly means

(A) beliefs
(B) results
(C) loyalties
(D) challenges
(E) emotions

Ⓐ Ⓑ Ⓒ Ⓓ Ⓔ

Q. Who was the first person *inducted* into the Basketball Hall of Fame as both player and coach?

8. The convicts made their escape by scaling the prison walls and stealing away under the cover of darkness.

Which most nearly captures the meaning of the word *stealing* in the line above?

(A) seizing
(B) taking
(C) slipping
(D) grabbing
(E) abducting

Ⓐ Ⓑ Ⓒ Ⓓ Ⓔ

PAIRED PASSAGES—A (NOT-SO) SPECIAL CASE

Don't let the paired passages worry you—they're not twice as hard as the single reading selections. In fact, students often find the paired passages the most interesting on the test. With paired passages, focus as you read on the relationship between the two passages. Just as with single passages, the questions following paired passages can help fill in the picture.

Q. Who holds the NHL record for most points in a career?

Questions following paired passages tend to be ordered, with the first few questions relating to the first passage, the next few to the second passage, and the final questions asking about the passages as a pair. This is the best way to tackle the questions in any case, even if the test makers mix in a question about both passages amidst questions on the first passage (it's been known to happen).

To do paired passages:

1. Skim the first passage, looking for the drift (as you would with a single passage).
2. Do the questions that relate to the first passage.
3. Skim the second passage, looking for the drift and thinking about how the second passage relates to the first.
4. Do the questions that relate to the second passage.
5. Now you're ready to do the questions that ask about the relationship between the two passages.

Alternately skimming passages and answering questions is especially important if you're short of time. You'll be able to answer at least some of the questions before time runs out. By the time you've looked at both passages and answered the questions about each passage, you'll have a firm sense of the relationship between the pair. That will help you to answer the last group of questions.

Active reading can help you answer these questions, too. Remember to ask yourself, "What are these passages about? What is each author's point? What is similar about the two passages? What is different?"

Answers to Vocabulary-in-Context Questions, pp. 64–65

1. (E)
2. (B)
3. (D)
4. (B)
5. (D)
6. (B)
7. (A)
8. (C)

WHAT TO DO WHEN TIME IS RUNNING OUT

It's always best to skim the passage before you hit the questions. But if you only have a few minutes left, here's how to score points even while time is running out.

You can answer Vocabulary-in-Context questions and many Little Picture questions without reading the passage. If the question has a line reference, locate the material you need to find your answer and follow the five-step method as usual. You won't have the overall picture to guide you, but you might be able to reach the correct answer just by understanding the "little picture."

REPLAY

Once you've mastered a concept, check it off.

The Basics of Critical Reading:

- ❑ How to read a passage
- ❑ Kaplan's Five-Step Method for Critical Reading questions
- ❑ Paired passages—a (not-so) special case
- ❑ What to do when time is running out

How to Do Specific Question Types:

- ❑ Big picture questions
- ❑ Little picture questions
- ❑ Vocabulary-in-context questions

7

Critical Reading Skills

HIGHLIGHTS

- Learn to skim passages effectively and efficiently
- Use the Kaplan Four-Step Paraphrasing Method
- Strengthen your ability to draw inferences

In the previous chapter, you learned the basics of Critical Reading—what it looks like, what to expect, how to read the passages, how to tackle the questions. This chapter will help you improve the Critical Reading skills tested on the SAT—skimming, paraphrasing, and drawing inferences. You already have these skills.

- *Skimming* means reading quickly and lightly. You do this when you look information up in a phone book, or glance at a newspaper article only long enough to get the gist of the story.
- When you restate something in your own words, that's *paraphrasing*. You do it all the time in daily life—when you give a phone message, or retell a story.
- When you deduce information from a statement or situation, you're *making inferences.* You do it every day. If your best friend stopped talking to you, you'd probably infer that your friend was mad at you, even if your friend didn't actually say so.

Two-Minute Drll

If you have just a few weeks to prep for the SAT, here's the best way to spend your time:

- Read the section on skimming.
- Hold off on the rest of the chapter until you've covered all the basics in this book. If you have time to come back, work on the paraphrasing and inference sections.

SKIMMING

Skimming is a specific reading style in which you read quickly and in less detail than usual. These two characteristics are what make skimming the best way to read SAT passages. You want to read quickly because time is limited, and you want to read lightly because the questions direct you to the details you need. Spending a lot of time with the passage before you see the questions just doesn't make sense. So skimming works well—as long as you read with three things in mind:

- The content of the passage
- The organization of the passage
- The author's purpose or point of view

If you have a general idea of these three things when you're done skimming, then you're ready for the questions.

Read This Quickly

Joe stood at the edge of town, a cigarette in his left hand, a bottle of bourbon in his right. He'd had tough ones before, but this was gonna be the end of him. He looked back towards the light of the city below him. "If only I could get Martinez to talk," he thought to himself. In a flash, Joe was back in the Mustang racing towards town. . . .

What was this little story about? Chances are, even with a quick read, you took away some information that helped you piece it together. That's because you've already developed your reading skills (you're reading this, right?).

Your challenge on the SAT is to apply these skills in a peculiar context and not to be intimidated by the passages they throw at you.

In order to be an effective skimmer, you need to practice. Treat your practice sessions as an opportunity to learn. In time, you'll notice improvement.

- Practice frequently, in short sessions.
- Use these methods every time you read.

How to Skim

To improve your reading speed, get your eyes to move quickly and lightly along each line of type. Think about the way you usually read. Do you dwell on each word, as if you were plodding through a field of mud? Or do your eyes move quickly over the page, as if you were walking on hard, dry ground?

The way your eyes habitually move across each line of type and return to the beginning of the next line is your tracking style. That's what you'll work on here. The object is to make it light and swift, rather than heavy and deliberate. Don't read each word separately. Move your eyes lightly over the page, grouping words. Improving your tracking style will help you perform your best when under pressure.

Here are some skimming tips:

Don't Subvocalize

Subvocalizing is "sounding out" words as you read. Even if you don't move your lips, you're probably subvocalizing if you read one word at a time. Subvocalizing costs you time—because you can't read faster than you speak. If you group words, you won't subvocalize.

Keep Asking Yourself Where the Author's Going

Stay alert for the author's signals. Each SAT passage takes you on a journey, and every passage contains phrases or paragraph breaks that signal the next phase of this journey. As you skim, notice where each passage changes course.

Keep Your "Footsteps" Light

Don't read a passage slowly and deliberately. On the other hand, don't race as fast as you can. The idea is to increase your reading rate slightly while remaining comfortable.

Skimming Exercises

Now try a few exercises to see how skimming works. Read the following paragraph word by word.

> The prohibitive prices of some exhibits, as well as the continued depression of the local economy, prevented the 1939 World's Fair from being a great financial success. In a cultural sense, however, the Fair was enormously successful, and a landmark event of the era. As one historian noted, the Fair became "a cultural document of American values and aspirations at a crucial crossroads." After a decade of hardship, many Americans were ready to embrace a vision of social harmony, prosperity, and a bright future.

Q. Who has won the most Olympic gold medals in U.S. track and field history?

Now read the same paragraph, concentrating phrase by phrase.

> The prohibitive prices/ of some exhibits, /as well as/ the continued depression/ of the local economy, /prevented/ the 1939 World's Fair/ from being/ a great financial success. /In a /cultural sense,/ however,/ the Fair/ was enormously successful,/ and a landmark event/ of the era./ As one historian noted,/ the Fair became / "a cultural document/ of American values and aspirations/ at a crucial crossroads." /After a decade /of hardship,/ many Americans/ were ready to embrace/ a vision of social harmony,/ prosperity,/ and a bright future.

Kaplan Rules

Don't put slash marks in your test booklet on the real SAT. You're allowed to, but it's a waste of time.

The point is to make "mental" slash marks so that you get in the habit of moving briskly through the passage.

Here's another paragraph. Put in the slash marks yourself, phrase by phrase.

> The theme of the 1939 World's Fair was "Building the World of Tomorrow." Indeed, the modern and the futuristic were everywhere apparent. The main symbols of the Fair were the Trylon and the Perisphere, a huge pyramid and orb which were lit up at night in a dazzling display. The most popular exhibit, sponsored by General Motors, was the Futurama, which claimed to provide visitors with a glimpse of

automotive America in 1960. Patrons were carried by individual moving chairs on a simulated cross-country voyage, along a superhighway which would allow drivers to reach speeds up to 100 miles an hour.

No two readers will mark up this paragraph the same way, because each person sees phrases differently. That's okay. What's important is to begin working phrase-by-phrase, instead of word-by-word.

Now try another method. Read the following paragraphs, letting your eyes move down the page, and coming to rest at only two places per line:

> Q. Who scored the winning goal in the 1999 women's World Cup?

The Catcher in the Rye, published in 1951, is the only novel written by J.D. Salinger in a career that lasted less than twenty years. It is the story of Holden Caulfield, a sensitive, rebellious New York City teen-ager taking his first hesitant steps into adulthood. Holden flees the confines of his snobbish Eastern prep school, searching for innocence and truth, but finds only "phoniness." Filled with humor and pathos, *The Catcher in the Rye* won wide critical acclaim at the time of its publication. In the four decades since then, however, it has become a true phenomenon, selling hundreds of thousands of copies each year, and Holden Caulfield has gained the status of a cultural icon. What accounts for this book's remarkable hold on generation after generation of American youth?

Holden Caulfield is the narrator of *The Catcher in the Rye*, and his narration is a stylistic tour de force, revealing Salinger's masterful ear for the linguistic idioms and rhythms of adolescent speech. Slang evolves continuously, of course, and yesterday's "in" expressions are usually passé by tomorrow. But Holden's characteristic means of expression—the vernacular of a teen-age social misfit, desperately trying to find his niche—transcends the particulars of time and place. Like another 1950s icon, James Dean in *Rebel Without a Cause*, Holden Caulfield has "outlived" his era and become an enduring symbol of sensitive youth, threatened by an indifferent society.

See how your eye takes in whole phrases, though you haven't read every word? That's another skimming method.

Remember, skim the passage before you turn to the questions. When you tackle the questions, you'll focus more tightly on parts of the passage. Many questions will direct you back to specific lines or paragraphs, so you won't be desperately searching for relevant information.

PARAPHRASING

What happens when your best friend misses a day of school? You probably tell her or him what went on that night on the phone, or the next day before class. If you did, you'd be paraphrasing—condensing a day's worth of events into a few minutes, highlighting the most important things. Critical Reading questions often ask you to do a similar thing. They ask what a passage, or part of it, says. The right answer accurately paraphrases the meaning of the passage or excerpt, that is, it restates the meaning without losing any important points. Let's see how this works. Here are a few sentences from a Critical Reading passage:

EXAMPLE

No doubt because it painted a less than flattering picture of American life in America for Asian immigrants, *East Goes West* was not well received by contemporary literary critics. According to them, Kang's book displayed a curious lack of insight regarding the American effort to accommodate those who had come over from Korea. The facet of the novel reviewers did find praiseworthy was Han's perseverance and sustained optimism in the face of adversity.

The passage indicates that the response of critics to *East Goes West* was one of

(A) irony regarding the difference between Han's expectations and reality

(B) admiration of the courage and creativity Kang showed in breaking from literary tradition

(C) confusion about the motivation of the protagonist

(D) qualified disapproval of Kang's perception of his adopted homeland

(E) anger that Kang had so viciously attacked American society

A Good Paraphrase

A good paraphrase accurately restates the meaning of the original, without adding or losing important points.

There's a lot going on in the passage, but don't let it confuse you. Follow our advice:

Kaplan's Four-Step Paraphrasing Method

1. Read the question stem. That's the partial sentence leading into the answer choices.
2. Read the lines you're referred to, searching for the relevant phrases. (If a question gives you a line reference, be sure to read a line or two before and after the keyed line.)
3. Predict a good paraphrase for what's being asked.
4. Find a similar answer choice.

Now apply Kaplan's method to the reading question above:

1–2. After reading the stem and relevant lines of the passage (in this case, we found them for you), the key phrases should have popped out: *not well received, a curious lack of insight,* and *the facet reviewers did find praiseworthy.*

3. Predicted paraphrase: The critics were displeased with Kang's view of the immigrant's experience, but approved of the hero's persistence.

4. Look for the answer choice that means the same as your paraphrase.

Choice (D) comes closest. *Qualified* means "modified" or "limited," so *qualified disapproval* captures both the negative and the positive reaction the reviewers had.

Notice that Choice (E) is too negative, and choice (B) is too positive. Choices (A) and (C) don't reflect what the excerpt says. So (D) is the answer.

Paraphrasing Practice

The excerpts on the following page will help you recognize a good paraphrase quickly. Follow the method you've just learned. Notice as you go if your paraphrase includes too much or too little information, or if it has the wrong focus. If so, adjust it.

Each excerpt is followed by a space in which you can write your own paraphrase. Compare your paraphrase with the answer choices and pick the best approximation. You'll find the answers on p. 80.

1. He was not in love with Margaret, and he believed, though one could never be sure, that she was not in love with him—that her preference was for the handsome young clergyman who read Browning with her every Tuesday afternoon. But he was aware also that she would marry him if he asked her; he knew that the hearts of four formidable parents were set on the match; and in his past experience his mother's heart had invariably triumphed over his less intrepid resolves.

   The protagonist believes that Margaret will marry him because (give the reason in your own words):

   ___

   ___

   Now find the best paraphrase:

   (A) she wouldn't have the resolve to refuse him
   (B) they are in love with each other
   (C) they both feel parental pressure
   (D) she knows the clergyman won't marry her
   (E) his mother will talk her into accepting him

   Ⓐ Ⓑ Ⓒ Ⓓ Ⓔ

2. Only with effort can the camera be forced to lie: basically it is an honest medium; so the photographer is much more likely to approach nature in a spirit of inquiry, of communion, instead of with the saucy swagger of self-dubbed "artists."

The distinction made in the passage between a photographer and an "artist" can best be summarized as which of the following (summarize the distinction in your own words):

____

____

Now find the best paraphrase:

(A) The photographer's job is to record the world, and the artist's is to embellish it.
(B) The photographer's work is realistic, while the artist's is impressionistic.
(C) The artist finds his inspiration in the urban environment, the photographer in nature.
(D) The photographer has a more open and unassuming attitude toward the natural world than the artist does.
(E) Photographers are more pretentious than artists are.

Ⓐ Ⓑ Ⓒ Ⓓ Ⓔ

3. The following excerpt is from a speech given by Frederick Douglass.

"What to the American slave is your Fourth of July? I answer, a day that reveals more to him than all other days of the year, the gross injustice and cruelty to which he is the constant victim. To him your celebration is a sham; your boasted liberty an unholy license; your national greatness, swelling vanity . . . ."

According to Douglass, for slaves, the Fourth of July (complete the sentence in your own words):

____

____

Now find the best paraphrase:

(A) highlights the hypocrisy of stated American ideals
(B) reveals the injustice of not being invited to participate
(C) is a reminder of the greatness of their homeland
(D) shows the depravity of the celebrants
(E) is a completely meaningless day

Ⓐ Ⓑ Ⓒ Ⓓ Ⓔ

MAKING INFERENCES

Inferences are conclusions you reach that are hinted at, but not directly stated, in the reading passage. When you infer, you're "reading between the lines." In Critical Reading:

- If you're given a line reference, be sure to read a line or two around it.
- Always look for evidence in the passage to support an inference.

Many SAT questions test your power to make accurate inferences.

Q. Name one of the four managers who have skippered both the New York Yankees and the New York Mets.

EXAMPLE

My father was a justice of the peace, and I supposed that he possessed the power of life and death over all men and could hang anybody that offended him. This distinction was enough for me as a general thing; but the desire to become a steamboat man kept intruding, nevertheless. I first wanted to be a cabin boy, so that I could come out with a white apron on and shake a tablecloth over the side, where all my old comrades could see me. Later I thought I would rather be the deck hand who stood on the end of the stage plank with a coil of rope in his hand, because he was particularly conspicuous.

The author makes the statement that "I supposed he possessed the power of life and death over all men and could hang anybody that offended him" primarily to suggest the

(A) power held by a justice of the peace in a frontier town

(B) naive view that he held of his father's importance

(C) respect that the townspeople had for his father

(D) possibility of miscarriages of justice on the American frontier

(E) harsh environment in which he was brought up

The answer is implied here. The author doesn't say "my view of my father's importance at the time was naive." But the idea is implicit in the excerpt.

As the author explains it, he supposed at the time that his father was all powerful and that he could kill almost anyone. On a first reading, that probably struck you as odd. You also probably wondered why the son was proud of it. But read the passage carefully and you'll realize the tone is ironic. The author is making fun of his youthful ideas. So the correct answer has to be (B).

Don't Go Too Far with Inferences

SAT inferences tend to be straightforward and consistent with the overall idea of the passage. They are not extreme, complex, or subtle. In fact, they're incredibly predictable. (You can use this to your advantage.) That's why choices (A) and (E) go too far.

- Is it realistic that the author's father could hang anyone he wanted? Even if he could, would the author be proud of it? Very unlikely.
- Do the boy's early assumptions about his father's power indicate anything about the environment he grew up in? Not a thing.

Look at another question about the same excerpt:

EXAMPLE

The author decides that he would rather become a deck hand than a cabin boy because

(A) the job offers higher wages

(B) he believes that the work is easier

(C) he wants to avoid seeing his older friends

(D) deck hands often go on to become pilots

(E) the job is more visible to passersby

The author never says, "I decided to become a deck hand because the job was more visible to passersby." He does say he wanted to become a cabin boy so his old comrades could see him. And he adds the deck hand job would make him conspicuous. Between the lines, the correct answer, (E), is strongly implied.

Inference Practice

To sharpen your ability to deal with all kinds of inferences, do the following exercise. (Answers on p. 80.)

1. The graduating classes were the nobility of the school. Like travelers with exotic destinations on their minds, the graduates were remarkably forgetful. They came to school without their books, or tablets, or even pencils. Volunteers fell over themselves to secure replacements for the missing equipment. Even the teachers were respectful of the now quiet and aging seniors, and tended to speak to them, if not as equals, as beings only slightly lower than themselves.

   In the lines above, the author most likely mentions the eagerness of the "volunteers" in order to

   (A) indicate the ambition of younger school members
   (B) explain a double standard in teachers' attitudes
   (C) underline the respect with which seniors were treated
   (D) emphasize how careless seniors were with their equipment
   (E) point out a shortage in school supplies

   Ⓐ Ⓑ Ⓒ Ⓓ Ⓔ

2. Without knowing exactly what he'd done, Marc realized that he'd really done it now, and he felt the silence incriminating him. "Now wait just a minute. Hold on there," he said, producing a laugh from somewhere. Marc was the statesman of the class. People joked about how much money he was going to make coming out of law school. But he was groping for his words now, his eyes flickering over the countertop as if the words he was looking for were visible there.

In the lines above, Marc's reputation as "the statesman of the class" is most likely mentioned in order to indicate that

(A) he is noted for his diplomacy
(B) many people resent his success
(C) he is generally an articulate speaker
(D) he is a popular student on campus
(E) his ambitions are not realistic

Ⓐ Ⓑ Ⓒ Ⓓ Ⓔ

Q. How many track and field events make up the Olympic decathlon?

3. Everyone seems to agree that there is something wrong with the way science is being taught these days. But no one is at all clear about what went wrong or what is to be done about it. The term "scientific illiteracy" has become almost a cliché in educational circles. Graduate schools blame the colleges, colleges blame the high schools, the high schools blame the elementary schools, which, in turn, blame the family. I suggest that the scientific community is partly, perhaps largely, to blame.

In the lines above, the phrase "almost a cliché in educational circles" is used to indicate

(A) the lack of unity between different sectors of education
(B) the widespread concern about the way science is being taught
(C) the inability of many scientists to communicate effectively
(D) the ignorance displayed by the scientific community about literature
(E) the extent of agreement over specific educational reforms

Ⓐ Ⓑ Ⓒ Ⓓ Ⓔ

REPLAY

Once you've mastered a concept, check it off.

Building Reading Skills:

- ❏ Skimming
- ❏ Paraphrasing
- ❏ Making inferences

Answers to Paraphrasing and Inference Questions

Paraphrasing:

1. (C) Their parents want them to get married.
2. (D) A photographer is more open to nature and less pretentious than an "artist" is.
3. (A) The Fourth of July is a sham because the holiday celebrates freedom and they are not free.

Inferences:

1. (C)
2. (C)
3. (B)

ROUND 3

Math Skills Workout

8

The Rules: SAT Math

HIGHLIGHTS

- Understand the breakdown and setup of the Math section
- Study traditional Math strategies as well as picking numbers and backsolving

Mathematics is many things. It is linear algebra and complex analysis. It is topology and trigonometry. It is number theory and multivariable calculus. Mathematics is a huge and daunting field, which requires years of study to master. But SAT Math is different. To ace the SAT, you need only a small body of mathematical knowledge covering basic concepts in arithmetic, algebra, and geometry. These concepts have been distilled into 100 principles that you'll find in the "SAT Math Scouting Report" section of this book.

A solid grasp of these principles will get you a good SAT score. Understanding the ways in which these principles are tested—the twists and turns that the test makers throw into many SAT problems—can get you a great score.

This chapter explains:

- The SAT Math sections
- The SAT Math question types
- How to approach SAT Math problems
- Picking numbers
- Backsolving

Two-Minute Drill

This chapter will help you get a handle on the SAT Math section. You should read this chapter even if you have two weeks or fewer to prepare.

Kaplan Rules

You get as many points for an easy question as you do for a hard one.

Then, in chapters 9 through 14, you'll learn:

- When to use your calculator
- Specific strategies for solving Regular Math questions, Quantitative Comparisons (QCs), and Grid-ins
- How to avoid math traps the test makers have set
- How to make educated guesses on difficult math problems

HOW SAT MATH IS SET UP

There are three scored Math sections on the SAT:

- One 30-minute section with 25 Regular Math questions
- One 30-minute section with a set of 15 QCs and a set of ten Grid-ins
- One 15-minute section with ten Regular Math questions

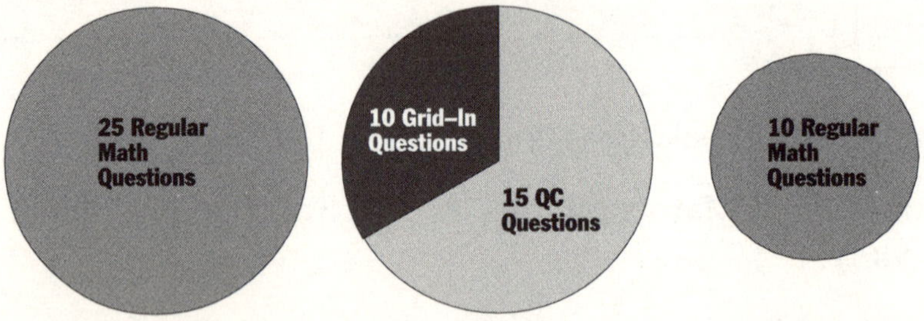

30 Minutes *30 Minutes* *15 Minutes*

Difficulty Level

All sets of SAT Math questions are designed to start off basic and gradually increase in difficulty.

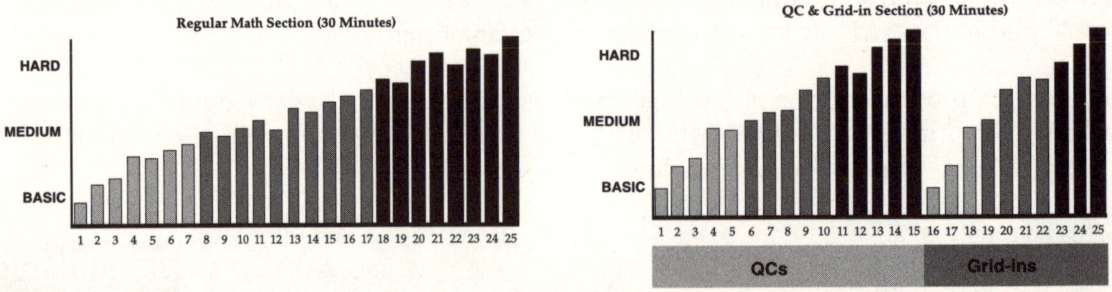

The ten Regular Math questions also get more difficult.

Q. How many strikes must a bowler roll to achieve a perfect game?

Always be aware of the difficulty level as you go through a question set. Easy problems call for different strategies. The harder the questions, the more traps you will encounter. If you know you're dealing with a hard question (even though it may look easy), you'll be prepared.

Know What to Expect

You'll save a lot of time on the SAT Math by knowing the directions. They take a fair amount of time to plow through and are the same for every test. With just a little prior experience, you'll know what to do with each question type so that you can skip the directions and go straight to the first question.

Kaplan Rules

Learn the directions now. Don't waste time on the day of the test.

At the start of each Math section you will find the following information:

Time—30 Minutes 25 Questions	Solve each of the following problems, decide which is the best answer choice, and darken the corresponding oval on the answer sheet. Use available space in the test booklet for scratchwork.

Notes:

(1) Calculator use is permitted.

(2) All numbers used are real numbers.

(3) Figures are provided for some problems. All figures are drawn to scale and lie in a plane UNLESS otherwise indicated.

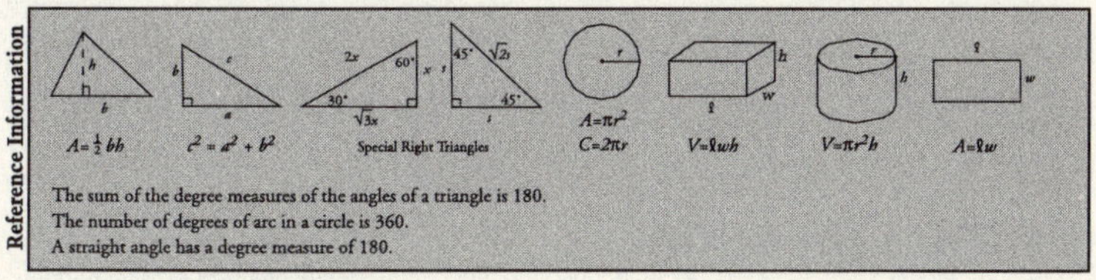

Note (2) means you won't have to deal with imaginary numbers, such as *i* (the square root of –1).

Note (3) tells you diagrams are drawn to scale, which means you can use these diagrams to estimate measurements. However, if the diagrams are labeled "Figure not drawn to scale," you can't do this.

Saying the figures "lie in a plane" simply means you are dealing with flat figures, like rectangles or circles, unless the question says otherwise.

The math information you're given includes many basic geometry formulas. By the day of the test you should know all these formulas by heart. But if you forget one at the last minute, you'll find them in the directions.

The Grid-ins and QCs have slightly different instructions, which we'll discuss in detail in chapter 10 and chapter 11.

HOW TO APPROACH SAT MATH

To maximize your Math score, you need to learn to use your time efficiently. Then you won't get bogged down on a single hard question and miss other problems you could have solved if you'd had more time.

Kaplan Rules

If you always mess up the same type of problem, circle it, skip it, and come back to it if you have time.

The key to working systematically is: Think about the question before you look for the answer. A few seconds spent up front looking for traps, thinking about your approach, and deciding whether to tackle the problem now or come back to it later will pay off in SAT points. On basic problems, you may know what to do right away. But on hard problems, the few extra seconds are time well spent.

Now apply it to the problem below:

EXAMPLE

12. At a certain diner, Joe orders three doughnuts and a cup of coffee and is charged $2.25. Stella ordered two doughnuts and a cup of coffee and is charged $1.70. What is the price of two doughnuts?

    (A) $0.55

    (B) $0.60

    (C) $1.10

    (D) $1.30

    (E) $1.80

Read Through the Question

This means the whole question. If you try to start solving the problem before reading it all the way through, you may end up doing unnecessary work.

Decide whether the question is basic, medium, or hard. All SAT Math questions are arranged in order of difficulty. Within a set, the first questions are basic, the middle ones moderately difficult, and the last ones are hard. Question 12 above is a moderately difficult word problem.

On difficult questions, watch out for Math Traps. Hard questions are often misleadingly worded to trip up careless readers. (For more on Math Traps, see chapter 13, "Avoid the Double-Team.")

Make sure you know what's being asked. Question 12 looks straightforward, but read through it carefully and you'll see a slight twist. You're asked to find the cost of two doughnuts, not one. Many people will find the price of a single doughnut and forget to double it.

What to Do When You Skip a Question

Circle it in your test booklet and make sure you skip it on your answer grid.

Decide Whether to Do the Problem or Skip It for Now

- If you have no idea what to do, skip the problem and circle it in your test booklet. Spend your time on the problems you can solve.
- If you think you can solve it, but it will take a lot of time, circle the question number in your test booklet and make a note to come back to it later if you have time.
- If you can eliminate one or more answer choices, do so and make an educated guess. Mark that you guessed in your test booklet, and try solving later if time permits. (For details on educated guessing, see chapter 14, "Slam-Dunk Strategies for Guessing.")

If You Do Tackle the Problem, Look for the Fastest Approach

Look for hidden information. On an easy question, all the information you need to solve the problem may be given up front, in the stem, or in a diagram. But in a harder question, you may need to look for hidden information that will help you solve the problem. Since questions are arranged in order of difficulty, you should be a little wary of question 12. If you get the answer too easily, you may have missed something. In this case, you're asked to find the price of two doughnuts, not one. For more on Hidden Instructions, see the chapter on SAT Math Traps.

Helpful Hint

When you skip a question, make a note in your test booklet to come back to it later, if you have time.

Look for shortcuts. Sometimes the obvious way of doing a problem is the long way. If the method you choose involves lots of calculating, look for another route. There's usually a shortcut you can use that won't involve tons of arithmetic.

In question 12, for example, the cost of doughnuts and coffee could be translated into two distinct equations using the variables d and c. You could find c in terms of d, then plug this into the other equation. But if you think carefully, you'll see there's a quicker way: The difference in price between three doughnuts and a cup of coffee and two doughnuts and a cup of coffee is the price of one doughnut. So one doughnut costs $\$2.25 - \$1.70 = \$0.55$. (Remember, you have to find the price of *two* doughnuts. Twice \$0.55 is \$1.10.)

Use a variety of strategies. Chapter 12, "Problem Solving," reviews many strategies for specific problem types that will help you get to the answer faster. You can also use special Kaplan methods, such as Picking Numbers and Backsolving. (For more on these methods, see pp. 88–92 in this chapter.)

Make an Educated Guess

If you're not sure what to do, or if you've tried solving a problem but got stuck, cut your losses. Eliminate any answer choices you can, and make an educated guess.

Let's say it's taking too long to solve the doughnut problem. Can you eliminate any answer choices? The price of two doughnuts and a cup of coffee is \$1.70. That means the cost of two doughnuts alone can't be \$1.80, which eliminates choice (E). Now you can choose between the remaining choices, and your odds of guessing correctly have improved. (See chapter 14, "Slam-Dunk Strategies for Guessing.")

If you practice using this approach to the Math problems on the SAT, you will save time and avoid mistakes on the day of the test.

Q. What is the longest field goal in NFL history?

(A) 100 yards

(B) 80 yards

(C) 63 yards

(D) 45 yards

(E) 29 yards

WHEN YOU'RE STUCK

The great thing about math, even if you hate it, is that there are usually a lot of different ways to get to the right answer. On the SAT, there are two methods in particular that are really useful when you don't see the straightforward way to solve the problem—picking numbers and backsolving. These strategies can take longer than traditional methods, but they're worth trying if you have enough time.

Picking Numbers

Sometimes you can get stuck on a math question just because it's too general or abstract. A good way to get a handle on such a question is to bring it down to earth and make it more explicit by temporarily substituting particular numbers. This "picking numbers" strategy works especially well with even/odd questions.

Q. In what sport is the term "half nelson" used?

EXAMPLE

If a is an odd integer and b is an even integer, which of the following must be odd?

(A) $2a + b$

(B) $a + 2b$

(C) ab

(D) a^2b

(E) ab^2

Rather than try to think this one through abstractly, it's easier for most people simply to pick numbers for a and b. There are rules that predict the evenness or oddness of sums, differences, and products, but there's no need to memorize these rules. When it comes to adding, subtracting, and multiplying evens and odds, what happens with one pair of numbers generally happens with all similar pairs.

Just say, for the time being, that $a = 3$ and $b = 2$. Plug those values into the answer choices, and there's a good chance that only one choice will be odd:

(A) $2a + b = 2(3) + 2 = 8$

(B) $a + 2b = 3 + 2(2) = 7$

(C) $ab = (3)(2) = 6$

(D) $a^2b = (3^2)(2) = 18$

(E) $ab^2 = (3)(2^2) = 12$

Choice (B) is the only odd one for $a = 3$ and $b = 2$, so it must be the one that's odd no matter what odd number a and even number b actually stand for. The answer is (B).

Another good situation for using the "picking numbers" strategy is when the answer choices to a percent problem are all percents.

EXAMPLE

From 1985 to 1990, the population of City *X* increased by 20 percent. From 1990 to 1995, the population increased by 30 percent. What was the percent increase in the population over the entire ten-year period 1985–1995?

(A) 10%

(B) 25%

(C) 50%

(D) 56%

(E) 60%

Kaplan Rules

On percents, 100 is an easy number to work with.

Instead of trying to solve this problem in the abstract, pick a number for the original 1985 population and see what happens. There's no need to pick a realistic number. You're better off picking a number that's easy to work with. And in percent problems the number that's easiest to work with is almost always 100. Say the 1985 population was 100, then what would the 1990 population be? Twenty percent more than 100 is 120. Now, if the 1990 population was 120, what would the 1995 population be? What's 30 percent more than 120? Be careful. Don't just add 30 to 120. You need to find 30 percent of 120 and add that on. Thirty percent of 120 is $(.30)(120) = 36$. Add 36 to 120 and you get a 1995 population of 156. What percent greater is 156 than 100? That's easy—that's why we picked 100 to start with. It's a 56 percent increase. The answer is (D).

A third good situation for using the "picking numbers" strategy is when the answer choices to a word problem are not numbers, but algebraic expressions.

EXAMPLE

If n apples cost p dollars, then how many dollars would q apples cost?

(A) $\frac{np}{q}$

(B) $\frac{nq}{p}$

(C) $\frac{pq}{n}$

(D) $\frac{n}{pq}$

(E) $\frac{p}{nq}$

SAT Math: The Warning Signs

- If your answer depends on calculating the weight of the moon, in kilograms, you've read something wrong.
- "One potato, two potato" is not a useful guessing technique.

Kaplan Rules

Avoid picking weird numbers like 0 and 1, as these often give several "possibly correct" answers.

The only thing that's hard about this question is that it uses variables instead of numbers. So, make it real. Pick numbers for the variables. Pick numbers that are easy to work with. Say $n = 2$, $p = 4$, and $q = 3$. Then the question becomes: "If two apples cost $4.00, how many dollars would three apples cost?" That's easy—$6.00. When $n = 2$, $p = 4$, and $q = 3$, the correct answer should equal 6. Plug those values into the answer choices and see which ones yield 6:

(A) $\frac{np}{q} = \frac{(2)(4)}{3} = \frac{8}{3}$

(B) $\frac{nq}{q} = \frac{(2)(3)}{3} = \frac{6}{3} = 2$

(C) $\frac{pq}{n} = \frac{(4)(3)}{2} = \frac{12}{2} = 6$

(D) $\frac{n}{pq} = \frac{2}{(4)(3)} = \frac{2}{12} = \frac{1}{6}$

(E) $\frac{p}{nq} = \frac{4}{(2)(3)} = \frac{4}{6} = \frac{2}{3}$

Choice (C) is the only one that yields 6, so it must be the correct answer.

When picking numbers for an abstract word problem like this one, it's important to try all five answer choices. Sometimes more than one choice will yield the correct result, in which case one or more choices work coincidentally with the numbers you picked. When that happens, pick another set of numbers to weed out the coincidences. Avoid picking weird numbers such as 0 and 1, as these often give several "possibly correct" answers.

Backsolving

On some Math questions, when you can't figure out the question, you can try working backwards from the answer choices. Plug the choices back into the question until you find the one that works.

Backsolving works best:

- When the question is a complex word problem and the answer choices are numbers
- When the alternative is setting up multiple algebraic equations

Don't backsolve:

- If the answer choices include variables
- On algebra questions or word problems that have ugly answer choices such as radicals and fractions (plugging them in takes too much time)

Complex Question, Simple Answer Choices

Speed Tip

To speed things up, start with the middle-range number. Since answer choices are always listed in increasing or decreasing order, you should start with choice (C). If it's too small, move to the bigger ones.

EXAMPLE

An office has 27 employees. If there are seven more women than men in the office, how many employees are women?

(A) 8

(B) 10

(C) 14

(D) 17

(E) 20

Sometimes backsolving is faster than setting up an equation.

The five answer choices represent the possible number of women in the office, so try them in the question stem. The choice that gives a total of 27 employees, with seven more women than men, will be the correct answer.

Plugging in choice (C) gives you 14 women in the office. Since there are seven more women than men, there are seven men in the office. But $14 + 7 < 27$. The sum is too small, so there must be more than 14 women. Eliminate answer choices (A), (B), and (C).

Either (D) or (E) will be correct. Plugging in (D) gives you 17 women in the office and $17 - 7$, or 10 men. $17 + 10 = 27$ employees total. Answer choice (D) is correct.

Algebra Problems for Which You Need to Solve Multiple Equations

EXAMPLE

If $a + b + c = 110$, $a = 4b$, and $3a = 2c$, then $b =$

(A) 6

(B) 8

(C) 9

(D) 10

(E) 14

You're looking for b, so plug in the answer choices for b in the question and see what happens. The choice that gives us 110 for the sum $a + b + c$ must be correct.

Start with the midrange number, 9, choice (C):

If $b = 9$, then $a = 4 \times 9 = 36$.

$2c = 3a = 3 \times 36 = 108$.

$c = 54$.

$a + b + c = 36 + 9 + 54 = 99$.

Since this is a smaller sum than 110, the correct value for b must be greater. Therefore, eliminate answer choices (A), (B), and (C).

Now plug in either (D) or (E) and see if it works. If it doesn't, the remaining choice must be correct.

Short of time? Try guessing between (D) and (E). But guess intelligently. Since (C) wasn't far wrong, you want a number just slightly bigger. That's choice (D).

Now work through the remaining chapters in the Math Skills Workout section to master other strategies that will help you to ace your test.

Q. In 1999 Mark McGwire and Sammy Sosa combined to hit 136 home runs. If McGwire hit four more than Sosa, how many home runs did McGwire hit?

(A) 93

(B) 70

(C) 66

(D) 61*

(E) 50

9

Equipment: Calculators

HIGHLIGHTS

- Practice with the calculator you'll bring to the test
- Use your calculator selectively
- Know the most common calculator mistakes and how to avoid them

You are allowed to use a calculator on the SAT. That's a mixed blessing. The good news is you can do computation faster. The bad news is you may be tempted to waste time using a calculator on questions that shouldn't involve lengthy computation.

Remember, you never *need* a calculator to solve an SAT problem. If you ever find yourself doing extensive calculation on the SAT—elaborate long division or long, drawn-out multiplication—stop and look again, because you probably missed a shortcut.

SHOULD I BRING A CALCULATOR?

You definitely want to bring your calculator on the day of the test. The fact is, there are some problems for which using the calculator will really come in handy. By using your calculator on particular problem types and by zeroing in on the parts of problems that need calculation, you can increase your score and save yourself time on the SAT.

Two-Minute Drill

If you have a week or two to prep for the SAT, be sure to read the section on common calculator mistakes.

WHAT KIND OF CALCULATOR SHOULD I BRING?

The best calculator to bring is one you're comfortable with. The most important thing is not how fancy your calculator is, but how good you are at using it. Remember, you won't be doing logs, trig functions, or preprogrammed formulas on the SAT. Most of the time you'll be multiplying and dividing.

You can use the following calculators on the SAT:

The More You Know About the SAT . . .

. . . the less you'll use your calculator.

Using a calculator too much could actually hurt your score. The better you are at the SAT, the less you'll need your calculator.

- A four-function calculator (that adds, subtracts, multiplies, divides)
- A scientific calculator (that also does radicals, exponents, etcetera)
- A graphing calculator (that displays the graph of an equation in a coordinate plane)

But the following are not allowed:

- A calculator that prints out your calculations
- A hand-held minicomputer or a laptop computer
- Any calculator with a typewriter keypad
- A calculator that "speaks," makes strange noises, or requires an electrical outlet for use

WHEN SHOULD I USE A CALCULATOR?

Calculators help the most on Grid-ins and the least on QCs.

The reason for this is that QCs are designed to be done very quickly, and rarely involve much computation—if you think you need a calculator on them, then you're probably missing something. Both Grid-ins and Regular Math will sometimes involve computation—never as the most important part of the question, but often as a final step.

Since Grid-ins don't give you answer choices to choose from, it's especially important to be sure of your work. Calculators can help you avoid careless errors.

Remember, a calculator can be useful when used selectively. Not all parts of a problem are necessarily easier on a calculator. Consider this problem:

EXAMPLE

If four grams of cadmium yellow pigment can make 3 kilograms of cadmium yellow oil paint, how many kilograms of paint could be produced from 86 grams of pigment?

This word problem has two steps. Step one is to set up the following proportion:

$$\frac{4 \text{ gms}}{3 \text{ kgs}} = \frac{86 \text{ gms}}{x \text{ kgs}}$$

A little algebraic engineering tells you that:

$$x \text{ kgs} = \frac{3 \text{ kgs} \times 86 \text{ gms}}{4 \text{ gms}}$$

Here's where you whip out that calculator. This problem has now been reduced down to pure calculation: $(3 \times 86) \div 4 = 64.5$.

Your calculator will also be especially useful for picking numbers and backsolving.

Check Your Batteries

The best calculator in the world won't help if the batteries are dead or if you forget to put them in. Make sure you have fresh batteries in your machine on the day of the test.

When You Pick Numbers

When you plug in real numbers to replace variables in complex equations, your calculator can speed things up. (See Picking Numbers in chapter 8, "The Rules: SAT Math.")

When You Backsolve

When you plug multiple-choice answers into a problem to see which answer is right, your calculator can speed up the process. (See Backsolving, in chapter 8.)

WHEN SHOULDN'T I USE A CALCULATOR?

Don't be fooled. On most SAT problems you may be tempted to use your calculator, but many questions will be easier without a calculator. That's particularly true on QCs.

Consider this problem:

EXAMPLE

Column A	Column B
The ratio of b to 7 is equal to the ratio of 143 to 188.	
b	7

Q. How many laps does it take to complete the Indianapolis 500 auto race?

Sure, you could set up the proportion $\frac{b}{7} = \frac{143}{188}$, grab your calculator, and cross multiply to find that $b = 5.324468085$. But why bother doing the calculation? Once you've set up the proportion, you can make a quick comparison without any further calculation. Your task is to compare b to 7. If $b = 7$, then $\frac{b}{7} = 1$. However, $\frac{b}{7}$ must be less than 1 since $\frac{143}{188} < 1$. Therefore, $b < 7$. Column B must be greater.

Be careful on non-QC questions, too. Consider this:

EXAMPLE

If $x^2 \times 8^2 = 49 \times 64 \times 81$, $x^2 =$

(A) 49^2

(B) 56^2

(C) 63^2

(D) 72^2

(E) 81^2

Now if you punch in $49 \times 64 \times 81$ you'll get 254,016. But that won't be too helpful. Look at the answer choices! Instead realize that:

$$(x^2) \times 8^2 = (49 \times 81) \times 64$$

8^2 is the same as 64, so get rid of the 64s on both sides. You get:

$$x^2 = 49 \times 81$$

So that's $x^2 = 7^2 \times 9^2$ or $x^2 = 7 \times 7 \times 9 \times 9$, which is 63×63 or 63^2.

No calculator required.

COMMON MISTAKE #1: CALCULATING BEFORE YOU THINK

On the Grid-in problem below, how should you use your calculator?

Calculator Abuse: The Warning Signs

- Punching in numbers before you've read the question.
- Hand cramps from punching in too many numbers.
- Repeatedly spelling *hello* or *Shell Oil* on your calculator rather than answering the question.

EXAMPLE

The sum of all the integers from 1 to 44, inclusive, is subtracted from the sum of all the integers from 7 to 50, inclusive. What is the result?

The Wrong Approach:

- Grab calculator.
- Punch in all the numbers.
- Put down an answer and hope you didn't hit any wrong buttons.

The wrong approach is to punch in all the numbers from 1 to 44, find their sum, then do the same for numbers 7 through 50, and subtract the first sum from the second. Doing that means punching 252 keys. The odds are you'll slip up somewhere, hit the wrong key, and get the wrong answer. Even if you don't, punching in all those numbers takes too much time.

The Kaplan Method

- Think first.
- Decide on the best way to solve it.
- Only then, use your calculator.

The right approach is to *think first.* The amount of computation involved in solving this directly tells you that there *must* be an easier way. You'll see this if you realize that both sums are of the same number of consecutive integers. Each integer in the first sum has a corresponding integer six units greater than it in the second sum, like so:

1	7
+2	+8
+3	+9
.	.
.	.
.	.
+42	+48
+43	+49
+44	+50
=	=

Q. Who holds the record for most career grand slam homers?

There are 44 pairs of integers that are six units apart. So the total difference between the two sums will be the difference between each pair of integers times the number of pairs.

Now take out your calculator, multiply 6 by 44, and get the correct answer of 264, with little or no time wasted.

HINT: *If you're punching buttons for long stretches at a time, you're approaching the problem the wrong way.*

COMMON MISTAKE #2: FORGETTING THE ORDER OF OPERATIONS

Watch out. Even when you use your calculator, you can't just enter numbers in the order they appear on the page—you've got to follow the order of operations. This is a very simple error but it can cost you lots of points.

Kaplan Rules

Different calculators do chain calculations different ways. Make sure you know how your calculator does chains so you don't miscalculate.

The order of operations, or PEMDAS, means you do whatever is in:

Parentheses first, then deal with

Exponents, then

Multiplication and

Division, and finally

Addition and

Subtraction

For example, say you want to find the value of the expression:

$$\frac{x^2 + 1}{x + 3} \quad \text{when } x = 7$$

If you just punched in "7 × 7 + 1 ÷ 7 + 3 =" you would get the wrong answer. The correct way to work it out is:

$$(7^2 + 1) \div (7 + 3) = (7 \times 7 + 1) \div (7 + 3) = (49 + 1) \div 10 = 50 \div 10 = 5$$

Combining a calculator with an understanding of when and how to use it can help you boost your score.

REPLAY

Once you've mastered a concept, check it off.

Calculators and the SAT:

- ❏ What kind of calculator should I bring?
- ❏ When should I use a calculator?
- ❏ When shouldn't I use a calculator?
- ❏ Common Mistakes

10

Grid-Ins

HIGHLIGHTS

- Familiarize yourself with grid formats, techniques, and rules
- Practice gridding in answers with fractions, mixed numbers, and decimals

In high school math class, you usually don't get five answer choices to choose from on a test. And you don't lose a quarter of a point for a wrong answer. Instead, you're given a problem and asked to find the answer.

The Grid-in section on the SAT is a lot like the math tests you're already used to taking. Unlike other questions on the SAT, Grid-ins have no multiple-choice answers and there's no penalty for wrong answers. You have to figure out your own answer and fill it in on a special grid. Note that some Grid-ins have only one correct answer, while others have several, or even a range of correct answers.

Two- Minute Drill

If you have two weeks or fewer to prep for the SAT, here's the best way to spend your time:

- Read this entire chapter. It's pretty short and the gridding tips that we discuss can help prevent you from making careless mistakes that can make a big difference in your score.
- Do the gridding drills at the end of the chapter.

Q. Who was the first NBA player to have 200 blocks and 200 steals in the same season?

THE FORMAT

You'll get ten Grid-ins, following the QCs, in one of the Math sections. To get an idea of what the instructions will look like on the day of the test, check out the example below.

For each question, you'll see a grid with four boxes and a column of ovals beneath each. First write your numerical answer in the boxes, one digit, decimal point, or fraction bar per box. Then fill in the corresponding ovals below.

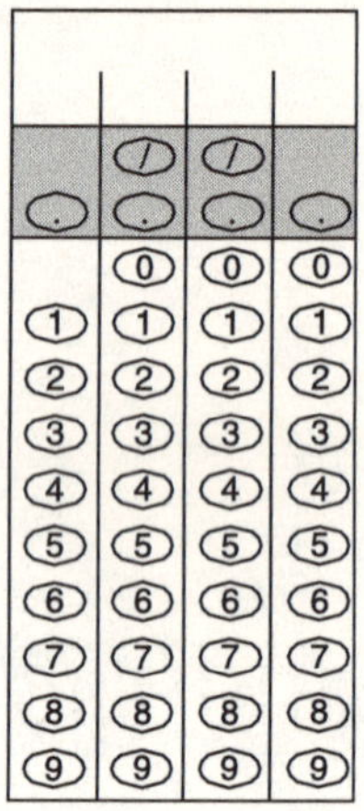

Warning:

- The computer cannot scan the numerical answer in the boxes; you must fill in the corresponding ovals.
- Fill in no more than one oval per column.
- Make the oval you grid match your number above that oval.

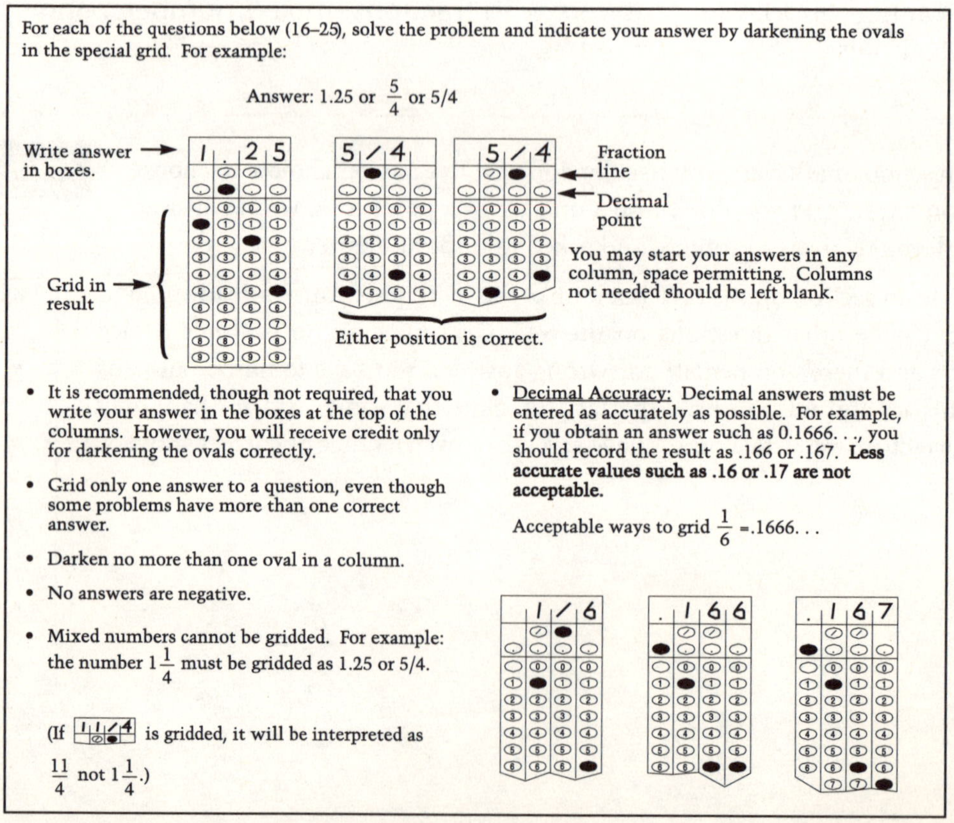

For each of the questions below (16–25), solve the problem and indicate your answer by darkening the ovals in the special grid. For example:

Answer: 1.25 or $\frac{5}{4}$ or 5/4

You may start your answers in any column, space permitting. Columns not needed should be left blank.

- It is recommended, though not required, that you write your answer in the boxes at the top of the columns. However, you will receive credit only for darkening the ovals correctly.
- Grid only one answer to a question, even though some problems have more than one correct answer.
- Darken no more than one oval in a column.
- No answers are negative.
- Mixed numbers cannot be gridded. For example: the number $1\frac{1}{4}$ must be gridded as 1.25 or 5/4.

(If 1 1 / 4 is gridded, it will be interpreted as $\frac{11}{4}$ not $1\frac{1}{4}$.)

- Decimal Accuracy: Decimal answers must be entered as accurately as possible. For example, if you obtain an answer such as 0.1666. . ., you should record the result as .166 or .167. **Less accurate values such as .16 or .17 are not acceptable.**

Acceptable ways to grid $\frac{1}{6}$ = .1666. . .

Grid instructions

FILLING IN THE GRID

The grid cannot accommodate:

- Negative answers
- Answers with variables
- Answers greater than 9,999
- Answers with commas
- Mixed numbers

Recommendation: Start your answer in the first column box. Do this even if your answer has only one or two figures. If you always start with the first column, your answers will always fit. Since there is no oval for 0 in the first column, grid an answer of 0 in any other column. (Technically, you can start in any column, but follow this rule to avoid mistakes.)

In a fractional answer, grid (/) in the correct column. The sign (/) separates the numerator from the denominator. It appears only in columns two and three.

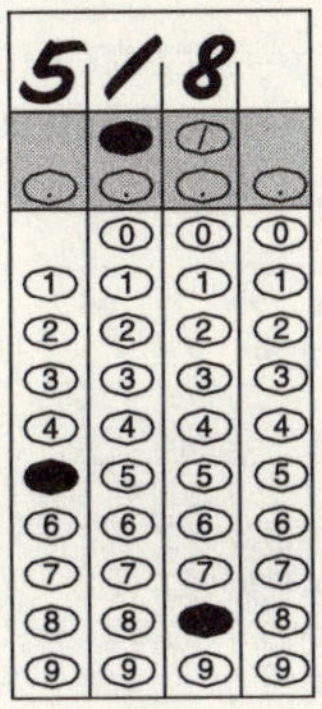

Example: If you get an answer of $\frac{5}{8}$. Grid (/) in col. two.

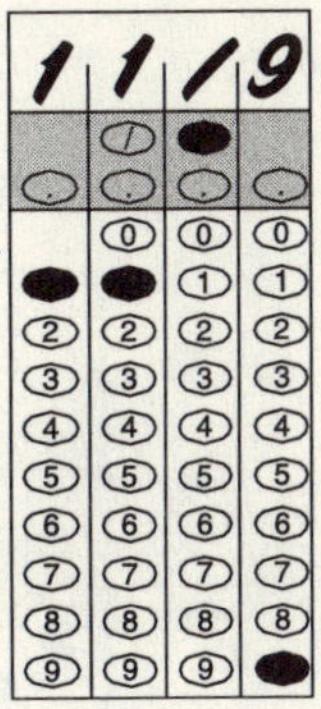

Example: If you get an answer of $\frac{11}{9}$. Grid (/) in col. three.

WARNING: *A fractional answer with four digits won't fit.*

Change mixed numbers to decimals or fractions before you grid. If you try to grid a mixed number, it will be read as a fraction, and be counted wrong. For example, $4\frac{1}{2}$ will be read as the fraction $\frac{41}{2}$, which is $20\frac{1}{2}$.

So first change mixed numbers to fractions or decimals, then grid in. In this case:

- Change $4\frac{1}{2}$ to $\frac{9}{2}$ and grid in as shown below.
- Or change $4\frac{1}{2}$ to 4.5 and grid in the decimal.

Two Grid-in Tips

1. Always start from the left.
2. Guess when you can. Skip it when you haven't a clue. Be sure to circle the question number in your test booklet if you skip it.

There's no wrong-answer penalty for Grid-ins. So if you have time, take an educated guess. It can't hurt.

Kaplan Rules

Bubble trouble: The computer scores only the numbers that are bubbled in, not what you've written on top of the grid. The only reason to write your answers out is to help you bubble in.

Kaplan Rules

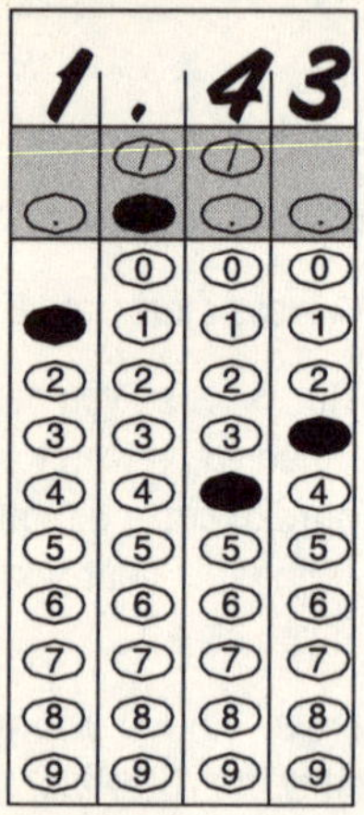

Always use the most accurate answer that fits. For example, 1.4 is not a substitute for 1.43.

Top Grid-in Screw-Ups

- Gridding in mixed numbers
- Making rounding errors
- Writing your answer and forgetting to grid it in
- Double bubble gridding two numbers in the same column (the computer reads this as an omission)
- Filling the wrong bubble under the right number—it's still considered a wrong answer

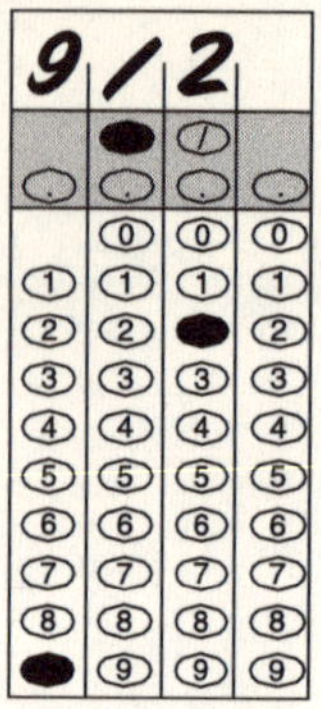

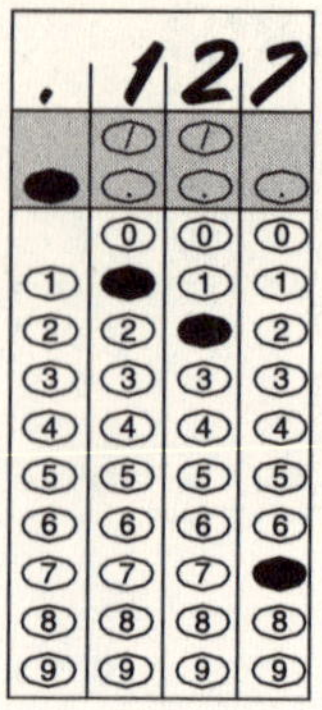

HINT: *Watch where you put your decimal points.*

- For a decimal less than 1, such as .127, enter the decimal point in the first box as shown in the figure above.
- Put a zero before the decimal point only if it's part of the answer—don't just put one there to make your answer look more accurate.
- Never grid a decimal point in the last column.

With long or repeating decimals, grid the first three digits only and plug in the decimal point where it belongs. Say three answers are .45454545, 82.452312, and 1.428743. Grid .454, 82.4, and 1.42, respectively.

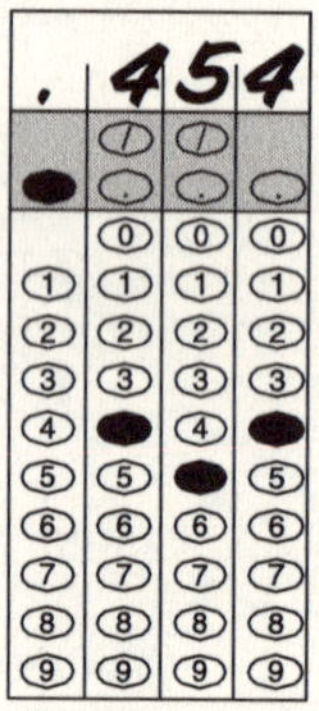

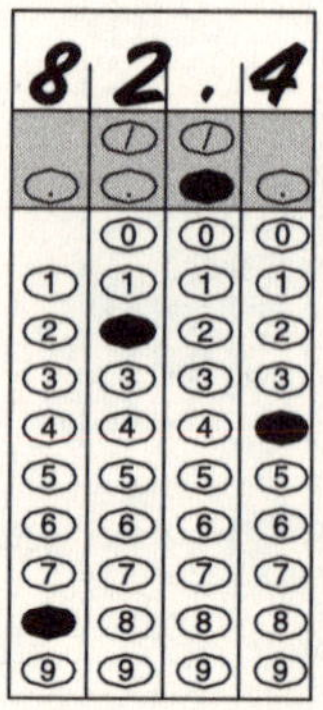

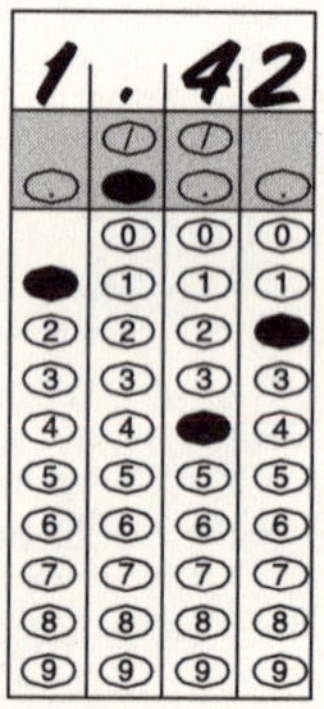

You could round 1.428743 up to the nearest hundredth (1.43), but it's not required. So don't bother, since you could make a mistake. Shorter, less accurate answers—such as 1.4—are wrong.

On Grid-ins with more than one right answer, choose one, and enter it.

Say you're asked for a two-digit integer that is a multiple of 2, 3, and 5. You might answer 30, 60, or 90. Whichever you grid would be right.

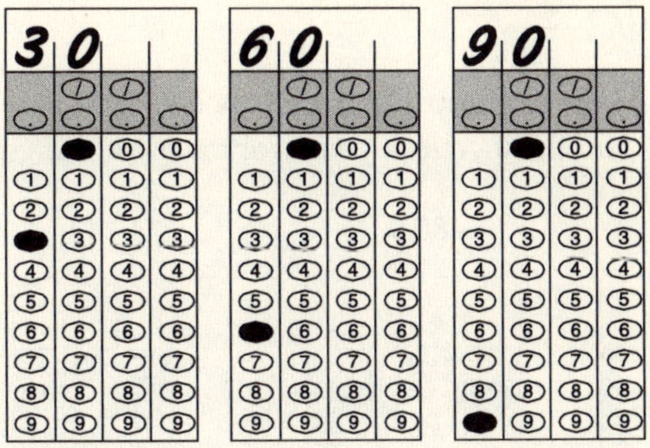

Q. For which NHL team is the octopus a good luck sign?

Some Grid-ins have a range of possible answers. Suppose you're asked to grid a value of m, given that $1 - 2m < m$ and $5m - 2 < m$. Solving for m in the first inequality, you find that $\frac{1}{3} < m$. Solving for m in the second inequality, you find that $m < \frac{1}{2}$. So $\frac{1}{3} < m < \frac{1}{2}$. Grid in any value between $\frac{1}{3}$ and $\frac{1}{2}$. (Gridding in $\frac{1}{3}$ or $\frac{1}{2}$ would be wrong.) When the answer is a range of values, it's often easier to work with decimals: $.333 < m < .5$. Then you can quickly grid .4 (or .35 or .45, etcetera) as your answer.

Write your answers in the number boxes. You will make fewer mistakes if you write your answers in the number boxes. You may think that gridding directly will save time, but writing first and then gridding ensures accuracy, which means more points.

PRACTICE GRIDDING

With just a little practice, you can master the gridding-in process. Complete the Grid-ins below, following our instructions. After you finish, check your work against the grids on p. 106.

126

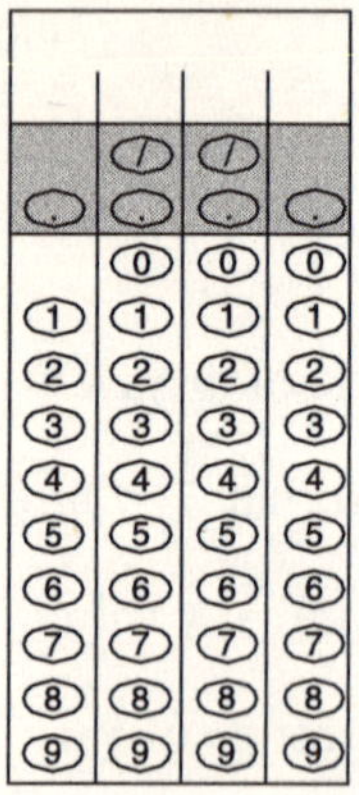

$\frac{3}{8}$

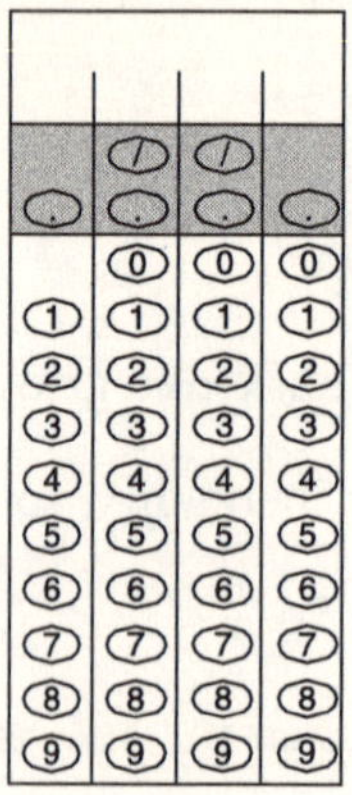

85.9

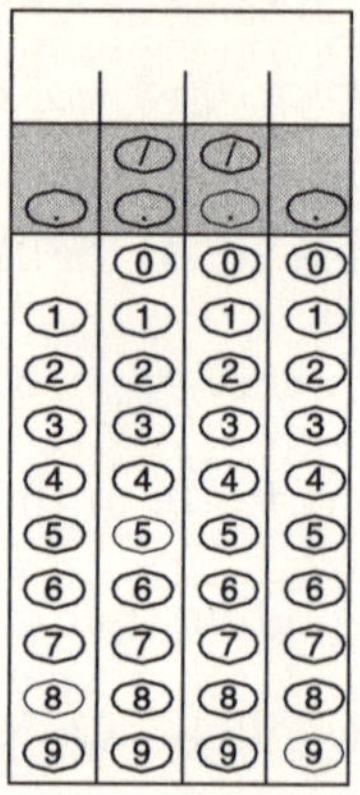

2,143

$5\frac{1}{2}$

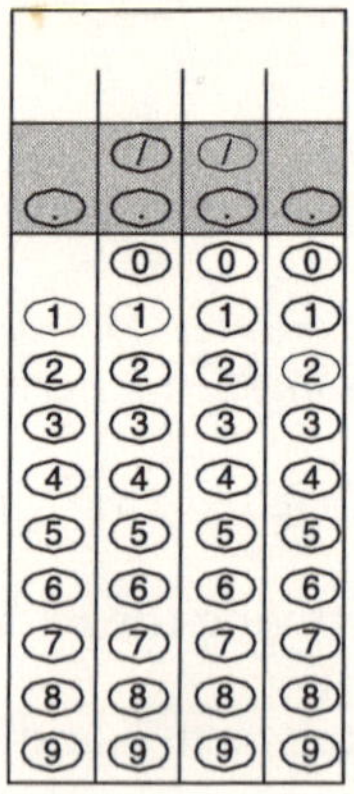

0

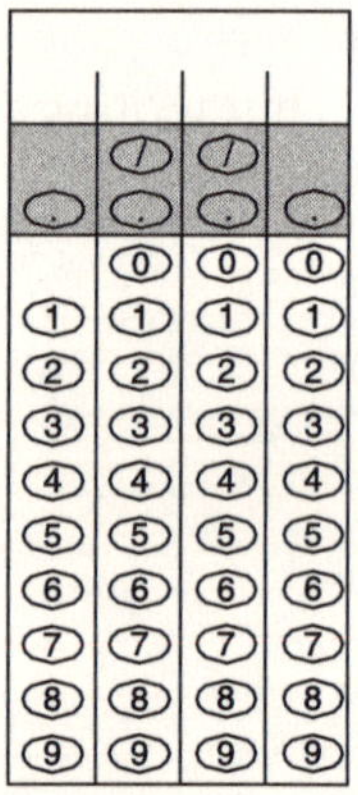

.141414

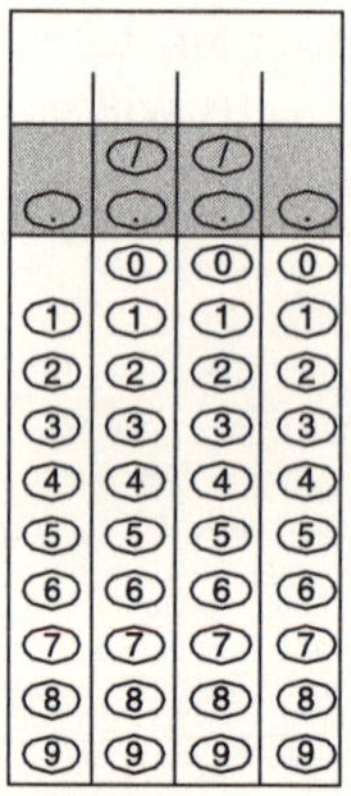

$\frac{14}{5}$

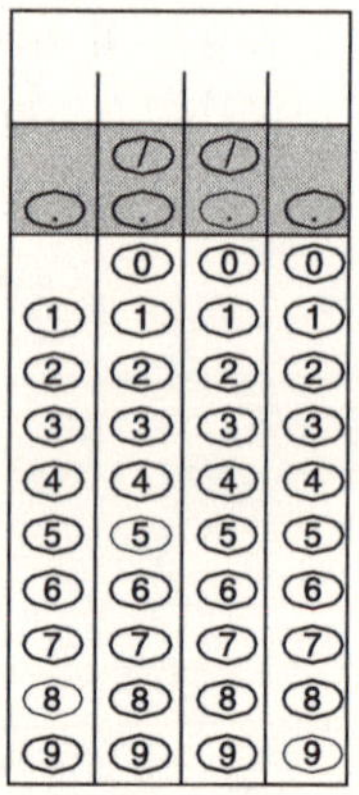

$1\frac{2}{3}$

8.175

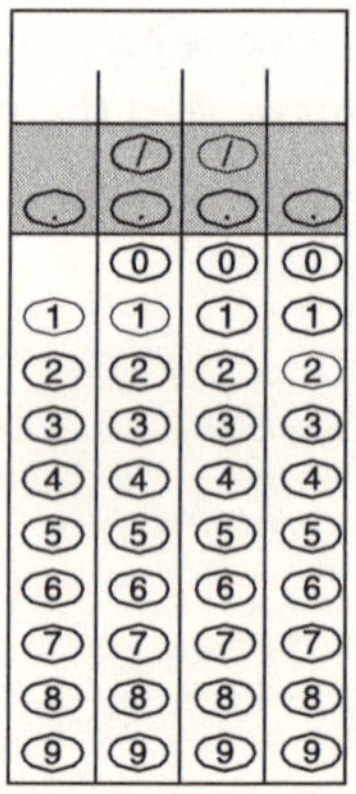

REPLAY

Once you've mastered a concept, check it off.

Grid-Ins:

❏ The format

❏ Filling in the grid

❏ Practice gridding

Gridding Answers

126

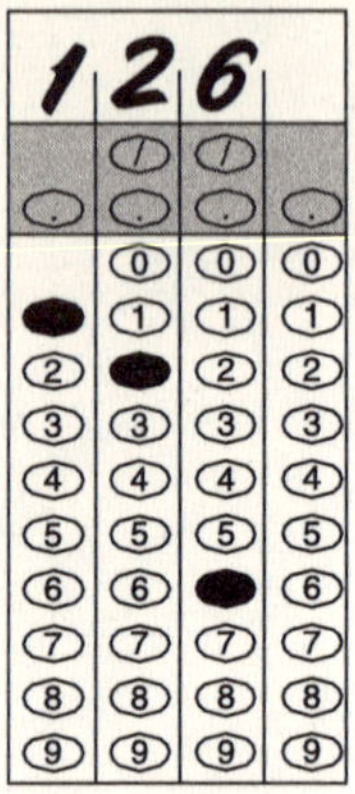

$\frac{3}{8}$

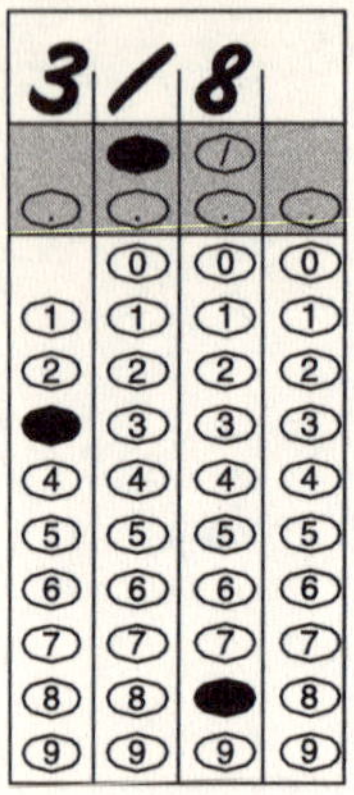

Or .375

85.9

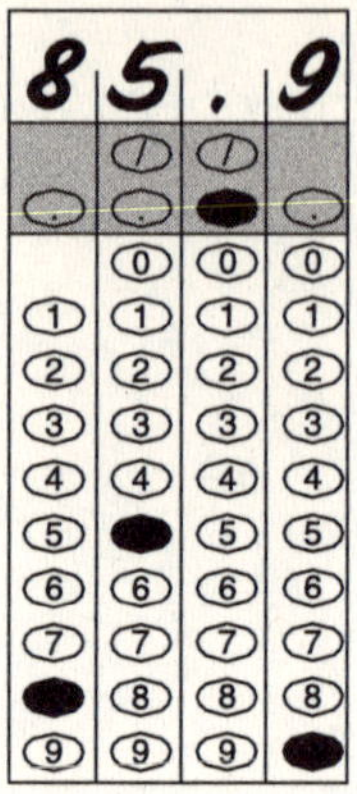

2,143

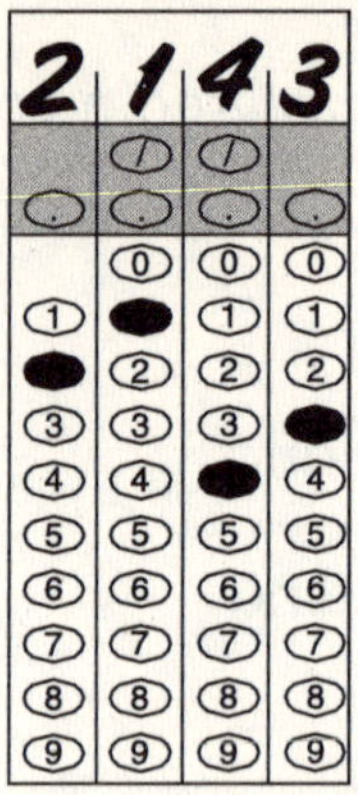

Omit the comma.

$5\frac{1}{2}$

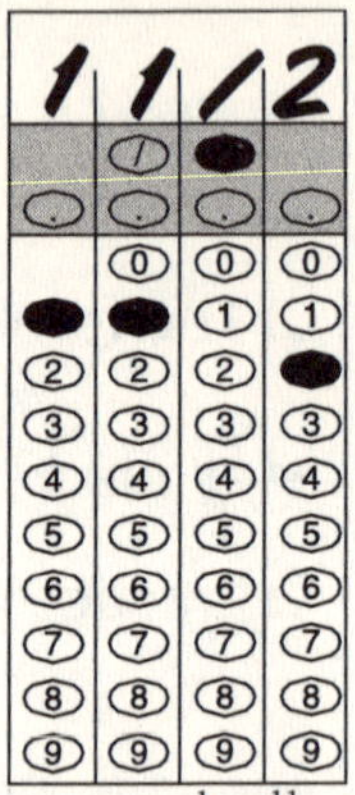

Convert $5\frac{1}{2}$ to $\frac{11}{2}$ (or 5.5); "5 1/2" is incorrect.

0

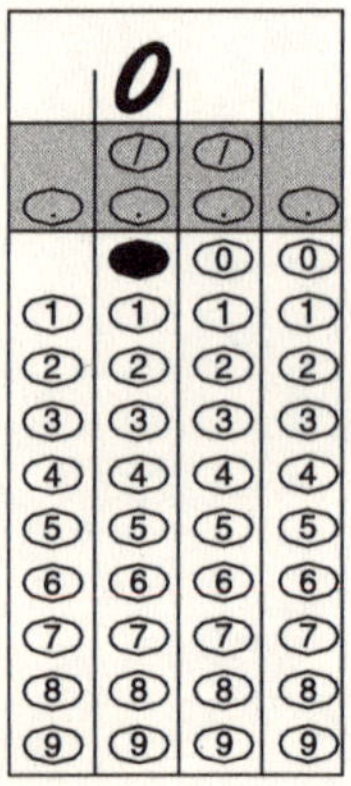

.141414

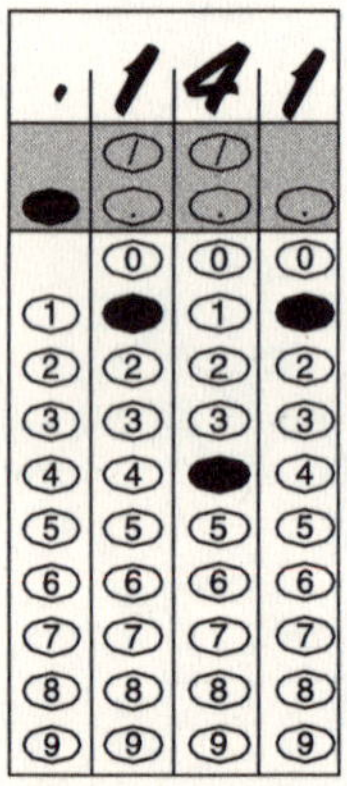

Place the decimal point in the first column and grid as many digits as possible.

$\frac{14}{5}$

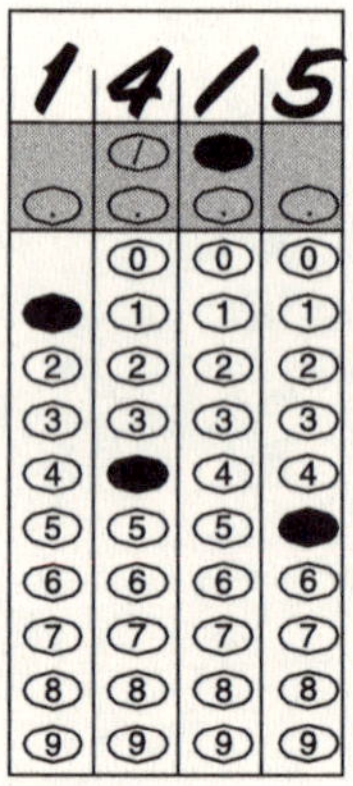

$1\frac{2}{3}$

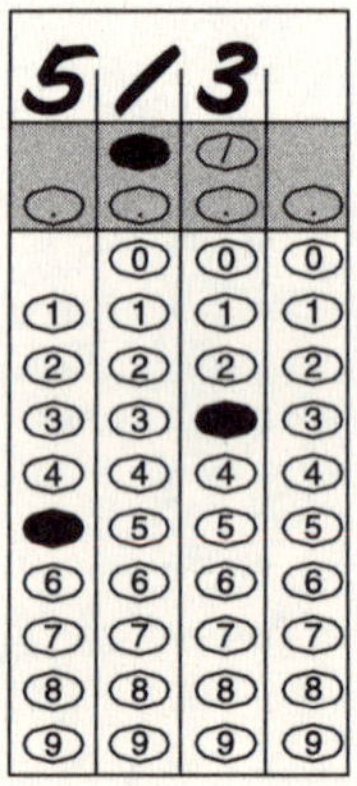

Convert $1\frac{2}{3}$ to $\frac{5}{3}$ (or 1.66 or 1.67); "12/3" is incorrect.

8.175

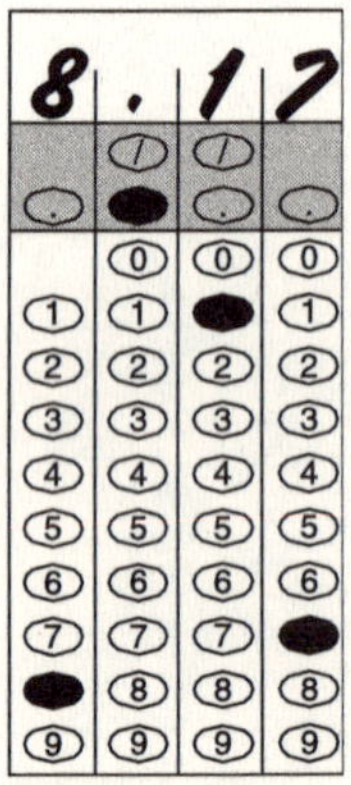

Or 8.18. Start in the left column and grid as many digits as possible.

11

Quantitative Comparisons

HIGHLIGHTS

- Understand the answer choices and the rules for choice (D)
- Master Kaplan's six strategies for tackling QCs
- Complete the Quantitative Comparisons Practice Set

In Quantitative Comparisons, instead of solving for a particular value, you need to compare two quantities. At first, QCs may appear really difficult because of their unfamiliar format. However, once you become used to them, they can be quicker and easier than the other types of math questions.

THE FORMAT

Where They Appear

The 15 QCs appear in the Math section that also contains the ten Grid-in questions. They are arranged in order of increasing difficulty.

The Questions

In each question, you'll see two mathematical expressions. They are boxed, one in Column A, the other in Column B. Your job is to compare them.

Two-Minute Drill

If you don't have much time to prep for the SAT, here's the best way to spend your time:

- Read p. 108.
- Learn the two rules for choice (D) on pp. 108–109.
- Do the practice problems on pp. 117–118. If you miss an answer, review the strategy before continuing.

Some questions include additional information about one or both quantities. This information is centered, unboxed, and essential to making the comparison.

HINT: *To score high on QCs, learn what the answer choices stand for.*

Kaplan Rules

If you remember anything from this chapter, it should be a thorough understanding of the four answer choices.

You won't have time to keep referring to the directions. You've got to know them cold.

(A) if Column A is greater

(B) if Column B is greater

(C) if the columns are equal

(D) if more information is needed to determine the relationship

(E) will not be scored

The Directions

The directions you'll see will look something like those on the next page. Familiarize yourself with them now.

DIRECTIONS FOR QUANTITATIVE COMPARISON QUESTIONS

Compare the boxed quantity in Column A with the boxed quantity in Column B. Select answer choice

A if Column A is greater;
B if Column B is greater;
C if the columns are equal; or
D if more information is needed to determine the relationship.

An E response will be treated as an omission.

Notes:

1. Some questions include information about one or both quantities. That information is centered and unboxed.
2. A symbol that appears in both Column A and Column B stands for the same thing in both columns.
3. All numbers used are real numbers.

EXAMPLES

	Column A	Column B	Answers
E1	3×4	$3 + 4$	● Ⓑ Ⓒ Ⓓ Ⓔ
	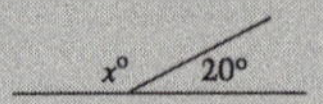		
E2	x	160	Ⓐ Ⓑ ● Ⓓ Ⓔ
	x and y are positive		
E3	$x + 1$	$y - 1$	Ⓐ Ⓑ Ⓒ ● Ⓔ

WARNING: *Never pick choice (E) as the answer to a QC.*

Two Rules for Answer Choice (D)

Choices (A), (B), and (C) all represent definite relationships between the quantities in Column A and Column B. But choice (D) represents a relationship that cannot be determined. Here are two things to remember about choice (D) that will help you decide when to pick it:

1. Choice (D) is never correct if both columns contain only numbers. The relationship between numbers is unchanging, but choice (D) means more than one relationship is possible.
2. Choice (D) is correct if you can demonstrate two different relationships between the columns. Suppose you ran across the following QC:

Column A	Column B
$2x$	$3x$

D-Day

As soon as you find that more than one relationship is possible, you know the answer is (D). Don't waste your time looking for other possibilities.

If x is a positive number, Column B is greater than Column A. If $x = 0$, the columns are equal. If x equals any negative number, Column B is less than Column A. Since more than one relationship is possible, the answer is (D). In fact, as soon as you find a second possibility, stop work and pick choice (D).

COMPARE, DON'T CALCULATE: KAPLAN'S SIX STRATEGIES

Here are six Kaplan strategies that will enable you to make quick comparisons. In the rest of this chapter you'll learn how they work and you'll try them on practice problems.

Kaplan Rules

Usually there's a simpler way to solve a QC than using your calculator.

Strategy 1: Compare Piece by Piece

This works on QCs that compare two sums or two products.

Strategy 2: Make One Column Look Like the Other

This is a great approach when the columns look so different that you can't compare them directly.

Strategy 3: Do the Same Thing to Both Columns

Change both columns by adding, subtracting, multiplying, or dividing by the same amount on both sides in order to make the comparison more apparent.

Strategy 4: Pick Numbers

Use this to get a handle on abstract algebra QCs.

Strategy 5: Redraw the Diagram

Redrawing a diagram can clarify the relationships between measurements.

Strategy 6: Avoid QC Traps

Stay alert for questions designed to fool you by leading you to the obvious, wrong answer.

Now learn how these strategies work.

STRATEGY 1: COMPARE PIECE BY PIECE

Q. Column A	Column B
Area of football field	Area of hockey rink

EXAMPLE

Column A	Column B
$w > x > 0 > y > z$	
$w + y$	$x + z$

In the problem above, there are four variables—*w*, *x*, *y*, and *z*. Compare the value of each "piece" in each column. If every "piece" in one column is greater than a corresponding "piece" in the other column and the only operation involved is addition, the column with the greater individual values will have the greater total value.

Kaplan Rules

Lengths and areas are always greater than zero.

From the given information we know that $w > x$ and $y > z$. Therefore, the first term in Column A, w, is greater than the first term in Column B, x. Similarly, the second term in Column A, y, is greater than the second term in Column B, z. Since each piece in Column A is greater than the corresponding piece in Column B, Column A must be greater; the answer is (A).

STRATEGY 2: MAKE ONE COLUMN LOOK LIKE THE OTHER

When the quantities in Columns A and B are expressed differently, you can often make the comparison easier by changing one column to look like the other. For example, if one column is a percent and the other a fraction, try converting the percent to a fraction.

EXAMPLE

Column A	Column B
$x(x-1)$	$x^2 - x$

Here Column A has parentheses, and Column B doesn't. So make Column A look more like Column B: Get rid of those parentheses. You end up with $x^2 - x$ in both columns, which means they are equal and the answer is (C).

Try another example, this time involving geometry.

EXAMPLE

Column A	Column B
The diameter of circle O is d and the area is a.	
$\frac{\pi d^2}{2}$	a

Make Column B look more like Column A by rewriting a, the area of the circle, in terms of the diameter, d. The area of any circle equals πr^2, with r as the radius.

Since the radius is half the diameter, we can plug in $\frac{d}{2}$ for r in the area formula to get $\pi\left(\frac{d}{2}\right)^2$ in Column B. Simplifying, we get $\frac{\pi d^2}{4}$. Since both columns contain π, we can simply compare $\frac{d^2}{2}$ with $\frac{d^2}{4}$. Since $\frac{d^2}{4}$ is half as much as $\frac{d^2}{2}$, and d^2 must be positive, Column A is greater.

Choice (A) is correct.

STRATEGY 3: DO THE SAME THING TO BOTH COLUMNS

Some QC questions become much clearer if you change not just the appearances, but the values of both columns. Treat them like two sides of an inequality, with the sign temporarily hidden.

You can add or subtract the same amount from both columns and multiply or divide by the same positive amount without altering the relationship. You can also square both columns if you're sure they're both positive. But watch out. Multiplying or dividing an inequality by a negative number reverses the direction of the inequality sign. Since it alters the relationship between the columns, avoid multiplying or dividing by a negative number.

Kaplan Rules

There are a number of traps to watch out for in QCs. QC traps may appear anywhere in the QC section, but they occur most often near the end because QCs are arranged in order of difficulty.

For more on traps, see the Top Ten SAT Math Traps in chapter 13, "Avoid the Double-Team."

HINT: *Don't multiply or divide both QC columns by a negative number.*

In the QC below, what could you do to both columns?

EXAMPLE

Column A		Column B
	$4a + 3 = 7b$	
$20a + 10$		$35b - 5$

All the terms in the two columns are multiples of 5, so divide both columns by 5 to simplify. You're left with $4a + 2$ in Column A and $7b - 1$ in Column B. This resembles the equation given in the centered information. In fact, if you add 1 to both columns, you have $4a + 3$ in Column A and $7b$ in Column B. The centered equation tells us they are equal. Thus choice (C) is correct.

In the next QC, what could you do to both columns?

EXAMPLE

Column A		Column B
	$y > 0$	
$1 + \frac{y}{(y+1)}$		$1 + \frac{1}{(1+y)}$

Solution: First subtract 1 from both sides. That gives you $\frac{y}{(1+y)}$ in Column A, and $\frac{1}{(1+y)}$ in Column B. Then multiply both sides by $(1 + y)$, which must be positive since y is positive. You're left comparing y with 1.

Kaplan Rules

Some surprising things can happen when you play around with negative numbers and fractions. Keep things like this in mind:

- When you square a positive fraction less than 1, the result is smaller than the original fraction.
- When you square a negative number, the result is a positive number.
- When you square 0 and 1, they stay the same.

You know y is greater than 0, but it could be a fraction less than 1, so it could be greater or less than 1. Since you can't say for sure which column is greater, the answer is (D).

STRATEGY 4: PICK NUMBERS

If a QC involves variables, try picking numbers to make the relationship clearer. Here's what you do:

- Pick numbers that are easy to work with.
- Plug in the numbers and calculate the values. Note the relationship between the columns.
- Pick another number for each variable and calculate the values again.

EXAMPLE

Column A		Column B
	$r > s > t > w > 0$	
$\frac{r}{t}$		$\frac{s}{w}$

Try $r = 4$, $s = 3$, $t = 2$, and $w = 1$. Then Column A $= \frac{r}{t} = \frac{4}{2} = 2$. And Column B $= \frac{s}{w} = \frac{3}{1} = 3$. So in this case Column B is greater than Column A.

Always Pick Another Number and Calculate Again

In the example above, we first found Column B was bigger. But that doesn't mean Column B is always bigger and that the answer is (B). It *does* mean the answer is not (A) or (C). But the answer could still be (D)—not enough information to decide.

If time is short, guess between (B) and (D). But whenever you can, pick another set of numbers and calculate again.

As best you can, make a special effort to find a second set of numbers that will alter the relationship. Here for example, try making r a lot larger. Pick $r = 30$ and keep the other variables as they were. Now Column A $= \frac{30}{2} = 15$. This time, Column A is greater than Column B, so answer choice (D) is correct.

HINT: *If the relationship between Columns A and B changes when you pick other numbers, (D) must be the answer.*

Pick Different Kinds of Numbers

Don't assume all variables represent positive integers. Unless you're told otherwise, variables can represent zero, negative numbers, or fractions. Since different kinds of numbers behave differently, always pick a different kind of number the second time around. In the example above, we plugged in a small positive number the first time and a larger number the second.

Speed Tip

If you're pressed for time, picking just one set of numbers will narrow it down to two choices. Guess from these.

In the next three examples, we pick different numbers and get different results. Since we can't find constant relationships between Columns A and B, in all these cases the answer is (D).

EXAMPLE

Column A	Column B
w	$-w$

If $w = 5$, Column A = 5 and Column B = –5, so Column A is greater.

If $w = -5$, Column A = –5 and Column B = 5, so Column B is greater.

EXAMPLE

Column A		Column B
	$x \neq 0$	
x		$\frac{1}{x}$

If $x = 3$, Column A = 3 and Column B = $\frac{1}{3}$, so Column A is greater.

If $x = \frac{1}{3}$, Column A = $\frac{1}{3}$ and Column B = $\frac{1}{\frac{1}{3}} = 3$, so Column B is greater.

EXAMPLE

Column A	Column B
x	x^2

If $x = \frac{1}{2}$, Column A = $\frac{1}{2}$ and Column B = $\frac{1}{4}$, so Column A is greater.

If $x = 2$, Column A = 2 and Column B = 4, so Column B is greater.

Don't Over (D) It

Choice (D) doesn't mean you can't determine which is greater—it means no one can.

If you frequently find (D) is your answer, double-check your work.

STRATEGY 5: REDRAW THE DIAGRAM

- Redraw a diagram if the one that's given misleads you.
- Redraw scale diagrams to exaggerate crucial differences.

Kaplan Rules

Remember:

Not all numbers are positive.

Not all numbers are integers.

Some geometry diagrams may be misleading. Two angles or lengths may look equal as drawn in the diagram, but the given information tells you that there is a slight difference in their measures. The best strategy is to redraw the diagram so that their relationship can be clearly seen.

EXAMPLE

Column A	Column B

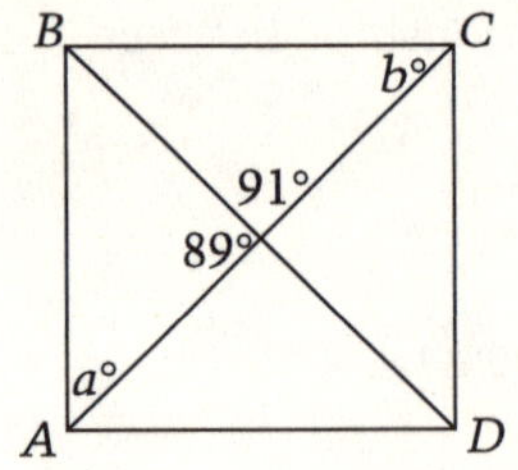

ABCD is a rectangle

a	b

Redraw this diagram to exaggerate the difference between the 89-degree angle and the 91-degree angle. In other words, make the larger angle much larger, and the smaller angle much smaller. The new rectangle that results is much wider than it is tall.

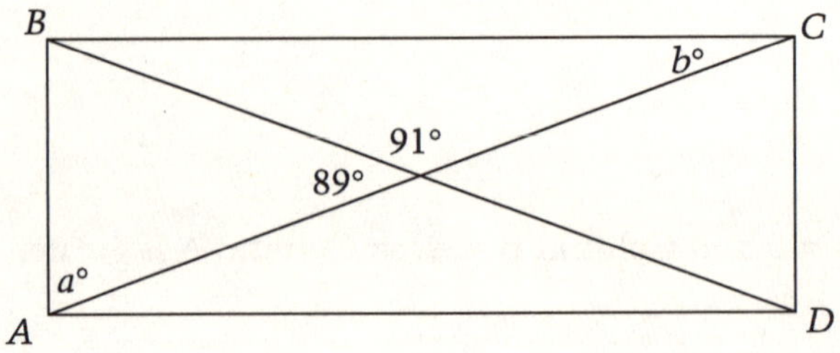

In the new diagram, where the crucial difference jumps out, a is clearly greater than b.

Q. True or False? Lisa Leslie scored 101 points in the first half of a high school basketball game.

STRATEGY 6: AVOID QC TRAPS

To avoid QC traps, always be alert. Don't assume anything. Be especially cautious near the end of the question set.

Don't Be Tricked by Misleading Information

EXAMPLE

Column A	Column B
John is taller than Bob.	
John's weight in pounds	Bob's weight in pounds

The test makers hope you think, "If John is taller, he must weigh more." But there's no guaranteed relationship between height and weight, so you don't have enough information. The answer is (D). Fortunately, problems like this are easy to spot if you stay alert.

Don't Assume

A common QC mistake is to assume that variables represent positive integers. As we saw in using the Picking Numbers strategy, fractions or negative numbers often show another relationship between the columns.

EXAMPLE

Column A	Column B
When 1 is added to the square of x the result is 37.	
x	6

It is easy to assume that x must be 6, since the square of x is 36. That would make choice (C) correct. However, it is possible that $x = -6$. Since x could be either 6 or -6, the answer is (D).

HINT: *Be aware of negative numbers!*

Don't Forget to Consider Other Possibilities

The following question appears at the end of the QC section.

EXAMPLE

Column A	Column B

$$\begin{array}{r} R \\ S \\ \underline{T} \\ 1W \end{array}$$

In the addition problem above, R, S, and T are different digits that are multiples of 3, and W is a digit.

Column A	Column B
W	8

Since you're told that R, S, and T are digits and different multiples of 3, most people will think of 3, 6, and 9, which add up to 18. That makes W equal to 8, and Columns A and B equal. But that's too obvious for a QC at the end of the section.

There's another possibility. Zero is also a multiple of 3. So the three digits could be 0, 3, and 9, or 0, 6, and 9, which give totals of 12 and 15, respectively. That means W could be 8, 2, or 5. Since the columns could be equal, or Column B could be greater, answer choice (D) must be correct.

Don't Second Guess the Answer Grid

There's no way to predict what the answer choice will be based on the pattern of previous answers. Don't try to guess answers blindly based on answer patterns. It's a waste of time.

Don't Fall for Look-Alikes

Q. Who retired as the only undefeated heavyweight boxing champion?

EXAMPLE

Column A	Column B
$\sqrt{5}+\sqrt{5}$	$\sqrt{10}$

At first glance, forgetting the rules of radicals, you might think these quantities are equal and that the answer is (C). But use some common sense to see this isn't the case. Each $\sqrt{5}$ in Column A is bigger than $\sqrt{4}$, so Column A is more than 4. The $\sqrt{10}$ in Column B is less than another familiar number, $\sqrt{16}$, so Column B is less than 4. The answer is (A).

Now use Kaplan's six strategies to solve nine typical QC questions. Then check your work against our solutions on p. 119.

TEST YOUR QC SMARTS

	Column A		Column B	
1.	$x^2 + 2x - 2$		$x^2 + 2x - 1$	Ⓐ Ⓑ Ⓒ Ⓓ Ⓔ
		$x = 2y$ $y > 0$		
2.	4^{2y}		2^x	Ⓐ Ⓑ Ⓒ Ⓓ Ⓔ
		$\frac{x}{y} = \frac{z}{4}$ x, y, and z are positive		
3.	$6x$		$2yz$	Ⓐ Ⓑ Ⓒ Ⓓ Ⓔ
		q, r, and s are positive integers $qrs > 12$		
4.	$\frac{qr}{5}$		$\frac{3}{s}$	Ⓐ Ⓑ Ⓒ Ⓓ Ⓔ
		$x > 1$ $y > 0$		
5.	y^x		$y^{(x+1)}$	Ⓐ Ⓑ Ⓒ Ⓓ Ⓔ
		$7p + 3 = r$ $3p + 7 = s$		
6.	r		s	Ⓐ Ⓑ Ⓒ Ⓓ Ⓔ

	Column A	Column B	
	In triangle *XYZ*, the measure of angle *X* equals the measure of angle *Y*.		
7.	The degree measure of angle *Z*	The degree measure of angle *X* plus the degree measure of angle *Y*	Ⓐ Ⓑ Ⓒ Ⓓ Ⓔ

....

$h > 1$

8.	The number of minutes in *h* hours	$\frac{60}{h}$	Ⓐ Ⓑ Ⓒ Ⓓ Ⓔ

....

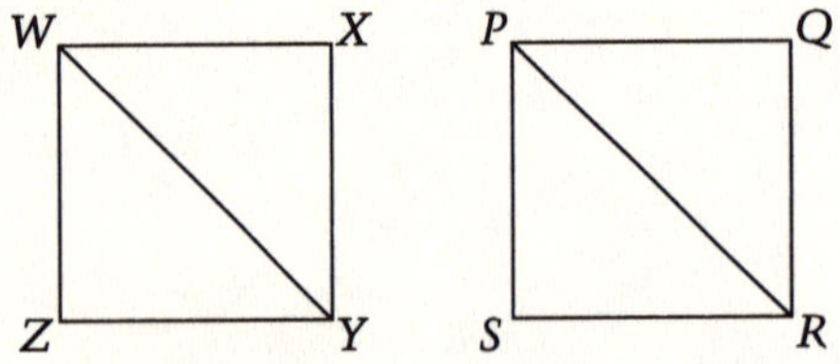

Square *A*　　　Square *B*

Note: Figures not drawn to scale.

9.	$\frac{\text{Perimeter of square } A}{\text{Perimeter of square } B}$	$\frac{\text{Length of } WY}{\text{Length of } PR}$	Ⓐ Ⓑ Ⓒ Ⓓ Ⓔ

Answers to QC Practice Set

1. (B) Comparing the respective pieces of the two columns, the only difference is the third piece: –2 in Column A and –1 in Column B. We don't know the value of x, but whatever it is, x^2 in Column A must have the same value as x^2 in Column B, and $2x$ in Column A must have the same value as $2x$ in Column B. Since any quantity minus 2 must be less than that quantity minus 1, Column B is greater than Column A.

2. (A) Replacing the x exponent in Column B with the equivalent value given in the problem, we're comparing 4^{2y} to 2^{2y}. Since y is greater than 0, raising 4 to the $2y$ power will result in a greater value than raising 2 to the $2y$ power.

3. (B) Do the same thing to both columns until they resemble the centered information. When we divide both columns by $6y$ we get $\frac{6x}{6y}$, or $\frac{x}{y}$ in Column A, and $\frac{2yz}{6y}$, or $\frac{z}{3}$ in Column B. Since $\frac{x}{y} = \frac{z}{4}$, and $\frac{z}{3} > \frac{z}{4}$ (because z is positive), $\frac{z}{3} > \frac{x}{y}$.

4. (D) Do the same thing to both columns to make them look like the centered information. When we multiply both columns by $5s$ we get qrs in Column A and 15 in Column B. Since qrs could be any integer greater than 12, it could be greater than, equal to, or less than 15.

5. (D) Try $x = y = 2$. Then Column A $= y^x = 2^2 = 4$. Column B $= y^{x+1} = 2^3 =$ 8, making Column B greater. But if $x = 2$ and $y = \frac{1}{2}$, Column A $= \left(\frac{1}{2}\right)^2 = \frac{1}{4}$ and Column B $= \left(\frac{1}{2}\right)^3 = \frac{1}{8}$. In this case, Column A is greater than Column B, so the answer is (D).

Q. Who was the Boston Red Sox pitcher who was sold to the New York Yankees prior to the 1920 season?

6. (D) Pick a value for p, and see what effect this has on r and s. If $p = 1$, $r = (7 \times 1) + 3 = 10$, and $s = (3 \times 1) + 7 = 10$, and the two columns are equal. But if $p = 0$, $r = (7 \times 0) + 3 = 3$, and $s = (3 \times 0) + 7 = 7$, and Column A is smaller than Column B. Since there are at least two different possible relationships, the answer is choice (D).

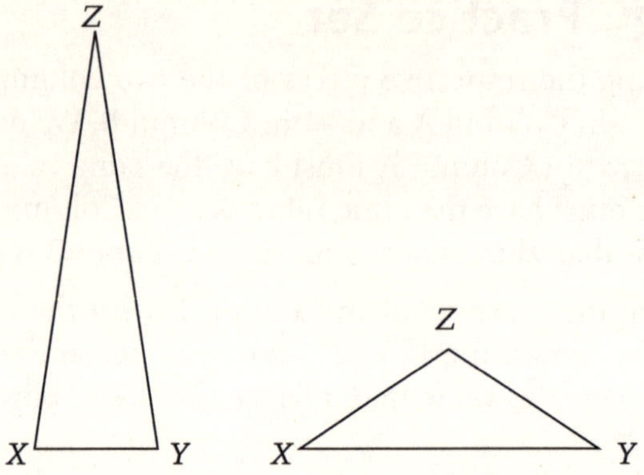

7. (D) Since angle X = angle Y, this is an isosceles triangle. We can draw two diagrams with X and Y as the base angles of an isosceles triangle. In one diagram, make the triangle tall and narrow, so that angle X and angle Y are very large, and angle Z is very small. In this case, column B is greater. In the second diagram, make the triangle short and wide, so that angle Z is much larger than angle X and angle Y. In this case, Column A is greater. Since more than one relationship between the columns is possible, the correct answer is choice (D).

8. (A) The "obvious" answer here is choice (C), because there are 60 minutes in an hour, and 60 appears in Column B. But the number of minutes in h hours would equal 60 times h, not 60 divided by h. Since h is greater than 1, the number in Column B will be less than the actual number of minutes in h hours, so Column A is greater. (A) is correct.

9. (C) We don't know the exact relationship between Square A and Square B, but it doesn't matter. The problem is actually just comparing the ratios of corresponding parts of two squares. Whatever the relationship between them is for one specific length in both squares, the same relationship will exist between them for any other corresponding length. If a side of one square is twice the length of a side of the second square, the diagonal will also be twice as long. The ratio of the perimeters of the two squares is the same as the ratio of the sides. Therefore, the columns are equal. (C) is correct.

REPLAY

Once you've mastered a concept, check it off.

Quantitative Comparisons:

- ❑ Compare piece by piece
- ❑ Make one column look like the other
- ❑ Do the same thing to both columns
- ❑ Pick numbers
- ❑ Redraw the diagram
- ❑ Avoid QC traps

12

Problem Solving

HIGHLIGHTS

Review ten popular question types and methods to solve each:

- Remainders
- Averages
- Ratios
- Rates
- Percents
- Combinations
- Simultaneous equations
- Symbolism
- Special triangles
- Multiple and oddball figures

Two-Minute Drill

If you have just a few weeks to prep for the SAT, here's how you should spend your time:

- In each of the ten sections, try the sample problems.
- Review any section where you have trouble.

The test makers are not paid to be creative. In fact, there are certain types of problems that they like to use again and again on the SAT. This chapter gives you ten of their favorite problem types, along with Kaplan's classic techniques for solving them.

REMAINDERS

Remainder questions can be easier than they look. You might think you have to solve for a certain value, but often you don't.

EXAMPLE

When n is divided by 7, the remainder is 4. What is the remainder when $2n$ is divided by 7?

(A) 0

(B) 1

(C) 2

(D) 3

(E) 4

Q. Who is the smallest player in NBA history?

The question above doesn't depend on knowing the value of n. In fact, n has an infinite number of possible values.

HINT: *Pick a number for* n.

Which number should you pick? Since the remainder when n is divided by 7 is 4, pick any multiple of 7 and add 4. The easiest multiple to work with is 7. So, $7 + 4 = 11$. Use 11 for n.

Plug 11 into the question and see what happens.

What is the remainder when $2n$ is divided by 7?

$$2(11) \div 7 =$$
$$22 \div 7 =$$
$$\frac{22}{7} = 3 \text{ remainder } 1$$

The remainder is 1 when $n = 11$. So the answer is (B). The remainder will also be 1 when $n =$ 18, 25, or 46.

QC Remainders

EXAMPLE

Column A	Column B
When p is divided by 5, the remainder is 3.	
When q is divided by 5, the remainder is 4.	
p	q

The centered information tells you that p can be any of the integers 3, 8, 13, 18, 23, . . . ; and that q can be any of the integers 4, 9, 14, 19, 24, and so forth. So how do p and q compare? You can't tell; p could be small and q big, or the other way around. The answer is (D), not enough information to decide.

Speed Tip

When picking a number for a remainder problem, add the remainder to the number you're dividing by.

Practice Problems: Remainders

REGULAR MATH

1. When z is divided by 8, the remainder is 5. What is the remainder when $4z$ is divided by 8?
   (A) 1
   (B) 3
   (C) 4
   (D) 5
   (E) 7

Ⓐ Ⓑ Ⓒ Ⓓ Ⓔ

QC

	Column A	Column B
	When x is divided by 6 the remainder is 3. When y is divided by 6 the remainder is 4.	
2.	x	y

Ⓐ Ⓑ Ⓒ Ⓓ Ⓔ

When m is divided by 5 the remainder is 2.
When n is divided by 5 the remainder is 1.

3.	The remainder when $m + n$ is divided by 5	The remainder when mn is divided by 5

Ⓐ Ⓑ Ⓒ Ⓓ Ⓔ

Answers to Remainders Problems

1. (C) Let $z = 13$ and plug in $4z = 4(13) = 52$, which leaves a remainder of 4 when divided by 8.
2. (D) We determine that x can be any of the integers 3, 9, 15, 21, . . . , and y can be any of the integers 4, 10, 16, 22, ... Since x could be greater than or less than y, the correct answer must be choice (D).
3. (A) The variable m can be any integer that ends in either a 2 or a 7; n can be any integer that ends in either a 1 or a 6. Plugging in will show that in any case, $m + n$ will leave a remainder of 3 when divided by 5, and mn will leave a remainder of 2 when divided by 5, so Column A is greater.

Use Your Head

Use common sense to learn about the size of the value you're asked to find. If all the terms listed are less than the given average, then the unknown term must be greater than the average to balance it out.

Likewise, if adding a new value, x, to a group of numbers raises the average value of the group, then x must be greater than the average of the original numbers.

AVERAGES

EXAMPLE

The average weight of five dogs in a certain kennel is 32 pounds. If four of the dogs weigh 25, 27, 19, and 35 pounds, what is the weight of the fifth dog?

(A) 28

(B) 32

(C) 49

(D) 54

(E) 69

Instead of giving you a list of values to plug into the average formula, SAT average questions often put a slight spin on the problem. They tell you the average of a group of terms and ask you to find the value of the missing term.

HINT: *Work with the sum.*

Let x = the weight of the fifth dog. Plug this into the average formula:

$$32 = \frac{25 + 27 + 19 + 35 + x}{5}$$

$$32 \times 5 = 25 + 27 + 19 + 35 + x$$

So the average weight of the dogs, times the number of dogs, equals the total weight of the dogs, or, mathematically:

Average × Number of Terms = Sum of Terms

Remember this manipulation of the average formula so that whenever you know the average of a group of terms and the number of terms, you can find the total sum.

Now you can solve for the weight of the fifth dog:

$$32 \times 5 = 25 + 27 + 19 + 35 + x$$
$$160 = 106 + x$$
$$54 = x$$

So the weight of the fifth dog is 54 pounds, choice (D).

Q. In 1968, who batted .301 for the lowest average ever to win a batting title?

Practice Problems: Averages

REGULAR MATH

1. The average (arithmetic mean) of six numbers is 16. If five of the numbers are 15, 37, 16, 9, and 23, what is the sixth number?

   (A) –20
   (B) –4
   (C) 0
   (D) 6
   (E) 16

   Ⓐ Ⓑ Ⓒ Ⓓ Ⓔ

2. Bart needs to buy five gifts with $80. If two of the gifts cost a total of $35, what is the average (arithmetic mean) amount Bart can spend on each of the remaining three gifts?

   (A) $45
   (B) $17
   (C) $16
   (D) $15
   (E) $10

   Ⓐ Ⓑ Ⓒ Ⓓ Ⓔ

3. The average (arithmetic mean) of five numbers is 8. If the average of two of these numbers is –6, what is the sum of the other three numbers?

   (A) 28
   (B) 34
   (C) 46
   (D) 52
   (E) 60

   Ⓐ Ⓑ Ⓒ Ⓓ Ⓔ

Answers to Averages Problems

1. (B) Average × Number of Terms = Sum of Terms

$$16 \times 6 = 15 + 37 + 16 + 9 + 23 + x$$
$$96 = 100 + x$$
$$-4 = x$$

2. (D) Bart has \$80 and spent \$35 on two gifts; therefore he has \$45 left to spend on the remaining three. So,

$$x = \frac{\$45}{3}$$
$$x = \$15$$

3. (D) Average × Number of Terms = Sum of Terms

The sum of all five numbers is

$$8 \times 5 = 40$$

The sum of two of these numbers is

$$(-6) \times 2 = -12$$

So, the difference of these two sums, $40 - (-12) = 52$, is the sum of the other numbers.

RATIOS

Train Your Brain

Use common sense to check your math on this example to the right. Most of the chips are nondefective, so the ratio must be greater than 1. If you reversed the terms and thought (C) was the answer, that would tell you that you did something wrong.

EXAMPLE

Out of every 50 chips produced in a certain factory, 20 are defective. What is the ratio of nondefective chips produced to defective chips produced?

(A) 2:5

(B) 3:5

(C) 2:3

(D) 3:2

(E) 5:2

HINT: *Identify the parts and the whole in the problem.*

Find the parts and the whole in the problem. In this case the total number of chips is the whole, and the number of nondefective chips and the number of defective chips are the parts that make up this whole.

You're given a part-to-whole ratio—the ratio of defective chips to all chips, and asked to find a part-to-part ratio—the ratio of nondefective chips to defective chips.

If 20 chips out of every 50 are defective, the remaining 30 chips must be nondefective. So the part-to-part ratio of nondefective to defective chips is 30/20, or 3/2, which is equivalent to 3:2—answer choice (D).

If you hadn't identified the part and the whole first, it would be easy to get confused and compare a part to the whole, like the ratios in answer choices (A) and (B).

This approach also works for ratio questions that ask you to find actual quantities. For example:

> Out of every five chips produced in a certain factory, two are defective. If 2,200 chips were produced, how many were defective?

Here you need to find a quantity—the number of defective chips.

HINT: *If you're looking for the actual quantities in a ratio, set up and solve a proportion.*

You're given a part-to-whole ratio (the ratio of defective chips to all chips), and the total number of chips produced. You can find the answer by setting up and solving a proportion.

$$\frac{\text{Number of defective chips}}{\text{Total number of chips}} = \frac{2}{5} = \frac{x}{2{,}200}$$

$$x = \text{Number of defective chips}$$

$$5x = 4{,}400$$

$$x = 880$$

HINT: *Remember that ratios compare only relative size—they don't tell you the actual quantities involved.*

Kaplan Rules

When you look at a ratio, make sure you know if you're dealing with *parts* to *parts* or *parts* to *whole.*

You also need to see if the parts that you're given add up to the whole. For example, the number of male and female students in a classroom must add up to the whole. The number of students with blond hair and the number of students with brown hair are parts, but do not necessarily add up to the whole.

Q. Which team achieved the NFL's only undefeated season?

Practice Problems: Ratios

REGULAR MATH

1. The ratio of right-handed pitchers to left-handed pitchers in a certain baseball league is 11:7. What fractional part of the pitchers in the league are left-handed?

   (A) $\frac{6}{7}$
   (B) $\frac{6}{11}$
   (C) $\frac{7}{11}$
   (D) $\frac{7}{18}$
   (E) $\frac{11}{18}$

Ⓐ Ⓑ Ⓒ Ⓓ Ⓔ

....

2. In a group of 24 people who are either homeowners or renters, the ratio of homeowners to renters is 5:3. How many homeowners are in the group?

   (A) 15
   (B) 14
   (C) 12
   (D) 9
   (E) 8

Ⓐ Ⓑ Ⓒ Ⓓ Ⓔ

....

3. Magazine *A* has a total of 28 pages, 16 of which are advertisements and 12 of which are articles. Magazine *B* has a total of 35 pages, all of them either advertisements or articles. If the ratio of the number of pages of advertisements to the number of pages of articles is the same for both magazines, then Magazine *B* has how many more pages of advertisements than Magazine *A*?

   (A) 2
   (B) 3
   (C) 4
   (D) 5
   (E) 6

Ⓐ Ⓑ Ⓒ Ⓓ Ⓔ

Answers to Ratios Problems

1. (D) The parts are the number of right-handed (11) and the number of left-handed pitchers (7). The whole is the total number of pitchers (right-handed + left-handed), which is 11 + 7, or 18. So:

$$\frac{\text{part}}{\text{whole}} = \frac{\text{left-handed}}{\text{total}} = \frac{7}{11+7} = \frac{7}{18}$$

2. (A) The parts are the number of homeowners (5) and the number of renters (3). The whole is the total (homeowners + renters). So:

$$\frac{\text{part}}{\text{whole}} = \frac{\text{homeowners}}{\text{homeowners + renters}} = \frac{5}{5+3} = \frac{5}{8}$$

Since we are trying to find an actual quantity, set up a proportion.

$$\frac{\text{Homeowners}}{\text{Total people}} = \frac{5}{8} = \frac{x}{24}$$

$$8x = 120$$

$$x = 15$$

Time Trouble

Use logic to narrow your choices. Most are homeowners, so the answer must be more than half of 24, or 12. Either (A) or (B) is the right answer.

3. (C) The $\frac{\text{part}}{\text{whole}}$ ratio of advertisements (16) to total pages (28) in Magazine *A* is $\frac{16}{28}$, or $\frac{4}{7}$. Magazine *B* has the same ratio, so if there are 35 pages in Magazine *B*, $\frac{4}{7} \times 35$—or 20 pages—are advertisements. Therefore, there are four more pages of advertisements in Magazine *B* than in Magazine *A*.

RATES

EXAMPLE

If eight oranges cost a dollars, b oranges would cost how many dollars?

(A) $8ab$

(B) $\frac{8a}{b}$

(C) $\frac{8}{ab}$

(D) $\frac{a}{8b}$

(E) $\frac{ab}{8}$

A rate is a ratio that compares quantities that are measured in different units. In the problem above the units are oranges and dollars.

What makes the rate problem above difficult is the presence of variables. It's hard to get a clear picture of the relationship between the units.

Q. A jogger always runs from her home to the park. If she averages 8 mph to the park and 6 mph back home, what is her average rate of speed?

HINT: *Pick numbers for the variables to make the relationship between the units clearer.*

Pick numbers for a and b that are easy to work with in the problem. Let $a = 16$. Then eight oranges cost \$16.00. So the cost per orange at this rate is $\frac{16 \text{ dollars}}{8 \text{ oranges}}$ = \$2 per orange. Let $b = 5$. So the cost of five oranges at this rate is five oranges × \$2.00 per orange = \$10.00.

Now plug in $a = 16$ and $b = 5$ into the answer choices to see which one gives you a value of 10.

Choice (A): $8 \times 16 \times 5 = 640$. Eliminate.

Choice (B): $\frac{8 \times 16}{5} = \frac{128}{5}$. Eliminate.

Choice (C): $\frac{8}{16 \times 5} = \frac{1}{10}$. Eliminate.

Choice (D): $\frac{16}{8 \times 5} = \frac{2}{5}$. Eliminate.

Choice (E): $\frac{16 \times 5}{8} = 10$.

Since (E) is the only one that gives the correct value, it is correct.

Practice Problems: Rates

REGULAR MATH

1. If David paints at the rate of h houses per day, how many houses does he paint in d days, in terms of h and d?

(A) $\frac{h}{d}$

(B) hd

(C) $h + \frac{d}{2}$

(D) $h - d$

(E) $\frac{d}{h}$

Ⓐ Ⓑ Ⓒ Ⓓ Ⓔ

....

2. Bill has to type a paper that is p pages long, with each page containing w words. If Bill types an average of x words per minute, how many hours will it take him to finish the paper?

(A) $60\ wpx$

(B) $\frac{wx}{60p}$

(C) $\frac{60wp}{x}$

(D) $\frac{wpx}{60}$

(E) $\frac{wp}{60x}$

Ⓐ Ⓑ Ⓒ Ⓓ Ⓔ

....

3. If Seymour drove 120 miles in x hours at constant speed, how many miles did he travel in the first 20 minutes of his trip?

(A) $60x$

(B) $3x$

(C) $\frac{120}{x}$

(D) $\frac{40}{x}$

(E) $\frac{6}{x}$

Ⓐ Ⓑ Ⓒ Ⓓ Ⓔ

Answers to Rates Problems

1. (B) Pick numbers for h and d. Let $h = 2$ and $d = 3$; that is, suppose he paints two houses per day and he paints for three days, so in three days he can paint six houses. You multiply the rate (h) by the number of days (d). The only answer choice that equals 6 when $h = 2$ and $d = 3$ is choice (B).

2. (E) Pick numbers for p, w, and x that work well in the problem. Let $p = 3$ and let $w = 100$. So there are three pages with 100 words per page, or 300 words total. Say he types five words a minute, so $x = 5$. So he types 5×60, or 300 words an hour. Therefore, it takes him one hour to type the paper. The only answer choice that equals 1 when $p = 3$, $w = 100$, and $x = 5$ is choice (E).

3. (D) Let $x = 4$. That means that he drove 120 miles in four hours, so his speed was $\frac{120 \text{ miles}}{4 \text{ hours}}$, or 30 miles per hour. Since 20 minutes $= \frac{1}{3}$ of an hour, the distance he traveled in the first 20 minutes is $\frac{1}{3}$ hours $\times$ 30 miles per hour = 10 miles. The only answer choice that equals 10 when $x = 4$ is choice (D).

PERCENTS

Memorize These

When you need to, you can figure out a percent equivalent on your calculator by dividing the numerator by the denominator. You'll save time by knowing some common percent equivalents.

$\frac{1}{5} = 20\%$

$\frac{1}{4} = 25\%$

$\frac{1}{3} = 33\frac{1}{3}\%$

$\frac{1}{2} = 50\%$

$\frac{2}{3} = 66\frac{2}{3}\%$

$\frac{3}{4} = 75\%$

EXAMPLE

Last year Julie's annual salary was $20,000. This year's raise brings her to an annual salary of $25,000. If she gets the same percent raise every year, what will her salary be next year?

(A) $27,500

(B) $30,000

(C) $31,250

(D) $32,500

(E) $35,000

In percent problems, you're usually given two pieces of information and asked to find the third. When you see a percent problem, remember:

- If you are solving for a percent:

$$\text{Percent} = \frac{\text{Part}}{\text{Whole}}$$

- If you need to solve for a part:

$$\text{Percent} \times \text{Whole} = \text{Part}$$

This problem asks for Julie's projected salary for next year—that is, her current salary plus her next raise.

You know last year's salary ($20,000) and you know this year's salary ($25,000), so you can find the difference between the two salaries:

$$\$25{,}000 - \$20{,}000 = \$5{,}000 = \text{her raise}$$

Now find the percent of her raise, by using the formula

$$\text{Percent} = \frac{\text{Part}}{\text{Whole}}$$

Since Julie's raise was calculated on last year's salary, divide by $20,000.

HINT: *Be sure you know which Whole to plug in. Here you're looking for a percent of $20,000, not $25,000.*

$$\text{Percent raise} = \frac{\$5{,}000}{\$20{,}000} = \frac{1}{4} = 25\%$$

You know she will get the same percent raise next year, so solve for the part. Use the formula Percent × Whole = Part. Her raise next year will be

$$25\% \times \$25{,}000 = \frac{1}{4} \times 25{,}000 = \$6{,}250$$

Add that sum to this year's salary and you have her projected salary: $25,000 + $6,250 = $31,250, or answer choice (C).

Make sure that you change the percent to either a fraction or a decimal before beginning calculations.

Q. Who was the amateur tennis player who won the 1968 U.S. Open?

Mirror Image

x percent of y = y percent of x

20% of 50 = 50% of 20

$$\frac{1}{5} \times 50 = \frac{1}{2} \times 20$$

$$10 = 10$$

Practice Problems: Percents

QC

	Column A	Column B	
1.	5% of 3% of 45	6.75	(A) (B) (C) (D) (E)

....

GRID-IN

2. Eighty-five percent of the members of a student organization registered to attend a certain field trip. If 16 of the members who registered were unable to attend, resulting in only 65 percent of the members making the trip, how many members are in the organization?

....

REGULAR MATH

3. If a sweater sells for $48 after a 25 percent markdown, what was its original price?

   (A) $56
   (B) $60
   (C) $64
   (D) $68
   (E) $72

(A) (B) (C) (D) (E)

Answers to Percents Problems

1. (B) Percent × Whole = Part. Five percent of (3 percent of 45) = .05 × (.03 × 45) = .05 × 1.35 = .0675, which is less than 6.75 in Column B.

2. (80) You need to solve for the Whole, so identify the Part and the Percent. If 85 percent planned to attend and only 65 percent did, 20 percent failed to attend, and you know that 16 students failed to attend.

   Percent × Whole = Part

   $$\frac{20}{100} \times \text{Whole} = 16$$

   $$\text{Whole} = 16 \times \frac{100}{20}$$

   $$\text{Whole} = 80$$

3. (C) We want to solve for the original price, the Whole. The percent markdown is 25 percent, so \$48 is 75 percent of the whole.

   Percent × Whole = Part

   75 percent × Original Price = \$48

   $$\text{Original Price} = \frac{\$48}{0.75} = \$64$$

Q. Michael Jordan's play-off record for the most points scored in a game is 63% of Wilt Chamberlain's record for the most points scored in a regular season game. How many points did Jordan score?

COMBINATIONS

EXAMPLE

If Alice, Betty, and Carlos sit in three adjacent empty seats in a movie house, how many different seating arrangements are possible?

(A) 3

(B) 4

(C) 5

(D) 6

(E) 8

Combination problems ask you to find the different possibilities that can occur in a given situation.

HINT: *Simply count the number of possibilities by listing them in a quick but systematic way.*

To solve this problem, let the first letter of each name stand for that person. First, find all the combinations with Alice in the first seat:

ABC

ACB

Using the same system, try Betty in the first seat, and then Carlos:

BAC

BCA

CAB

CBA

Q. What are the odds that a high school basketball player will make it to the NBA?

At this point we've exhausted every possibility. So there are six possible arrangements, and that's answer choice (D).

Some problems set up conditions that limit the possibilities somewhat. Some may ask for the number of distinct possibilities, meaning that if the same combination shows up twice in different forms, you should count it only once. Consider the following problem.

EXAMPLE

Set I: {2, 3, 4, 5}

Set II: {1, 2, 3}

If x is a number generated by multiplying a number from Set I by a number from Set II, how many possible values of x are greater than 5?

(A) 3

(B) 4

(C) 5

(D) 6

(E) 7

Warning

Don't use complex formulas to solve combinations problems. SAT combinations questions are simple enough that you can write down the possibilities and count them.

Again, list the possibilities in a systematic way, pairing off each number in the first set with each number in the second set, so every combination is included:

$2 \times 1 = 2$	$4 \times 1 = 4$
$2 \times 2 = 4$	$4 \times 2 = 8$
$2 \times 3 = 6$	$4 \times 3 = 12$
$3 \times 1 = 3$	$5 \times 1 = 5$
$3 \times 2 = 6$	$5 \times 2 = 10$
$3 \times 3 = 9$	$5 \times 3 = 15$

How many of these values are greater than 5? Going down the list: 6, 6, 9, 8, 12, 10, and 15. Although there are seven answers for x that are greater than 5, two of them are the same. So there are six different values of x greater than 5, not seven. The answer is (D).

HINT: *Always write down the possibilities as you organize them, so you can count them accurately, and so you don't count the same combination twice.*

Practice Problems: Combinations

REGULAR MATH

1. A three-digit code is made up of three different digits from the set {2,4,6,8}. If 2 is always the first digit in the code, how many three-digit codes can be formed?

   (A) 16
   (B) 12
   (C) 10
   (D) 8
   (E) 6

Ⓐ Ⓑ Ⓒ Ⓓ Ⓔ

QC

Column A	Column B

Five people attend a meeting. Each person shakes hands once with every other person at the meeting.

	Column A	Column B
2.	The total number of handshakes that take place	15

Ⓐ Ⓑ Ⓒ Ⓓ Ⓔ

REGULAR MATH

3. Three people stop for lunch at a hot dog stand. If each person orders one item and there are three items to choose from, how many different combinations of food could be purchased? (Assume that order doesn't matter; e.g., a hot dog and two sodas are considered the same as two sodas and a hot dog.)

   (A) 6
   (B) 9
   (C) 10
   (D) 18
   (E) 27

Ⓐ Ⓑ Ⓒ Ⓓ Ⓔ

Answers to Combinations Problems

1. (E) Every code starts with 2, so the last two digits determine the number of possibilities. The last two digits could be: 46, 48, 64, 68, 84, and 86. That makes six combinations that fit the conditions.

2. (B) Be careful not to count each handshake twice. Call the five people *A*, *B*, C, *D*, and E. We can pair them off like this:

   A with *B*, *C*, *D*, and *E* (four handshakes)

   B with *C*, *D*, and *E* (three more—note that we leave out *A*, since the handshake between *A* and *B* is already counted)

   C with *D* and *E* (two more)

   D with *E* (one more)

   The total is 4 + 3 + 2 + 1, or 10 handshakes.

3. (C) To find the number, let's call the three items they can purchase *A*, *B*, and *C*. The possibilities:

   All three order the same thing: *AAA*, *BBB*, *CCC*

   Two order the same thing: *AAB*, *AAC*, *BBA*, *BBC*, *CCA*, *CCB*

   All three order something different: *ABC*

   So there are ten different ways the three items could be ordered.

Q. Who is the only person to play in the Major League Baseball All-Star Game and the NFL Pro Bowl Game?

SIMULTANEOUS EQUATIONS

Kaplan Rules

When subtracting one equation from another, be sure to distribute the minus sign to each term. In the example to the left,

$$-p - 2q = -14$$

EXAMPLE

If $p + 2q = 14$ and $3p + q = 12$, then $p =$

(A) –2

(B) –1

(C) 1

(D) 2

(E) 3

In order to get a numerical value for each variable, you need as many different equations as there are variables to solve for. So, if you have two variables, you need two independent equations.

You could tackle this problem by solving for one variable in terms of the other, and then plugging this expression into the other equation. But the simultaneous equations that appear on the SAT can usually be handled in an easier way.

HINT: *Combine the equations—by adding or subtracting them—to cancel out all but one of the variables.*

You can't eliminate p or q by adding or subtracting the equations in their present form. But if you multiply the second equation by 2:

$$2(3p + q) = 2(12)$$
$$6p + 2q = 24$$

Now when you subtract the first equation from the second, the qs will cancel out so you can solve for p:

$$\begin{array}{r} 6p + 2q = 24 \\ \underline{-[p + 2q = 14]} \\ 5p + 0 = 10 \end{array}$$

If $5p = 10$, $p = 2$.

Practice Problems: Simultaneous Equations

Kaplan Rules

Simultaneous equations on the SAT are almost always easy to combine.

REGULAR MATH

1. If $x + y = 8$ and $y - x = -2$, then $y =$

   (A) -2
   (B) 3
   (C) 5
   (D) 8
   (E) 10

(A) (B) (C) (D) (E)

GRID-IN

2. If $4a + 3b = 19$ and $a + 2b = 6$, then $a + b =$

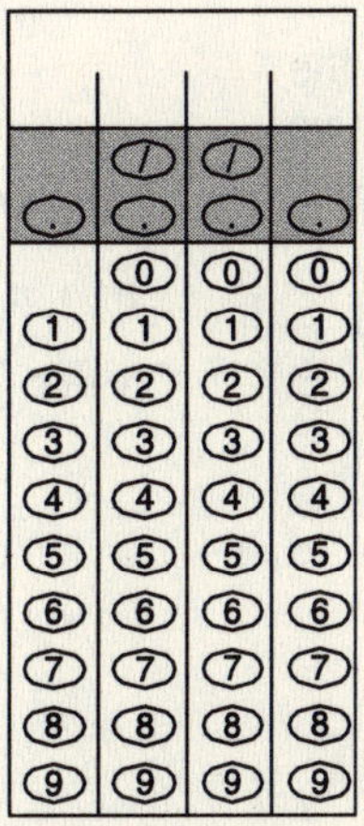

REGULAR MATH

3. If $m - n = 5$ and $2m + 3n = 15$, then $m + n =$

   (A) 1
   (B) 6
   (C) 7
   (D) 10
   (E) 15

(A) (B) (C) (D) (E)

Answers to Simultaneous Equations Problems

1. (B) When you add the two equations, the *x*s cancel out and you find that $2y = 6$, so $y = 3$.

2. (5) Adding the two equations, you find that $5a + 5b = 25$. Dividing by 5 shows that $a + b = 5$.

3. (C) Multiply the first equation by 2, then subtract the first equation from the second to eliminate the *m*s and find that $5n = 5$, or $n = 1$:

$$\begin{array}{r} 2m + 3n = 15 \\ -2m + 2n = -10 \\ \hline 5n = 5 \\ n = 1 \end{array}$$

Plugging this value for n into the first equation shows that $m = 6$:

$$m - n = 5$$
$$m - 1 = 5$$
$$m = 6$$

So $m + n = 7$:

$$m + n = 6 + 1 = 7$$

Choice (C) is correct.

Q. Who has played in the most consecutive Major League Baseball games?

SYMBOLISM

You should be quite familiar with the arithmetic symbols +, –, ×, ÷, and %. Finding the value of 10 + 2, 18 – 4, 4 × 9, or 96 ÷ 16 is easy.

However, on the SAT, you may come across bizarre symbols. You may even be asked to find the value of 10 ★ 2, 5 ❄ 7, 10 ✸ 6, or 65 ❤ 2.

The SAT test makers put strange symbols in questions to confuse or unnerve you. Don't let them. The question stem always tells you what the strange symbol means. Although this type of question may look difficult, it is really an exercise in plugging in. Look at the following example:

> **Kaplan Rules**
>
> Intimidated by symbols?
>
> The test makers put symbolism on the SAT to test your ability to think. Once you get over your fear of seeing something completely unknown, you'll realize the math is usually quite easy.

EXAMPLE

If a ★ b = $\sqrt{a + b}$ for all non-negative numbers, what is the value of 10 ★ 6 ?

(A) 0

(B) 2

(C) 4

(D) 8

(E) 16

To solve, just plug in 10 for *a* and 6 for *b* into the expression $\sqrt{a + b}$. That equals $\sqrt{10 + 6}$ or $\sqrt{16}$ or 4, choice (C).

How about a more involved symbolism question?

EXAMPLE

If a ▲ means to multiply by 3 and a ✸ means to divide by –2, what is the value of ((8✸)▲)✸ ?

(A) –6

(B) 0

(C) 2

(D) 3

(E) 6

HINT: *When a symbolism problem includes parentheses, do the operations inside the parentheses first.*

First find 8✸. This means to divide 8 by –2, which is –4. Working out to the next set of parentheses, we have (–4)▲, which means to multiply –4 by 3, which is –12. Lastly, we find (–12) ✸, which means to divide –12 by –2, which is 6, choice (E).

HINT: *When two or three questions include the same symbol, expect the last question to be the most difficult, and be extra careful.*

Practice Problems: Symbolism

QC

Column A	Column B

If $x \neq 0$, let ♠x be defined by ♠$x = x - \frac{1}{x}$

1. –3 | ♠–3 Ⓐ Ⓑ Ⓒ Ⓓ Ⓔ

....

REGULAR MATH

2. If r ❤ $s = r(r - s)$ for all integers r and s, then 4 ❤ (3 ❤ 5) equals

   (A) –8
   (B) –2
   (C) 2
   (D) 20
   (E) 40 Ⓐ Ⓑ Ⓒ Ⓓ Ⓔ

....

Questions 3 and 4 refer to the following definition:

$c \bigstar d = \frac{(c - d)}{c}$, where $c \neq 0$.

3. 12 ★ 3 =

   (A) –3
   (B) $\frac{1}{4}$
   (C) $\frac{2}{3}$
   (D) $\frac{3}{4}$
   (E) 3 Ⓐ Ⓑ Ⓒ Ⓓ Ⓔ

....

4. If $9 \bigstar 4 = 15 \bigstar k$, then $k =$

(A) 3
(B) 6
(C) $\frac{20}{3}$
(D) $\frac{25}{3}$
(E) 9

(A) (B) (C) (D) (E)

Answers to Symbolism Problems

1. (B) Plug in –3 for x: $\spadesuit x = -3 - \frac{1}{-3} = -3 + \frac{1}{3} = -2\frac{2}{3}$, which is greater than –3 in Column A.

2. (E) Start in the parentheses and work out: $(3 \heartsuit 5) = 3(3 - 5) = 3(-2) = -6$; $4 \heartsuit (-6) = 4[4 - (-6)] = 4(10) = 40$.

3. (D) Plug in 12 for c and 3 for d: $\frac{12 - 3}{12} = \frac{9}{12} = \frac{3}{4}$.

4. (C) Plug in on both sides of the equation:

$$\frac{9 - 4}{9} = \frac{15 - k}{15}$$

$$\frac{5}{9} = \frac{15 - k}{15}$$

Cross-multiply and solve for k:

$$75 = 135 - 9k$$

$$-60 = -9k$$

$$\frac{-60}{-9} = k$$

$$\frac{20}{3} = k$$

Q. If  means pitched a perfect game, who is the only player to have  in World Series history?

SPECIAL TRIANGLES

The Specials

The test makers often put triangles on the SAT to test your knowledge of special triangles.

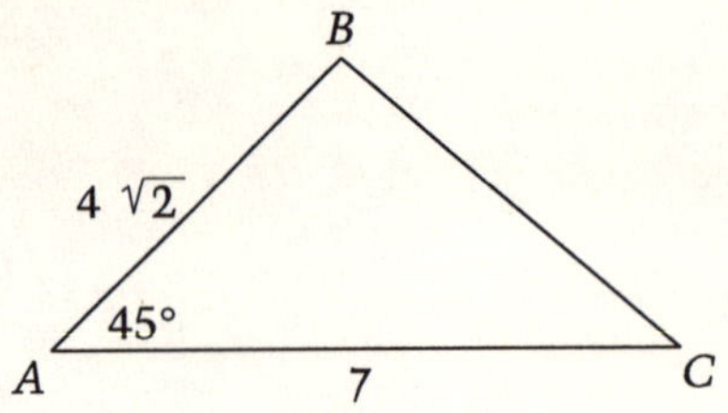

Note: Figure not drawn to scale.

EXAMPLE

In the triangle above, what is the length of side *BC*?

(A) 4

(B) 5

(C) $4\sqrt{2}$

(D) 6

(E) $5\sqrt{2}$

HINT: *Look for the special triangles in geometry problems.*

Special triangles contain a lot of information. For instance, if you know the length of one side of a 30-60-90 triangle, you can easily work out the lengths of the others. Special triangles allow you to transfer one piece of information around the whole figure.

The following are the special triangles you should look for on the SAT.

Speed Tip

Popular right triangles:

- 3-4-5
- 5-12-13

or multiples of these, such as:

- 6-8-10
- 10-24-26

Equilateral Triangles

All interior angles are 60° and all sides are of the same length.

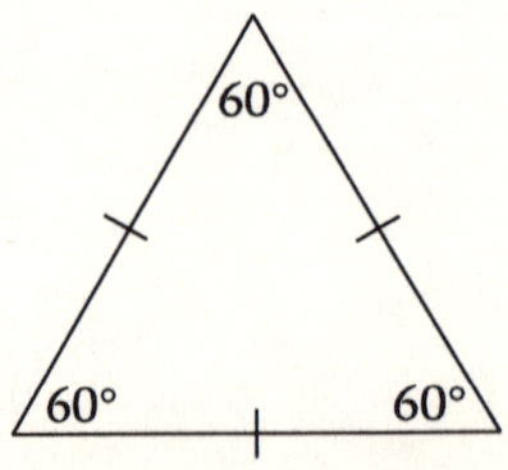

Isosceles Triangles

Two sides are of the same length and the angles facing these sides are equal.

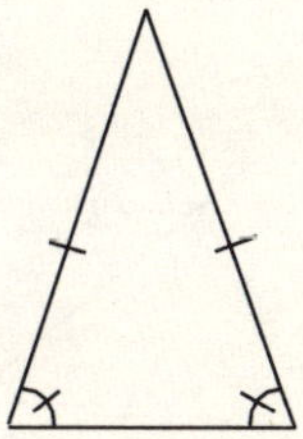

Right Triangles

Contain a 90° angle. The sides are related by the Pythagorean theorem. $a^2 + b^2 = c^2$ where a and b are the legs and c is the hypotenuse.

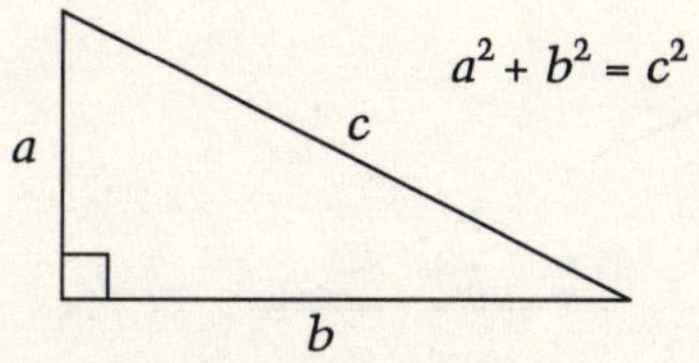

The "Special" Right Triangles

Many triangle problems contain "special" right triangles, whose side lengths always come in predictable ratios. If you recognize them, you won't have to use the Pythagorean theorem to find the value of a missing side length.

The 3-4-5 Right Triangle

(Be on the lookout for multiples of 3-4-5 as well.)

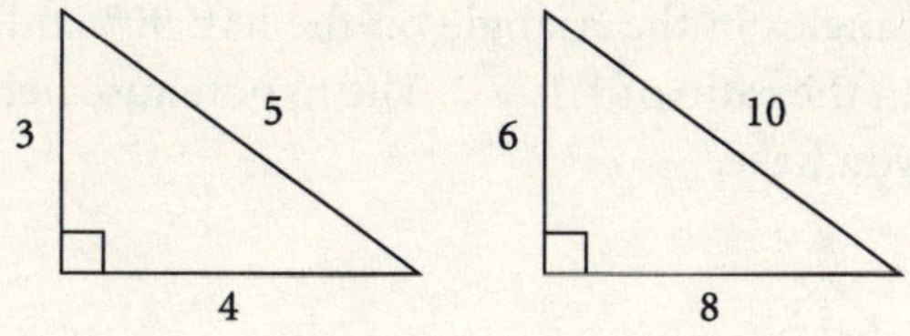

Q. What two sports both hold events in the "half-pipe"?

If You Have a Bad Memory . . .

If you forget the triangle ratios, you can find a description of the isosceles right triangle and 30-60-90 triangle in the information box at the start of every Math section on the SAT.

The Isosceles Right Triangle

(Note the side ratio—$1:1:\sqrt{2}$.)

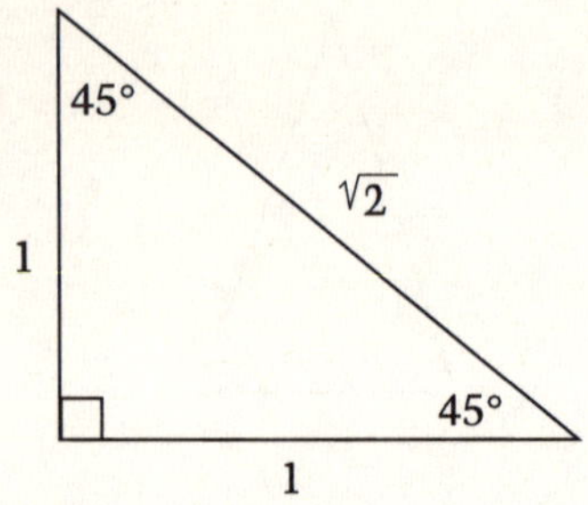

The 30-60-90 Right Triangle

(Note the side ratio—$1:\sqrt{3}:2$, and which side is opposite which angle.)

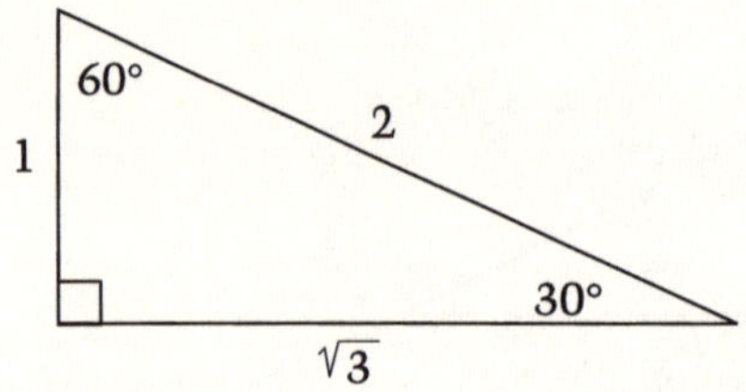

Getting back to our example, you can drop a vertical line from *B* to line *AC*. This divides the triangle into two right triangles.

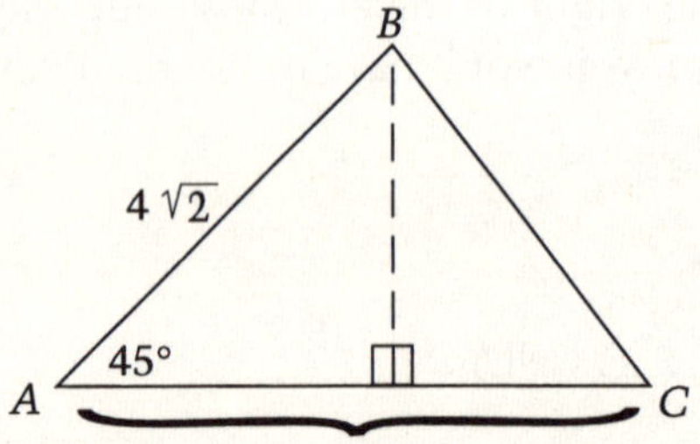

That means you know two of the angles in the triangle on the left: 90° and 45°. So this is an isosceles right triangle, with sides in the ratio of $1:1:\sqrt{2}$. The hypotenuse here is $4\sqrt{2}$, so both legs have length 4. Filling this in, you have:

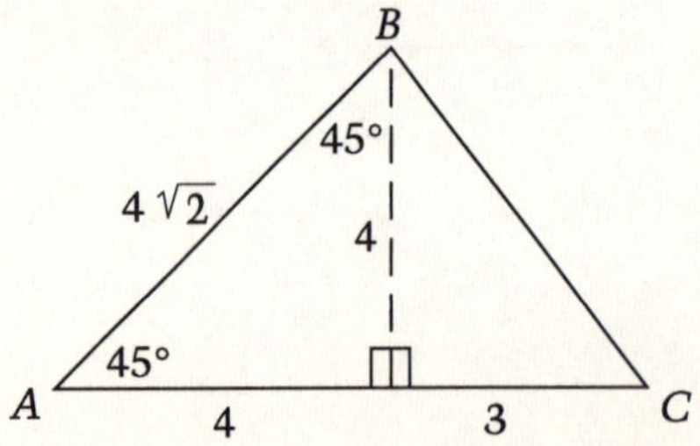

Now you can see that the legs of the smaller triangle on the right must be 4 and 3, making this a 3-4-5 right triangle, and the length of hypotenuse *BC* is 5.

Practice Problems: Special Triangles

REGULAR MATH

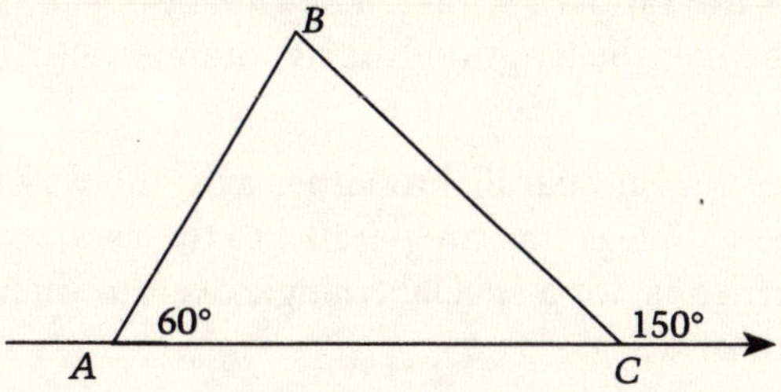

Note: Figure not drawn to scale.

Q. How many degrees does an ice skater rotate when doing a triple axel?

1. In triangle ABC above, if $AB = 4$, then $AC =$

(A) 10
(B) 9
(C) 8
(D) 7
(E) 6

Ⓐ Ⓑ Ⓒ Ⓓ Ⓔ

QC

Column A	Column B

In the coordinate plane, point R has coordinates (0, 0) and point S has coordinates (9, 12).

	Column A	Column B
2.	The distance from R to S	16

Ⓐ Ⓑ Ⓒ Ⓓ Ⓔ

REGULAR MATH

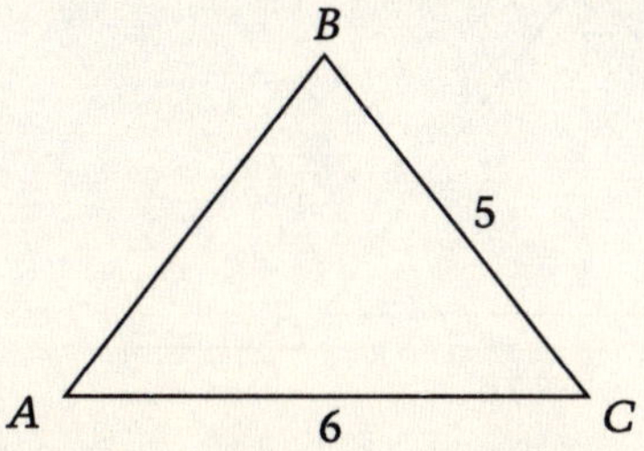

3. If the perimeter of triangle ABC above is 16, what is its area?

(A) 8
(B) 9
(C) 10
(D) 12
(E) 15

Ⓐ Ⓑ Ⓒ Ⓓ Ⓔ

Answers to Special Triangles Problems

1. (C) Angle *BCA* is supplementary to the angle marked 150°, so angle *BCA* = 180° – 150° = 30°. Since the sum of interior angles of a triangle is 180°, angle *A* + angle *B* + angle *BCA* = 180°, so angle *B* = 180° – 60° – 30° = 90°. So triangle *ABC* is a 30-60-90 right triangle, and its sides are in the ratio 1: $\sqrt{3}$: 2. The side opposite the 30°, *AB*, which we know has length 4, must be half the length of the hypotenuse, *AC*. Therefore *AC* = 8, and that's answer choice (C).

2. (B) Draw a diagram. Since *RS* isn't parallel to either axis, the way to compute its length is to create a right triangle with legs that are parallel to the axes, so their lengths are easy to find. If the triangle formed is not a special triangle, we can then use the Pythagorean theorem to find the length of *RS*.

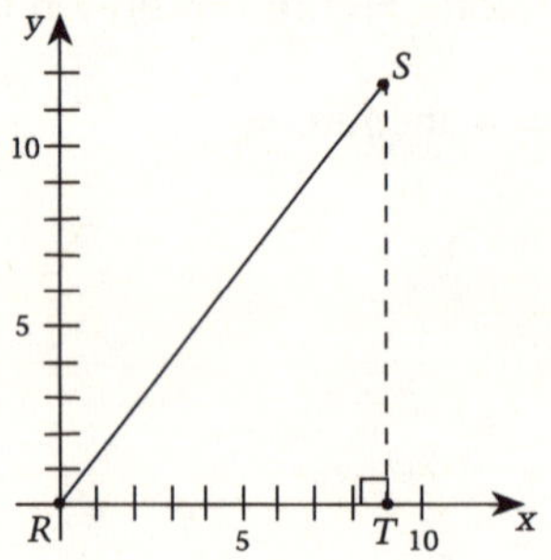

Since *S* has a *y*-coordinate of 12, it's 12 units above the *x*-axis, so the length of *ST* must be 12. And since *T* is the same number of units to the right of the *y*-axis as *S*, given by the *x*-coordinate of 9, the distance from the origin to *T* must be 9. So we have a right triangle with legs of 9 and 12. You should recognize this as a multiple of the 3-4-5 triangle. 9 = 3 × 3; 12 = 3 × 4; so the hypotenuse *RS* must be 3 × 5, or 15. That's the value of Column A, so Column B is greater.

3. (D) To find the area you need to know the base and height. If the perimeter is 16, then *AB* + *BC* + *AC* = 16; that is, *AB* = 16 – 5 – 6 = 5. Since *AB* = *BC*, this is an isosceles triangle. If you drop a line from vertex *B* to *AC*, it will divide the base in half. This divides up the triangle into two smaller right triangles:

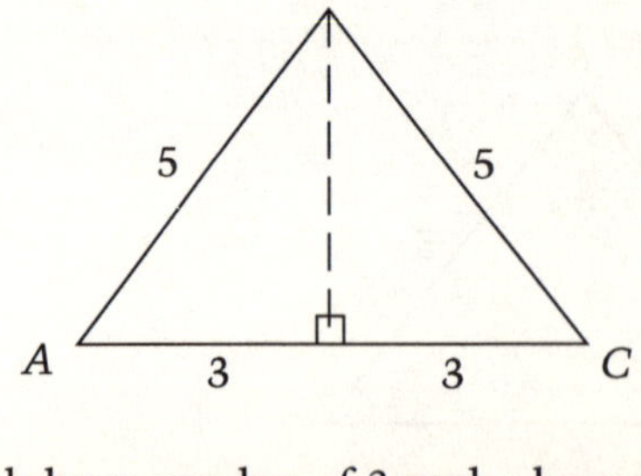

These right triangles each have one leg of 3 and a hypotenuse of 5; therefore they are 3-4-5 right triangles. So the missing leg (which is also the height of triangle *ABC*) must have length 4. We now know that the base of *ABC* is 6 and the height is 4, so the area is $\frac{1}{2} \times 6 \times 4$, or 12, answer choice (D).

MULTIPLE AND ODDBALL FIGURES

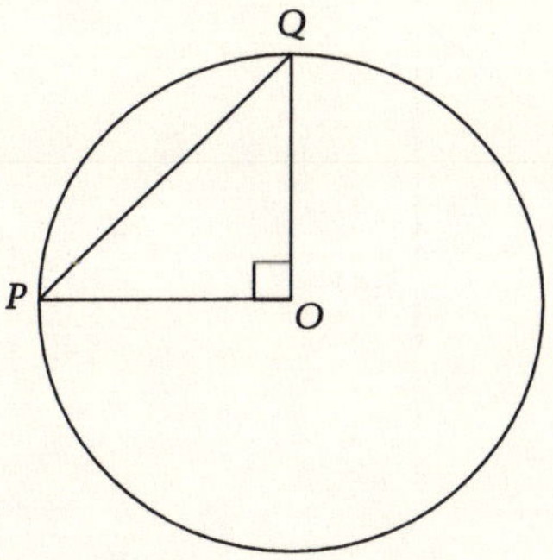

EXAMPLE

In the figure above, if the area of the circle with center O is 9π, what is the area of triangle POQ ?

(A) 4.5

(B) 6

(C) 9

(D) 3.5π

(E) 4.5π

Breaking Up Is Easy

When you see a shape that isn't a triangle, rectangle, or circle, try breaking it into familiar figures.

In a problem that combines figures, you have to look for the relationship between the figures.

HINT: *Look for pieces the figures have in common.*

For instance, if two figures share a side, information about that side will probably be the key.

In this case the figures don't share a side, but the triangle's legs are important features of the circle—they are radii. You can see that $PO = OQ$ = the radius of circle O.

The area of the circle is 9π. The area of a circle is πr^2, where r = the radius. So $9\pi = \pi r^2$, $9 = r^2$, and the radius = 3. The area of a triangle is $\frac{1}{2}$ base times height. Therefore, the area of ΔPOQ is $\frac{1}{2}(\text{leg}_1 \times \text{leg}_2) = \frac{1}{2}(3 \times 3) = \frac{9}{2} = 4.5$, answer choice (A).

Q.

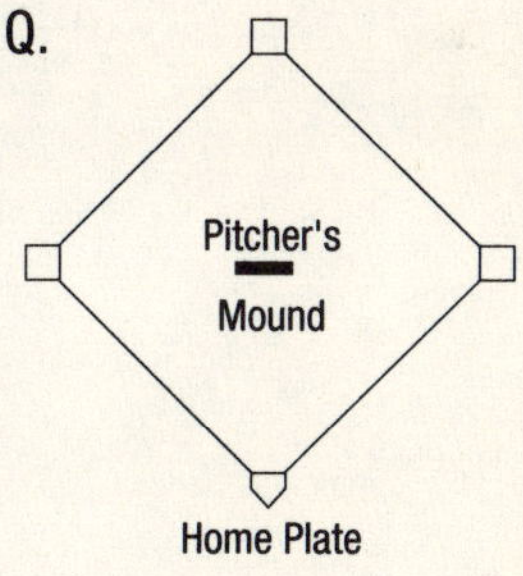

Assume that a baseball diamond is a square with sides of 90 feet and the pitcher's mound is located at the intersection of the square's diagonals. How far is it from the pitcher's mound to home plate?

But what if, instead of a number of familiar shapes, you are given something like this?

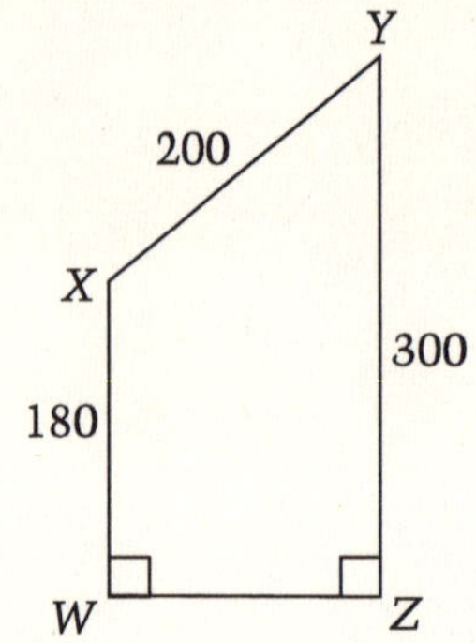

EXAMPLE

What is the perimeter of quadrilateral *WXYZ* ?

(A) 680

(B) 760

(C) 840

(D) 920

(E) 1,000

Kaplan Rules

Multiple figures are almost always made up of either several familiar shapes put together, or one familiar shape with a recognizable piece shaded or cut out of it.

Try breaking the unfamiliar shape into familiar ones. Once this is done, you can use the same techniques that you would for multiple figures. Perimeter is the sum of the lengths of the sides of a figure, so you need to find the length of *WZ*. Drawing a perpendicular line from point *X* to side *YZ* will divide the figure into a right triangle and a rectangle. Call the point of intersection *A*.

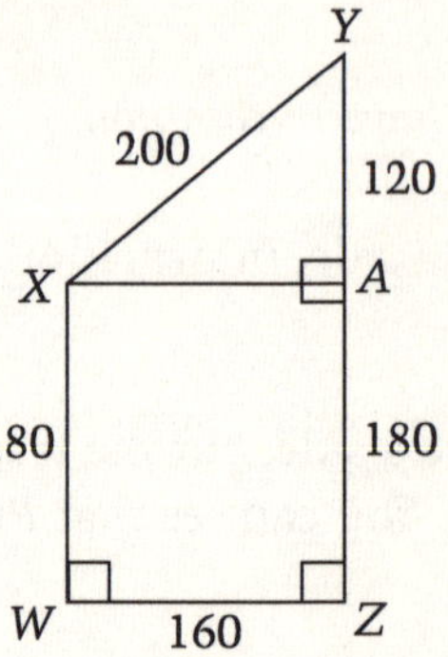

Opposite sides of a rectangle have equal length, so $WZ = XA$ and $WX = ZA$. *WX* is labeled as 180, so $ZA = 180$. Since *YZ* measures 300, *AY* is $300 - 180 = 120$. In right triangle *XYA*, hypotenuse $XY = 200$ and leg $AY = 120$; you should recognize this as a multiple of a 3-4-5 right triangle. The hypotenuse is 5×40, one leg is 3×40, so *XA* must be 4×40 or 160. (If you didn't recognize this special right triangle you could have used the Pythagorean theorem to find the length of *XA*.) Since $WZ = XA = 160$, the perimeter of the figure is $180 + 200 + 300 + 160 = 840$, answer choice (C).

Practice Problems: Multiple and Oddball Figures

REGULAR MATH

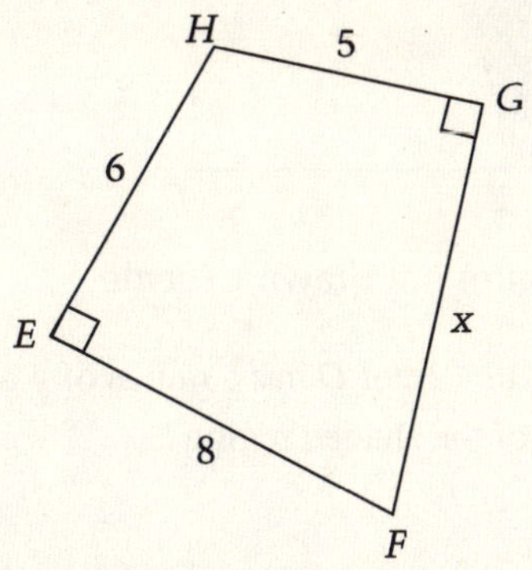

1. What is the value of x in the figure above?

   (A) 4
   (B) $3\sqrt{3}$
   (C) $3\sqrt{5}$
   (D) $5\sqrt{3}$
   (E) 9

Q. In boxing, what do the letters "TKO" stand for?

Ⓐ Ⓑ Ⓒ Ⓓ Ⓔ

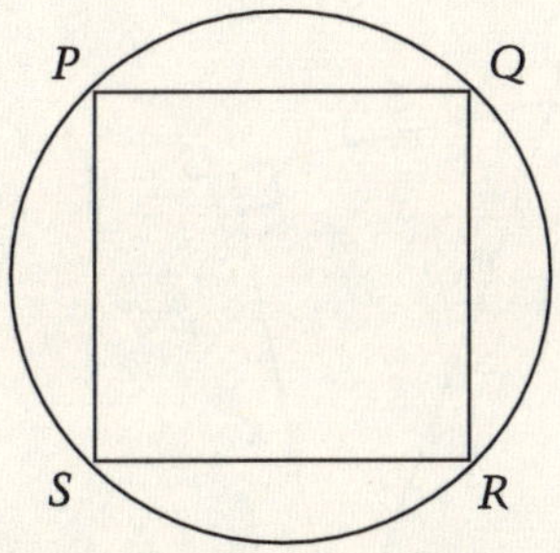

2. In the figure above, square $PQRS$ is inscribed in a circle. If the area of square $PQRS$ is 4, what is the radius of the circle?

   (A) 1
   (B) $\sqrt{2}$
   (C) 2
   (D) $2\sqrt{2}$
   (E) $4\sqrt{2}$

Ⓐ Ⓑ Ⓒ Ⓓ Ⓔ

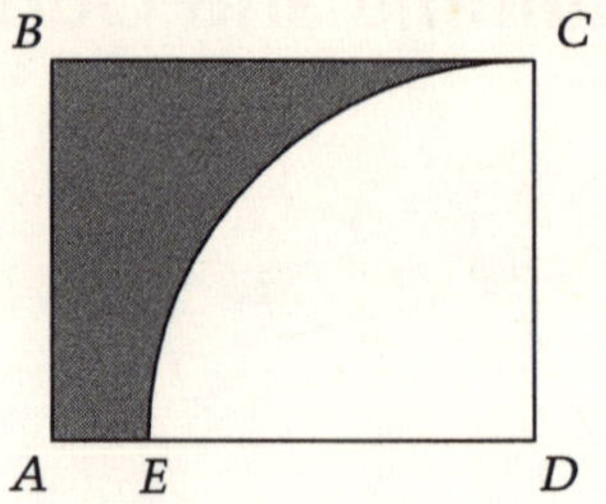

Note: Figure not drawn to scale.

3. In the figure above, the quarter circle with center D has a radius of 4 and rectangle $ABCD$ has a perimeter of 20. What is the perimeter of the shaded region?

(A) $20 - 8\pi$
(B) $10 + 2\pi$
(C) $12 + 2\pi$
(D) $12 + 4\pi$
(E) $4 + 8\pi$

Ⓐ Ⓑ Ⓒ Ⓓ Ⓔ

Answers to Multiple and Oddball Figures Problems

1. (D) Draw a straight line from point H to point F, to divide the figure into two right triangles.

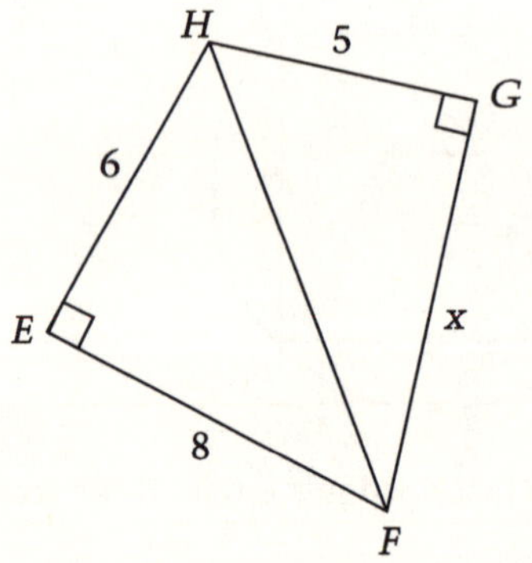

ΔEFH is a 3-4-5 right triangle with a hypotenuse of length 10. Use the Pythagorean theorem in ΔFGH to find x:

$$x^2 + 5^2 = 10^2$$
$$x^2 + 5^2 = 100$$
$$x^2 = 75$$
$$x = \sqrt{75}$$
$$x = \sqrt{25}\sqrt{3}$$
$$x = 5\sqrt{3}$$

2. (B) Draw in diagonal QS and you will notice that it is also a diameter of the circle.

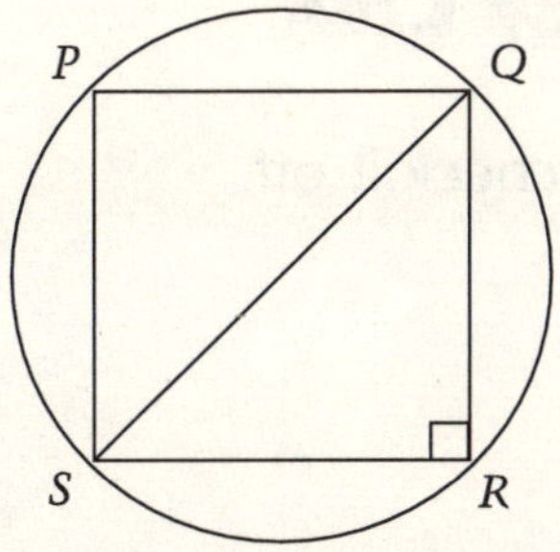

Since the area of the square is 4 its sides must each be 2. Think of the diagonal as dividing the square into two isosceles right triangles. Therefore, the diagonal = $2\sqrt{2}$ = the diameter; the radius is half this amount, or $\sqrt{2}$.

3. (C) The perimeter of the shaded region is $BC + AB + AE$ + arc EC. The quarter circle has its center at D, and point C lies on the circle, so side DC is a radius of the circle and equals 4.

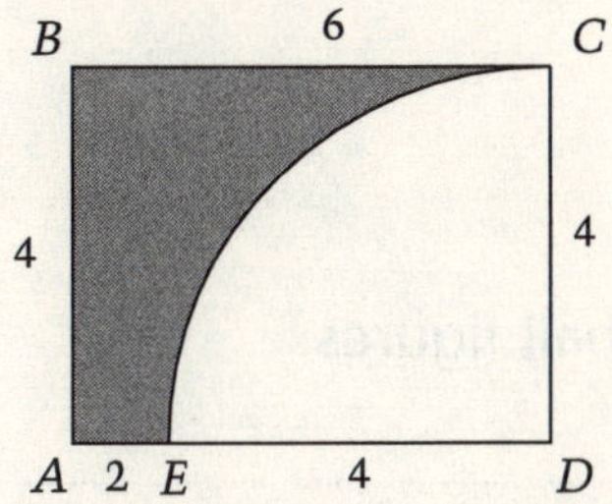

Opposite sides of a rectangle are equal, so AB is also 4. The perimeter of the rectangle is 20, and since the two short sides account for 8, the two longer sides must account for 12, making BC and AD each 6. To find AE, subtract the length of ED, another radius of length 4, from the length of AD, which is 6; $AE = 2$.

Since arc EC is a quarter circle, the length of the arc EC is $\frac{1}{4}$ of the circumference of a whole circle with radius 4: $\frac{1}{4} \times 2\pi r = \frac{1}{4} \times 8\pi = 2\pi$.

So the perimeter of the shaded region is $6 + 4 + 2 + 2\pi = 12 + 2\pi$.

You Can Look It Up

A list of the 100 Math Principles you need to know can be found in the "SAT Math Scouting Report" chapter. Review it to see what areas you might need to brush up on.

REPLAY

Once you've mastered a concept, check it off.

Classic Problem-Solving Techniques:

- ❑ Remainders
- ❑ Averages
- ❑ Ratios
- ❑ Rates
- ❑ Percents
- ❑ Combinations
- ❑ Simultaneous equations
- ❑ Symbolism
- ❑ Special triangles
- ❑ Multiple and oddball figures

13

Avoid the Double-Team (Math Traps)

HIGHLIGHTS

- Study the most common SAT Math traps and how to avoid them
- Train yourself to recognize wrong and tricky answer choices
- Pick up tips and hints on how to solve problems
- Complete the Math Traps Practice Sets

It's time for us to let you in on a little secret that will allow you to breeze through the entire SAT, get into any college you want, succeed in life, and find eternal happiness.

If you believed a word of the preceding paragraph, you need to pay special attention to this chapter. This chapter presents ten common SAT traps. Traps lure you into one answer, usually one that's easy to get to. But they conceal the correct answer, which requires some thought. If you're not wary of traps on the SAT, they may trip you up. Learn to recognize common traps and you'll gain more points.

HINT: *If you see what appears to be a basic problem late in a question set, there is probably a trap.*

Two-Minute Drill

If you have only a week or two to prep for the SAT, here's the best way to spend your time:

- Skim the chapter, paying special attention to the "Top Ten Trap" sidebars.
- Do the first practice set on p. 160. If you miss an answer, identify the trap that caught you and study that section.
- Do the second practice set on p. 174. Identify any trap that caught you and study that section. If you get all the answers right, you're strong at avoiding traps.

Kaplan's Favorite Trap

When the hands of your watch show 12:30, how many degrees separate the hour hand from the minute hand?

The obvious answer is 180 degrees. That's a trap. (At 12:30 the hour hand doesn't point directly at the 12; it's halfway between the 12 and the 1.) The test makers hoped that you would jump to the obvious answer, without taking the time to think it through.

Over the years, the SAT has had plenty of problems like this one. Traps catch unwary students who forget to think through the problem before they answer it. How do you prevent yourself from falling for other SAT Math traps? Read this chapter.

WATCH OUT FOR TRAPS

The following ten questions have one thing in common—they all have traps. Take 12 minutes to try to work through all of them. Then check your answers on p. 164.

1. Jackie purchased a new car in 1990. Three years later she sold it to a dealer for 40 percent less than she paid for it in 1990. The dealer then added 20 percent onto the price he paid and resold it to another customer. The price the final customer paid for the car was what percent of the original price Jackie paid in 1990?
   (A) 40 percent
   (B) 60 percent
   (C) 72 percent
   (D) 80 percent
   (E) 88 percent
   Ⓐ Ⓑ Ⓒ Ⓓ Ⓔ

2. In a class of 27 students, the average (arithmetic mean) score of the boys on the final exam was 83. If the average score of the 15 girls in the class was 92, what was the average of the whole class?
   (A) 86.2
   (B) 87.0
   (C) 87.5
   (D) 88.0
   (E) 88.2
   Ⓐ Ⓑ Ⓒ Ⓓ Ⓔ

....

3. Mike's coin collection consists of quarters, dimes, and nickels. If the ratio of the number of quarters to the number of dimes is 5:2, and the ratio of the number of dimes to the number of nickels is 3:4, what is the ratio of the number of quarters to the number of nickels?
   (A) 5 to 4
   (B) 7 to 5
   (C) 10 to 6
   (D) 12 to 7
   (E) 15 to 8
   Ⓐ Ⓑ Ⓒ Ⓓ Ⓔ

....

	Column A		Column B	
		$p > q > 1$		
4.	$p^2 - q^2$		$(p - q)^2$	Ⓐ Ⓑ Ⓒ Ⓓ Ⓔ

....

A, *B*, and *C* are points on a line such that point *A* is 12 units away from point *B* and point *B* is four units away from point *C*.

5.	The distance from point *A* to point *C*	16	Ⓐ Ⓑ Ⓒ Ⓓ Ⓔ

6.

Column A	Column B
The area of a square with a perimeter of 14	Twice the area of a square with a perimeter of 7

Ⓐ Ⓑ Ⓒ Ⓓ Ⓔ

7. If $n \neq 0$, then which of the following must be true?

I. $n^2 > n$
II. $2n > n$
III. $n + 1 > n$

(A) I only
(B) II only
(C) III only
(D) I and III only
(E) I, II, and III

Ⓐ Ⓑ Ⓒ Ⓓ Ⓔ

> Q. Who holds the record for consecutive victories on the LPGA tour?

8. At a certain restaurant, the hourly wage for a waiter is 20 percent greater than the hourly wage for a dishwasher, and the hourly wage for a dishwasher is half as much as the hourly wage for a cook's assistant. If a cook's assistant earns \$8.50 an hour, how much less than a cook's assistant does a waiter earn each hour?

(A) \$2.55
(B) \$3.40
(C) \$4.25
(D) \$5.10
(E) \$5.95

Ⓐ Ⓑ Ⓒ Ⓓ Ⓔ

9. A car traveled from A to B at an average speed of 40 miles per hour and then immediately traveled back from B to A at an average speed of 60 miles per hour. What was the car's average speed for the round-trip, in miles per hour?

(A) 45
(B) 48
(C) 50
(D) 52
(E) 54

Ⓐ Ⓑ Ⓒ Ⓓ Ⓔ

10. The tickets for a certain raffle are consecutively numbered. If Louis sold the tickets numbered from 75 to 148 inclusive, how many raffle tickets did he sell?

(A) 71
(B) 72
(C) 73
(D) 74
(E) 75

Ⓐ Ⓑ Ⓒ Ⓓ Ⓔ

HOW MATH TRAPS WORK AND HOW TO AVOID THEM

Q. Who is the only college football player to win the Heisman Trophy twice?

How did you do? If you got any wrong answers, unless you calculated incorrectly, chances are you got caught in a trap. The same traps occur again and again on the SAT. Learn how they work and how to avoid them. Once you can deal with traps, you'll do much better on the harder math questions.

To see how they work, let's take another look at the ten sample questions. Each contains one of the Top Ten Math Traps.

Trap 1: Percent Increase/Decrease

EXAMPLE

Jackie purchased a new car in 1990. Three years later she sold it to a dealer for 40 percent less than she paid for it in 1990. The dealer then added 20 percent onto the price he paid and resold it to another customer. The price the final customer paid for the car was what percent of the original price Jackie paid in 1990?

(A) 40 percent
(B) 60 percent
(C) 72 percent
(D) 80 percent
(E) 88 percent

Top Ten Trap #1

To get a combined percent increase or decrease, don't just add the percents.

The Wrong Answer

The increase/decrease percentage problem usually appears at the end of a section and invariably contains a trap. Most students will figure that taking away 40 percent, and then adding 20 percent gives you an overall loss of 20 percent, and pick choice (D), 80 percent, as the correct answer.

The Trap

When a quantity is increased or decreased by a percent more than once, you cannot simply add and subtract the percents to get the answer.

In this kind of percent problem:

- The first percent change is a percent of the starting amount.
- The second change is a percent of the new amount.

Avoiding the Trap

Percents can be added and subtracted only when they are percents of the same amount.

Finding the Right Answer

We know:

- The 40 percent less that Jackie got for the car is 40 percent of her original price.
- The 20 percent the dealer adds on is 20 percent of what the dealer paid, a much smaller amount.
- Adding on 20 percent of that smaller amount is not the same thing as adding back 20 percent of the original price.

So We Can Solve the Problem

- Use 100 for a starting quantity, whether or not it makes sense in the real situation. The problem asks for the relative amount of change. So you can take any starting number, and compare it with the final result. Because you're dealing with percents, 100 is the easiest number to work with.

HINT: *Pick 100 as the starting quantity and see what happens.*

- If Jackie paid $100.00 for the car, what is 40 percent less?
- In the case of $100.00, each percent equals $1.00, so she sold it for $60.00.
- If the dealer charges 20 percent more than his purchase price, he's raising the price by 20 percent of $60.00, which is $12.00 (not 20 percent of $100.00, which is $20.00).
- Therefore the dealer sold the car again for $60.00 + $12.00, or $72.00.
- Finally, what percent of the starting price ($100.00) is $72.00? It's 72 percent. So the correct answer here is choice (C).

Trap 2: Weighted Averages

Top Ten Trap #2

Don't just average the averages.

EXAMPLE

In a class of 27 students, the average (arithmetic mean) score of the boys on the final exam was 83. If the average score of the 15 girls in the class was 92, what was the average of the whole class?

(A) 86.2

(B) 87.0

(C) 87.5

(D) 88.0

(E) 88.2

The Wrong Answer

If you simply average 83 and 92 to come up with 87.5 as the class average, you fell for the trap.

Stumped?

Use logic. There are more girls than boys, so the average would be closer to the girls' average—92. The only choices that are closer to 92 than 83 are (D) and (E).

The Trap

You cannot combine averages of different quantities by taking the average of those averages.

In an average problem, if one value occurs more frequently than others it is "weighted" more. Remember that the average formula calls for the sum of all the terms, divided by the total number of terms.

Avoiding the Trap

Work with the sums, not the averages.

Answer Key for Trap Exercise on pp. 160–161

1. (C)
2. (D)
3. (E)
4. (A)
5. (D)
6. (A)
7. (C)
8. (B)
9. (B)
10. (D)

Finding the Right Answer

If 15 of the 27 students are girls, the remaining 12 must be boys. We can't just add 83 to 92 and divide by two. In this class there are more girls than boys, and therefore the girls' test scores are "weighted" more—they contribute more to the class average. So the answer must be either (D) or (E). To find each sum, multiply each average by the number of terms it represents. After you have found the sums of the different terms, find the combined average by plugging the sums into the average formula.

$$\text{Total class average} = \frac{\text{Sum of girls' scores} + \text{Sum of boys' scores}}{\text{Total number of students}}$$

$$= \frac{(\#\text{ of girls} \times \text{girls' average score}) + (\#\text{ of boys} \times \text{boys' average score})}{\text{Total number of students}}$$

$$= \frac{15(92) + 12(83)}{27} = \frac{1{,}380 + 996}{27} = 88$$

So the class average is 88, answer choice (D).

Trap 3: Ratio:Ratio:Ratio

Money, Money, Money

Don't be distracted by money. In the example to the right, we care only about the *number* of coins, not their value.

EXAMPLE

Mike's coin collection consists of quarters, dimes, and nickels. If the ratio of the number of quarters to the number of dimes is 5:2, and the ratio of the number of dimes to the number of nickels is 3:4, what is the ratio of the number of quarters to the number of nickels?

(A) 5:4

(B) 7:5

(C) 10:6

(D 12:7

(E) 15:8

The Wrong Answer

If you chose 5:4 as the correct answer, you fell for the classic ratio trap.

The Trap

Parts of different ratios don't always refer to the same whole.

In the classic ratio trap, two different ratios each share a common part that is represented by two different numbers. The two ratios do not refer to the same whole, however, so they are not in proportion to each other. To solve this type of problem, restate both ratios so that the numbers representing the common part (in this case "dimes") are the same. Then all the parts will be in proportion and can be compared to each other.

Q. What is the average annual income of a:
—high school dropout?
—high school graduate?
—associate degree holder?
—college graduate?

Avoiding the Trap

Make sure parts of ratios refer to the same whole.

Finding the Right Answer

To find the ratio of quarters to nickels, restate both ratios so that the number of dimes is the same in both. We are given two ratios:

Quarters:dimes = 5:2 Dimes:nickels = 3:4

The number corresponding to dimes in the first ratio is 2.
The number corresponding to dimes in the second ratio is 3.
To restate the ratios, find the least common multiple of 2 and 3.
The least common multiple of 2 and 3 is 6.

Restate the ratios with the number of dimes as 6:

Quarters:dimes = 15:6 Dimes:nickels = 6:8

The ratios are still in their original proportions, but now they're in proportion to each other and they refer to the same whole.

The ratio of quarters to dimes to nickels is 15:6:8, so the ratio of quarters to nickels is 15:8, which is answer choice (E).

Top Ten Trap #3

Don't take one number from one ratio and compare it to another number from another ratio.

Trap 4: Expressions That Look Equal—But Aren't

EXAMPLE

Column A		Column B
	$p > q > 1$	
$p^2 - q^2$		$(p - q)^2$

The Wrong Answer

If you said the expressions were equal, you'd be wrong.

Top Ten Trap #4

Don't be fooled by appearances.

The Trap

At first glance the expressions look like they're equal—but they're not.

This common SAT trap happens most often in QCs. Problems like this trap students who are too hasty, who answer on the basis of appearance, without considering the mathematical rules involved.

Avoiding the Trap

If two quantities seem obviously equal, double-check your answer, using your math knowledge and the techniques discussed in chapter 11, Quantitative Comparisons.

This is an example of the general rule that whenever an answer to a question late in a section looks obviously correct, it probably isn't.

Finding the Right Answer

In this case you can use the make-one-column-look-more-like-the-other technique discussed in chapter 11.

Factor Column A and rewrite Column B:

Column A	Column B
$(p - q)(p + q)$	$(p - q)(p - q)$

Stumped?

Pick numbers.

If $p = 3$ and $q = 2$, then

$p^2 - q^2 = 5$ and $(p - q)^2 = 1$.

Column A is bigger, so you know the answer must be either (A) or (D).

Now use the do-the-same-thing-to-both-columns technique. Both columns contain $(p - q)$. You know than $p > q$, so $p - q$ is a positive number. Therefore, you can divide both columns by $p - q$:

Column A	Column B
$p + q$	$p - q$

Since q is positive, adding q in Column A will get you more than subtracting q in Column B. Column A is greater, so the answer is (A).

This trap does not apply only to quadratics. Below are some other quantities that the hasty student might mistake as equal. Go through this list and make sure you can tell why these expressions are not equal except for special cases.

- $(x + y)^2$ does NOT equal $x^2 + y^2$
- $(2x)^2$ does NOT equal $2x^2$
- $x^{20} - x^{18}$ does NOT equal x^2
- $x^3 + x^3$ does NOT equal x^6
- $\sqrt{x} + \sqrt{x}$ does NOT equal $\sqrt{2x}$
- $\sqrt{x} - \sqrt{y}$ does NOT equal $\sqrt{x - y}$
- $\frac{1}{x} + \frac{1}{y}$ does NOT equal $\frac{1}{x + y}$

You could prove that any of these quantities need not be equal using the Picking Numbers technique.

Trap 5: Unspecified Order

Top Ten Trap #5

Don't assume that there's just one way to draw the diagram.

EXAMPLE

Column A	Column B
A, *B*, and *C* are points on a line such that point *A* is 12 units away from point *B* and point *B* is 4 units away from point *C*.	
The distance from point *A* to point *C*	16

The Wrong Answer

First you should always draw a diagram to help you visualize the relationship between the points.

In this diagram, the distance from *A* to *C* is 16, which is the same as Column B. But choice (C) is not the right answer.

The Trap

Don't assume that there is only one arrangement of the points—in this case, alphabetical order. We are not told what the relationship between *A* and *C* is. In fact *C* could lie to the left of *B*, like so:

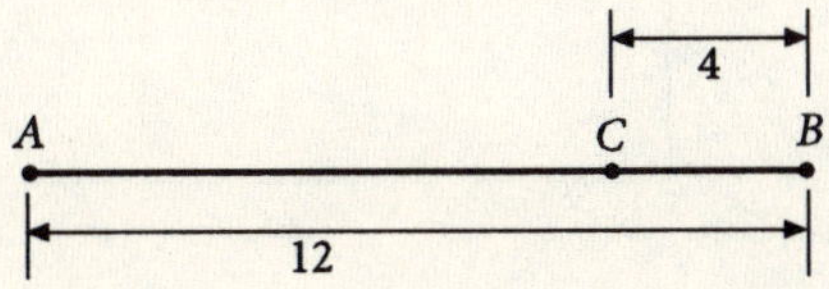

Avoiding the Trap

Don't assume points lie in the order they are given or in alphabetical order. Look for alternatives.

Finding the Right Answer

In this case, the distance from *A* to *C* is 8, which is less than Column B. Since we have two possible relationships between the columns, the answer must be (D)—you can't be certain from the data given.

Q. Who holds the NFL record for most yards rushing in one game?

Trap 6: Length:Area Ratios

Top Ten Trap #6

The ratio of areas is not the same as the ratio of lengths.

EXAMPLE

Column A	Column B
The area of a square with a perimeter of 14	Twice the area of a square with a perimeter of 7

The Wrong Answer

Twice the perimeter doesn't mean twice the area. Choice (C) is wrong.

The Trap

In proportional figures, the ratio of the areas is not the same as the ratio of the lengths.

Avoiding the Trap

Understand that the ratio of the areas of proportional figures is the square of the ratio of corresponding linear measures.

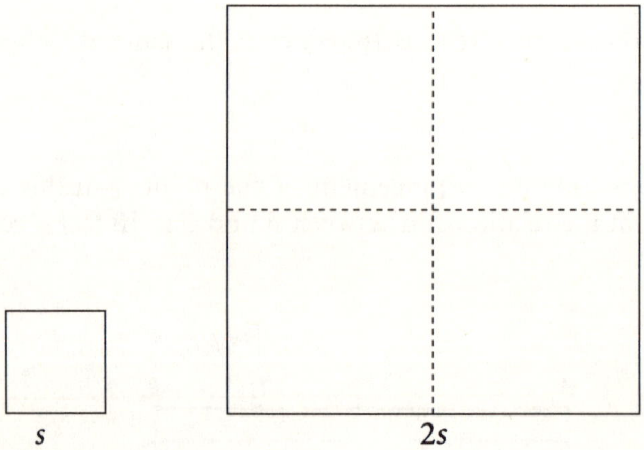

Finding the Right Answer

One way to solve this QC would be to actually compute the respective areas.

> Q. Assume a hockey puck has a radius of $1\frac{1}{2}$ inches and is $\frac{1}{2}$ inch thick. What is its volume?

A square of perimeter 14 has side length $\frac{14}{4} = 3.5$. Its area then is $(3.5)^2 = 12.25$.

On the other hand, the area of the square in Column B is $\left(\frac{7}{4}\right)^2 = (1.75)^2 = 3.0625$.

Even twice that area is still less than the 12.25 in Column A. The answer is (A).

A quicker and more clever way to dodge this trap is to understand the relationship between the linear ratio and the area ratio of proportional figures. In proportional figures, the area ratio is the square of the linear ratio.

In the example above, we are given two squares with sides in a ratio of 14:7 or 2:1.

Using the rule above, we square the linear 4:1 ratio. The areas of the two figures will be in a four-to-one ratio.

The same goes for circles:

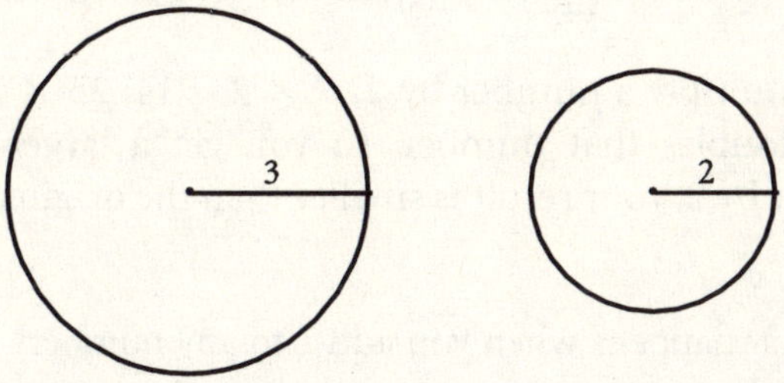

In the figure above, we are given two circles with radii in a 3:2 ratio. Using the rule above, we square the linear 3:2 ratio. The areas of the two circles will be in a 9:4 ratio.

Trap 7: Not All Numbers Are Positive Integers

EXAMPLE

If $n \neq 0$, then which of the following must be true?

I. $n^2 > n$

II. $2n > n$

III. $n + 1 > n$

(A) I only
(B) II only
(C) III only
(D) I and III only
(E) I, II, and III

Top Ten Trap #7

Not all numbers are positive integers. Don't forget to consider 0, fractions, and negative numbers.

The Wrong Answer

In the example above, if you considered only positive integers greater than 1 for the value of n, you would assume that all three statements are true. However, that is not the case.

The Trap

Not all numbers are positive integers. Don't forget there are negative numbers and fractions as well. This is important because negative numbers and fractions between 0 and 1 behave very differently from positive integers.

Avoiding the Trap

When picking numbers for variables, consider fractions and negative numbers.

Finding the Right Answer

Looking at statement I, you may assume that when you square a number, you end up with a larger number as a result. For example, $4^2 = 16$, or $10^2 = 100$. However, when you square a fraction between 0 and 1, the result is quite different: $\left(\frac{1}{2}\right)^2 = \frac{1}{4}$. $\left(\frac{1}{10}\right)^2 = \frac{1}{100}$, so you get a smaller number.

In statement II, what happens when you multiply a number by 2? $7 \times 2 = 14$; $25 \times 2 = 50$. Multiplying any positive number by 2 doubles that number, so you get a larger result. However, if you multiply a negative number by 2, your result is smaller than the original number. For example, $-3 \times 2 = -6$.

Q. What New York Liberty star was the women's college basketball Player of the Year in 1995 and led Connecticut to the national title?

Finally, look at statement III. What happens when you add 1 to any number? Adding 1 to any number gives you a larger number as a result. For example, $5 + 1 = 6$; $\frac{1}{2} + 1 = 1\frac{1}{2}$; and $-7 + 1 = -6$.

Therefore, only statement III must be true, so choice (C) is correct. If you didn't consider fractions or negative numbers, you would have fallen into the trap and answered the question incorrectly.

HINT: *This trap appears most often in QC problems, so watch out.*

Trap 8: Hidden Instructions

EXAMPLE

At a certain restaurant, the hourly wage for a waiter is 20 percent greater than the hourly wage for a dishwasher, and the hourly wage for a dishwasher is half as much as the hourly wage for a cook's assistant. If a cook's assistant earns \$8.50 an hour, how much less than a cook's assistant does a waiter earn each hour?

(A) \$2.55

(B) \$3.40

(C) \$4.25

(D) \$5.10

(E) \$5.95

Top Ten Trap #8

Make sure you're answering the question that's asked. Hint: underline the last phrase in the question.

The Wrong Answer

To solve this problem, you must find the hourly wage of the waiter.

The cook's assistant earns \$8.50 an hour. The dishwasher earns half of this—\$4.25 an hour. The waiter earns 20 percent more than the dishwasher—$\$4.25 \times 1.2 = \$5.10$.

So the waiter earns \$5.10 an hour, and you might reach automatically to fill in answer choice (D). But (D) is the wrong answer.

The Trap

A small step, easily overlooked, can mean the difference between a right and wrong answer.

In this case the word is *less*. After spending all this time finding the waiter's hourly wage, in their moment of triumph many students skip right over the vital last step. They overlook that the question asks not what the waiter earns, but how much less than the cook's assistant the waiter earns.

Peek-a-Boo

Hidden instructions come in many forms. Watch out for questions that give all the information in one unit (say, minutes) and ask you for the answer in another unit (say, seconds or hours). Read carefully and solve for the correct quantity.

Avoiding the Trap

Make sure you answer the question that's being asked. Watch out for hidden instructions.

Finding the Right Answer

You have figured out that the waiter earns $5.10 an hour. And the cook's assistant earns $8.50 an hour. To find out how much less than the cook's assistant the waiter earns, subtract the waiter's hourly wage from the cook's assistant's hourly wage.

The correct answer is (B).

Trap 9: Average Rates

EXAMPLE

A car traveled from *A* to *B* at an average speed of 40 miles per hour and then immediately traveled back from *B* to *A* at an average speed of 60 miles per hour. What was the car's average speed for the round-trip, in miles per hour?

(A) 45

(B) 48

(C) 50

(D) 52

(E) 54

Top Ten Trap #9

Any time it says "average rate" in the question, be alert: You usually can't just average the rates to get the right answer.

The Wrong Answer

Do you see which answer choice looks too good to be true? The temptation is simply to average 40 and 60. The answer is "obviously" 50 (C). But 50 is wrong.

The Trap

To get an average speed, you can't just average the rates.

Why is the average speed not 50 mph? Because the car spent more time traveling at 40 mph than at 60 mph. Each leg of the round trip was the same distance, but the first leg, at the slower speed, took more time.

Stumped?

Use common sense. The car spent more time at 40 mph so the answer will be less than 50—i.e., weighted more heavily towards 40 (remember weighted averages, trap #2).

If you saw this much but couldn't get the answer, you could guess between (A) and (B). (More on guessing in chapter 14.)

Avoiding the Trap

You can solve almost any Average Rate problem with this general formula:

$$\text{Average Rate} = \frac{\text{Total Distance}}{\text{Total Time}}$$

Use the given information to figure out the total distance and the total time. But how can you do that when many problems don't specify the distances?

Finding the Right Answer

In our sample above, we are told that a car went from *A* to *B* at 40 miles per hour and back from *B* to *A* at 60 miles per hour. In other words, it went half the total distance at 40 mph and half the total distance at 60 mph.

How do you use the formula:

$$\text{Average Rate} = \frac{\text{Total Distance}}{\text{Total Time}}$$

if you don't know the total distance?

Q. What sport has the highest average player salary?

HINT: *Pick a number! Pick any number you want for the total distance.*

Divide that total distance into half distances. Calculate the time needed to travel each half distance at the different rates.

HINT: *Pick a number that's easy to work with.*

A good number to pick here would be 240 miles for the total distance, because you can figure in your head the times for two 120-mile legs at 40 mph and 60 mph:

$$A \text{ to } B\text{: } \frac{120 \text{ miles}}{40 \text{ miles per hour}} = 3 \text{ hours}$$

$$B \text{ to } A\text{: } \frac{120 \text{ miles}}{60 \text{ miles per hour}} = 2 \text{ hours}$$

Total time = 5 hours

Now plug "total distance = 240 miles" and "total time = 5 hours" into the general formula:

$$\text{Average Rate} = \frac{\text{Total Distance}}{\text{Total Time}} = \frac{240 \text{ miles}}{5 \text{ hours}} = 48 \text{ miles per hour}$$

Correct answer choice: (B).

Trap 10: Counting Numbers

Top Ten Trap #10

You just can't subtract the first number from the last number; you have to add one.

EXAMPLE

The tickets for a certain raffle are consecutively numbered. If Louis sold the tickets numbered from 75 to 148 inclusive, how many raffle tickets did he sell?

(A) 71

(B) 72

(C) 73

(D) 74

(E) 75

The Wrong Answer

If you subtract 75 from 148 and get 73 as the answer, you are wrong.

The Trap

Subtracting the first and last integers in a range will give you the difference of the two numbers. It won't give you the number of integers in that range.

Avoiding the Trap

To count the number of integers in a range, subtract and then add 1.

If you forget the rule, pick two small numbers that are close together, such as 1 and 4. Obviously, there are four integers from 1 to 4, inclusive. But if you had subtracted 1 from 4, you would have gotten 3.

In the diagram below, you can see that 3 is actually the distance between the integers, if the integers were on a number line or a ruler.

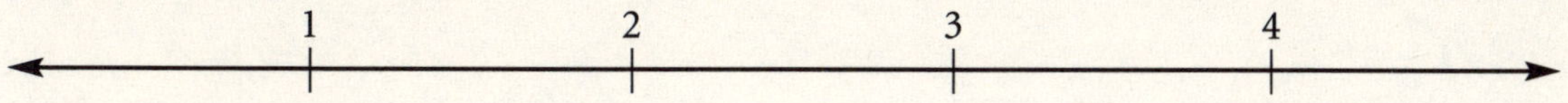

Finding the Right Answer

In the problem above, subtract 75 from 148. The result is 73. Add 1 to this difference to get the number of integers. That gives you 74. The correct answer choice is (D).

The word "inclusive" tells you to include the first and last numbers given. So, for example, "the integers from 5 to 15 inclusive" would include 5 and 15. Questions always make it clear whether you should include the outer numbers or not, since the correct answer hinges on this point.

MORE PRACTICE

Now that you can recognize the Top Ten Traps, try the following test. This time, try to identify the trap in each problem. Check your answers on p. 177.

	Column A	Column B	

A car traveled the first half of a 100-kilometer distance at an average speed of 120 kilometers per hour, and it traveled the remaining distance at an average speed of 80 kilometers per hour.

	Column A	Column B	
1.	The car's average speed, in kilometers per hour, for the 100 kilometers	100	Ⓐ Ⓑ Ⓒ Ⓓ Ⓔ

....

The ratio of $\frac{1}{4}$ to $\frac{2}{5}$ is equal to the ratio of $\frac{2}{5}$ to x.

	Column A	Column B	
2.	x	$\frac{3}{5}$	Ⓐ Ⓑ Ⓒ Ⓓ Ⓔ

....

	Column A	Column B	
3.	$14 - 6$	$\sqrt{14^2 - 6^2}$	Ⓐ Ⓑ Ⓒ Ⓓ Ⓔ

....

	Column A	Column B	
4.	$\frac{a+b}{3}$	$a+b$	Ⓐ Ⓑ Ⓒ Ⓓ Ⓔ

....

John buys 34 books at $6.00 each, and 17 at $12.00 each.

	Column A	Column B	
5.	The average price John pays per book	$9.00	Ⓐ Ⓑ Ⓒ Ⓓ Ⓔ

....

Column A	Column B

On a certain highway Town X lies 50 miles away from Town Y, and Town Z lies 80 miles from Town X.

	Column A	Column B	
6.	The number of minutes a car traveling at an average speed of 60 miles per hour takes to travel from Town Y to Town Z	30	Ⓐ Ⓑ Ⓒ Ⓓ Ⓔ

....

a, b, and c are positive numbers; $b < c$

	Column A	Column B	
7.	$(a + b)^2$	$a^2 + c^2$	Ⓐ Ⓑ Ⓒ Ⓓ Ⓔ

....

	Column A	Column B	
8.	The area of a circle with a diameter of 3	The sum of the areas of three circles each with a diameter of 1	Ⓐ Ⓑ Ⓒ Ⓓ Ⓔ

....

Jane invests her savings in a fund that adds 10 percent interest to her savings at the end of every year.

	Column A	Column B	
9.	The percent by which her money has increased after three years	31 percent	Ⓐ Ⓑ Ⓒ Ⓓ Ⓔ

....

$x > 1$

	Column A	Column B	
10.	$7^{2x} - 7^x$	7^x	Ⓐ Ⓑ Ⓒ Ⓓ Ⓔ

....

11. Pump 1 can drain a 400-gallon water tank in 1.2 hours. Pump 2 can drain the same tank in 1.8 hours. How many minutes longer than pump 1 would it take pump 2 to drain a 100-gallon tank?
    (A) 0.15
    (B) 1.2
    (C) 6
    (D) 9
    (E) 18

Ⓐ Ⓑ Ⓒ Ⓓ Ⓔ

....

12. Volumes 12 through 30 of a certain encyclopedia are located on the bottom shelf of a bookcase. If the volumes of the encyclopedia are numbered consecutively, how many volumes of the encyclopedia are on the bottom shelf?
(A) 17
(B) 18
(C) 19
(D) 29
(E) 30

13. A reservoir is at full capacity at the beginning of summer. By the first day of fall, the level in the reservoir is 30 percent below full capacity. Then during the fall a period of heavy rains raises the level by 30 percent. After the rains, the reservoir is at what percent of its full capacity?
(A) 100 percent
(B) 95 percent
(C) 91 percent
(D) 85 percent
(E) 60 percent

Q. Only two coaches have made 12 NCAA Final Four appearances. John Wooden is one. Who is the other?

14. Two classes, one with 50 students, the other with 30, take the same exam. The combined average of both classes is 84.5. If the larger class averages 80, what is the average of the smaller class?
(A) 87.2
(B) 89.0
(C) 92.0
(D) 93.3
(E) 94.5

15. In a pet shop, the ratio of puppies to kittens is 7:6 and the ratio of kittens to guinea pigs is 5:3. What is the ratio of puppies to guinea pigs?
(A) 7:3
(B) 6:5
(C) 13:8
(D) 21:11
(E) 35:18

16. A typist typed the first n pages of a book, where $n > 0$, at an average rate of 12 pages per hour and typed the remaining n pages at an average rate of 20 pages per hour. What was the typist's average rate, in pages per hour, for the entire book?
(A) $14\frac{2}{3}$
(B) 15
(C) 16
(D) 17
(E) 18

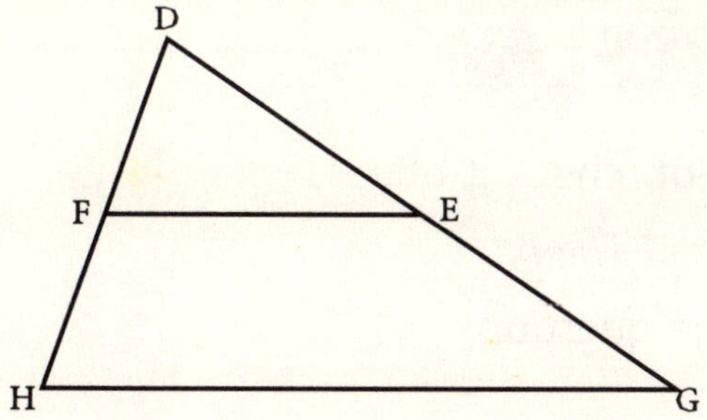

17. In triangle DGH above, $DE = EG$, $EF \parallel GH$, and the area of triangle DGH is 30. What is the area of triangle DEF ?
    (A) 7.5
    (B) 15
    (C) 22.5
    (D) 60
    (E) It cannot be determined from the information given.

Ⓐ Ⓑ Ⓒ Ⓓ Ⓔ

Did You Fall for the Traps?

How did you do? Did you spot the trap in each problem? Use the answers below to see what your weaknesses are. Each wrong answer represents one trap you need to work on. Go back and reread the section on that trap. Then try the problems again, until you answer correctly.

1. (B) Trap 9: Average rates
2. (A) Trap 3: Ratio:ratio:ratio
3. (B) Trap 4: Expressions that look equal—but aren't
4. (D) Trap 7: Not all numbers are positive integers
5. (B) Trap 2: Weighted averages
6. (D) Trap 5: Unspecified order
7. (D) Trap 4 : Expressions that look equal—but aren't
8. (A) Trap 6: Length:area ratio
9. (A) Trap 1: Percent increase/decrease
10. (A) Trap 4: Expressions that look equal—but aren't
11. (D) Trap 8: Hidden instructions
12. (C) Trap 10: Counting numbers
13. (C) Trap 1: Percent increase/decrease
14. (C) Trap 2: Weighted averages
15. (E) Trap 3: Ratio:ratio:ratio
16. (B) Trap 9: Average rates
17. (A) Trap 6: Length:area ratios

Q. What is the mascot of the University of California at Santa Cruz?

REPLAY

Once you've mastered a concept, check it off.

How Traps Work and How to Avoid Them:

❑ The wrong way to answer the questions

❑ Avoiding the traps

❑ Finding the right answers

Kaplan's Top Ten SAT Math Traps:

❑ Percent increase/decrease

❑ Weighted averages integers

❑ Ratio:ratio:ratio

❑ Expressions that look equal—but aren't

❑ Unspecified order

❑ Length:area ratios

❑ Not all numbers are positive

❑ Hidden instructions

❑ Average rates

❑ Counting numbers

14

Slam-Dunk Strategies for Guessing

HIGHLIGHTS

- Master the five strategies for making educated guesses
- See when to eliminate unreasonable or obvious choices
- Practice eyeballing geometry diagrams
- Learn to guess with confidence on Grid-ins

Obviously, the best way to find the answer is to actually solve the problem. But if you're stuck or running out of time, guessing can be a good alternative.

The Regular Math and QC sections, like the Verbal sections, are scored to discourage random guessing. For every question you get right you earn a whole point. For every question you get wrong, you lose a fraction of a point. So if you guess at random on a number of questions, the points you gain from correct guesses are canceled out by the points you lose on incorrect guesses, for no overall gain or loss.

But you can make *educated guesses*. This raises the odds of guessing correctly, so the fractional points you lose no longer cancel out all the whole points you gain. You have just raised your score.

To make an educated guess, eliminate answer choices you know to be wrong, and guess from what's left. Of course, the more answer choices you can eliminate, the better chance you have of guessing the correct answer from what's left over.

Two-Minute Drill

Guessing is an important strategy for scoring points, so read this chapter carefully, even if you only have a week or two to prep for the SAT. It's a short chapter, and there are no shortcuts to learning how to guess accurately.

FIVE STRATEGIES

In the pages that follow, you'll find five strategies for guessing intelligently on all types of math problems.

Eliminate Unreasonable Answer Choices

Before you guess, think about the problem, and decide which answers don't make sense. Take as an example the following problem:

EXAMPLE

The ratio of men to women in a certain room is 13:11. If there are 429 men in the room, how many women are there?

(A) 143

(B) 363

(C) 433

(D) 507

(E) 792

Solution:

- The ratio of men to women is 13:11, so there are more men than women.
- Since there are 429 men, there must be fewer than 429 women.
- So you can eliminate choices (C), (D), and (E).
- The answer must be either (A) or (B), so guess. The correct answer is (B).

Guessing Is Easy

Quick. Guess the right answer. William H. Harrison's middle name was:

- Hazel
- Hello
- Henry
- Hal
- Herbert

Except for the class clown who said Hazel, most people can safely eliminate two of the five choices. That means you've got a one-in-three chance of guessing Henry.

If you went into the SAT determined not to guess, you would have missed this great opportunity to score a point. If you can eliminate at least one answer, you should guess.

Eliminate the Obvious on Hard Questions

On the hard questions late in a set, obvious answers are usually wrong. So eliminate them when you guess. That doesn't hold true for early, easy questions, when the obvious answer could be right.

Now apply the rule. In the following difficult problem, which obvious answer should you eliminate?

EXAMPLE

A number x is increased by 30 percent and then the result is decreased by 20 percent. What is the final result of these changes?

(A) x is increased by 10 percent

(B) x is increased by 6 percent

(C) x is increased by 4 percent

(D) x is decreased by 5 percent

(E) x is decreased by 10 percent

Q. Which school has produced the most Heisman Trophy winners?

If you picked (A) as the obvious choice to eliminate, you'd be right. Most people would combine the decrease of 20 percent with the increase of 30 percent, getting a net increase of 10 percent. That's the easy, obvious answer, but not the correct answer. If you must guess, avoid (A). The correct answer is (C).

Eyeball Lengths, Angles, and Areas on Geometry Problems

Use diagrams that accompany geometry problems to help you eliminate wrong answer choices. First make sure that the diagram is drawn to scale. Diagrams are always drawn to scale unless there's a note like this: "Note: Figure not drawn to scale." If it's not, don't use this strategy. If it is, estimate quantities or eyeball the diagram. Then eliminate answer choices that are way too large or too small.

Stuck?

- Stuck on a QC or Regular Math question? Eliminate at least one answer choice and guess.
- Stuck on a Grid-in? You won't lose points for guessing wrong on Grid-ins. So go ahead and guess.

Length

When a geometry question asks for a length, use the given lengths to estimate the unknown length. Measure off the given length by making a nick in your pencil with your thumbnail. Then hold the pencil against the unknown length on the diagram to see how the lengths compare.

In the following problem, which answer choices can you eliminate by eyeballing?

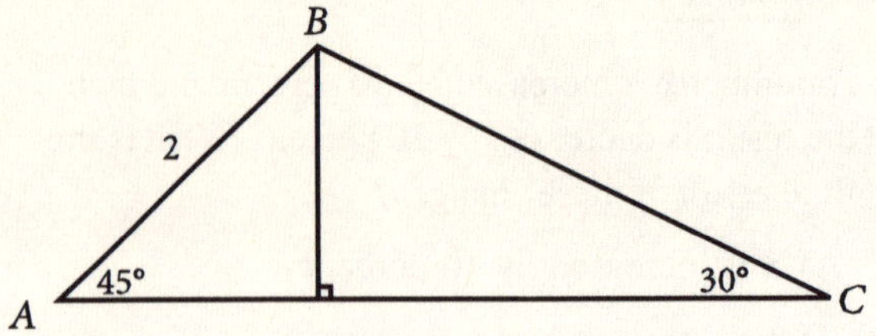

EXAMPLE

In the figure above, what is the length of *BC*?

(A) $\sqrt{2}$

(B) 2

(C) $2\sqrt{2}$

(D) 4

(E) $4\sqrt{2}$

Q. How high is an NBA rim?

Solution:

- *AB* is 2, so measure off this length on your pencil.
- Compare *BC* with this length.
- *BC* appears almost twice as long as *AB*, so *BC* is about 4.
- Since $\sqrt{2}$ is about 1.4, and *BC* is clearly longer than *AB*, choices (A) and (B) are too small.
- Choice (E) is much greater than 4, so eliminate that.
- Now guess between (C) and (D). The correct answer is (C).

Angles

You can also eyeball angles. To eyeball an angle, compare the angle with a familiar angle, such as a straight angle (180°), a right angle (90°), or half a right angle (45°). The corner of a piece of paper is a right angle, so use that to see if an angle is greater or less than 90°.

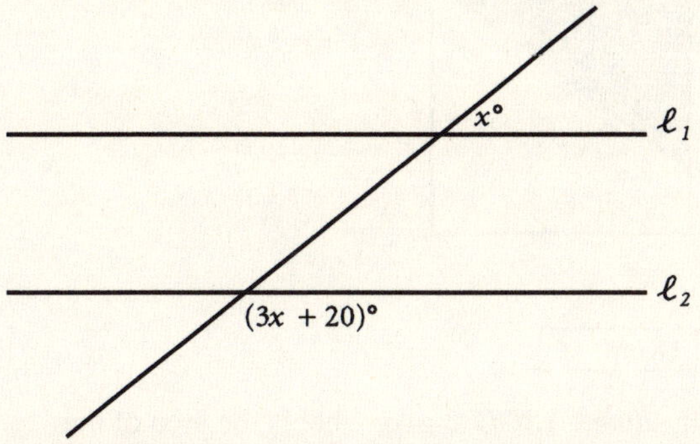

EXAMPLE

In the figure above, if $\ell_1 \parallel \ell_2$, what is the value of x?

(A) 130

(B) 100

(C) 80

(D) 50

(E) 40

Solution:

- You see that x is less than 90 degrees, so eliminate choices (A) and (B).
- Since x appears to be much less than 90 degrees, eliminate choice (C).
- Now pick between (D) and (E). In fact, the correct answer is (E).

Areas

Eyeballing an area is similar to eyeballing a length. You compare an unknown area in a diagram to an area that you do know.

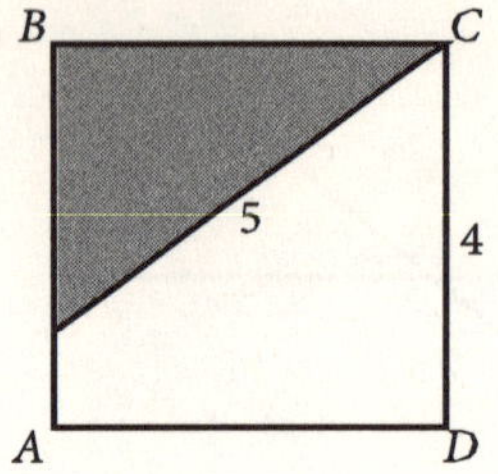

EXAMPLE

In square *ABCD* above, what is the area of the shaded region?

(A) 10

(B) 9

(C) 8

(D) 6

(E) 4

Solution:

- Since ABCD is a square, it has area 4^2, or 16.
- The shaded area is less than one-half the size of the square, so its area must be less than 8.
- Eliminate answer choices (A), (B), and (C). The correct answer is (D).

Eliminate Choice (D) on Some QCs

If both columns of a QC contain only concrete numbers, choice (D)—"the relationship cannot be determined"—can't be right. With no variables in either column, there must be one consistent relationship, even if you can't find it. If you don't know the answer, eliminate (D) as unreasonable and guess.

EXAMPLE

Column A	Column B
The largest prime factor of 1,224	18

Each column contains only numbers—so eliminate choice (D) and guess. If you were extra clever, you may also have seen that since 18 isn't prime, and Column A contains a prime number, the answer cannot be (C) either. The correct answer is (B).

Find the Range on Grid-ins—then Guess

On Grid-ins, there are no answer choices to eliminate, but you won't lose points for guessing. So if you are stuck, try to estimate the general range of the answer, and guess.

Here are some examples of hard Grid-in questions.

EXAMPLE

1. If the three-digit number $11Q$ is a prime number, what digit is represented by Q?
2. The sum of five consecutive odd integers is 425. What is the greatest of these integers?
3. A triangle has one side of length 3 and another of length 7. If the length of the third side is a solution to the equation $x^2 - 2x = 63$, what is the length of the third side?

Q. Name the Japanese slugger who has hit more home runs than any other player in pro baseball history.

Solutions:

1. Since Q is a digit, it must be one of the integers 0 through 9. Eliminate all the even digits, since they are divisible by 2. And eliminate 5, since any number ending with 5 is divisible by 5. You can also eliminate 1 and 7, because they are divisible by 3 (the digits add up to a multiple of 3). You are left with 3 and 9 to pick between. The correct answer is 3.
2. Since the integers are consecutive, they are all about the same size. So the number we are looking for is an odd number around $425 \div 5$, which is 85. The right answer is 89.
3. Even if you can't solve that quadratic, you know that one side of a triangle has to be less than the sum and greater than the difference of the other two sides. So the third side is less than $7 + 3$, or 10, and greater than $7 - 3$, or 4. Since solutions to SAT quadratics are usually integers, pick an integer from 5 to 9. If you picked 9, you'd be right.

HINT: *Read "SAT Math Scouting Report" in the "SAT Locker Room" section.*

REPLAY

Once you've mastered a concept, check it off.

Math Guessing:

❏ Eliminate unreasonable answer choices

❏ Eliminate the obvious on hard questions

❏ Eyeball lengths, angles, and areas on geometry problems

❏ Eliminate choice (D) on some QCs

❏ Find the range on Grid-ins—then guess

ROUND 4

Ready, Set, Go!

15

In the Zone: Stress Management

HIGHLIGHTS

- Unearth your sources of stress and learn how to manage them
- Take stock of your strengths and weaknesses
- Imagine yourself succeeding
- Practice proper breathing and exercise techniques
- Prepare for the final countdown

The countdown has begun. Your date with THE TEST is looming on the horizon. Anxiety is on the rise. The butterflies in your stomach have gone ballistic. Perhaps you feel as if the last thing you ate has turned into a lead ball. Your thinking is getting cloudy. Maybe you think you won't be ready. Maybe you already know your stuff, but you're going into panic mode anyway. Worst of all, you're not sure of what to do about it.

Don't panic! It is possible to tame that anxiety and stress—before and during the test. We'll show you how. You won't believe how quickly and easily you can deal with that killer anxiety.

Lack of control is one of the prime causes of stress. A ton of research shows that if you don't have a sense of control over what's happening in your life you can easily end up feeling helpless and hopeless. So, just having concrete things to do and to think about—taking control—will help reduce your stress. This section shows you how to take control during the days leading up to taking the test.

Two-Minute Drill

If you have only a week or two to prep for the SAT, you may just want to skim this chapter. If you're feeling stressed out, take the time to read it carefully. It will help you relax!

IDENTIFY THE SOURCES OF STRESS

In the space provided, jot down anything you identify as a source of your test-related stress. The idea is to pin down that free-floating anxiety so that you can take control of it. Here are some common examples to get you started:

- I always freeze up on tests.
- I'm nervous about the math (or the vocabulary or reading, etcetera).
- I need a good/great score to go to Acme College.
- My older brother/sister/best friend/girl- or boyfriend did really well. I *must* match their scores or do better.
- My parents, who are paying for school, will be really disappointed if I don't test well.
- I'm afraid of losing my focus and concentration.
- I'm afraid I'm not spending enough time preparing.
- I study like crazy but nothing seems to stick in my mind.
- I always run out of time and get panicky.
- I feel as though thinking is becoming like wading through thick mud.

Avoid Must-y Thinking

Let go of "must-y" thoughts, those notions that you must do something in a certain way—for example, "I must get a great score, or else!" or "I must meet Mom and Dad's expectations!"

Sources of Stress:

____

____

____

____

____

____

____

____

____

____

Q. How many Super Bowls did former Devner Bronco quarterback and future Hall-of-Famer John Elway lose before finally winning in 1998?

Take a few minutes to think about the things you've just written down. Then rewrite them in some sort of order. List the statements you most associate with your stress and anxiety first, and put the least disturbing items last. Chances are, the top of the list is a fairly accurate description of exactly how you react to test anxiety, both physically and mentally. The later items usually describe your fears (disappointing Mom and Dad, looking bad, etcetera). As you write the list, you're forming a hierarchy of items so you can deal first with the anxiety provokers that bug you most. Very often, taking care of the major items from the top of the list goes a long way towards relieving overall testing anxiety. You probably won't have to bother with the stuff you placed last.

TAKE STOCK OF YOUR STRENGTHS AND WEAKNESSES

Take one minute to list the areas of the test that you are good at. They can be general ("algebra") or specific ("quadratic equations"). Put down as many as you can think of, and if possible, time yourself. Write for the entire time; don't stop writing until you've reached the one-minute stopping point.

Strong Test Subjects:

____

____

____

____

____

____

____

Next, take one minute to list areas of the test you're not so good at, just plain bad at, have failed at, or keep failing at. Again, keep it to one minute, and continue writing until you reach the cutoff. Don't be afraid to identify and write down your weak spots! In all probability, as you do both lists you'll find you are strong in some areas and not so strong in others. Taking stock of your assets *and* liabilities lets you know the areas you don't have to worry about, and the ones that will demand extra attention and effort.

Weak Test Subjects:

____

____

____

____

____

____

____

____

Facing your weak spots gives you some distinct advantages. It helps a lot to find out where you need to spend extra effort. Increased exposure to tough material makes it more familiar and less intimidating. (After all, we mostly fear what we don't know and are probably afraid to face.) You'll feel better about yourself because you're dealing directly with areas of the test that bring on your anxiety. You can't help feeling more confident when you know you're actively strengthening your chances of earning a higher overall test score.

Very Superstitious

Stress expert Stephen Sideroff, Ph.D., tells of a client who always stressed out before, during, and even after taking tests. Yet, she always got outstanding scores. It became obvious that she was thinking superstitiously—subconsciously believing that the great scores were a result of her worrying. She also didn't trust herself, and believed that if she didn't worry she wouldn't study hard enough. Sideroff convinced her to take a risk and work on relaxing before her next test. She did, and her test results were still as good as ever—which broke her cycle of superstitious thinking.

Q. Who set the decathlon world record after failing to qualify for the event at the 1992 Olympic trials?

Now, go back to the "good" list, and expand it for two minutes. Take the general items on that first list and make them more specific; take the specific items and expand them into more general conclusions. Naturally, if anything new comes to mind, jot it down. Focus all of your attention and effort on your strengths. Don't underestimate yourself or your abilities. Give yourself full credit. At the same time, don't list strengths you don't really have; you'll only be fooling yourself.

Expanding from general to specific might go as follows. If you listed "Verbal" as a broad topic you feel strong in, you would then narrow your focus to include areas of this subject about which you are particularly knowledgeable. Your areas of strength might include analogies, ability to decipher unfamiliar words through knowledge of Latin, ability to recognize vocabulary bridges, etcetera.

Whatever you know comfortably (that is, almost as well as you know the back of your hand) goes on your "good" list. Okay. You've got the picture. Now, get ready, check your starting time, and start writing down items on your expanded "good" list.

Strong Test Subjects: An Expanded List:

Stress Tip

Don't work in a messy or cramped area. Before you sit down to study, clear yourself a nice, open space. And, make sure you have books, paper, pencils—whatever tools you will need—within easy reach before you sit down to study.

After you've stopped, check your time. Did you find yourself going beyond the two minutes allotted? Did you write down more things than you thought you knew? Is it possible you know more than you've given yourself credit for? Could that mean you've found a number of areas in which you feel strong?

You just took an active step towards helping yourself. Notice any increased feelings of confidence? Enjoy them.

Here's another way to think about your writing exercise. Every area of strength and confidence you can identify is much like having a reserve of solid gold at Fort Knox. You'll be able to draw on your reserves as you need them. You can use your reserves to solve difficult questions, maintain confidence, and keep test stress and anxiety at a distance. The encouraging thing is that every time you recognize another area of strength, succeed at coming up with a solution, or get a good score on a test, you increase your reserves. And, there is absolutely no limit to how much self-confidence you can have or how good you can feel about yourself.

IMAGINE YOURSELF SUCCEEDING

This next little group of exercises is both physical and mental. It's a natural follow-up to what you've just accomplished with your lists.

First, get yourself into a comfortable sitting position in a quiet setting. Wear loose clothes. If you wear glasses, take them off. Then, close your eyes and breathe in a deep, satisfying breath of air. Really fill your lungs until your rib cage is fully expanded and you can't take in any more. Then, exhale the air completely. Imagine you're blowing out a candle with your last little puff of air. Do this two or three more times, filling your lungs to their maximum and emptying them totally. Keep your eyes closed, comfortably but not tightly. Let your body sink deeper into the chair as you become even more comfortable.

Stress Tip

If you want to play music, keep it low and in the background. Music with a regular, mathematical rhythm—reggae, for example—aids the learning process. A recording of ocean waves is also soothing.

With your eyes shut you can notice something very interesting. You're no longer dealing with the worrisome stuff going on in the world *outside* of you. Now you can concentrate on what happens *inside* you. The more you recognize your own physical reactions to stress and anxiety, the more you can do about them. You may not realize it, but you've begun to regain a sense of being in control.

Let images begin to form on the "viewing screens" on the back of your eyelids. You're experiencing visualizations from the place in your mind that makes pictures. Allow the images to come easily and naturally; don't force them. Imagine yourself in a relaxing situation. It might be in a special place you've visited before or one you've read about. It can be a fictional location that you create in your imagination, but a real-life memory of a place or situation you know is usually better. Make it as detailed as possible and notice as much as you can.

Stay focused on the images as you sink farther back into your chair. Breathe easily and naturally. You might have the sensations of any stress or tension draining from your muscles and flowing downward, out your feet and away from you.

Take a moment to check how you're feeling. Notice how comfortable you've become. Imagine how much easier it would be if you could take the test feeling this relaxed and in this state of ease. You've coupled the images of your special place with sensations of comfort and relaxation. You've also found a way to become relaxed simply by visualizing your own safe, special place.

Now, close your eyes and start remembering a real-life situation in which you did well on a test. If you can't come up with one, remember a situation in which you did something (academic or otherwise) that you were really proud of—a genuine accomplishment. Make the memory as detailed as possible. Think about the sights, the sounds, the smells, even the tastes

Q. True or False? Super Bowl MVP and Hall-of-Famer Joe Montana was not a first-round draft choice.

associated with this remembered experience. Remember how confident you felt as you accomplished your goal. Now start thinking about the upcoming test. Keep your thoughts and feelings in line with that successful experience. Don't make comparisons between them. Just imagine taking the upcoming test with the same feelings of confidence and relaxed control.

This exercise is a great way to bring the test down to earth. You should practice this exercise often, especially when the prospect of taking the exam starts to bum you out. The more you practice it, the more effective the exercise will be for you.

EXERCISE YOUR FRUSTRATIONS AWAY

Whether it is jogging, walking, biking, mild aerobics, pushups, or a pickup basketball game, physical exercise is a very effective way to stimulate both your mind and body and to improve your ability to think and concentrate. A surprising number of students get out of the habit of regular exercise, ironically because they're spending so much time prepping for exams. Also, sedentary people—this is a medical fact—get less oxygen to the blood and hence to the head than active people. You can live fine with a little less oxygen; you just can't think as well.

Any big test is a bit like a race. Thinking clearly at the end is just as important as having a quick mind early on. If you can't sustain your energy level in the last sections of the exam, there's too good a chance you could blow it. You need a fit body that can weather the demands any big exam puts on you. Along with a good diet and adequate sleep, exercise is an important part of keeping yourself in fighting shape and thinking clearly for the long haul.

Take a Hike, Pal

When you're in the middle of studying and hit a wall, take a short, brisk walk. Breathe deeply and swing your arms as you walk. Clear your mind. (And, don't forget to look for flowers that grow in the cracks of the sidewalk.)

There's another thing that happens when students don't make exercise an integral part of their test preparation. Like any organism in nature, you operate best if all your "energy systems" are in balance. Studying uses a lot of energy, but it's all mental. When you take a study break, do something active instead of raiding the fridge or vegging out in front of the TV. Take a five- to ten-minute activity break for every 50 or 60 minutes that you study. The physical exertion gets your body into the act, which helps to keep your mind and body in sync. Then, when you finish studying for the night and hit the sack, you won't lie there, tense and unable to sleep because your head is overtired and your body wants to pump iron or run a marathon.

One warning about exercise, however: It's not a good idea to exercise vigorously right before you go to bed. This could easily cause sleep onset problems. For the same reason, it's also not a good idea to study right up to bedtime. Make time for a "buffer period" before you go to bed: For 30 to 60 minutes, just take a hot shower, meditate, simply veg out.

THE DANGERS OF DRUGS

Using drugs (prescription or recreational) specifically to prepare for and take a big test is definitely self-defeating. (And if they're illegal drugs, you may end up with a bigger problem than the SAT on your hands.) Except for the drugs that occur naturally in your brain, every drug has major drawbacks—and a false sense of security is only one of them.

You may have heard that popping uppers helps you study by keeping you alert. If they're illegal, definitely forget about it. They wouldn't really work anyway, since amphetamines make it hard to retain information. Mild stimulants, such as coffee, cola, or over-the-counter caffeine pills can sometimes help as you study, since they keep you alert. On the down side, they can also lead to agitation, restlessness, and insomnia. Some people can drink a pot of high-octane coffee and sleep like a baby. Others have one cup and start to vibrate. It all depends on your tolerance for caffeine. Remember, a little anxiety is a good thing. The adrenaline that gets pumped into your bloodstream helps you stay alert and think more clearly. But, too much anxiety and you can't think straight at all.

Instead, go for endorphins—the "natural morphine." Endorphins have no side effects and they're free—you've already got them in your brain. It just takes some exercise to release them. Running around on the basketball court, bicycling, swimming, aerobics, power walking—these activities cause endorphins to occupy certain spots in your brain's neural synapses. In addition, exercise develops staying power and increases the oxygen transfer to your brain. Go into the test naturally.

Nutrition and Stress: The Dos and Don'ts

Do eat:

- Fruits and vegetables (raw is best, or just lightly steamed or nuked)
- Low-fat protein such as fish, skinless poultry, beans, and legumes
- Whole grains such as brown rice, whole wheat bread, and pastas

Don't eat:

- Refined sugar; sweet, high-fat snacks (simple carbohydrates like sugar make stress worse and fatty foods lower your immunity)
- Salty foods (they deplete potassium, which you need for nerve functions)

TAKE A DEEP BREATH . . .

Here's another natural route to relaxation and invigoration. It's a classic isometric exercise that you can do whenever you get stressed out—just before the test begins, even *during* the test. It's very simple and takes just a few minutes.

Close your eyes. Starting with your eyes and—*without holding your breath*—gradually tighten every muscle in your body (but not to the point of pain) in the following sequence:

1. Close your eyes tightly.
2. Squeeze your nose and mouth together so that your whole face is scrunched up. (If it makes you self-conscious to do this in the test room, skip the face-scrunching part.)
3. Pull your chin into your chest, and pull your shoulders together.
4. Tighten your arms to your body, then clench your hands into tight fists.
5. Pull in your stomach.
6. Squeeze your thighs and buttocks together, and tighten your calves.
7. Stretch your feet, then curl your toes (watch out for cramping in this part).

At this point, every muscle should be tightened. Now, relax your body, one part at a time, in *reverse order*, starting with your toes. Let the tension drop out of each muscle. The entire process might take five minutes from start to finish (maybe a couple of minutes during the test). This clenching and unclenching exercise should help you to feel very relaxed.

The Relaxation Paradox

Forcing relaxation is like asking yourself to flap your arms and fly. You can't do it, and every push and prod only gets you more frustrated. Relaxation is something you don't work at. You simply let it happen. Think about it. When was the last time you tried to force yourself to go to sleep, and it worked?

AND KEEP BREATHING

Conscious attention to breathing is an excellent way of managing test stress (or any stress, for that matter). The majority of people who get into trouble during tests take shallow breaths. They breathe using only their upper chests and shoulder muscles, and may even hold their breath for long periods of time. Conversely, the test taker who by accident or design keeps breathing normally and rhythmically is likely to be more relaxed and in better control during the entire test experience.

So, now is the time to get into the habit of relaxed breathing. Do the next exercise to learn to breathe in a natural, easy rhythm. By the way, this is another technique you can use during the test to collect your thoughts and ward off excess stress. The entire exercise should take no more than three to five minutes.

With your eyes still closed, breathe in slowly and deeply through your nose. Hold the breath for a bit, and then release it through your mouth. The key is to breathe slowly and deeply by using your diaphragm (the big band of muscle that spans your body just above your waist) to draw air in and out naturally and effortlessly. Breathing with your diaphragm encourages relaxation and helps minimize tension. Try it and notice how relaxed and comfortable you feel.

QUICK TIPS FOR THE DAYS JUST BEFORE THE EXAM

- The best test takers do less and less as the test approaches. Taper off your study schedule and take it easy on yourself. You want to be relaxed and ready on the day of the test. Give yourself time off, especially the evening before the exam. By that time, if you've studied well, everything you need to know is firmly stored in your memory banks.
- Positive self-talk can be extremely liberating and invigorating, especially as the test looms closer. Tell yourself things such as, "I choose to take this test" rather than "I have to"; "I will do well" rather than "I hope things go well"; "I can" rather than "I cannot." Be aware of negative, self-defeating thoughts and images and immediately counter any you become aware of. Replace them with affirming statements that encourage your self-esteem and confidence. Create and practice doing visualizations that build on your positive statements.

Q. What sports event was revolutionalized by the "Fosbury Flop"?

- Get your act together sooner rather than later. Have everything (including choice of clothing) laid out days in advance. Most important, know where the test will be held and the easiest, quickest way to get there. You will gain great peace of mind if you know that all the little details—gas in the car, directions, etcetera—are firmly in your control before the day of the test.
- Experience the test site a few days in advance. This is very helpful if you are especially anxious. If at all possible, find out what room your part of the alphabet is assigned to, and try to sit there (by yourself) for a while. Better yet, bring some

practice material and do at least a section or two, if not an entire practice test, in that room. In this case, familiarity doesn't breed contempt, it generates comfort and confidence.

- Forego any practice on the day before the test. It's in your best interest to marshal your physical and psychological resources for 24 hours or so. Even race horses are kept in the paddock and treated like princes the day before a race. Keep the upcoming test out of your consciousness; go to a movie, take a pleasant hike, or just relax. Don't eat junk food or tons of sugar. And—of course—get plenty of rest the night before. Just don't go to bed too early. It's hard to fall asleep earlier than you're used to, and you don't want to lie there thinking about the test.

HANDLING STRESS DURING THE TEST

The biggest stress monster will be the test itself. Fear not; there are methods of quelling your stress during the test.

- Keep moving forward instead of getting bogged down in a difficult question or passage. You don't have to get everything right to achieve a fine score. So, don't linger out of desperation on a question that is going nowhere even after you've spent considerable time on it. The best test takers skip difficult material temporarily in search of the easier stuff. They mark the ones that require extra time and thought. This strategy buys time and builds confidence so you can handle the tough stuff later.
- Don't be thrown if other test takers seem to be working more busily and furiously than you are. Continue to spend your time patiently but doggedly thinking through your answers; it's going to lead to higher-quality test taking and better results. Don't mistake the other people's sheer activity as signs of progress and higher scores.
- *Keep breathing!* Weak test takers tend to share one major trait: They forget to breathe properly as the test proceeds. They start holding their breath without realizing it, or they breathe erratically or arrhythmically. Improper breathing hurts confidence and accuracy. Just as important, it interferes with clear thinking.
- Some quick isometrics during the test—especially if concentration is wandering or energy is waning—can help. Try this: Put your palms together and press intensely for a few seconds. Concentrate on the tension you feel through your palms, wrists, forearms, and up into your biceps and shoulders. Then, quickly release the pressure. Feel the difference as you let go. Focus on the warm relaxation that floods through the muscles. Now you're ready to return to the task.
- Here's another isometric that will relieve tension in both your neck and eye muscles. Slowly rotate your head from side to side, turning your head and eyes to look as far back over each shoulder as you can. Feel the muscles stretch on one side of your neck as they contract on the other. Repeat five times in each direction.

What Are "Signs of a Winner," Alex?

Here's some advice from a Kaplan instructor who won big on *Jeopardy!*™ In the green room before the show, he noticed that the contestants who were quiet and "within themselves" were the ones who did great on the show. The contestants who did not perform as well were the ones who were fact-cramming, talking a lot, and generally being manic before the show. Lesson: Spend the final hours leading up to the test getting sleep, meditating, and generally relaxing.

> Q. What NCAA men's basketball team holds the record for the longest winning streak?

With what you've just learned here, you're armed and ready to do battle with the test. This book and your studies will give you the information you'll need to answer the questions. It's all firmly planted in your mind. You also know how to deal with any excess tension that might come along, both when you're studying for and taking the exam. You've experienced everything you need to tame your test anxiety and stress. You're going to get a great score.

16

Peaking at the Right Time

HIGHLIGHTS

- Find out what to do in the time before, during, and after the test
- Improve your test mentality with confidence and the right attitude

Is it starting to feel like your whole life is a build-up to the SAT? You've known about it for years, worried about it for months, and now spent at least a few hours in solid preparation for it. As the test gets closer, you may find your anxiety is on the rise. You shouldn't worry. After the preparation you've received from this book, you're in good shape for the test.

Two-Minute Drill

Even if you're short on time, read this entire chapter. It tells you how to use your time wisely before, during, and after the test.

GAME PLAN

To calm any pretest jitters you may have, this chapter leads you through a sane game plan for the last week.

The Week Before the Test

Review the Replay lists in the chapters. Are there major holes in your preparation? If there are, choose a few of these areas to work on—but don't overload. You can't cram for the SAT.

Take a full-length SAT. If you haven't done so already, take the practice test in this book. Actual SATs released by ETS are available in libraries and bookstores. You could also pick up Kaplan's *Fast Track SAT*, or get from your guidance counselor a copy of *Taking the SAT I*, a College Board publication with a practice test. All of these are good practice for the real thing.

Things Not to Do the Night Before the Test

- Try to copy the dictionary onto your fingernails.
- Stay up all night watching all the *Friday the 13th* movies.
- Eat a large double anchovy, sausage, and pepper pizza with a case of chocolate soda.
- Send away for brochures from vocational schools.
- Start making flashcards.
- Tattoo yourself.

Two Days Before the Test

Do your last studying—a few more practice problems, a few more vocabulary words, and call it quits.

The Night Before the Test

Don't study. Get together the following items:

- A calculator with fresh batteries
- A watch
- A few No. 2 pencils
- Erasers
- Photo ID card
- Your admission ticket from ETS
- A snack—there are two breaks and you'll probably get hungry

Know exactly where you're going and exactly how you're getting there.

Relax the night before the test. Read a good book, take a bubble bath, watch TV. Get a good night's sleep. Go to bed at a reasonable hour and leave yourself extra time in the morning.

The Morning of the Test

Eat breakfast. Make it something substantial, but not anything too heavy or greasy. Don't drink a lot of coffee if you're not used to it; bathroom breaks cut into your time.

Dress in layers so that you can adjust to the temperature of the test room.

Read something. Warm up your brain with a newspaper or a magazine. You shouldn't let the SAT be the first thing you read that day.

Be sure to get there early.

Q. Who is credited with saying, "It ain't over till it's over"?

During the Test

Don't be shaken. If you find your confidence slipping, remind yourself how well you've prepared. You know the structure of the test; you know the instructions; you've studied for every question type.

Even if something goes really wrong, don't panic. If the test booklet is defective—two pages are stuck together or the ink has run—try to stay calm. Raise your hand, tell the proctor you need a new book. If you accidentally misgrid your answer page or put the answers in the wrong section, again don't panic. Raise your hand, tell the proctor. He or she might be able to arrange for you to regrid your test after it's over, when it won't cost you any time.

Don't think about which section is experimental. Remember, you never know for sure which section won't count. Besides, you can't work on any other section during that section's designated time slot.

Need More Help?

Call 1-800-KAP-TEST if you have any questions about the SAT or want more information about our other books or courses. You can also check out our Website at www.kaptest.com.

After the Test

Once the test is over, put it out of your mind. If you don't plan to take the test again, give this book away and start thinking about more interesting things.

You might walk out of the SAT thinking that you blew it. You probably didn't. You tend to remember the questions that stumped you, not the many that you knew. If you're really concerned, you can call ETS within 24 hours to find out about canceling your score. But there is usually no good reason to do so. Remember, you can retake the test as many times as you want, and most colleges consider only your highest scores.

If you want more help, or just want to know more about the SAT, college admissions, or Kaplan prep courses for the PSAT, SAT, and ACT, give us a call at 1-800-KAP-TEST. We're here to answer your questions and to help you in any way that we can.

Good luck!

ROUND 5

Scrimmage: Practice Test and Explanations

SAT

Practice Test

HOW TO TAKE THIS PRACTICE TEST

Before taking this practice test, find a quiet room where you can work uninterrupted for two and a half hours. Make sure you have a comfortable desk, your calculator, and several No. 2 pencils.

Use the answer sheet provided to record your answers. (You can cut it out or photocopy it.)

Once you start this practice test, don't stop until you've finished. Remember—you can review any questions within a section, but you may not go back or forward a section.

You'll find an answer key, score conversion charts, and explanations following the test.

Good luck.

SAT Practice Test Answer Sheet

Remove (or photocopy) this answer sheet and use it to complete the practice test. (See answer key following the test when finished.)

Start with number 1 for each section. If a section has fewer questions that answer spaces, leave the extra spaces blank.

SECTION 1

1 (A) (B) (C) (D) (E)	11 (A) (B) (C) (D) (E)	21 (A) (B) (C) (D) (E)	31 (A) (B) (C) (D) (E)
2 (A) (B) (C) (D) (E)	12 (A) (B) (C) (D) (E)	22 (A) (B) (C) (D) (E)	32 (A) (B) (C) (D) (E)
3 (A) (B) (C) (D) (E)	13 (A) (B) (C) (D) (E)	23 (A) (B) (C) (D) (E)	33 (A) (B) (C) (D) (E)
4 (A) (B) (C) (D) (E)	14 (A) (B) (C) (D) (E)	24 (A) (B) (C) (D) (E)	34 (A) (B) (C) (D) (E)
5 (A) (B) (C) (D) (E)	15 (A) (B) (C) (D) (E)	25 (A) (B) (C) (D) (E)	35 (A) (B) (C) (D) (E)
6 (A) (B) (C) (D) (E)	16 (A) (B) (C) (D) (E)	26 (A) (B) (C) (D) (E)	36 (A) (B) (C) (D) (E)
7 (A) (B) (C) (D) (E)	17 (A) (B) (C) (D) (E)	27 (A) (B) (C) (D) (E)	37 (A) (B) (C) (D) (E)
8 (A) (B) (C) (D) (E)	18 (A) (B) (C) (D) (E)	28 (A) (B) (C) (D) (E)	38 (A) (B) (C) (D) (E)
9 (A) (B) (C) (D) (E)	19 (A) (B) (C) (D) (E)	29 (A) (B) (C) (D) (E)	39 (A) (B) (C) (D) (E)
10 (A) (B) (C) (D) (E)	20 (A) (B) (C) (D) (E)	30 (A) (B) (C) (D) (E)	40 (A) (B) (C) (D) (E)

right in section 1

wrong in section 1

SECTION 2

1 (A) (B) (C) (D) (E)	11 (A) (B) (C) (D) (E)	21 (A) (B) (C) (D) (E)	31 (A) (B) (C) (D) (E)
2 (A) (B) (C) (D) (E)	12 (A) (B) (C) (D) (E)	22 (A) (B) (C) (D) (E)	32 (A) (B) (C) (D) (E)
3 (A) (B) (C) (D) (E)	13 (A) (B) (C) (D) (E)	23 (A) (B) (C) (D) (E)	33 (A) (B) (C) (D) (E)
4 (A) (B) (C) (D) (E)	14 (A) (B) (C) (D) (E)	24 (A) (B) (C) (D) (E)	34 (A) (B) (C) (D) (E)
5 (A) (B) (C) (D) (E)	15 (A) (B) (C) (D) (E)	25 (A) (B) (C) (D) (E)	35 (A) (B) (C) (D) (E)
6 (A) (B) (C) (D) (E)	16 (A) (B) (C) (D) (E)	26 (A) (B) (C) (D) (E)	36 (A) (B) (C) (D) (E)
7 (A) (B) (C) (D) (E)	17 (A) (B) (C) (D) (E)	27 (A) (B) (C) (D) (E)	37 (A) (B) (C) (D) (E)
8 (A) (B) (C) (D) (E)	18 (A) (B) (C) (D) (E)	28 (A) (B) (C) (D) (E)	38 (A) (B) (C) (D) (E)
9 (A) (B) (C) (D) (E)	19 (A) (B) (C) (D) (E)	29 (A) (B) (C) (D) (E)	39 (A) (B) (C) (D) (E)
10 (A) (B) (C) (D) (E)	20 (A) (B) (C) (D) (E)	30 (A) (B) (C) (D) (E)	40 (A) (B) (C) (D) (E)

right in section 2

wrong in section 2

SECTION 3

1 (A) (B) (C) (D) (E)	11 (A) (B) (C) (D) (E)	21 (A) (B) (C) (D) (E)	31 (A) (B) (C) (D) (E)
2 (A) (B) (C) (D) (E)	12 (A) (B) (C) (D) (E)	22 (A) (B) (C) (D) (E)	32 (A) (B) (C) (D) (E)
3 (A) (B) (C) (D) (E)	13 (A) (B) (C) (D) (E)	23 (A) (B) (C) (D) (E)	33 (A) (B) (C) (D) (E)
4 (A) (B) (C) (D) (E)	14 (A) (B) (C) (D) (E)	24 (A) (B) (C) (D) (E)	34 (A) (B) (C) (D) (E)
5 (A) (B) (C) (D) (E)	15 (A) (B) (C) (D) (E)	25 (A) (B) (C) (D) (E)	35 (A) (B) (C) (D) (E)
6 (A) (B) (C) (D) (E)	16 (A) (B) (C) (D) (E)	26 (A) (B) (C) (D) (E)	36 (A) (B) (C) (D) (E)
7 (A) (B) (C) (D) (E)	17 (A) (B) (C) (D) (E)	27 (A) (B) (C) (D) (E)	37 (A) (B) (C) (D) (E)
8 (A) (B) (C) (D) (E)	18 (A) (B) (C) (D) (E)	28 (A) (B) (C) (D) (E)	38 (A) (B) (C) (D) (E)
9 (A) (B) (C) (D) (E)	19 (A) (B) (C) (D) (E)	29 (A) (B) (C) (D) (E)	39 (A) (B) (C) (D) (E)
10 (A) (B) (C) (D) (E)	20 (A) (B) (C) (D) (E)	30 (A) (B) (C) (D) (E)	40 (A) (B) (C) (D) (E)

right in section 3

wrong in section 3

Remove (or photocopy) this answer sheet and use it to complete the practice test.

Start with number 1 for each section. If a section has fewer questions that answer spaces, leave the extra spaces blank.

SECTION 4

1 A B C D E	11 A B C D E	21 A B C D E	31 A B C D E
2 A B C D E	12 A B C D E	22 A B C D E	32 A B C D E
3 A B C D E	13 A B C D E	23 A B C D E	33 A B C D E
4 A B C D E	14 A B C D E	24 A B C D E	34 A B C D E
5 A B C D E	15 A B C D E	25 A B C D E	35 A B C D E
6 A B C D E	16 A B C D E	26 A B C D E	36 A B C D E
7 A B C D E	17 A B C D E	27 A B C D E	37 A B C D E
8 A B C D E	18 A B C D E	28 A B C D E	38 A B C D E
9 A B C D E	19 A B C D E	29 A B C D E	39 A B C D E
10 A B C D E	20 A B C D E	30 A B C D E	40 A B C D E

\# right in section 4

\# wrong in section 4

If section 4 of your test book contains math questions that are not multiple choice, continue to item 16 below. Otherwise, continue to item 16 above.

16 17 18 19 20 21 22 23 24 25

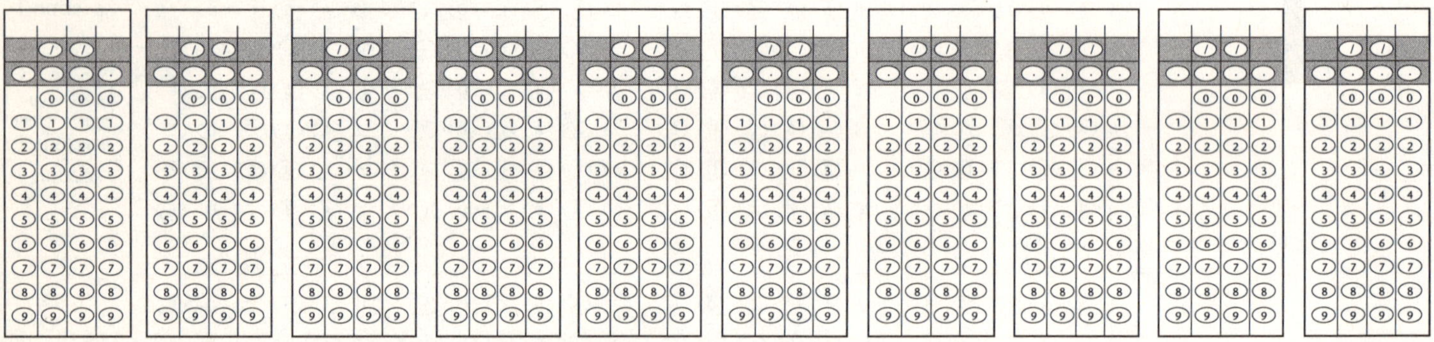

SECTION 5

1 A B C D E	11 A B C D E	21 A B C D E	31 A B C D E
2 A B C D E	12 A B C D E	22 A B C D E	32 A B C D E
3 A B C D E	13 A B C D E	23 A B C D E	33 A B C D E
4 A B C D E	14 A B C D E	24 A B C D E	34 A B C D E
5 A B C D E	15 A B C D E	25 A B C D E	35 A B C D E
6 A B C D E	16 A B C D E	26 A B C D E	36 A B C D E
7 A B C D E	17 A B C D E	27 A B C D E	37 A B C D E
8 A B C D E	18 A B C D E	28 A B C D E	38 A B C D E
9 A B C D E	19 A B C D E	29 A B C D E	39 A B C D E
10 A B C D E	20 A B C D E	30 A B C D E	40 A B C D E

\# right in section 5

\# wrong in section 5

SECTION 6

1 A B C D E	11 A B C D E	21 A B C D E	31 A B C D E
2 A B C D E	12 A B C D E	22 A B C D E	32 A B C D E
3 A B C D E	13 A B C D E	23 A B C D E	33 A B C D E
4 A B C D E	14 A B C D E	24 A B C D E	34 A B C D E
5 A B C D E	15 A B C D E	25 A B C D E	35 A B C D E
6 A B C D E	16 A B C D E	26 A B C D E	36 A B C D E
7 A B C D E	17 A B C D E	27 A B C D E	37 A B C D E
8 A B C D E	18 A B C D E	28 A B C D E	38 A B C D E
9 A B C D E	19 A B C D E	29 A B C D E	39 A B C D E
10 A B C D E	20 A B C D E	30 A B C D E	40 A B C D E

\# right in section 6

\# wrong in section 6

Time—30 Minutes
30 Questions

For each of the following questions, choose the best answer and darken the corresponding oval on the answer sheet.*

Select the lettered word or set of words that best completes the sentence.

Example:

Today's small, portable computers contrast markedly with the earliest electronic computers, which were ----.

(A) effective
(B) invented
(C) useful
(D) destructive
(E) enormous

Ⓐ Ⓑ Ⓒ Ⓓ ●

1 More insurers are limiting the sale of property insurance in coastal areas and other regions ---- natural disasters.

(A) safe from
(B) according to
(C) despite
(D) which include
(E) prone to

2 Roman legions ---- the mountain ---- of Masada for three years before they were able to seize it.

(A) dissembled . . bastion
(B) assailed . . symbol
(C) besieged . . citadel
(D) surmounted . . dwelling
(E) honed . . stronghold

3 Unlike his calmer, more easygoing colleagues, the senator was ----, ready to quarrel at the slightest provocation.

(A) whimsical
(B) irascible
(C) gregarious
(D) ineffectual
(E) benign

4 Although historians have long thought of Genghis Khan as a ---- potentate, new research has shown he was ---- by many of his subjects.

(A) tyrannical . . abhorred
(B) despotic . . revered
(C) redundant . . venerated
(D) jocular . . esteemed
(E) peremptory . . invoked

5 Jill was ---- by her employees because she often ---- them for not working hard enough.

(A) deified . . goaded
(B) loathed . . berated
(C) disregarded . . eulogized
(D) cherished . . derided
(E) execrated . . lauded

6 Reconstructing the skeletons of extinct species like dinosaurs is ---- process that requires much patience and effort by paleontologists.

(A) a nascent
(B) an aberrant
(C) a disheveled
(D) a worthless
(E) an exacting

7 Nearly ---- by disease and the destruction of their habitat, koalas are now found only in isolated parts of eucalyptus forests.

(A) dispersed
(B) compiled
(C) decimated
(D) infuriated
(E) averted

8 Deep ideological ---- and internal power struggles ---- the government.

(A) disputes . . facilitated
(B) similarities . . protracted
(C) distortions . . accelerated
(D) agreements . . stymied
(E) divisions . . paralyzed

9 Medical experts have viewed high doses of vitamins as a popular remedy whose value is, as yet, ----.

(A) medicinal
(B) prescribed
(C) recommended
(D) unproven
(E) beneficial

*The directions on the actual SAT will vary slightly.

GO ON TO THE NEXT PAGE ➡

Choose the lettered pair of words that is related in the same way as the pair in capital letters.

Example:

FLAKE : SNOW ::

(A) storm : hail
(B) drop : rain
(C) field : wheat
(D) stack : hay
(E) cloud : fog

Ⓐ ● Ⓒ Ⓓ Ⓔ

10 TROUT : FISH ::

(A) grain : sand
(B) human : mammal
(C) river : stream
(D) chicken : egg
(E) frog : toad

11 INHALE : LUNGS ::

(A) swallow : stomach
(B) attack : heart
(C) ache : head
(D) pump : blood
(E) travel : foot

12 BRAGGART : BOAST ::

(A) laggard : tarry
(B) hypocrite : speak
(C) extrovert : brood
(D) mendicant : compromise
(E) boor : gratify

13 ALLEVIATE : PAIN ::

(A) soothe : antidote
(B) depreciate : value
(C) contract : job
(D) deviate : standard
(E) officiate : safety

14 INFURIATE : ANNOY ::

(A) admire : respect
(B) indulge : lure
(C) terrify : frighten
(D) satiate : deprive
(E) vex : startle

15 MISERLY : MAGNANIMITY ::

(A) greedy : mirth
(B) transient : stupefaction
(C) admirable : fastidiousness
(D) innocent : culpability
(E) offensive : avarice

GO ON TO THE NEXT PAGE ➡

Answer the questions below based on the information in the accompanying passages.

Questions 16–23 are based on the following passage.

In this excerpt, a Nobel Prize–winning scientist discusses ways of thinking about extremely long periods of time.

There is one fact about the origin of life which is reasonably certain. Whenever and wherever it happened, it started a very long time ago, so long ago that it is extremely difficult to form any realistic idea of such vast stretches of time. The shortness of human life necessarily limits the span of direct personal recollection.

Human culture has given us the illusion that our memories go further back than that. Before writing was invented, the experience of earlier generations, embodied in stories, myths, and moral precepts to guide behavior, was passed down verbally or, to a lesser extent, in pictures, carvings, and statues. Writing has made more precise and more extensive the transmission of such information and, in recent times, photography has sharpened our images of the immediate past. Even so, we have difficulty in contemplating steadily the march of history, from the beginnings of civilization to the present day, in such a way that we can truly experience the slow passage of time. Our minds are not built to deal comfortably with periods as long as hundreds or thousands of years.

Yet when we come to consider the origin of life, the time scales we must deal with make the whole span of human history seem but the blink of an eyelid. There is no simple way to adjust one's thinking to such vast stretches of time. The immensity of time passed is beyond our ready comprehension. One can only construct an impression of it from indirect and incomplete descriptions, just as a blind man laboriously builds up, by touch and sound, a picture of his immediate surroundings.

The customary way to provide a convenient framework for one's thoughts is to compare the age of the universe with the length of a single earthly day. Perhaps a better comparison, along the same lines, would be to equate the age of our earth with a single week. On such a scale the age of the universe, since the Big Bang, would be about two or three weeks. The oldest macroscopic fossils (those from the start of the Cambrian Period*) would have been alive just one day ago. Modern man would have appeared in the last 10 seconds and agriculture in the last one or two. Odysseus** would have lived only half a second before the present time.

Even this comparison hardly makes the longer time scale comprehensible to us. Another alternative is to draw a linear map of time, with the different events marked on it. The problem here is to make the line long enough to show our own experience on a reasonable scale, and yet short enough for convenient reproduction and examination. But perhaps the most vivid method is to compare time to the lines of print themselves. Let us make a 200-page book equal in length to the time from the start of the Cambrian to the present; that is, about 600 million years. Then each full page will represent roughly three million years, each line about ninety thousand years and each letter or small space about fifteen hundred years. The origin of the earth would be about seven books ago and the origin of the universe (which has been dated only approximately) ten or so books before that. Almost the whole of recorded human history would be covered by the last two or three letters of the book.

If you now turn back the pages of the book, slowly reading *one letter at a time*—remember, each letter is fifteen hundred years—then this may convey to you something of the immense stretches of time we shall have to consider. On this scale the span of your own life would be less than the width of a comma.

*Cambrian: the earliest period in the Paleozoic era, beginning about 600 million years ago.

**Odysseus: the most famous Greek hero of antiquity; he is the hero of Homer's *The Odyssey*, which describes the aftermath of the Trojan War (ca. 1200 B.C.).

16 The word *span* in line 6 most nearly means

(A) rate of increase
(B) value
(C) bridge
(D) extent
(E) accuracy

GO ON TO THE NEXT PAGE ➡

17 The phrase *to a lesser extent* in line 13, indicates that, before the invention of writing, the wisdom of earlier generations was

(A) rejected by recent generations when portrayed in pictures, carvings, or statues
(B) passed down orally, or not at all
(C) transmitted more effectively by spoken word than by other means
(D) based on illusory memories that turned fact into fiction
(E) more strongly grounded in science than in the arts

18 The author most likely describes the impact of writing (lines 14–17) in order to

(A) illustrate the limitations of the human memory
(B) provide an example of how cultures transmit information
(C) indicate how primitive preliterate cultures were
(D) refute an opinion about the origin of human civilization
(E) explain the difference between historical facts and myth

19 The word *ready* in line 29 most nearly means

(A) set
(B) agreeable
(C) immediate
(D) apt
(E) willing

20 The analogy of the "blind man" (line 32) is presented primarily to show that

(A) humans are unable to comprehend long periods of time
(B) myths and legends fail to give an accurate picture of the past
(C) human history is only a fraction of the time since life began
(D) humans refuse to learn the lessons of the past
(E) long periods of time can only be understood indirectly

21 In lines 40–44, the author mentions the Big Bang and the Cambrian Period in order to demonstrate which point?

(A) The age of the earth is best understood using the time scale of a week.
(B) Agriculture was a relatively late development in human history.
(C) No fossil record exists before the Cambrian Period.
(D) Convenient time scales do not adequately represent the age of the earth.
(E) The customary framework for thinking about the age of the universe should be discarded permanently.

22 According to lines 52–56, one difficulty of using a linear representation of time is that

(A) linear representations of time do not meet accepted scientific standards of accuracy
(B) prehistoric eras overlap each other, making linear representation deceptive
(C) the more accurate the scale, the more difficult the map is to copy and study
(D) there are too many events to represent on a single line
(E) our knowledge of pre-Cambrian time is insufficient to construct an accurate linear map

23 The author of this passage discusses several kinds of time scales primarily in order to illustrate the

(A) difficulty of assigning precise dates to past events
(B) variety of choices faced by scientists investigating the origin of life
(C) evolution of efforts to comprehend the passage of history
(D) immensity of time since life began on earth
(E) development of the technology of communication

GO ON TO THE NEXT PAGE ➡

Questions 24–30 are based on the following passage.

The following excerpt is from a speech delivered in 1873 by Susan B. Anthony, a leader in the women's rights movement of the 19th century.

Friends and fellow-citizens: I stand before you tonight under indictment for the alleged crime of having voted at the last Presidential election, without having a lawful right to vote. It shall be my work this evening to prove to you that in thus voting, I not only committed no crime, but, instead, simply exercised my citizen's rights, guaranteed to me and all United States citizens by the National Constitution, beyond the power of any State to deny.

The preamble of the Federal Constitution says: "We, the people of the United States, in order to form a more perfect union, establish justice, insure domestic tranquillity, provide for the common defense, promote the general welfare, and secure the blessings of liberty to ourselves and our posterity, do ordain and establish this Constitution for the United States of America."

It was we, the people; not we, the white male citizens; nor yet we, the male citizens; but we, the whole people, who formed the Union. And we formed it, not to give the blessings of liberty, but to secure them; not to the half of ourselves and the half of our posterity, but to the whole people—women as well as men. And it is a downright mockery to talk to women of their enjoyment of the blessings of liberty while they are denied the use of the only means of securing them provided by this democratic-republican government—the ballot.

For any State to make sex a qualification that must ever result in the disfranchisement* of one entire half of the people is a violation of the supreme law of the land. By it the blessings of liberty are forever withheld from women and their female posterity. To them this government had no just powers derived from the consent of the governed. To them this government is not a democracy. It is not a republic. It is an odious aristocracy; a hateful oligarchy of sex; this oligarchy of sex, which makes father, brothers, husband, sons, the oligarchs over the mother and sisters, the wife and daughters of every household—which ordains all men sovereigns, all women subjects, carries dissension, discord and rebellion into every home of the nation.

Webster, Worcester and Bouvier all define a citizen to be a person in the United States, entitled to vote and hold office.

The one question left to be settled now is: Are women persons? And I hardly believe any of our opponents will have the hardihood to say they are not. Being persons, then, women are citizens; and no State has a right to make any law, or to enforce any old law, that shall abridge their privileges or immunities. Hence, every discrimination against women in the constitutions and laws of the several States is today null and void, precisely as is every one against Negroes.

*_disfranchisement_: to deprive of the right to vote.

24 In the first paragraph, Anthony states that her action in voting was

(A) illegal, but morally justified
(B) the result of her keen interest in national politics
(C) legal, if the Constitution is interpreted correctly
(D) an illustration of the need for a women's rights movement
(E) illegal, but worthy of leniency

25 Which best captures the meaning of the word *promote* in line 15?

(A) further
(B) organize
(C) publicize
(D) commend
(E) motivate

26 By saying "we, the people . . . the whole people, who formed the Union" (lines 19–21), Anthony means that

(A) the founders of the nation conspired to deprive women of their rights
(B) some male citizens are still being denied basic rights
(C) the role of women in the founding of the nation is generally ignored
(D) society is endangered when women are deprived of basic rights
(E) all people deserve to enjoy the rights guaranteed by the Constitution

GO ON TO THE NEXT PAGE ➡

27 By "the half of our posterity" (lines 23–24), Anthony means

(A) the political legacy passed down from her era
(B) future generations of male United States citizens
(C) those who wish to enjoy the blessings of liberty
(D) current and future opponents of the women's rights movement
(E) future members of the democratic-republican government

28 In the fifth paragraph, lines 31–46, Anthony's argument rests mainly on the strategy of convincing her audience that

(A) any state which denies women the vote undermines its status as a democracy
(B) women deprived of the vote will eventually raise a rebellion
(C) the nation will remain an aristocracy if the status of women does not change
(D) women's rights issues should be debated in every home
(E) even an aristocracy cannot survive without the consent of the governed

29 The word *hardihood* in line 52 could best be replaced by

(A) endurance
(B) vitality
(C) nerve
(D) opportunity
(E) stupidity

30 When Anthony warns that "no State . . . shall abridge their privileges" (lines 54–55), she means that

(A) women should be allowed to live a life of privilege
(B) women on trial cannot be forced to give up their immunity
(C) every state should repeal its outdated laws
(D) governments may not deprive citizens of their rights
(E) the rights granted to women must be decided by the people, not the state

IF YOU FINISH BEFORE TIME IS CALLED, YOU MAY CHECK YOUR WORK ON THIS SECTION ONLY. DO NOT TURN TO ANY OTHER SECTION IN THE TEST. **STOP**

Time—30 Minutes 25 Questions	Solve each of the following problems, decide which is the best answer choice, and darken the corresponding oval on the answer sheet. Use available space in the test booklet for scratchwork.*

Notes:

(1) Calculator use is permitted.

(2) All numbers used are real numbers.

(3) Figures are provided for some problems. All figures are drawn to scale and lie in a plane UNLESS otherwise indicated.

Reference Information

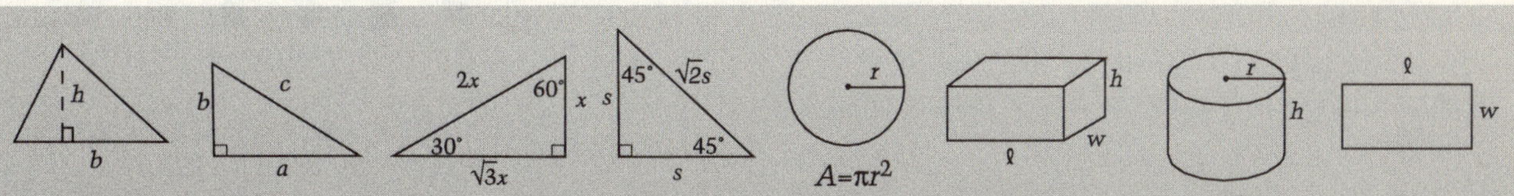

$A=\frac{1}{2}bh$ $c^2 = a^2 + b^2$ Special Right Triangles $A=\pi r^2$ $C=2\pi r$ $V=\ell wh$ $V=\pi r^2 h$ $A=\ell w$

The sum of the degree measures of the angles of a triangle is 180.
The number of degrees of arc in a circle is 360.
A straight angle has a degree measure of 180.

1 Which of the following must be equal to 30 percent of x ?

(A) $30x$

(B) $3x$

(C) $\frac{3x}{10}$

(D) $\frac{3x}{100}$

(E) $\frac{3x}{1000}$

2 $(2 \times 10^4) + (5 \times 10^3) + (6 \times 10^2) + (4 \times 10^1) =$

(A) 2,564
(B) 20,564
(C) 25,064
(D) 25,604
(E) 25,640

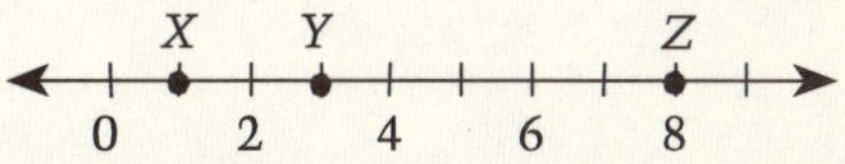

3 On the number line shown above, the length of YZ is how much greater than the length of XY ?

(A) 3
(B) 4
(C) 5
(D) 6
(E) 7

4 If $2^{x+1} = 16$, what is the value of x ?

(A) 2
(B) 3
(C) 4
(D) 5
(E) 6

*The directions on the actual SAT will vary slightly.

GO ON TO THE NEXT PAGE ➡

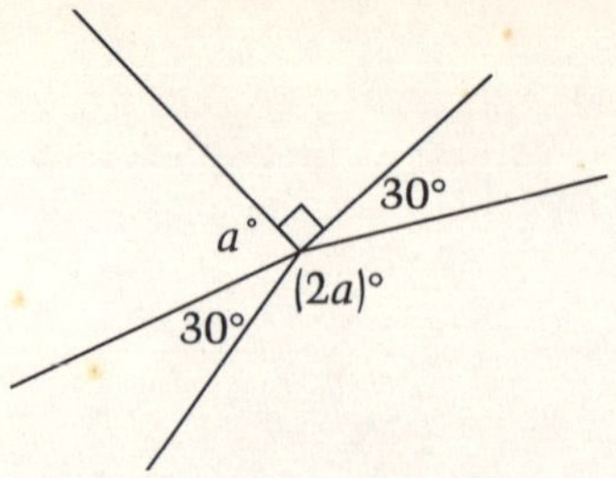

Note: Figure not drawn to scale.

5 In the figure above, what is the value of a ?

(A) 50
(B) 55
(C) 60
(D) 65
(E) 70

6 A machine labels 150 bottles in 20 minutes. At this rate, how many minutes does it take to label 60 bottles?

(A) 2
(B) 4
(C) 6
(D) 8
(E) 10

7 If $x - 1$ is a multiple of 3, which of the following must be the next greater multiple of 3?

(A) x
(B) $x + 2$
(C) $x + 3$
(D) $3x$
(E) $3x - 3$

8 When x is divided by 5, the remainder is 4. When x is divided by 9, the remainder is 0. Which of the following is a possible value for x ?

(A) 24
(B) 45
(C) 59
(D) 109
(E) 144

9 In triangle ABC, $AB = 6$, $BC = 12$, and $AC = x$. Which of the following cannot be a value of x ?

(A) 6
(B) 7
(C) 8
(D) 9
(E) 10

10 The average of 20, 70, and x is 40. If the average of 20, 70, x, and y is 50, then $y =$

(A) 100
(B) 80
(C) 70
(D) 60
(E) 30

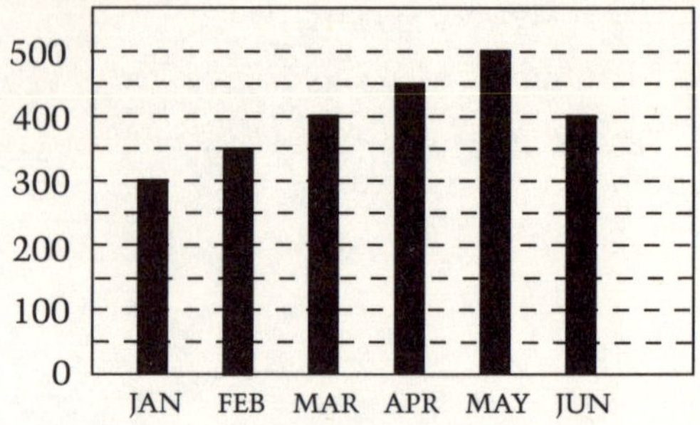

NUMBER OF BOOKS BORROWED
FROM MIDVILLE LIBRARY

11 According to the graph above, the number of books borrowed during the month of January was what fraction of the total number of books borrowed during the first six months of the year?

(A) $\frac{1}{8}$
(B) $\frac{1}{7}$
(C) $\frac{1}{6}$
(D) $\frac{3}{16}$
(E) $\frac{5}{12}$

12 If 40 percent of r is equal to s, then which of the following is equal to 10 percent of r ?

(A) $4s$
(B) $2s$
(C) $\frac{s}{2}$
(D) $\frac{s}{4}$
(E) $\frac{s}{8}$

GO ON TO THE NEXT PAGE ➡

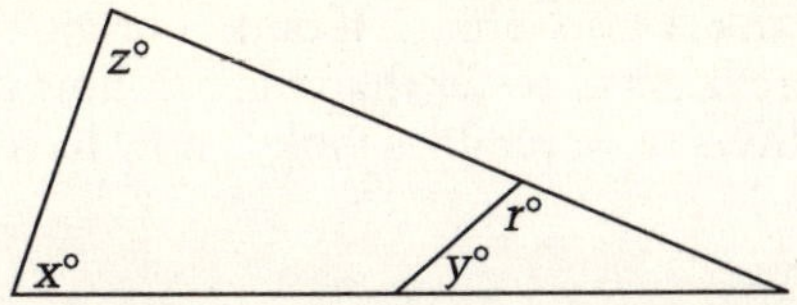

13 In the figure above, which of the following must be true?

(A) $x + r = z + y$
(B) $x + r = z - y$
(C) $x - y = z + r$
(D) $x - r = y - z$
(E) $x + y = z + r$

14 If a *prifact number* is a nonprime integer such that each factor of the integer other than 1 and the integer itself is a prime number, which of the following is a *prifact number*?

(A) 12
(B) 18
(C) 21
(D) 24
(E) 28

15 If $3x + y = 14$, and x and y are positive integers, each of the following could be the value of $x + y$ EXCEPT

(A) 12
(B) 10
(C) 8
(D) 6
(E) 4

16 A certain deck of cards contains r cards. After the cards are distributed evenly among s people, 8 cards are left over. In terms of r and s, how many cards did each person receive?

(A) $\frac{s}{8-r}$

(B) $\frac{r-s}{8}$

(C) $\frac{r-8}{s}$

(D) $s - 8r$

(E) $rs - 8$

17 If d is an integer, which of the following CANNOT be an integer?

(A) $\frac{d}{2}$

(B) $\frac{\sqrt{d}}{2}$

(C) $2d$

(D) $d\sqrt{2}$

(E) $d + 2$

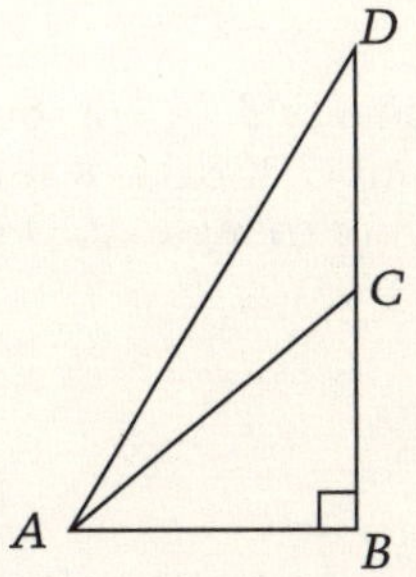

18 In the figure above, the area of triangle ABC is 6. If $BC = CD$, what is the area of triangle ACD?

(A) 6
(B) 8
(C) 9
(D) 10
(E) 12

19 The ratio of x to y to z is 3 to 6 to 8. If $y = 24$, what is the value of $x + z$?

(A) 11
(B) 33
(C) 44
(D) 66
(E) 88

20 What is the minimum number of rectangular tiles, each 12 centimeters by 18 centimeters, needed to completely cover five flat rectangular surfaces, each 60 centimeters by 180 centimeters?

(A) 50
(B) 100
(C) 150
(D) 200
(E) 250

GO ON TO THE NEXT PAGE ➡

21 If $x + y = 11$, $y + z = 14$, and $x + z = 13$, what is the value of $x + y + z$?

(A) 16
(B) 17
(C) 18
(D) 19
(E) 20

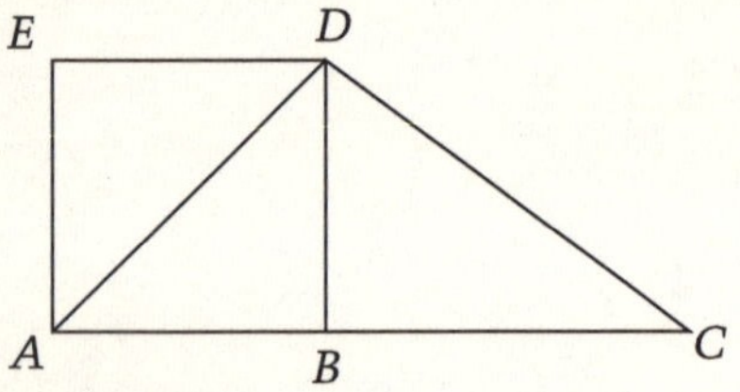

22 In the figure above, side AB of square $ABDE$ is extended to point C. If $BC = 8$ and $CD = 10$, what is the perimeter of triangle ACD ?

(A) $18 + 6\sqrt{2}$
(B) $24 + 6\sqrt{2}$
(C) $26 + 6\sqrt{2}$
(D) 30
(E) 36

23 If $r < 0$ and $(4r - 4)^2 = 36$, what is the value of r ?

(A) -2
(B) -1
(C) $-\frac{1}{2}$
(D) $-\frac{1}{4}$
(E) $-\frac{1}{8}$

24 Five liters of water were poured from tank A into tank B, and 10 liters of water were then poured from tank A into tank C. If tank A originally had 10 more liters of water than tank C, how many more liters of water does tank C now have than tank A ?

(A) 0
(B) 5
(C) 10
(D) 15
(E) 20

25 If a cube has a surface area of $36n^2$ square feet, what is its volume in cubic feet, in terms of n ?

(A) $n^3\sqrt{6}$
(B) $6n^3\sqrt{6}$
(C) $36n^3$
(D) $36n^3\sqrt{6}$
(E) $216n^3$

IF YOU FINISH BEFORE TIME IS CALLED, YOU MAY CHECK YOUR WORK ON THIS SECTION ONLY. DO NOT TURN TO ANY OTHER SECTION IN THE TEST. **STOP**

Time—30 Minutes
35 Questions

For each of the following questions, choose the best answer and darken the corresponding oval on the answer sheet.

Select the lettered word or set of words that best completes the sentence.

Example:

Today's small, portable computers contrast markedly with the earliest electronic computers, which were ----.

(A) effective
(B) invented
(C) useful
(D) destructive
(E) enormous

Ⓐ Ⓑ Ⓒ Ⓓ ●

1 The rain is so rare and the land is so ---- that few of the men who work there see much ---- in farming.

(A) plentiful . . hope
(B) barren . . difficulty
(C) productive . . profit
(D) infertile . . future
(E) dry . . danger

2 The principal declared that the students were not simply ignoring the rules, but openly ---- them.

(A) accepting
(B) redressing
(C) reviewing
(D) flouting
(E) discussing

3 Some critics believe that the ---- of modern art came with dadaism, while others insist that the movement was a ----.

(A) zenith . . sham
(B) pinnacle . . triumph
(C) decline . . disaster
(D) acceptance . . success
(E) originality . . fiasco

4 She would never have believed that her article was so ---- were it not for the ---- of correspondence that followed its publication.

(A) interesting . . dearth
(B) inflammatory . . lack
(C) controversial . . spate
(D) commonplace . . influx
(E) insignificant . . volume

5 The writings of the philosopher Descartes are ----; many readers have difficulty following his complex, intricately woven arguments.

(A) generic
(B) trenchant
(C) reflective
(D) elongated
(E) abstruse

6 The prisoner was ---- even though he presented evidence clearly proving that he was nowhere near the scene of the crime.

(A) abandoned
(B) indicted
(C) exculpated
(D) exhumed
(E) rescinded

7 Many biologists are critical of the film's ---- premise that dinosaurs might one day return.

(A) scientific
(B) tacit
(C) speculative
(D) unwitting
(E) ambiguous

8 Mozart composed music with exceptional ----; he left no rough drafts because he was able to write out his compositions in ---- form.

(A) audacity . . original
(B) facility . . finished
(C) incompetence . . ideal
(D) prestige . . orchestral
(E) independence . . concise

9 Known for their devotion, dogs were often used as symbols of ---- in Medieval and Renaissance art.

(A) resistance
(B) benevolence
(C) generosity
(D) fidelity
(E) antagonism

10 It is ---- that a people so capable of treachery and brutality should also exhibit such a tremendous capacity for heroism.

(A) unfortunate
(B) explicable
(C) paradoxical
(D) distressing
(E) appalling

GO ON TO THE NEXT PAGE ➡

Choose the lettered pair of words that is related in the same way as the pair in capital letters.

Example:

FLAKE : SNOW ::

(A) storm : hail
(B) drop : rain
(C) field : wheat
(D) stack : hay
(E) cloud : fog

Ⓐ ● Ⓒ Ⓓ Ⓔ

11 CHARLATAN : SCRUPULOUS ::

(A) confidant : virtuous
(B) laborer : stalwart
(C) officer : mutinous
(D) dullard : irritable
(E) tyrant : just

12 GREED : ACQUIRE ::

(A) fear : disguise
(B) inertia : persuade
(C) gluttony : eat
(D) conformity : agree
(E) ignorance : speak

13 PARRY : BLOW ::

(A) counter : argument
(B) sidestep : offense
(C) defer : ruling
(D) stumble : pitfall
(E) shine : light

14 MALIGN : SLURS ::

(A) satisfy : treaties
(B) persecute : complaints
(C) torment : whispers
(D) court : debates
(E) flatter : compliments

15 LENTIL : LEGUME ::

(A) rice : cereal
(B) nutrition : food
(C) horseshoe : pony
(D) husk : corn
(E) baker : cake

16 INDULGE : APPETITE ::

(A) filter : impurity
(B) infuriate : anger
(C) coddle : emotion
(D) humor : whim
(E) liberate : freedom

17 MELLIFLUOUS : SOUND ::

(A) musical : entertainment
(B) fragrant : smell
(C) pale : color
(D) raucous : discussion
(E) auspicious : occasion

18 GUFFAW : LAUGH ::

(A) sniffle : sneeze
(B) whoop : cough
(C) yell : talk
(D) snore : sleep
(E) chuckle : sigh

19 CELESTIAL : HEAVENS ::

(A) planetary : orbit
(B) scientific : experiment
(C) nautical : ships
(D) solar : heat
(E) viscous : matter

20 ENERVATE : VITALITY ::

(A) consolidate : power
(B) energize : action
(C) daunt : courage
(D) estimate : worth
(E) admit : guilt

21 OLIGARCHY : FEW ::

(A) government : majority
(B) authority : consent
(C) constitution : country
(D) monarchy : one
(E) discrimination : minority

22 UNTRUTHFUL : MENDACIOUSNESS ::

(A) circumspect : caution
(B) timid : behavior
(C) agile : physique
(D) sensitive : patient
(E) trusting : honesty

23 INEXCUSABLE : JUSTIFY ::

(A) isolated : abandon
(B) unassailable : attack
(C) affable : like
(D) famous : admire
(E) splendid : revere

GO ON TO THE NEXT PAGE ➡

Answer the questions below based on the information in the accompanying passages.

Questions 24–35 are based on the following passage.

In the following passage, a 19th-century American writer recalls his boyhood in a small town along the Mississippi River.

My father was a justice of the peace, and I supposed he possessed the power of life and death over all men and could hang anybody that offended him. This was distinction enough for me as a general thing; but the desire to be a steamboatman kept intruding, nevertheless. I first wanted to be a cabin boy, so that I could come out with a white apron on and shake a tablecloth over the side, where all my old comrades could see me. Later I thought I would rather be the deck hand who stood on the end of the stage plank with a coil of rope in his hand, because he was particularly conspicuous.

But these were only daydreams—too heavenly to be contemplated as real possibilities. By and by one of the boys went away. He was not heard of for a long time. At last he turned up as an apprentice engineer or "striker" on a steamboat. This thing shook the bottom out of all my Sunday-school teachings. That boy had been notoriously worldly and I had been just the reverse—yet he was exalted to this eminence, and I was left in obscurity and misery. There was nothing generous about this fellow in his greatness. He would always manage to have a rusty bolt to scrub while his boat was docked at our town, and he would sit on the inside guard and scrub it, where we could all see him and envy him and loathe him.

He used all sorts of steamboat technicalities in his talk, as if he were so used to them that he forgot common people could not understand them. He would speak of the "labboard" side of a horse in an easy, natural way that would make you wish he was dead. And he was always talking about "St. Looy" like an old citizen. Two or three of the boys had long been persons of consideration among us because they had been to St. Louis once and had a vague general knowledge of its wonders, but the day of their glory was over now. They lapsed into a humble silence, and learned to disappear when the ruthless "cub" engineer approached. This fellow had money, too, and hair oil, and he wore a showy brass watch chain, a leather belt, and used no suspenders. No girl could withstand his charms. He "cut out" every boy in the village. When his boat blew up at last, it diffused a tranquil contentment among us such as we had not known for months. But when he came home the next week, alive, renowned, and appeared in church all battered up and bandaged, a shining hero, stared at and wondered over by everybody, it seemed to us that the partiality of Providence for an undeserving reptile had reached a point where it was open to criticism.

This creature's career could produce but one result, and it speedily followed. Boy after boy managed to get on the river. Four sons of the chief merchant, and two sons of the county judge became pilots, the grandest position of all. But some of us could not get on the river—at least our parents would not let us.

So by and by I ran away. I said I would never come home again till I was a pilot and could return in glory. But somehow I could not manage it. I went meekly aboard a few of the boats that lay packed together like sardines at the long St. Louis wharf, and very humbly inquired for the pilots, but got only a cold shoulder and short words from mates and clerks. I had to make the best of this sort of treatment for the time being, but I had comforting daydreams of a future when I should be a great and honored pilot, with plenty of money, and could kill some of these mates and clerks and pay for them.

24 The author makes the statement that "I supposed he . . . offended him" (lines 1–4) primarily to suggest the

(A) power held by a justice of the peace in a frontier town
(B) naive view that he held of his father's importance
(C) respect in which the townspeople held his father
(D) possibility of miscarriages of justice on the American frontier
(E) harsh environment in which he was brought up

25 As used in line 4, the word *distinction* most nearly means

(A) difference
(B) variation
(C) prestige
(D) desperation
(E) clarity

26 The author decides that he would rather become a deck hand than a cabin boy (lines 6–12) because

(A) the job offers higher wages
(B) he believes that the work is easier
(C) he wants to avoid seeing his older friends
(D) deck hands often go on to become pilots
(E) the job is more visible to passersby

GO ON TO THE NEXT PAGE ➡

27 The author most likely mentions his "Sunday-school teachings" in lines 18–19 in order to emphasize

(A) the influence of his early education in later life
(B) his sense of injustice at the engineer's success
(C) his disillusionment with longstanding religious beliefs
(D) his determination to become an engineer at all costs
(E) the unscrupulous nature of the engineer's character

28 The author most likely concludes that the engineer is not "generous" (line 22) because he

(A) has no respect for religious beliefs
(B) refuses to share his wages with friends
(C) flaunts his new position in public
(D) takes a pride in material possessions
(E) ignores the disappointment of other people's ambitions

29 The author most probably mentions the use of "steamboat technicalities" (lines 28–30) in order to emphasize the engineer's

(A) expertise after a few months on the job
(B) fascination for trivial information
(C) ignorance on most other subjects
(D) desire to appear sophisticated
(E) inability to communicate effectively

30 The word *consideration* in line 35 most nearly means

(A) generosity
(B) deliberation
(C) contemplation
(D) unselfishness
(E) reputation

31 According to the passage, the "glory" of having visited St. Louis (lines 36–38) was over because

(A) the boys' knowledge of St. Louis was much less detailed than the engineer's
(B) St. Louis had changed so much that the boys' stories were no longer accurate
(C) the boys realized that traveling to St. Louis was not a mark of sophistication
(D) the engineer's account revealed that the boys' stories were lies
(E) travel to St. Louis had become too commonplace to be envied

32 The author describes the engineer's appearance (lines 41–42) primarily in order to

(A) suggest one reason why many people found the engineer impressive
(B) convey the way steamboatmen typically dressed
(C) emphasize the inadequacy of his own wardrobe
(D) contrast the engineer's behavior with his appearance
(E) indicate his admiration for fashionable clothes

33 In lines 50–52, the author's response to the engineer's survival is one of

(A) thankfulness for what he believes is God's providence
(B) astonishment at the engineer's miraculous escape
(C) reflection on the occupational hazards of a steamboating career
(D) outrage at his rival's undeserved good fortune
(E) sympathy for the extent of the engineer's wounds

34 The major purpose of the passage is to

(A) sketch the peaceful life of a frontier town
(B) relate the events that led to a boy's first success in life
(C) portray the unsophisticated ambitions of a boy
(D) describe the characteristics of a small-town boaster
(E) give a humorous portrayal of a boy's conflicts with his parents

35 At the end of the passage, the author reflects on

(A) his new ambition to become either a mate or a clerk
(B) the wisdom of seeking a job in which advancement is easier
(C) the prospect of abandoning a hopeless search for fame
(D) the impossibility of returning home and asking his parents' pardon
(E) his determination to keep striving for success in a glorious career

IF YOU FINISH BEFORE TIME IS CALLED, YOU MAY CHECK YOUR WORK ON THIS SECTION ONLY. DO NOT TURN TO ANY OTHER SECTION IN THE TEST. **STOP**

Time—30 Minutes
25 Questions

Solve each of the following problems, decide which is the best answer choice, and darken the corresponding oval on the answer sheet. Use available space in the test booklet for scratchwork.*

Notes:

(1) Calculator use is permitted.

(2) All numbers used are real numbers.

(3) Figures are provided for some problems. All figures are drawn to scale and lie in a plane UNLESS otherwise indicated.

Reference Information

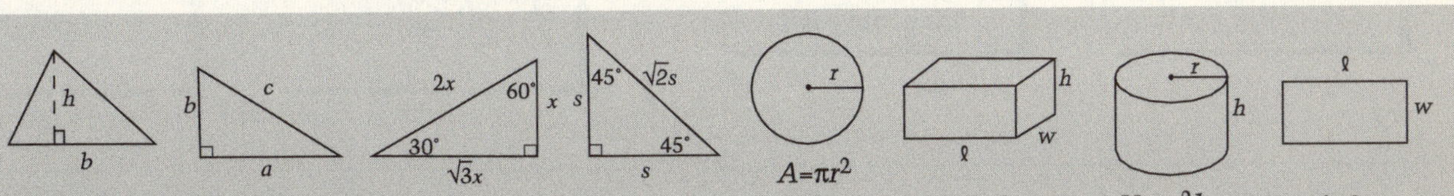

$A=\frac{1}{2}bh$ $c^2 = a^2 + b^2$ Special Right Triangles $A=\pi r^2$ $C=2\pi r$ $V=\ell wh$ $V=\pi r^2 h$ $A=\ell w$

The sum of the degree measures of the angles of a triangle is 180.
The number of degrees of arc in a circle is 360.
A straight angle has a degree measure of 180.

DIRECTIONS FOR QUANTITATIVE COMPARISON QUESTIONS

Compare the boxed quantity in Column A with the boxed quantity in Column B. Select answer choice

A if Column A is greater;
B if Column B is greater;
C if the columns are equal; or
D if more information is needed to determine the relationship.

An E response will be treated as an omission.

Notes:

1. Some questions include information about one or both quantities. That information is centered and unboxed.
2. A symbol that appears in both Column A and Column B stands for the same thing in both columns.
3. All numbers used are real numbers.

EXAMPLES

	Column A	Column B	Answers
E1	3×4	$3 + 4$	● Ⓑ Ⓒ Ⓓ Ⓔ
	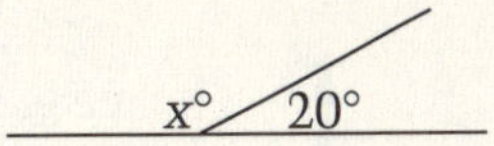		
E2	x	160	Ⓐ Ⓑ ● Ⓓ Ⓔ
	x and y are positive		
E3	$x + 1$	$y - 1$	Ⓐ Ⓑ Ⓒ ● Ⓔ

GO ON TO THE NEXT PAGE ➡

*The directions on the actual SAT will vary slightly.

	Column A	Column B
1	$\frac{3}{8} + \frac{2}{5}$	1
2	The cost of six pens at two for 22 cents	The cost of five pens at 22 cents each

$$2a + b = 17$$
$$b - 3 = 2$$

	Column A	Column B
3	a	b
4	$x - 2(y + z)$	$x - 2y - 2z$

a, b, and c are positive integers such that $a + b + c = 150$.

	Column A	Column B
5	The mean of a, b, and c	The median of a, b, and c

For all numbers x and y, let $x \circledast y = (x + y)^3$.

	Column A	Column B
6	$4 \circledast 5$	$0 \circledast 9$

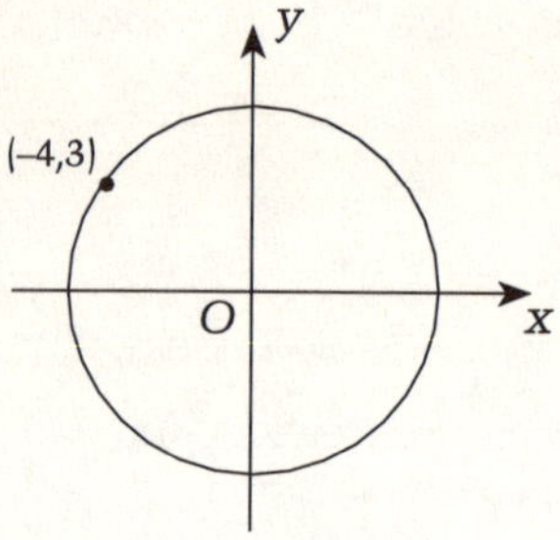

	Column A	Column B
7	The circumference of circle O	30

Jimmy owns a plant he waters every other day.

	Column A	Column B
8	The number of times Jimmy waters the plant during a certain week	The number of times Jimmy waters the plant during the following week

A certain line in the rectangular coordinate plane contains the points $(1, 1)$, $(3, r)$, $(s, 9)$, and $(6, 11)$.

	Column A	Column B
9	r	s

$$r^2 + 4 = 21$$

	Column A	Column B
10	r	4

GO ON TO THE NEXT PAGE ➡

Column A	Column B

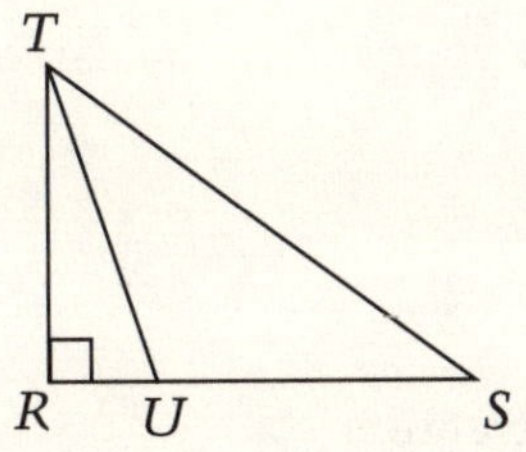

In right triangle RST, $RT = US = 6$ and $RU < 2$.

	Column A	Column B
11	The perimeter of RST	24

At a science fair, five students are semifinalists for first- and second-place prizes.

	Column A	Column B
12	The total number of ways to select the two science fair prize winners	10

$x > 0$
$0 < x^2 < 1$

	Column A	Column B
13	$1 - x^2$	$1 - x$

Column A	Column B

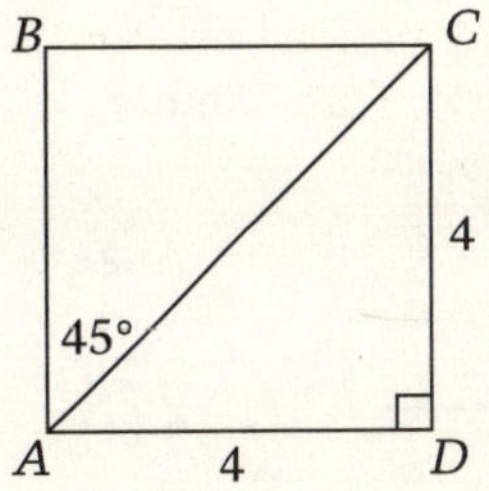

Note: Figure not drawn to scale.

	Column A	Column B
14	The length of AB	4

t is a positive integer.

	Column A	Column B
15	The number of distinct prime factors of $2t$	The number of distinct prime factors of $8t$

GO ON TO THE NEXT PAGE ➡

DIRECTIONS FOR STUDENT-PRODUCED RESPONSE QUESTIONS

For each of the questions below (16–25), solve the problem and indicate your answer by darkening the ovals in the special grid. For example:

Answer: 1.25 or $\frac{5}{4}$ or 5/4

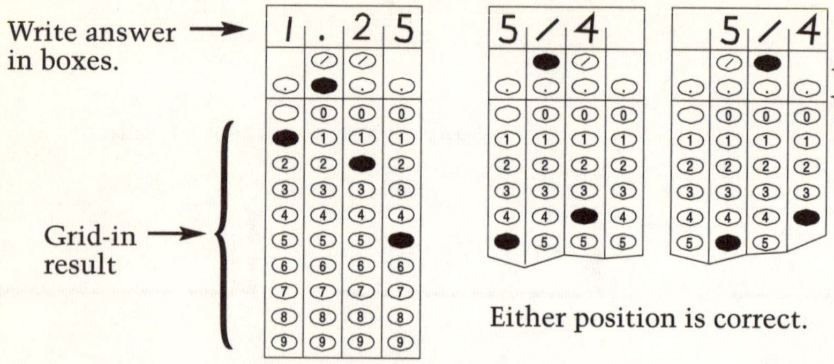

Fraction line

Decimal point

You may start your answers in any column, space permitting. Columns not needed should be left blank.

Either position is correct.

- It is recommended, though not required, that you write your answer in the boxes at the top of the columns. However, you will receive credit only for darkening the ovals correctly.
- Grid only one answer to a question, even though some problems have more than one correct answer.
- Darken no more than one oval in a column.
- No answers are negative.
- Mixed numbers cannot be gridded. For example: the number $1\frac{1}{4}$ must be gridded as 1.25 or 5/4.

(If 1 1 / 4 is gridded, it will be interpreted as $\frac{11}{4}$, not $1\frac{1}{4}$.)

- Decimal Accuracy: Decimal answers must be entered as accurately as possible. For example, if you obtain an answer such as 0.1666..., you should record the result as .166 or .167. **Less accurate values such as .16 or .17 are not acceptable.**

Acceptable ways to grid $\frac{1}{6}$ = .1666. . .

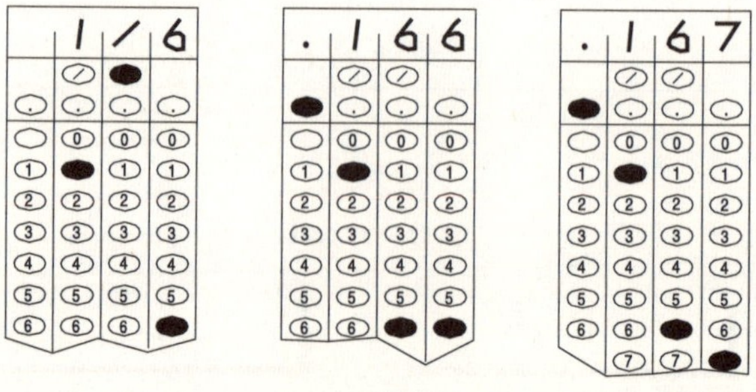

16 If $A = 2.54$ and $20B = A$, what is the value of B ?

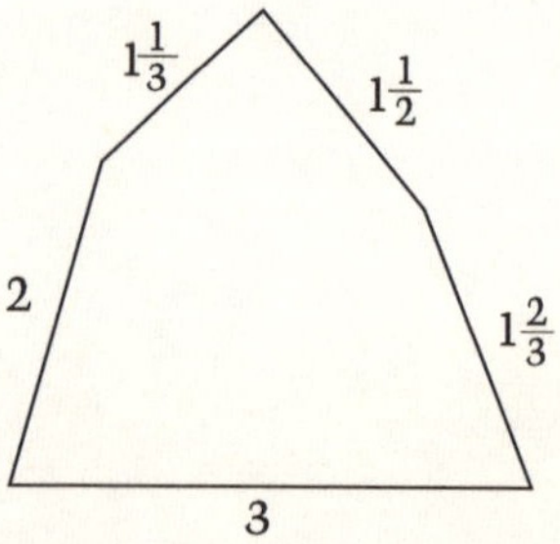

17 What is the perimeter of the figure shown above?

GO ON TO THE NEXT PAGE ➡

18 If $\frac{h}{3}$ and $\frac{h}{4}$ are integers, and if $75 < h < 100$, what is one possible value of h ?

19 A retailer buys 16 shirts at $4.50 each, and she sells all 16 shirts for $6.75 each. If the retailer purchases more of these shirts at $4.50 each, what is the greatest number of these shirts that she can buy with the profit she made on the 16 shirts?

20 Lines ℓ and m intersect at a point to form four angles. If one of the angles formed is 15 times as large as an adjacent angle, what is the measure, in degrees, of the smaller angle?

21 If $x = -4$ when $x^2 + 2xr + r^2 = 0$, what is the value of r ?

22 Let $n* = n^2 - n$ for all positive numbers n.

What is the value of $\frac{1}{4}* - \frac{1}{2}*$?

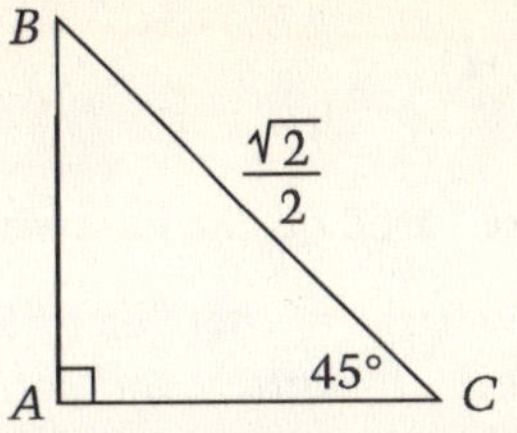

23 What is the area of ΔABC shown above?

24 If x is a factor of 8,100 and if x is an odd integer, what is the greatest possible value of x ?

25 In a certain class, $\frac{1}{2}$ of the male students and $\frac{2}{3}$ of the female students speak French. If there are $\frac{3}{4}$ as many girls as boys in the class, what fraction of the entire class speaks French?

IF YOU FINISH BEFORE TIME IS CALLED, YOU MAY CHECK YOUR WORK ON THIS SECTION ONLY. DO NOT TURN TO ANY OTHER SECTION IN THE TEST.

STOP

Time—15 Minutes
13 Questions

Answer the questions below based on the information in the accompanying passages.

Questions 1–13 are based on the following passages.

The controversy over the authorship of Shakespeare's plays began in the 18th century and continues to this day. Here, the author of Passage 1 embraces the proposal that Francis Bacon actually wrote the plays, while the author of Passage 2 defends the traditional attribution to Shakespeare himself.

Passage 1

Anyone with more than a superficial knowledge of Shakespeare's plays must necessarily entertain some doubt concerning their true authorship. Can scholars honestly accept the idea that such masterworks were written by a shadowy actor with limited formal education and a social position that can most charitably be called "humble"? Obviously, the author of the plays must have traveled widely, yet there is no record that Shakespeare ever left his native England. Even more obviously, the real author had to have intimate knowledge of life within royal courts and palaces, yet Shakespeare was a commoner, with little firsthand experience of the aristocracy. No, common sense tells us that the plays must have been written by someone with substantial expertise in the law, the sciences, classics, foreign languages, and the fine arts—someone, in other words, like Shakespeare's eminent contemporary, Sir Francis Bacon.

The first person to suggest that Bacon was the actual author of the plays was Reverend James Wilmot. Writing in 1785, Wilmot argued that someone of Shakespeare's educational background could hardly have produced works of such erudition and insight. But a figure like Bacon, a scientist and polymath* of legendary stature, would certainly have known about, for instance, the circulation of the blood as alluded to in *Coriolanus.* And as an aristocrat, Bacon would have possessed the familiarity with court life required to produce a *Love's Labour's Lost*.

Delia Bacon (no relation to Sir Francis) was next to make the case for Francis Bacon's authorship. In 1856, in collaboration with Nathaniel Hawthorne, she insisted that it was ridiculous to look for the creator of Hamlet among "that dirty, doggish group of players, who come into the scene [of the play Hamlet] summoned like a pack of hounds to his service." Ultimately, she concluded that the plays were actually composed by a committee consisting of Bacon, Edmund Spenser, Walter Raleigh, and several others.

Still, some might wonder why Bacon, if indeed the plays were wholly or partly his work, would not put his own name on them. But consider the political climate of England in Elizabethan times. Given that it would have been politically and personally damaging for a man of Bacon's position to associate himself with such controversial plays, it is quite understandable that Bacon would hire a lowly actor to take the credit—and the consequences.

But perhaps the most convincing evidence of all comes from the postscript of a 1624 letter sent to Bacon by Sir Tobie Matthew. "The most prodigious wit that I ever knew . . . is your lordship's name," Matthew wrote, "though he be known by another." That name, of course, was William Shakespeare.

**polymath*—a person of wide and varied learning

Passage 2

Over the years, there have been an astonishing number of persons put forth as the "true author" of Shakespeare's plays. Some critics have even gone so far as to claim that only a "committee" could have possessed the abundance of talent and energy necessary to produce Shakespeare's thirty-seven plays. Among the individual figures most seriously promoted as "the real Shakespeare" is Sir Francis Bacon. Apparently, the fact that Bacon wrote most of his own work in academic Latin does nothing to deter those who would crown him the premier stylist in the English language.

Although the entire controversy reeks of scholarly gamesplaying, the issue underlying it is worth considering: how could an uneducated actor create such exquisite works? But the answer to that is easy. Shakespeare's dramatic gifts had little to do with encyclopedic knowledge, complex ideas, or a fluency with great systems of thought. Rather, Shakespeare's genius was one of common sense and perceptive intuition—a genius that grows not out of book-learning, but out of a deep understanding of human nature and a keen grasp of basic emotions, passions, and jealousies.

One of the most common arguments advanced by skeptics is that the degree of familiarity with the law exhibited in a *Hamlet* or a *Merchant of Venice* can only have been achieved by a lawyer or other man of affairs. The grasp of law evidenced in these plays, however, is not a detailed knowledge of formal law, but a more general understanding of so-called "country law." Shakespeare was a landowner —an extraordinary achievement in itself for an ill-paid Elizabethan actor—and so would have been

GO ON TO THE NEXT PAGE ➡

knowledgeable about legal matters related to the buying, selling, and renting of real estate. Evidence of such a common understanding of land regulations can be found, for instance, in the gravedigging scene of *Hamlet.*

So no elaborate theories of intrigue and secret identity are necessary to explain the accomplishment of William Shakespeare. Scholars who have made a career of ferreting out "alternative bards" may be reluctant to admit it, but literary genius can flower in any socioeconomic bracket. Shakespeare, in short, was Shakespeare—an observation that one would have thought was obvious to everyone.

1 In line 2, *entertain* most nearly means

(A) amuse
(B) harbor
(C) occupy
(D) cherish
(E) engage

2 In Passage 1, the author draws attention to Shakespeare's social standing as a "commoner" (line 13) in order to cast doubt on the Elizabethan actor's

(A) aptitude for writing poetically
(B) knowledge of foreign places and habits
(C) ability to support himself by playwriting
(D) familiarity with life among persons of high rank
(E) understanding of the problems of government

3 *Coriolanus* and *Love's Labour's Lost* are mentioned in lines 28–31 as examples of works that

(A) only Francis Bacon could have written
(B) exhibit a deep understanding of human nature
(C) resemble works written by Francis Bacon under his own name
(D) portray a broad spectrum of Elizabethan society
(E) reveal expertise more likely held by Bacon than Shakespeare

4 In Passage 1, the quotation from Delia Bacon (lines 36–39) conveys a sense of

(A) disdain for the disreputable vulgarity of Elizabethan actors
(B) resentment at the way Shakespeare's characters were portrayed
(C) regret that conditions for Elizabethan actors were not better
(D) doubt that Shakespeare could actually have created such unsavory characters
(E) disappointment at the incompetence of Elizabethan actors

5 The author of Passage 1 maintains that Bacon did not put his own name on the plays attributed to Shakespeare because he

(A) regarded writing as an unsuitable occupation for an aristocrat
(B) wished to protect himself from the effects of controversy
(C) preferred being known as a scientist and politician rather than as a writer
(D) did not want to associate himself with lowly actors
(E) sought to avoid the attention that fame brings

6 In the first paragraph of Passage 2, the author calls into question Bacon's likely ability to

(A) write in a language with which he was unfamiliar
(B) make the transition between scientific writing and playwriting
(C) produce the poetic language evident in the plays
(D) cooperate with other members of a committee
(E) single-handedly create thirty-seven plays

7 The word *premier* in line 69 most nearly means

(A) earliest
(B) influential
(C) inaugural
(D) greatest
(E) original

GO ON TO THE NEXT PAGE ➡

8 In line 76, the word *encyclopedic* most nearly means

(A) technical
(B) comprehensive
(C) abridged
(D) disciplined
(E) specialized

9 The author of Passage 2 cites Shakespeare's status as a landowner in order to

(A) prove that Shakespeare was a success as a playwright
(B) refute the claim that Shakespeare had little knowledge of aristocratic life
(C) prove that Shakespeare didn't depend solely on acting for his living
(D) dispute the notion that Shakespeare was a commoner
(E) account for Shakespeare's apparent knowledge of the law

10 In lines 100–103, the author maintains that literary genius

(A) is not dependent on a writer's external circumstances
(B) must be based on an inborn comprehension of human nature
(C) is enhanced by the suffering that poverty brings
(D) frequently goes unrecognized among those of modest means and position
(E) can be stifled by too much book-learning and academic training

11 The author of Passage 2 would probably respond to the speculation in the fourth paragraph of Passage 1 by pointing out that

(A) Shakespeare's plays would not have seemed particularly controversial to Elizabethan audiences
(B) The extent and range of Bacon's learning has been generally exaggerated
(C) such scenarios are farfetched and unnecessary if one correctly understands Shakespeare's genius
(D) Bacon would not have had the knowledge of the lower classes required to produce the plays
(E) the claim implies that Shakespeare was disreputable when in fact he was a respectable landowner

12 The author of Passage 1 would probably respond to the skepticism expressed in lines 67–70 by making which of the following statements?

(A) The similarities between English and Latin make it plausible that one person could write well in both languages.
(B) Plays written in Latin would not have been likely to attract a wide audience in Elizabethan England.
(C) The premier stylist in the English language is more likely to have been an eminent scholar than an uneducated actor.
(D) Writing the plays in Latin would have shielded Bacon from much of the political damage he wanted to avoid.
(E) The style of the plays is notable mostly for the clarity of thought behind the lines rather than their musicality or beauty.

13 In line 105, "observation" most nearly means

(A) inspection
(B) measurement
(C) research
(D) comment
(E) memorandum

IF YOU FINISH BEFORE TIME IS CALLED, YOU MAY CHECK YOUR WORK ON THIS SECTION ONLY. DO NOT TURN TO ANY OTHER SECTION IN THE TEST.

STOP

Time—15 Minutes
10 Questions

Solve each of the following problems, decide which is the best answer choice, and darken the corresponding oval on the answer sheet. Use available space in the test booklet for scratchwork.

Notes:

(1) Calculator use is permitted.

(2) All numbers used are real numbers.

(3) Figures are provided for some problems. All figures are drawn to scale and lie in a plane UNLESS otherwise indicated.

Reference Information

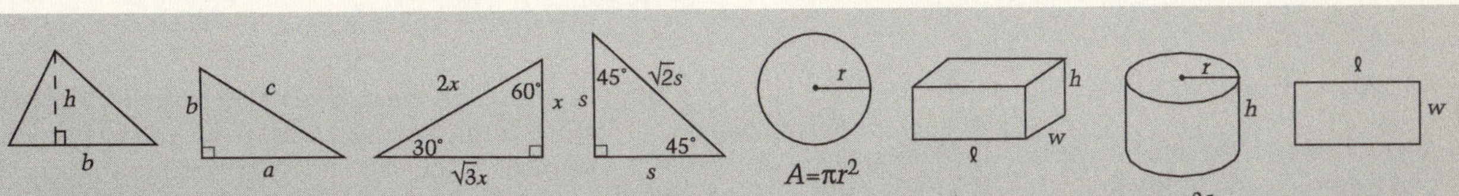

$A=\frac{1}{2}bh$ $c^2=a^2+b^2$ Special Right Triangles $A=\pi r^2$ $C=2\pi r$ $V=\ell wh$ $V=\pi r^2h$ $A=\ell w$

The sum of the degree measures of the angles of a triangle is 180.
The number of degrees of arc in a circle is 360.
A straight angle has a degree measure of 180.

1 If $p=-2$ and $q=3$, then $p^3q^2+p^2q=$

(A) −84
(B) −60
(C) 36
(D) 60
(E) 84

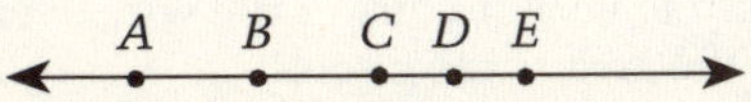

Note: Figure not drawn to scale.

2 In the figure above, B is the midpoint of AC and D is the midpoint of CE. If $AB=5$ and $BD=8$, what is the length of DE ?

(A) 8
(B) 6
(C) 5
(D) 4
(E) 3

N	P
2	7
4	13
6	19
8	25

3 Which of the following equations describes the relationship of each pair of numbers (N, P) in the table above?

(A) $P=N+5$
(B) $P=2N+3$
(C) $P=2N+5$
(D) $P=3N+1$
(E) $P=3N-1$

GO ON TO THE NEXT PAGE ➡

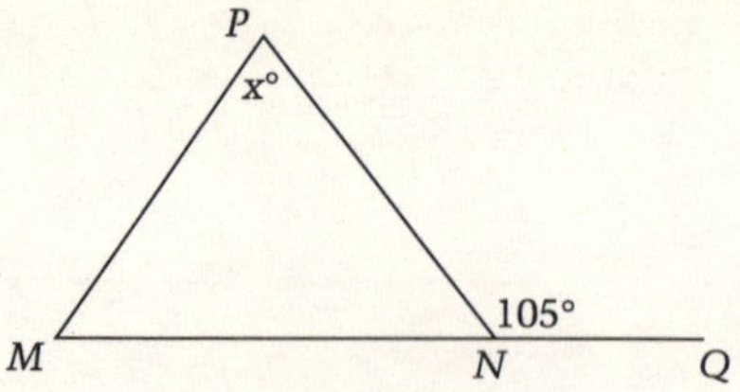

Note: Figure not drawn to scale.

4 In the figure above, MQ is a straight line. If $PM = PN$, what is the value of x ?

(A) 30
(B) 45
(C) 60
(D) 75
(E) 90

5 Marty has exactly five blue pens, six black pens, and four red pens in his knapsack. If he pulls out one pen at random from his knapsack, what is the probability that the pen is either red or black?

(A) $\frac{11}{15}$
(B) $\frac{2}{3}$
(C) $\frac{1}{2}$
(D) $\frac{1}{3}$
(E) $\frac{1}{5}$

6 Two hot dogs and a soda cost \$3.25. If three hot dogs and a soda cost \$4.50, what is the cost of two sodas?

(A) \$0.75
(B) \$1.25
(C) \$1.50
(D) \$2.50
(E) \$3.00

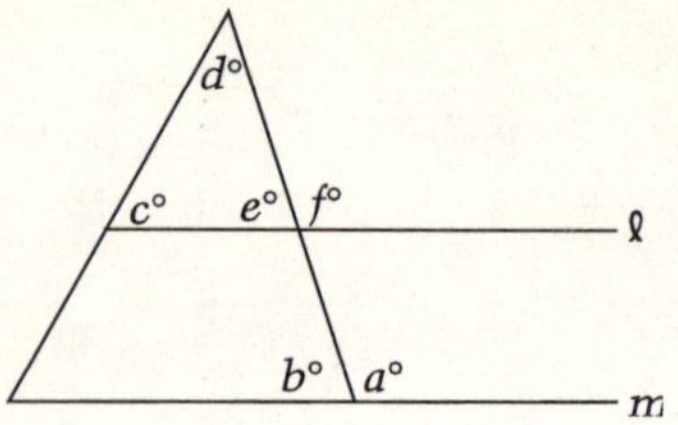

7 In the figure above, if $\ell \parallel m$, which of the following must be equal to a ?

(A) $b + c$
(B) $b + e$
(C) $c + d$
(D) $d + e$
(E) $d + f$

8 A certain phone call costs 75 cents for the first three minutes plus 15 cents for each additional minute. If the call lasted x minutes and x is an integer greater than 3, which of the following expresses the cost of the call, in dollars?

(A) $0.75(3) + 0.15x$
(B) $0.75(3) + 0.15(x + 3)$
(C) $0.75 + 0.15(3 - x)$
(D) $0.75 + 0.15(x - 3)$
(E) $0.75 + 0.15x$

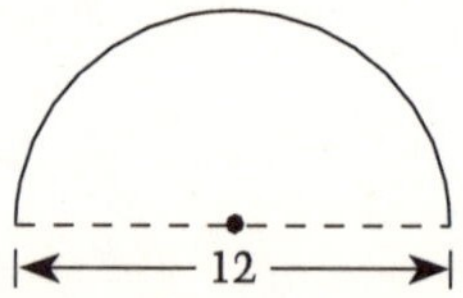

9 The figure above shows a piece of wire in the shape of a semicircle. If the piece of wire is bent to form a circle without any of the wire overlapping, what is the area of the circle?

(A) 6π
(B) 9π
(C) 12π
(D) 18π
(E) 36π

10 If $a^2 - a = 72$, and b and n are integers such that $b^n = a$, which of the following cannot be a value for b ?

(A) –8
(B) –2
(C) 2
(D) 3
(E) 9

IF YOU FINISH BEFORE TIME IS CALLED, YOU MAY CHECK YOUR WORK ON THIS SECTION ONLY. DO NOT TURN TO ANY OTHER SECTION IN THE TEST. **STOP**

ANSWER KEY ON FOLLOWING PAGE ➡

Answer Key

Section 1

1. E
2. C
3. B
4. B
5. B
6. E
7. C
8. E
9. D
10. B
11. A
12. A
13. B
14. C
15. D
16. D
17. C
18. B
19. C
20. E
21. A
22. C
23. D
24. C
25. A
26. E
27. B
28. A
29. C
30. D

Section 2

1. C
2. E
3. A
4. B
5. E
6. D
7. B
8. E
9. A
10. B
11. A
12. D
13. D
14. C
15. E
16. C
17. D
18. A
19. C
20. E
21. D
22. B
23. C
24. D
25. B

Section 3

1. D
2. D
3. A
4. C
5. E
6. B
7. C
8. B
9. D
10. C
11. E
12. C
13. A
14. E
15. A
16. D
17. B
18. C
19. C
20. C
21. D
22. A
23. B
24. B
25. C
26. E
27. B
28. C
29. D
30. E
31. A
32. A
33. D
34. C
35. E

Section 4

1. B
2. B
3. A
4. C
5. D
6. C
7. A
8. D
9. C
10. D
11. B
12. A
13. A
14. D
15. C
16. .127
17. 9.5 or 19/2
18. 84 or 96
19. 8
20. 45/4, 11.2, or 11.3
21. 4
22. 1/16, .062, or .063
23. 1/8 or .125
24. 2025
25. 4/7 or .571

Section 5

1. B
2. D
3. E
4. A
5. B
6. C
7. D
8. B
9. E
10. A
11. C
12. C
13. D

Section 6

1. B
2. E
3. D
4. A
5. B
6. C
7. C
8. D
9. B
10. C

Compute Your Raw Score

First, check your answers against the answer key on the previous page, and count up the number right and the number wrong for each section (there are boxes on your answer sheet to record these numbers). Remember not to count omissions as wrong.

Then figure out your raw scores using the table below. The Verbal raw score is equal to the total right in the three Verbal sections minus one-fourth of the number wrong in those sections. The Math raw score is equal to the total right in the three Math sections minus one-fourth of the number wrong in the two Regular Math sections and minus one-third the number wrong in the QCs. (Remember: There is no deduction for wrong answers in the Grid-ins.) Round each raw score to the nearest whole number.

Finally, use the tables on the next page to convert each raw score to a range of scaled scores.

	Number Right		Number Wrong		Raw Score
Section 1:	[ ]	– [.25 x	[ ]]	=	[ ]
Section 3:	[ ]	– [.25 x	[ ]]	=	[ ]
Section 5:	[ ]	– [.25 x	[ ]]	=	[ ]
			Verbal Raw Score:		[ ] (Rounded)
Section 4A: (Questions 1 to 15)	[ ]	– [.33 x	[ ]]	=	[ ]
Section 4B: (Questions 16 to 25)	[ ]		(No wrong-answer penalty)	=	[ ]
Section 2:	[ ]	– [.25 x	[ ]]	=	[ ]
Section 6:	[ ]	– [.25 x	[ ]]	=	[ ]
			Math Raw Score:		[ ] (Rounded)

Convert Your Score

Verbal

Raw	Scaled	Raw	Scaled	Raw	Scaled
–3 or less	200	22	450	48	620
–2	230	23	460	49	630
–1	270	24	470	50	640
0	290	25	470	51	640
1	300	26	480	52	650
2	310	27	490	53	660
3	320	28	490	54	670
4	330	29	500	55	670
5	330	30	510	56	670
6	340	31	510	57	680
7	350	32	520	58	690
8	360	33	530	59	690
9	370	34	530	60	700
10	370	35	540	61	710
11	380	36	550	62	720
12	390	37	550	63	730
13	390	38	560	64	730
14	400	39	570	65	740
15	410	40	570	66	750
16	410	41	580	67	760
17	420	42	590	68	770
18	430	43	590	69	780
19	430	44	600	70	790
20	440	45	600	71 or more	800
21	450	46	610		
		47	610		

Math

Raw	Scaled	Raw	Scaled	Raw	Scaled
–1 or less	200	19	440	40	600
0	220	20	450	41	610
1	240	21	460	42	620
2	260	22	470	43	630
3	280	23	480	44	640
4	300	24	480	45	650
5	310	25	490	46	650
6	330	26	500	47	660
7	340	27	510	48	670
8	350	28	520	49	680
9	360	29	520	50	690
10	370	30	530	51	700
11	380	31	530	52	720
12	390	32	540	53	730
13	400	33	550	54	740
14	410	34	560	55	760
15	420	35	560	56	770
16	430	36	570	57	780
17	430	37	580	58	790
18	440	38	590	59	800
		39	600	60	800

Don't take these scores too literally. Practice test conditions cannot precisely mirror real test conditions. Your actual SAT scores will almost certainly vary from your practice test scores.

Your score on the practice test gives you a rough idea of your range on the actual exam. If you don't like your score, it's not too late to do something about it. Work your way way through this book again, and turn to Kaplan's *SAT Verbal Workbook* and *SAT Math Workbook* for even more help.

Practice Test Answers and Explanations

SECTION 1

1. E

It's easy enough to understand that insurers don't like to insure property in places where natural disasters are likely to happen. The term **prone to** in (E) means "having a tendency to," so it is correct.

2. C

If it took Roman legions three years to seize Masada, we can predict that they spent a long time "surrounding or isolating" the mountain "fortress or stronghold" of Masada before they were finally able to take it. (C) is the best choice. (B) **assailed**, meaning "attacked," would make sense in the first blank, and (E) **stronghold** and (A) **bastion** would fit, too. But (A), (B), and (E)'s first-position words don't make sense when plugged in.

besieged: surrounded with armed forces
citadel: fortress
assailed: attacked
bastion: fortified area
dissembled: concealed
honed: sharpened

3. B

If the senator was **unlike** "his calmer, more easygoing colleagues" and "ready to quarrel at the slightest provocation," it's fair to infer that the senator was short-tempered or extremely irritable. The best choice is (B)—**irascible**.

irascible: easily angered
whimsical: fanciful, erratic, or unpredictable
gregarious: sociable, friendly
ineffectual: futile, unproductive
benign: harmless or gentle

4. B

You don't have to know that Genghis Khan was a violent dictator to get this question right. What's important to know is that the first word of the sentence, *although*, implies that the two blanks have to contain words that contrast with each other. (B) is the best choice—although historians had thought that Genghis Khan was a **despotic** potentate, new research shows that many of his subjects nevertheless **revered** him. Although (A) **tyrannical** is synonymous with *despotic*, (A)'s second-blank choice, **abhorred,** doesn't provide the predicted contrast. Choice (C) **venerated** doesn't really contrast with **redundant**. And in (E), it doesn't make sense to say that Khan's subjects **invoked** him despite his **peremptory** reputation.

despotic: oppressive, dictatorial
potentate: dictator
revered: worshipped, adored
abhorred: hated
venerated: highly respected
redundant: repetitive
jocular: jolly
peremptory: putting an end to debate
invoke: call upon for help

5. B

The word *because* in the middle of the sentence lets us know that the words in the blanks will be consistent in meaning, which means that they will share the same type of charge. We can predict two positive words, like "Jill was appreciated by her employees because she often forgave" the fact that they were lazy, or two negative words like "Jill was disliked by her employees because she often scolded them" for being lazy. (B) matches the latter prediction—Jill was **loathed** by her employees because she often **berated** them for not working hard enough. No other choice besides (B) contains two like charges.

loathed: hated
berated: scolded
deified: made godlike
lauded: praised or celebrated
derided: made fun of
execrated: condemned, cursed

6. E

If "reconstructing the skeletons of extinct species like dinosaurs . . . requires much patience and effort by paleontologists," we can predict that such an activity is a "painstaking or tough, demanding process." (E) **exacting** is our best choice.

exacting: requiring lots of attention and extreme accuracy
nascent: introductory or starting
aberrant: abnormal

7. C

Because of disease and the destruction of their habitat, koalas are now found only in isolated parts of eucalyptus forests. The word in the blank must mean something like "killed off" or "destroyed," since things like "disease and habitat destruction" are destructive processes. (C) is our best choice—"nearly **decimated** or wiped out by disease and habitat destruction," koalas are now found only in isolated parts of eucalyptus forests. (A) **dispersed,** meaning "scattered," may have been a little tempting, but there's no reason to assume that the koalas were scattered around the forests due to "disease and habitat destruction."

dispersed: scattered
compiled: categorized, collected, arranged
averted: avoided

8. E

Looking at the first blank first, if there were "internal power struggles" in the government, then it's likely that the government had something like "deep ideological differences or conflicts." For the second blank, we can predict that these conflicts and power struggles harmed or crippled the government. Although choice (C)'s first-blank choice, **distortions,** sounds negative, like "differences or conflicts," choices (A) and (E) make *more* sense. We can easily imagine "deep ideological **disputes**" or "deep ideological **divisions**" going hand in hand with "internal power struggles," but it's hard to imagine ideological **distortions.**

Now we can turn to (A) and (E)'s second-blank choices. (A) doesn't make sense given the context of the sentence—why would "deep ideological **disputes** and internal power struggles **facilitate** the government"? (E) is the best choice—"deep ideological **divisions** and internal power struggles **paralyzed** the government."

distortions: perversions, twisted versions
facilitate: assist
stymied: frustrated, impeded

9. D

The terms *popular remedy* and *as yet* are key in this sentence. Large doses of vitamins are popularly thought to be good, but their effectiveness has not been proven at this time. (D) **unproven** is the correct answer. Answer choices (A), (B), (C), and (E) are wrong because they imply that medical experts understand and approve of large doses, which clearly contradicts the sentence.

10. B

A **TROUT** is a type of **FISH,** just as a **human** is a type of **mammal.**

11. A

Bridge: If you **INHALE** something, it goes into your **LUNGS**. If you **swallow** something, it goes into your **stomach.**

12. A

A **BRAGGART** is, by definition, someone who **BOASTs.** A **laggard** is, by definition, someone who **tarries.** A speaker, not a **hypocrite,** is someone who, by definition, **speaks,** so (B) is wrong.

laggard: lingerer, one who lags behind
extrovert: someone very outgoing
tarry: to dawdle, be late, delay
hypocrite: someone who pretends to be what he or she is not

13. B

To **ALLEVIATE** is to reduce **PAIN,** just as to **depreciate** is to reduce **value.** In choice (D), to **deviate** is to move away from some set **standard**. That's not the same as lowering a **standard.**

14. C

Bridge: To **INFURIATE** someone is to **ANNOY** him or her a great deal. In correct choice (C), to **terrify** someone is to **frighten** him or her a great deal.

satiate: to satisfy

15. D

Someone **MISERLY** is not characterized by **MAGNANIMITY,** or generousness. Similarly, someone **innocent** is not characterized by **culpability.**

transient: wandering from place to place
stupefaction: overwhelming amazement
fastidiousness: the quality of being painstaking or particular
avarice: greed
magnanimity: generosity
culpability: guilt

The Time Passage

Next up is a fairly abstract science passage. This particular passage is perhaps a little bit harder than the ones you're going to encounter on the test—but don't be intimidated by the subject matter. Even if your passage is written by a Nobel Prize winner, it's going to contain ideas that you can relate to, and probably some ideas that you've seen before.

The topic of the passage is how difficult it is to comprehend long stretches of time. Paragraph two tells us that our minds aren't built to handle the idea of thousands of years passing. We have *some* conception of the past through the art, writing, and photography of previous generations, but the scale of longer time periods eludes us. Paragraphs four and five attempt to bridge this gap by providing a few everyday yardsticks; the time the human race has been around is compared to a few seconds in a week, or a few letters in a book. Essentially, that's all you need to take from your first reading of the passage; the details you can come back to later.

16. D

Here, in paragraph one, the author's talking about why we find it difficult to understand vast stretches of time. We're told that the "span" of what we can remember is limited because our lives are relatively short. So *span* in this context means the *amount* of time we're able to recollect—the (D) **extent.**

(A) **rate of increase,** (B) **value,** and (E) **accuracy** are all correct definitions of *span,* but they're not aspects of memory as discussed in the passage. And (C) **bridge,** the most common definition, doesn't fit at all.

HINT: *The golden rule about vocabulary questions on the Critical Reading section is that they test vocabulary IN CONTEXT. You're being asked how a particular word is used in the passage, not how it's usually defined.*

17. C

Before writing, we're told, the wisdom of generations was passed down in two ways—verbally, and "to a lesser extent," in pictures, carvings, and statues. This means that the wisdom of the past was transmitted less effectively by nonverbal means, and thus (C) **more effectively by the spoken word than by other means.**

Choices (A) and (B) *distort* this idea. Nowhere are we told that wisdom was rejected. And since spoken words *and* pictures were both used, it was obviously not an all or nothing proposition. (E) doesn't make much sense. How could there be an emphasis on science before writing existed? (D), finally, makes no sense at all—the author never says that all ancient wisdom was fiction.

18. B

This is a Little Picture question asking about the purpose of a detail. The question asks why the author discusses the impact of writing. Looking at the lines around the line reference given, we're told that writing has made the transmission of information about the past a lot more precise and extensive. Pictures and photography are also mentioned as ways in which the experience of the past has been passed down. So choice (B)'s correct here—writing is mentioned as an **example** of how cultures record knowledge about the past.

(A) is a distortion—the author is showing us something about the past, not why we remember hardly anything. He never implies any criticism of preliterate cultures, so choice (C) is out too. Choices (D) and (E) are wrong because the author never mentions them in the context referred to or in the whole passage.

19. C

Another Vocabulary-in-Context question. The word *ready* can mean several things—choices (A), (C), (D), and (E) are all possible meanings. In this context, however, it most nearly means **immediate,** choice (C). In the sentence before the cited line, the author says "there is no simple way" to understand vast stretches of time. And in the sentence following the cited line, the author compares the way we understand time to the way a blind man "laboriously" constructs a picture of his surroundings. This implies that our understanding of time is a difficult and time-consuming task, not something we can do *readily* or **immediately.**

20. E

Another question asking about the *purpose behind* part of the author is argument. Give the context a quick scan. Once again, the author's talking about how difficult it is to understand vast stretches of time. We're told that it's like a blind man building up a sensory picture of his surroundings. This is an **indirect** process, so choice (E) is right.

Choice (C) is dealt with later in paragraph four, so you can eliminate it right away.

Choice (A) is too sweeping. The author never says that human beings are *completely* **unable to comprehend time.** (B) and (D) have nothing to do with the passage.

21. A

Inference skills are required here. What is the author's underlying point in mentioning the Big Bang and the Cambrian Period? The author *introduces* this discussion in the cited passage by saying that **a week** provides a better yardstick for the age of the earth than a day. The Big Bang and the Cambrian Period are used as examples to support this point. So (A) is right—it's the point about the time scale that the author's trying to demonstrate.

Choices (D) and (E) both distort the point in different ways. The author is not suggesting that the time scale of a day should be totally abandoned—just that the week is a better scale. The development of (B) **agriculture** is another supporting example like the Big Bang and the Cambrian Period, but it's not the author's central point here. Finally, **fossils** have nothing to do with the question at hand, so (C) is easily eliminated.

22. C

A more straightforward comprehension question this time. When we go back to the lines referred to, we're told about the problem with linear maps: When you produce one that's big enough to show us on it, the map becomes too big to study and reproduce conveniently. (C) gets the right paraphrase here. Notice especially the match up in synonyms for "convenient reproduction" and "examination."

(A), (B), and (E) aren't supported here—there's nothing about **overlapping** periods, **scientific standards,** or ignorance about **pre-Cambrian times** in the passage. (D) doesn't address the problem. The question is about getting our human experience on the map.

23. D

What's the overall point the author is trying to prove?

The Big Picture is that life started on earth so long ago that it is difficult for us to comprehend. Everything that follows is meant to illustrate this point, including the time scales. Don't let the material confuse you. The point is (D)—**the immensity of time** since the origin of **life.**

(C) is tricky to reject because it's an aspect of the larger argument, but it's not the whole point. The other wrong choices mention issues that the author hardly touches on. In paragraphs four to six, the author's *not* concerned with getting dates right (A), the question of how life actually began (B), or the (E) **development of communication.**

The Susan B. Anthony Passage

This humanities passage is from a speech by Susan B. Anthony, a 19th-century women's rights leader. Anthony admits at the outset that she was recently charged with the "crime" of voting. Her intention is to prove that her vote was no crime, but rather the exercise of her Constitutional rights, which no state should be allowed to impinge upon. This generates the passage's big idea: that Anthony—and by extension all women—should be allowed to vote. You may have found Anthony's style a little dated or confusing. Don't worry; the questions will help you focus on specific details.

24. C

The important thing here is to see what exactly Anthony is saying. The question stem is keyed to the first paragraph. In the second sentence she states that she "not only committed no crime, but . . . simply exercised my citizen's rights, guaranteed me . . . by the National Constitution." The words *no crime* are the first important clue. You can immediately rule out (A) and (E) because they say she believes the act was illegal. The second part of the line discusses the Constitution, so (C) is clearly a restatement of her argument.

(B) and (D) both make sense, but she does not state these points in the first paragraph. Therefore, they are wrong.

25. A

The most common meaning of "promote" is to move up—to a higher position, rank, or job. This doesn't make sense, though, in the phrase "promote the general welfare." "General welfare" means the good of all people, so to (A) **further** it, makes the most sense.

(B) **organize** and (C) **publicize** both could apply to the general welfare, but not as well as (A). They refer more to promotion as you would do with a concert or sports event. (D) **commend** means "praise," which seems silly in the context given, as does (E) **motivate.**

HINT: *In Vocabulary-in-Context questions, the right answer is usually not the most common meaning of the given word. Be sure to reread the context.*

26. E

Anthony points out that no subgroup was excluded by the wording of the preamble of the Constitution. " . . . we formed it . . . to secure [the blessings of liberty,] not to the half of ourselves . . . but to . . . women as well as men." Therefore (E) is correct. **All people deserve to enjoy the rights of the Constitution.**

Anthony never claims that the Founding Fathers plotted to deny women their rights (A). (B) is incorrect because the author's concern is women's rights and not rights of any other group. Though **some male citizens may still be denied basic rights,** (B) goes against the gist of what is being said. (C) is like (A) in that it's a claim Anthony never makes. Finally, though (D) is a point that Anthony does make, she doesn't make it until the next paragraph.

27. B

We're still looking at the same part of the passage.

Look at the structure of the quoted sentence: "We didn't do it only for X, but for X *and* Y." *Posterity* means "future generations," which would include men and women. So the X, the "half of our posterity," refers to the posterity of those who already enjoy the blessings of liberty. In other words, men. (B) is the right choice.

(A) has nothing to do with what Anthony is discussing. Since the construction of the sentence makes it clear that the "half of our posterity" is not the whole of those who want to vote, (C) is out. There's no way of saying that one-half of the people are and will be opponents of women's rights, so (D) is wrong. And (E) wrongly suggests that in the future, one half of the country's population will be members of government.

28. A

Reread the keyed paragraph. Anthony is saying that a state that prohibits women from voting violates federal law—the Constitution. Therefore it becomes "an odious aristocracy, a hateful oligarchy." Neither of these things is a democracy. (A) is the correct answer.

Anthony mentions rebellion, but she doesn't mean the kind of violent rebellion (B) talks about. (C) is wrong because of the word *remain.* The nation is not and never has been an aristocracy. (D) plays off the same sentence as (B) does, but instead of going too far, it doesn't go far enough. Anthony wants the laws against women voting repealed; she doesn't want them merely discussed. (E) is totally wrong because at no point is Anthony arguing that an aristocracy should be preserved.

29. C

You might readily associate *hardihood* with (A) **endurance** and (B) **vitality,** but a quick check back in context shows you these aren't correct. Anthony says she doesn't believe her opponents would have the ---- to say women aren't "persons." Saying such an offensive thing would take a lot of **nerve,** choice (C). It might also take a lot of **stupidity** (E), but that's too strong a word, considering Anthony's diplomatic tone.

30. D

The stem keys you to the second to last sentence of the passage. *Abridge* means "deprive," so Anthony is saying that no state can deprive citizens of their rights. (D) states exactly this.

In (A), *privilege* means "luxury," but voting is a basic right, not a luxury. (B) comes out of nowhere; there's no discussion of courts in this passage. (C) plays off Anthony's reference to "any old law." She's not talking about *any* outdated laws in this passage; she means any law *that prohibits women from voting.* Anthony never addresses how the laws will be changed, only that they must be changed, so (E) is out.

antagonism: hostility

SECTION 2

1. C

Use the formula Percent × Whole = Part.

30 percent is $\frac{30}{100}$, or $\frac{3}{10}$. So $\frac{3}{10} \times x$ = part, and choice (C) is correct.

2. E

$2 \times 10^4 = 20{,}000$. $5 \times 10^3 = 5{,}000$. $6 \times 10^2 = 600$. $4 \times 10^1 = 40$. So the sum is 25,640.

3. A

Find the length of each segment, and then subtract the length of *XY* from the length of *YZ*. *Y* is at 3 on the number line and *Z* is at 8, so the length of *YZ* is $8 - 3 = 5$. *X* is at 1 on the number line and *Y* is at 3, so the length of *XY* is $3 - 1 = 2$. So the length of *YZ* is $5 - 2 = 3$ greater than the length of *XY*.

4. B

To find the value of x, you need to change 16 into a power of 2: $16 = 2^4$. Therefore, $2^{x+1} = 2^4$. So $x + 1 = 4$, or $x = 3$.

5. E

The number of degrees around a point is 360. Therefore:

$$90 + 30 + 2a + 30 + a = 360$$
$$150 + 3a = 360$$
$$3a = 210$$
$$a = 70$$

6. D

If a machine labels 150 bottles in 20 minutes, it labels 15 bottles every 2 minutes. To label 60, or 4 × 15, bottles would take 4 × 2, or 8 minutes.

7. B

To find the next multiple of 3, simply add 3 to the expression: $x - 1 + 3 = x + 2$, choice (B).

If this is unclear, pick a number for x. If $x = 4$, $4 - 1 = 3$; the next greatest multiple of 3 is 6. Plugging 4 for x into each answer choice, we find that only choice (B) gives us 6.

8. E

Since x leaves a remainder of 4 when divided by 5, it must end in either a 4 or a 9, so choice (B) can be eliminated. Since x leaves no remainder when divided by 9, it is evenly divisible by 9. Of the remaining choices only 144 is divisible by 9.

9. A

The sum of the lengths of any two sides of a triangle must be greater than the length of the third side. So $AB + AC$ must be greater than BC; $6 + x > 12$. If $x = 6$, $6 + 6 = 12$ is not greater than 12, so x cannot equal 6.

10. B

Number of terms × average = sum of the terms. For the first group, $3 \times 40 = 120$, so the sum of 20, 70, and x is 120. For the second group, $4 \times 50 = 200$, so $20 + 70 + x + y = 200$. Since the sum of the first three terms is 120, $120 + y = 200$, $y = 80$.

11. A

Looking at the graph, you can see that the number of books borrowed in January was 300. To find the total number of books borrowed during the first six months of the year, add the values of each bar: $300 + 350 + 400 + 450 + 500 + 400 = 2{,}400$ books. So the number of books borrowed in January is $\frac{300}{2400}$ or $\frac{1}{8}$ of the total number of books borrowed during the first six months of the year.

12. D

We're told that 40% of $r = s$. The value of 40% of r is 4 times the value of 10% of r, so 10% of $r = \frac{1}{4} \times s = \frac{s}{4}$.

An alternative method is to pick numbers. Since you're dealing with percents, let $r = 100$. 40% of $r = s$, so 40% of $100 = 40 = s$. You're asked which answer choice is equal to 10% of r; 10% of $100 = 10$. Now plug the value for s into the answer choices to see which ones give you 10:

(A) $4s = 4 \times 40 = 160$. Eliminate.

(B) $2s = 2 \times 40 = 80$. Eliminate.

(C) $\frac{s}{2} = \frac{40}{2} = 20$. Eliminate.

(D) $\frac{s}{4} = \frac{40}{4} = 10$. Works!

(E) $\frac{s}{8} = \frac{40}{8} = 5$. Eliminate.

Since (D) is the only choice that produces the desired result, it is the correct answer. But remember, when picking numbers you need to check all the answer choices; if more than one works, pick new numbers and plug them in until only one answer choice works.

13. D

The two overlapping triangles share a common angle, which we can label $p°$. Since the interior angles of any triangle add up to 180°, we have two equations: $x + z + p = 180$ and $y + r + p = 180$. Subtracting p from both sides of each equation, we have $x + z = 180 - p$ and $y + r = 180 - p$. Since $x + z$ and $y + r$ both equal the same quantity, $x + z$ and $y + r$ must be equal to each other. Rearranging $x + z = y + r$, we get $x - r = y - z$, which matches choice (D).

14. C

Check the answer choices. If a number has even one factor (not including 1 and itself) that is not a prime number, eliminate that choice:

(A) 12: 4 is not prime. Eliminate.

(B) 18: 6 is not prime. Eliminate.

(C) 21: 3 and 7 are its only other factors, and both are prime. Correct!

(D) 24: 6 is not prime. Eliminate.

(E) 28: 4 is not prime. Eliminate.

15. E

Try different possible values for x and y, eliminating the incorrect answer choices. Since x is multiplied by 3, let's begin with the smallest positive integer value for x: 1. If $3(1) + y = 14$, then $y = 11$, and $x + y = 12$. So choice (A) is out.

If $3(2) + y = 14$, then $y = 8$, and $x + y = 10$. So choice (B) is out. If $3(3) + y = 14$, then $y = 5$, and $x + y = 8$. So choice (C) is also out. If you're really clever, you'll see at this point that answer choice (E) is impossible (which makes it the right choice). After all, the next smallest possible value of x is 4, and since x and y must both be positive integers, neither one can equal 0. (Zero is *not* positive—or negative.) So the sum of x and y must be greater than 4. (Sure enough, if $x = 4$, then $y = 2$, and $x + y = 6$, eliminating choice (D) as well.)

16. C

When the r cards are distributed, there are 8 left over, so the number of cards distributed is $r - 8$. Divide the number of cards distributed by the number of people. Since there are s people, each person gets $\frac{r-8}{s}$ cards.

Another approach is to pick numbers. Let $r = 58$ and $s = 10$; if $58 - 8$ or 50 cards were distributed evenly among 10 people, each would receive 5 cards. Plug the values you picked for r and s into the answer choices to see which ones give you 5:

(A) $\frac{s}{8-r} = \frac{10}{8-58} = -\frac{1}{5}$. Eliminate.

(B) $\frac{r-s}{8} = \frac{58-10}{8} = 6$. Eliminate.

(C) $\frac{r-8}{s} = \frac{58-8}{10} = 5$. Works!

(D) $s - 8r = 10 - (8 \times 58) = -454$. Eliminate.

(E) $rs - 8 = (58 \times 10) - 8 = 572$. Eliminate.

Since (C) is the only answer choice that gives you 5, it is the correct answer. But be sure to check all the answer choices when picking numbers.

17. D

Check each answer choice to see which doesn't work:

(A) $\frac{d}{2}$: If d is an even integer, say 2, then $\frac{d}{2} = \frac{2}{2} = 1$ is an integer. Eliminate.

(B) $\frac{\sqrt{d}}{2}$: If d is a perfect square with an even square root, say $d = 4$, then $\frac{\sqrt{4}}{2} = \frac{2}{2} = 1$ is an integer. Eliminate.

(C) $2d$: This will always produce an even integer; if $d = 3$, $2d = 2 \times 3 = 6$ is an integer. Eliminate.

(D) $d\sqrt{2}$ CANNOT produce an integer. An integer would result if $\sqrt{2}$ is multiplied by another multiple of $\sqrt{2}$, which is impossible because d must be an integer. So (D) is correct.

Let's check (E) just to make sure.

(E) $d + 2$: This will always produce an integer; if $d = 5$, $d + 2 = 5 + 2 = 7$ is an integer. Eliminate.

18. A

The area of a triangle = $\frac{1}{2}$(base × height). Since the area of ΔABC is 6, $\frac{1}{2}(AB \times BC) = 6$. If you consider CD as the base of ΔACD, you will notice that its height is represented by altitude AB. So the area of $\Delta ACD = \frac{1}{2}(CD \times AB)$. Since $CD = BC$, the area of ΔACD can be expressed as $\frac{1}{2}(BC \times AB)$, which you know equals 6.

19. C

Since the ratio of x to y to z is 3:6:8, if $y = 24$ or 4×6, x and z must also be multiplied by 4 for the ratio to hold. So $x = 4 \times 3 = 12$ and $z = 4 \times 8 = 32$, and $x + z = 44$.

20. E

Each of the five surfaces is 60 by 180 centimeters, so tiles measuring 12 by 18 centimeters can be laid down in 5 rows of 10 to exactly cover one surface. There are 5 surfaces so $5 \times 5 \times 10 = 250$ tiles are needed.

21. D

If you add the 3 equations together, you find that $2x + 2y + 2z = 38$; dividing both sides by 2 shows that $x + y + z = 19$, answer choice (D).

22. B

The perimeter of triangle $ACD = AD + AB + BC + CD$. You are given the lengths of BC and CD, so you need to find the lengths of AD and AB. Angle DBC is a right angle because it is supplementary to $\angle DBA$, one of the 4 right angles of square $ABDE$. Since right triangle DBC has sides of length 8 and 10, you should recognize it as a 6-8-10 right triangle (a multiple of the 3-4-5 right triangle) and realize that $BD = 6$. (If you didn't recognize this, you could have used the Pythagorean theorem to find the length of BD.) BD is also a side of the square and since all sides of a square are equal, $AB = 6$.

So triangle DBA is an isosceles right triangle with sides in the ratio of $1:1:\sqrt{2}$. That means hypotenuse AD is equal to the length of a side times $\sqrt{2}$, so $AD = 6\sqrt{2}$. Now you can find the perimeter of triangle ACD: $6\sqrt{2} + 6 + 8 + 10 = 24 + 6\sqrt{2}$.

23. C

$(4r - 4)^2 = 36$, so $4r - 4$ could equal 6 or -6, since the result is 36 when each of these integers is squared. But the problem states that $r < 0$, so try -6. $4r - 4 = -6$, $4r = -2$, and $r = -\frac{2}{4} = -\frac{1}{2}$, answer choice (C). (If you try $4r - 4 = 6$ you'll find $r = 2\frac{1}{2}$, which cannot be correct for this question since $r < 0$.)

24. D

Tank *A* originally contained 10 more liters of water than tank *C*, so represent the initial number of liters in each tank in terms of tank *A:*

tank $A = a$

tank $C = a - 10$

5 liters of water are poured from *A* to *B*, and an additional 10 liters are poured from *A* to *C*. A total of 15 liters are removed from tank *A* so it now contains $a - 15$ liters of water. 10 liters are added to tank *C* so it now contains $a - 10 + 10 = a$ liters. So tank C contains 15 more liters of water than tank *A*.

25. B

The surface area of a cube is $6e^2$, where $e =$ the length of an edge of the cube. Since the surface area is $36n^2$:

$$6e^2 = 36n^2$$
$$e^2 = 6n^2$$
$$e = n\sqrt{6}$$

The volume of a cube is e^3. To solve for the volume in terms of *n*, plug in the value for an edge that you just found: Volume $= e^3 = (n\sqrt{6})^3 = 6n^3\sqrt{6}$, answer choice (B).

SECTION 3

1. D

This is not a difficult question. The use of the word *and* tells us that we're looking for a word to fill the first blank which is consistent with "scarcity of rain"—a word like *dry.* We can, therefore, eliminate (A) and (C) at once. Since farming conditions are "bad," our second blank should express the idea that there's no point in trying to work there. By that criterion, choices (B) and (E) can be eliminated. This leaves us with (D) **future.** (D)'s first word, **infertile,** also fits perfectly, so (D) is the correct answer.

barren: not productive

2. D

The structural clue in this sentence is *not only . . . but,* which suggests that the students were doing something even worse than ignoring the rules. The only word that fits here is **flouting,** choice (D).

flouting: mocking, treating with contempt

3. A

The word *while* following the comma in the second part of the sentence tells us that there will be a contrast between what some critics believe about dadaism and what *others* "insist the movement was." The best choice is (A)—"some critics believe that the **zenith** of modern art came with dadaism, while others insist the movement was a **sham.**" Other choices have single words that would make sense in one of the blanks, but none of the pairs except (A) expresses the contrast that is implied by the sentence.

zenith: highest point
sham: hoax

4. C

In this question you are asked to make a logical connection between two parts of a sentence. It is clear that the content of the journalist's article either had no impact, in which case there was little or no response from the public, or it attracted a great deal of attention and was followed by a lot of correspondence. (C) is the correct answer. The author would never have thought her article was **controversial** were it not for the **spate** of correspondence. The other answer choices are wrong because they sound contradictory when plugged into the sentence. For example, in choice (A), if the article were **interesting,** one would expect it to be followed by a lot of correspondence—not by a **dearth,** or lack of it. In choice (D), if the article were **commonplace** (ordinary), why would an **influx** of letters follow its publication?

spate: a sudden flood or rush
dearth: lack
inflammatory: likely to arouse strong feeling or anger
influx: flow coming in

5. E

If many readers have difficulty following Descartes's complex, intricately woven arguments, then it's likely that his writings are something like *complicated, esoteric,* or *obscure.* The best choice is (E) **abstruse.**

abstruse: difficult to understand
generic: common, general
trenchant: extremely perceptive, insightful

6. B

The phrase *even though* indicates contrast. So, even though the prisoner "presented evidence clearly proving that he was nowhere near the scene of the crime," he was **indicted** or formally charged with committing the crime.

exculpated: absolved, proved to be innocent
exhumed: removed from a grave
rescinded: cancelled, taken back

7. C

A *premise* is a proposition which is used as the basis for an argument—or a story. If scientists are critical of the premise for a movie, we can infer that they are so because they consider it to be unscientific, without basis in fact, or **speculative.** (C) is therefore the correct answer. (A) is wrong, because if the premise, or underlying argument, were **scientific** then it would hardly be open to criticism by scientists. (B) is wrong because there's no reason to think that the theme of the return of the dinosaurs is unexpressed in the movie.

tacit: silent; understood but unexpressed

8. B

Looking at the second blank first, if Mozart "left no rough drafts," it's probably "because he was able to write out his compositions in a complete, unrevised form." So, for the second blank, (B) **finished** looks best. (E) **concise** is also possible, so let's try (B) and (E) in the first blank. We've already seen that Mozart didn't need to revise his compositions—therefore, it makes sense to say that he "composed music with exceptional *ease* or **facility.**" (E) **independence** is just too ambiguous to fit in to the context of the sentence.

concise: using as few words as possible, to the point

9. D

If dogs are "known for their devotion," then it's likely that they "were often used as symbols of *faithfulness, loyalty,* or **fidelity**" in Medieval and Renaissance art. (A) **resistance** and (E) **antagonism** are not what we're looking for, and choices (B) and (C), while positive, don't relate to the idea of *devotion.*

antagonism: hostility

10. C

In this sentence we find a description of two contradictory characteristics which exist in the same group of people. On the one hand, they are brutal; on the other, they are heroic. Such an occurrence is termed a *paradox* and therefore (C) **paradoxical** is the correct answer. Choices (A), (D), and (E) are wrong; it is **unfortunate, distressing,** and **appalling** that they are brutal—but not that they are heroic.

paradoxical: like a riddle; opposed to common sense but true
explicable: able to be explained

11. E

A **CHARLATAN** is, by definition, not **SCRUPULOUS.** A **tyrant** is a ruler who uses power oppressively and unjustly. So a **tyrant** is, by definition, not **just.**

charlatan: a fraud or a quack, someone who pretends to have more knowledge or skill than he or she possesses

12. C

GREED is the desire to **ACQUIRE** large amounts of things. **Gluttony** is the desire to **eat** large amounts, so (C) is the best answer.

(A) won't work; someone who experiences **fear** may or may not want to **disguise** himself or herself. In (B), it may be hard to **persuade** someone characterized by **inertia,** but **inertia** isn't the desire to **persuade** large amounts.

inertia: apathy, inactivity

13. A

The word **BLOW** is being used to mean "a swipe or punch." To **PARRY** means "to deflect, ward off," so our bridge is "to **PARRY** a **BLOW** is to deflect it." (A) shares the same bridge—to **counter** an **argument** is to deflect it.

In choice (B), you might **sidestep** or avoid an argument or issue, but there isn't really any clear connection between **sidestep** and **offense.** In (C), to **defer** isn't to deflect or ward off a **ruling.**

pitfall: a trap or hidden danger
defer: put off or delay

14. E

By definition, **SLURS** are words that **MALIGN,** just as **compliments** are words that **flatter.** The other choices don't fit this bridge. For instance, in (C), **whispers** aren't necessarily words that **torment.**

15. A

A **LENTIL** is classified as a **LEGUME,** a bean or pea, in the same way that **rice** is classified as a **cereal.**

Even if you didn't know that a **LENTIL** is a **LEGUME,** you might have been able to arrive at the answer by eliminating all choices with no good bridges. For example, in (B) **food** may or may not provide **nutrition,** or nourishment.

husk: the outer covering of a kernel or seed

16. D

To **INDULGE** an **APPETITE** is to satisfy it. Similarly, to **humor** a **whim** is to satisfy it.

In (A), you can **filter** out an **impurity,** but it doesn't make sense to say that to **filter** out an **impurity** is to satisfy it. (C) might have been a tempting choice, since the word **coddle** is similar to **indulge.** But **coddle** doesn't have a necessary connection to **emotion.**

coddle: to overindulge, pamper

17. B

Bridge: **MELLIFLUOUS** means "sweet **SOUND**ing." **Fragrant** means "sweet **smell**ing."

In (D), a **raucous discussion** would be a harsh-sounding, noisy debate.

mellifluous: sweet sounding, melodious
fragrant: sweet smelling
raucous: harsh or grating

18. C

By definition, a **GUFFAW** is loud, unrestrained **LAUGH**ing. In the same way, a **yell** is loud, unrestrained **talk**ing.

19. C

The word **CELESTIAL** means "having to do with the **HEAVENS**." The word **nautical** means "having to do with **ships.**"

celestial: having to do with the heavens
nautical: having to do with ships
viscous: thick and gluey

20. C

To **ENERVATE** is to lessen or decrease **VITALITY.** In (C), to **daunt** is to lessen **courage.**

You could have worked backwards by eliminating answer choices with inappropriate or weak bridges. For example, in (A), one can **consolidate power** by securing and strengthening one's position, but that bridge doesn't work with the stem words. Choice (B) has a weak bridge, too: To **energize** is to fill with energy, but that doesn't always result in **action.** If you plug the stem words into (D)'s bridge, you get, "To enervate is to assess the vitality of something." It doesn't sound sensible, so (D) is out, too. In (E) to **admit guilt** is to confess. That couldn't be true of the stem as well. By process of elimination, (C) is correct.

enervate: to lessen or decrease vitality
daunt: to subdue or dismay
energize: to fill with energy
estimate: to assess the worth of something

21. D

An **OLIGARCHY** is, by definition, a form of government in which power is held by a **FEW** people. Answer choice (D) is analogous to this: A **monarchy** is a form of government in which power is held by **one** person.

If the definition of **OLIGARCHY** posed a problem, you could again eliminate wrong answers. For instance, in choice (A), the terms **government** and **majority** are not always linked. Similarly, in (B), **authority** and **consent** don't necessarily go together. In (C), a **country** may or may not have a **constitution.**

oligarchy: a form of government in which power is held by a few people
monarchy: a form of government in which power is held by one person
constitution: a set of principles according to which a nation is governed

22. A

Bridge: Someone who is **UNTRUTHFUL** is characterized by **MENDACIOUSNESS.** Choice (A) is correct: Someone who is **circumspect** is characterized by **caution.**

What if you don't know what *mendaciousness* or *circumspect* mean? You must try to eliminate wrong answers. Remember that the stem words and the correct answer choice will have the same strong bridge. Work backwards. Does (B) have a strong bridge? A person who is **timid** exhibits a certain type of **behavior**—that's not a strong connection. Similarly, (C)'s bridge is weak: Everyone has a **physique** of some kind, not just **agile** people. Answer choices (D) and (E) can also be eliminated because they have weak bridges. That leaves us with (A).

mendaciousness: lying
circumspect: cautious or watchful

23. B

The bridge can be stated as: Something that is **INEXCUSABLE** is impossible to **JUSTIFY.** Likewise, in (B), something that is **unassailable** is impossible to **attack.**

unassailable: not open to attack or question
affable: friendly and polite
revere: to feel deep respect or awe for

The Twain Passage

This excerpt from Mark Twain's *Life on the Mississippi* should be amusing and easy to read. All the humor comes from the same technique—using deadpan, matter-of-fact language to describe the exaggerated daydreams and jealousies of a boy's life.

The central point here is the author's envy of the engineer, and many of the questions focus on this. The author starts with his own glamorous ideas about steamboating, then spends most of the passage on the show-off engineer. The passage finishes with the author's own failure to find work as a pilot. The slightly old-fashioned style isn't hard to follow, but several questions focus on the author's figurative use of words.

24. B

The key word in the sentence is *supposed.* Of course, a justice of the peace *doesn't* possess unlimited power, but because of inexperience the author "supposed" he did. (B) accurately uses *naive* (inexperienced, gullible) to characterize the author's misconception. Three of the wrong choices assume that the father really *did* have unlimited powers and explain this in different ways—frontier justice (A, D), public support (C). (E) mistakenly views the boy's description of his father as an indication that the boy's childhood environment was harsh.

25. C

Distinction has several meanings, including those in (A), (B), (C), and (E). The key to its use here is context: In the previous sentence the author is talking about his naive ideas of his father's great power. **Prestige,** (C), suggesting high status and honor, fits this context; the other three don't. (D) is not a meaning of *distinction* at all.

26. E

This question asks about the literal meaning of the sentence, but inference and context help, too. The sentence explains that the author wanted the job because a deck hand was "conspicuous," or easily seen. The previous sentence stresses standing "where all my old comrades could see me," so you can deduce that the author wants to be seen and admired in what he imagines is a glamorous profession (E).

(A) and (B) invent advantages that are not mentioned, and miss the humor by suggesting common-sense economic motivations. (C) assumes that if the author could be seen by his "old comrades" in the first job, he must want *not* to be seen by them in a different job; but this is false, since he'd be "conspicuous" in the second job, too. (D) brings in an ambition—becoming a pilot—that the author doesn't develop until the end of the passage.

27. B

Again, context helps you to figure out the answer to the question. The **Sunday-school** reference is explained in the next sentence. The engineer had been "worldly"—which is what Sunday-school probably taught students not to be—and the author had been "just the reverse." In other words, the author followed his Sunday-school teachings and the engineer didn't—yet the engineer gets the glory. The underlying idea is that this was unjust, choice (B).

(A) is never mentioned. (C) takes the Sunday-school reference literally and misses the humorous tone. (D) invents an ambition that the author never mentions; his reaction is pure envy, not frustrated ambition. (E) misconstrues the reference to the engineer as "worldly"; it means he didn't take Sunday-school seriously, not that he was **unscrupulous** (dishonest or crooked).

28. C

To get this question, you need to read the sentence that follows. The engineer was not generous because he sat about where "we all could see him and envy him." The implication is that great people should be generous by not showing off or (C) **flaunting** their success.

(A) refers to the Sunday-school comment, but that was about undeserved greatness, not lack of generosity. (B) and (D) interpret *generous* in the literal sense of not caring for money, but the author is using the word figuratively. (E) relates to the author's unfulfilled desire to work on a steamboat, but the engineer is not thinking about the author, he is just showing off.

29. D

The engineer does everything for the purpose of showing off. He talks the jargon of the trade to make himself look knowledgeable, or (D) **sophisticated.**

Reading between the lines, we realize he's not an expert (A), and doesn't care about knowledge for its own sake (B). His (C) **ignorance** on other subjects is not mentioned; in fact, he has a working knowledge of St. Louis. (E) takes literally the phrase about how the engineer "forgot common people could not understand"—he couldn't **communicate effectively.** But the author says the engineer talked "as if" he forgot common people. In other words he didn't *fail* to communicate, he *chose not* to, to impress others.

30. E

The first four choices are all common meanings of *consideration,* but the context makes it clear that the figurative use in (E) is meant. The boys had "consideration" because they knew something about St. Louis, but their glory is over because the engineer knows much more. Prestige, respect, or (E) **reputation** supplies the meaning that fits. Boys are not likely to have the qualities of **generosity, deliberation, contemplation,** or **unselfishness** as a result of knowing a little about St. Louis.

31. A

The context makes it clear that the engineer had, or at least seemed to have, much more familiarity with St. Louis than the other boys with their "vague knowledge"; their "glory" is ended because he can talk rings around them about St. Louis (A).

There's no indication that (B) **St. Louis has changed,** or that the boys had been lying—their knowledge was "vague," not false (D). Reading between the lines, it's clear that travel to St. Louis was still rare enough to seem enviable (E). As for choice (C), the passage implies just the opposite.

32. A

With his "hair oil . . . showy brass watch chain, [and] leather belt," the engineer was obviously out to impress (A). The next sentence confirms that, telling us "no girl could withstand his charms."

The author never says the young man's dress is typical (B). (C) and (E) are both wrong; the emphasis here is on the engineer's charms, not the author's wardrobe or fashion ideas. (D) won't work because the engineer's behavior is as showy and superficial as his clothes.

33. D

As often in these questions, wrong choices give flat-footed, literal interpretations where the author is being humorous. (A) misunderstands the reference to Providence—the author is criticizing providence, not thanking it, because it has spared an "undeserving reptile," the engineer. So the author feels resentment, or (D) **outrage,** because the engineer's good luck seems **undeserved.**

Choice (B) sounds believable at first, but the passage doesn't emphasize the lucky escape—it focuses on people's sense that the engineer got better than he deserved. (C) and (E) are never mentioned.

34. C

The passage focuses on the author's ambition to work on a steamboat and his envy of the engineer. This makes (C) and (D) the strongest choices, so you need to decide between them. Looking at (D), the passage certainly emphasizes the engineer's **boastfulness,** but only within the framework of the author's dreams and ambitions (paragraphs one and five) and the author's reactions to the engineer. So (C) describes the *whole* passage whereas (D) describes only the long central paragraphs. In a *major purpose/major focus* question, the answer that sums up the *whole* passage will be correct.

The (A) **life** of the **town** is barely suggested. (B) is wrong because the passage's events don't end in **success**—although in reality, Mark Twain did go on to become a pilot. The author's (E) **conflict with his parents** is mentioned only briefly, toward the end of paragraph four.

35. E

The last paragraph discusses the author's failed attempts to become a pilot, and his daydreams that he will still become one, so (E) works best. Mates and clerks are mentioned as ignoring the author, but he never considers becoming either a (A) **mate or a clerk,** looking for some other job (B), giving up his aim of being a pilot (C), or asking his parents' forgiveness (D).

SECTION 4

1. B

You could find the answer by calculating the value of Column A, but there's a shortcut. You should see that both fractions in Column A are less than $\frac{1}{2}$. Therefore, their sum must be less than 1, and Column B is greater than Column A.

2. B

The cost of 6 pens at 2 for 22 cents is $\frac{22}{2}$ cents $\times$ 6, or \$0.66, which is the value of Column A. The cost of 5 pens at 22 cents each is \$1.10, and that's the value of Column B. So Column B is greater, and choice (B) is correct.

3. A

You can solve for b using the second equation: $b - 3 = 2$, so $b = 5$. Plug in 5 for b in the first equation and solve for a: $2a + 5 = 17$, $2a = 12$, $a = 6$. So Column A is greater than Column B, and choice (A) is correct.

4. C

Make one column look more like the other. Perform the multiplication in Column A: $x - 2(y + z)$ becomes $x - 2y - 2z$, which is the same expression as in Column B. Therefore, choice (C) is correct.

5. D

The mean (or average) of a group of terms is equal to the sum of the terms divided by the number of terms. You don't know the values of a, b, or c, but you do know that they sum to 150. So in Column A their mean is $\frac{150}{3} = 50$. The median is the middle term in a group of terms in numerical order. All you know about

a, b, and c is that their sum is 150. It is possible that $a = 1$, $b = 2$, and $c = 147$; if so, the median would be 2 and in this case Column A would be greater. But what if $a = b = c = 50$? Then the median would be 50 and the columns would be equal. Since more than one relationship between the columns is possible, the answer must be choice (D).

6. C

Plug the values from each column into the given expression:

Column A = $(4 + 5)^3$ or $(9)^3$.

Column B = $(0 + 9)^3$ or $(9)^3$.

Since the values in both columns are equal, choice (C) is correct.

7. A

To find the circumference of circle *O*, you need to find the length of its radius. Draw a right triangle as shown below:

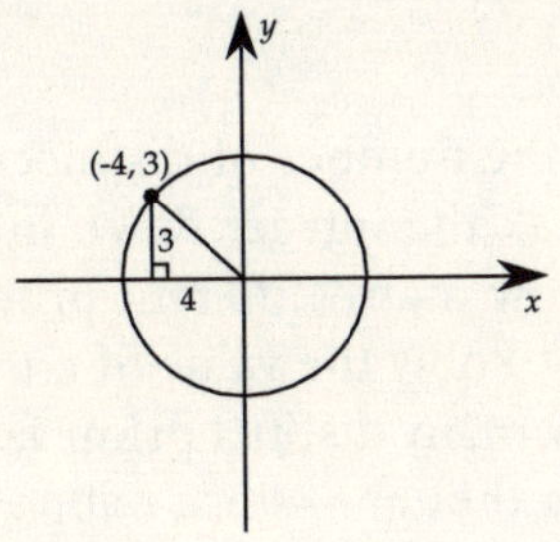

The lengths of the legs of the triangle are 4 and 3. You should recognize that this is a special 3-4-5 right triangle, so the length of the hypotenuse, which is also the radius of the circle, must be 5. Since circumference = $2\pi r$, the circumference of circle $O = 10\pi$. Since π is approximately 3.14, the circumference of circle *O* is greater than 30; Column A is greater than Column B.

8. D

If Jimmy waters his plant every other day, the number of times he waters it in one week depends upon whether he waters it the first day of the week or not. If he does, then he will water the plant the first, third, fifth, and seventh days for a total of 4 times that week. So Column A can be 4. Then the following week he will water it on the second, fourth, and sixth days for a total of 3 times. So Column B is 3, which makes Column A greater in this case. However, it's possible that in a given week he doesn't water the plant until the second day of the week. Then he will water it only 3 times that week and 4 times the following week. In this case, Column A is 3 and Column B is 4, making Column B greater. So Column A can be either greater than or less than Column B, and the answer must be choice (D).

9. C

To find the values of r and s, you need to find the slope of the line. Plug coordinates (1, 1) and (6, 11) into the slope formula:

$$\text{Slope} = \frac{y_2 - y_1}{x_2 - x_1}$$

$$= \frac{11 - 1}{6 - 1}$$

$$= \frac{10}{5}$$

$$= 2$$

So the slope of the line is 2.

Now find the value of r using coordinates (1, 1) and (3, r):

$$2 = \frac{r - 1}{3 - 1}$$

$$2 = \frac{r - 1}{2}$$

$$4 = r - 1$$

$$5 = r$$

Then find the value of s using coordinates (s, 9) and (6, 11):

$$2 = \frac{11-9}{6-s}$$

$$2 = \frac{2}{6-s}$$

$$12 - 2s = 2$$

$$-2s = -10$$

$$s = 5$$

The values in both columns are the same, and choice (C) is correct.

10. D

$r^2 + 4 = 21$, so $r^2 = 17$. You might think this means that r in Column A is greater than 4 in Column B, since $r^2 = 17$ while 4^2 equals only 16. But r can have a positive or negative value, since a negative squared also produces a positive. If r has a positive value, Column A is greater; if r has a negative value, Column B is greater. Since more than one relationship is possible, the answer is choice (D).

11. B

The perimeter of a triangle is equal to the sum of the lengths of its sides. You're given that $RT = US = 6$ and $RU < 2$. This means that RS must be less than 8. However, if $RS = 8$, then triangle RST would be a special right triangle with side lengths in a ratio of 3:4:5. So the length of ST would be 10, and the perimeter would be 6 + 8 + 10, or 24. But RS is less than 8, which means the perimeter must be less than 24. Therefore, Column B is greater than Column A, and choice (B) is correct.

12. A

Think of the 5 students as *A, B, C, D,* and *E* and then systematically consider all the possible winning combinations. If A wins 1st place, then *B, C, D,* or *E* could win 2nd; if *B* wins 1st place, then *A, C, D,* or *E* could win 2nd; if C wins 1st place, then *A, B, D,* or *E* could win 2nd; if *D* wins 1st place, then *A, B, C,* or *E* could win 2nd; if *E* wins 1st place, then *A, B, C,* or *D* could win 2nd. This is a total of 20 different combinations, so Column A is greater than 10 in Column B.

13. A

Since x^2 is a positive fraction less than 1, its positive square root, x, must also be a fraction less than 1, which you are told is positive. When a positive fraction less than 1 is squared, the result is a positive fraction smaller than the original. Therefore, $x^2 < x$.

For example, $\left(\frac{1}{2}\right)^2 < \frac{1}{2}$, since $\left(\frac{1}{2}\right)^2 = \frac{1}{4}$. So in Column A you're subtracting a positive value from 1, and in Column B you're subtracting a larger positive value from 1, so Column A must be greater.

14. D

Do not assume that $ABCD$ is a square and that $AB = BC = AD = 4$. You know that triangle ACD is an isosceles right triangle and angle CAD is a 45° angle, which means that angle BAD is a right angle. However, no information is given about the lengths of AB and BC, or whether angles ABC and BCD are right angles. If necessary, redraw the diagram to see this. So the relationship cannot be determined and answer choice (D) is correct.

15. C

To determine the number of distinct prime factors of an integer, break the integer down into its prime factors and see how many different prime factors it has. Since you don't know the value of t, there is no way to determine how many distinct prime factors it has. This isn't a problem though—since t appears as a factor in both of the columns, we can eliminate it from each without affecting the relationship between the columns. So that leaves 2 in Column A and 8 in Column B. The only prime factor of 2 is 2, and the prime factorization of 8 is $2 \times 2 \times 2$. While 2 appears as a factor three times in Column B, there is still only one distinct prime factor in each, so the columns are equal.

16. .127

If $A = 2.54$ and $20B = A$, then $20B = 2.54$. So $B = \frac{2.54}{20}$ or .127.

17. 9.5 or 19/2

The perimeter of the figure is equal to the sum of the lengths of its sides: $2 + 1\frac{1}{3} + 1\frac{1}{2} + 1\frac{2}{3} + 3 = 9\frac{1}{2}$, which is $\frac{19}{2}$ expressed as an improper fraction, or 9.5 expressed as a decimal.

18. 84 or 96

If $\frac{h}{3}$ and $\frac{h}{4}$ are both integers, then h must be a multiple of 3×4, or 12. Since it's given that h is between 75 and 100, h must be 84 or 96.

19. 8

The profit made by the retailer on the shirts is equal to the difference between the selling price and the cost for each shirt, multiplied by the number of shirts: (\$6.75 – \$4.50) × 16 = \$2.25 × 16 = \$36.00 profit. To find the number of \$4.50 shirts that can be bought for \$36.00, you need to divide \$36.00 by \$4.50, and $\frac{36}{4.5} = 8$.

20. 45/4 or 11.2 or 11.3

Draw a diagram and label it according to the given information:

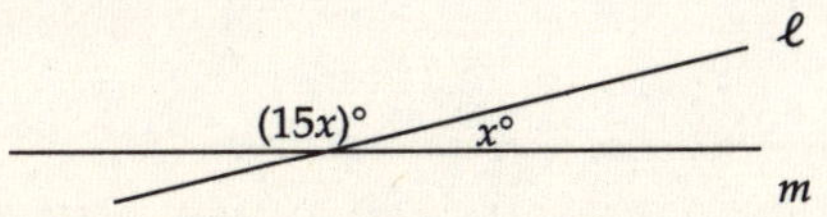

Let the smaller angle measure $x°$. Since the other angle formed is 15 times as large, label it $(15x)°$. Notice that these two angles are supplementary, that is, they add up to 180°. Therefore:

$$x + 15x = 180$$
$$16x = 180$$
$$x = \frac{45}{4}$$

So the smaller angle is $\frac{45}{4}$ degrees, which can also be gridded in decimal form as 11.2 or 11.3.

21. 4

Before you plug in –4 for x, you should factor the given equation:

$$x^2 + 2xr + r^2 = 0$$
$$(x + r)(x + r) = 0$$
$$(x + r)^2 = 0$$

Now plug in –4 for x to solve for r: $(-4 + r)^2 = 0$, $-4 + r = 0$, and $r = 4$.

22. 1/16 or .062 or .063

Plug the values into the given definition:

$$\frac{1}{4}* = \left(\frac{1}{4}\right)^2 - \frac{1}{4} = \frac{1}{16} - \frac{1}{4} = \frac{1}{16} - \frac{4}{16} = \frac{-3}{16}$$

$$\frac{1}{2}* = \left(\frac{1}{2}\right)^2 - \frac{1}{2} = \frac{1}{4} - \frac{1}{2} = \frac{-1}{4}$$

So:

$$\frac{1}{4}* - \frac{1}{2}* = \frac{-3}{16} - \left(\frac{-1}{4}\right) = \frac{-3}{16} - \left(-\frac{4}{16}\right) = \frac{1}{16}$$

This can also be gridded as .062 or .063.

23. 1/8 or .125

You should recognize that right ΔABC is a 45-45-90 triangle, with side lengths in a ratio of $1:1:\sqrt{2}$. Therefore, the length of the two equal legs AB and AC is $\frac{1}{2}$.

To find the area of the triangle, plug the values of the base and height (the lengths of the two equal legs) into the area formula:

Area of a triangle $= \frac{1}{2}(\text{base} \times \text{height})$

$$= \frac{1}{2}\left(\frac{1}{2}\right)^2$$

$$= \frac{1}{2}\left(\frac{1}{4}\right)$$

$$= \frac{1}{8}, \text{ or } .125$$

24. 2025

You're given that x is a factor of 8,100 and it's an odd integer. To find the greatest possible value of x, begin factoring 8,100 by using its smallest prime factor, 2, as one of the factors. Continue factoring out a 2 from the remaining factors until you find an odd one as shown below:

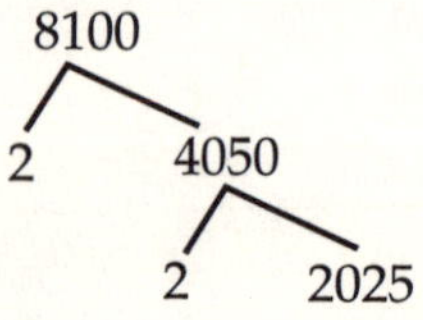

8,100

$2 \times 4{,}050$

$2 \times 2{,}025$

Since 2,025 is odd, you can stop factoring; it is the greatest odd factor of 8,100.

25. 4/7 or .571

Translate the problem into math: Let b = number of boys; let g = number of girls. So $b + g$ = total number of students in the class.

$\frac{1}{2}$ of the boys speak French, so $\frac{1}{2}b$ = the number of boys who speak French.

$\frac{2}{3}$ of the girls speak French, so $\frac{2}{3}g$ = the number of girls who speak French.

Therefore, $\frac{1}{2}b + \frac{2}{3}g$ = total French speakers.

So the fraction of the class that speaks French

$$= \frac{\frac{1}{2}b + \frac{2}{3}\left(\frac{3}{4}b\right)}{b + g}$$

Since there are $\frac{3}{4}$ as many girls as boys in the class, $g = \frac{3}{4}b$. Plug in $\frac{3}{4}b$ for g into the fraction above.

Fraction of the class that speaks French:

$$= \frac{\frac{1}{2}b + \frac{2}{3}\left(\frac{3}{4}b\right)}{b + \frac{3}{4}b}$$

$$= \frac{\frac{1}{2}b + \frac{1}{2}b}{\frac{7}{4}b}$$

$$= \frac{b}{\frac{7}{4}b}$$

$$= \frac{4}{7}, \text{ or } .571$$

SECTION 5

The Shakespeare Pair

These paired passages present two opposing arguments on a single subject, the subject here being "Who Really Wrote Shakespeare's Plays?" The author of the first passage maintains that Francis Bacon actually wrote the plays, basing that conclusion on the assertion that Shakespeare didn't have the education and social experience necessary to create such sophisticated plays. The author of the second passage takes issue with that, claiming that Shakespeare's genius grew out of a deep understanding of human nature rather than any wide learning or arcane knowledge.

1. B

A Vocabulary-in-Context question. Here we're asked the definition of the word *entertain* in line 2, where it is used in the phrase "entertain some doubt." Well, when you entertain doubt, or entertain an idea, you are holding it in your head. You are **harboring** it, in the sense of **to harbor** as "to be host to." So choice (B) is correct.

The other choices are all acceptable dictionary definitions of the verb *entertain,* but none fits the context as well as choice (B) does. (A) **amuse** is a common synonym for *entertain,* but how does one amuse doubt? (C) **occupy** and (E) **engage** are closer, but they don't fit the sentence either. One's *mind* is occupied or engaged, but the doubt itself is not occupied or engaged. Meanwhile, (D) **cherish** adds a sense of valuing the entertained thing, as if it were something desirable.

2. D

The author claims that the person who actually wrote the plays must have had "intimate knowledge of life within royal courts and palaces," but that Shakespeare was just a commoner, without that kind of "firsthand experience" of the aristocracy. He wants to cast doubt on Shakespeare's **familiarity with the life of [aristocrats]**, or choice (D).

Shakespeare's ability to (A) **write poetically** and his (C) **ability to support himself as a playwright** never come up in Passage 1. The **knowledge of foreign places** mentioned in (B) does come up, but being a commoner is not necessarily related to Shakespeare's apparent lack of travel. Choice (E) is the closest wrong choice, since the aristocracy was the **government** in Elizabethan England, but the issue is his knowledge of all aspects of aristocratic life.

3. E

Two Shakespearian plays—*Coriolanus* and *Love's Labour's Lost*—are mentioned in lines 28–31 in connection with the allegedly specialized knowledge they contain. They support the point that the educated aristocrat Bacon was a more likely author than was the undereducated commoner Shakespeare. So (E) answers the question best.

Choice (A) is a clever wrong choice, but it's too extreme. The author's not trying to prove that *only* Bacon could have written these plays, just that Bacon was far more likely than Shakespeare to have written them. The **deep understanding of human nature** mentioned in (B) is something brought up in Passage 2, not Passage 1. The author is not comparing the two plays to **works written by Bacon,** as (C) claims. And (D) is wrong since nothing about society is mentioned with regard to *Coriolanus.* Also, it's not the **broad spectrum of society** the author alludes to with regard to *Love's Labour's Lost,* but rather the knowledge of just the upper range of society.

4. A

It's clear that Ms. Bacon is looking down on actors, of which Shakespeare was one, regarding them with the **disdain** expressed in correct choice (A).

She's not **resentful** at how the **characters are portrayed,** choice (B), since she's talking about the characters themselves and what they tell us about real-life actors. Given her opinion of actors, she certainly doesn't **regret that their conditions weren't better,** choice (C). (D) is closer, but it's a distortion. She never doubts that anyone could **create such characters;** she doubts that the author of the plays could *be like* such a character. And finally, in (E), there's no evidence in the quote that Ms. Bacon thinks the actors are inept at their art, just that they are vulgar and lowly persons.

5. B

This question sends you back to paragraph 4 of Passage 1, where Bacon's preference for anonymity is explained. The author claims that, because the plays were "controversial," Bacon felt that associating himself with them would have been "politically and personally damaging." So **he wished to protect himself from the effects of controversy,** choice (B).

(A) is wrong, since Bacon did publish a lot of writing under his own name. (C) is plausible, but it's not the reason given in paragraph 4 or anywhere else in the first passage. (D) tries to confuse us by introducing the subject of **lowly actors** from the preceding paragraph. And (E) is a fabrication since we know that Bacon was already famous from his other writings.

6. C

This question takes us to the first paragraph of Passage 2, where the emphasis is on language ability. The author doubts that Bacon, a writer primarily of academic Latin, would have had the ability to produce the exalted English in which the plays were written. That makes (C) the best answer.

(A) is a distortion. Just because Bacon wrote most of his own work in another language doesn't mean that he was **unfamiliar** with English. (B)'s emphasis on the difficult switch from **scientific writing** to **writing plays** is close, but language rather than the type of writing is the focus. There's no reason to surmise that the author doubts Bacon's ability to **cooperate** on a **committee,** choice (D). Finally, (E) is wrong because there is no evidence in the first paragraph that the author has doubts about Bacon's ability to produce that amount of work.

7. D

Back to Vocabulary-in-Context. This question asks about *premier* as it is used in the phrase "premier stylist in the English language." The author definitely wants to indicate the sublime language of the plays here, so *premier* is being used in the sense of "of the first rank," or, as choice (D) has it, **greatest.** (A), (C), and (E) all play on the sense of premier as "first in sequence" (*inaugural,* by the way, means "marking the commencement or beginning"), but the author is not referring here to *when* Shakespeare wrote. He's writing about how *well* Shakespeare wrote. On the other hand, (B) **influential** misses on two counts—first, it's not a definition of *premier* in any context, and second, the issue of influence on other writers is not brought up here.

8. B

The next Vocabulary-in-Context question concerns the adjective *encyclopedic* in line 76, where it's used to modify the noun "knowledge." The author says that Shakespeare's genius was one of common sense and perceptive intuition, not encyclopedic knowledge, which is related to great book-learning. So the knowledge described as "encyclopedic" is wide-ranging and in-depth—**comprehensive,** in other words, choice (B).

(A) **technical** is close to the sense of the context, but it's not a synonym of *encyclopedic,* so it really won't work here. (C) won't work either, since **abridged** (meaning "condensed") cannot describe the kind of exhaustive knowledge the author is describing here. And while it may take discipline to gain encyclopedic knowledge, *encyclopedic* itself cannot be defined as **disciplined,** so cut (D). Finally, (E) **specialized** isn't quite right, since it implies a narrowness of focus.

9. E

The reference to Shakespeare's status as a landowner comes in the third paragraph of Passage 2, where it is brought up to show that Shakespeare would have been "knowledgeable about legal matters related to . . . real estate." That makes (E) the best answer, "legal matters" being equivalent to **the law.**

(A) is interesting, since the author does say that owning land was quite an accomplishment for a playwright, but it has nothing to do with his knowledge of the law. (B) is off, since owning land doesn't make one automatically friendly with the highborn set. (C) is wrong, because Shakespeare's financial state is just a side issue; it's not the point of bringing up Shakespeare's landowning status. And (D) doesn't fit, since no one doubts that **Shakespeare was a commoner.**

10. A

This question directs us to lines 100–103, where the author claims that literary genius "can flower in any socioeconomic bracket." That implies that genius has little to do with a person's social and financial position—or, as correct choice (A) has it—genius doesn't depend **on a writer's external circumstances.**

(B) fails by bringing in the notion of **comprehension of human nature** from elsewhere in the passage. (C) is a common cliché, but there's no evidence here that the author felt that Shakespeare's genius was **enhanced by poverty.** In fact, this author implies that Shakespeare wasn't even all that poor. (D) may be a true statement, but recognition of genius isn't really under discussion here; it's the simple existence of genius. And (E) is a distortion; the author claims that at least one kind of genius does not *stem* from **book-learning and academic training,** but that doesn't mean that those things would **stifle** *literary genius.*

11. C

Go back to the fourth paragraph of Passage 1, where our first author claims that Bacon may have "hired a lowly actor" like Shakespeare to put his name to the plays and take the heat of controversy. How would our second author respond to this claim? The second author, remember, writes in the concluding paragraph of Passage 2 that "no elaborate theories of intrigue and secret identity are necessary to explain the accomplishment of William Shakespeare." Surely author 2 would regard the **scenario** described in Passage 1 as just this kind of **unnecessary** theory, so (C) is the best guess for how author 2 would react.

As for choice (A), author 2 may or may not agree that the plays were **controversial** in their time, so (A) won't work. (B) gets the thrust of author 2's argument wrong. Author 2 denigrates the notion that Bacon wrote the plays *not* by arguing that Bacon wasn't a great scholar, but by arguing that it didn't require a great scholar to write the plays. (D) tries to turn author 1's argument on its head. A nice idea, perhaps, but author 2 shows no hint of doing anything of the kind. And (E) brings up the notion of Shakespeare's social *respectability,* which really isn't of much concern to author 2.

12. C

What would be author 1's reaction to author 2's skepticism that Bacon, the author of Latin treatises, could be the "premier stylist in the English language"? Well, author 1's repeated assertions of Bacon's scholarly genius and Shakespeare's lack of education are both reflected in choice (C), which makes it a good bet as the correct answer.

(A)'s mention of the **similarities between Latin and English** is enough to kill this choice, since author 1 mentions no such similarities in the passage. (B) is a true statement, perhaps, but it doesn't really address the issue. (D) is fairly nonsensical, since it would weaken author 1's entire theory about why Bacon hired Shakespeare. Finally, (E) makes a good point, but again, there is no hint of this sentiment in author 1's statements.

13. D

Always check back to the passage to figure out the meaning of a Vocab-in-Context word. Here, the word "observation" refers to the phrase that "Shakespeare, in short, was Shakespeare"—a jokey comment on the author's part. None of the other choices fits the context of an informal remark, so (D) is correct here.

SECTION 6

1. B

Plug in −2 for p and 3 for q: $p^3q^2 + p^2q = (-2)^3 3^2 + (-2)^2 3 = (-8)(9) + 4(3)$, or $(-72) + 12 = -60$. (Note that a negative number raised to an *even* power becomes positive, but raised to an *odd* power stays negative.)

2. E

Keep track of the lengths you know on the diagram. B is the midpoint of AC so $AB = BC$. Since $AB = 5$, $BC = 5$. $BD = 8$, so $BC + CD = 8$. $BC = 5$, so $5 + CD = 8$, $CD = 3$. D is the midpoint of CE, so $CD = DE = 3$.

3. D

Try each answer choice until you find one that works for all of the pairs of numbers.

Choice (A), $P = N + 5$ works for 2 and 7, but not for 4 and 13.

Choice (B), $P = 2N + 3$ also works for 2 and 7, but not for 4 and 13.

Choice (C), $P = 2N + 5$, doesn't work for 2 and 7.

Choice (D), $P = 3N + 1$, works for all four pairs of numbers, so that's the answer.

4. A

$\angle PNM$ is supplementary to $\angle PNQ$, so $\angle PNM + 105° = 180°$, and $\angle PNM = 75°$. Since $PM = PN$, triangle MPN is an isosceles and $\angle PMN = \angle PNM = 75°$. The interior angles of a triangle sum to 180°, so $75 + 75 + x = 180$, and $x = 30$.

5. B

Probability is defined as the number of desired events divided by the total number of possible events. There are 5 + 6 + 4, or 15 pens in the knapsack. If he pulls out 1 pen, there are 15 different pens he might pick, or 15 possible outcomes. The desired outcome is that the pen be either red or black.

The group of acceptable pens consists of 4 + 6, or 10 pens. So the probability that one of these pens will be picked is 10 out of 15, or $\frac{10}{15}$, which we can reduce to $\frac{2}{3}$.

6. C

Pick variables for the two items and translate the given information into algebraic equations. Let h = the price of a hot dog and s = the price of a soda. The first statement is translated as $2h + s = \$3.25$, and the second as $3h + s = \$4.50$. If you subtract the first equation from the second, the s is eliminated so you can solve for h:

$$\begin{array}{r} 3h + s = \$4.50 \\ -2h + s = \$3.25 \\ \hline h \quad = \$1.25 \end{array}$$

Plug this value for h into the first equation to solve for s:

$$2(\$1.25) + s = \$3.25$$
$$\$2.50 + s = \$3.25$$
$$s = \$0.75$$

So two sodas would cost $2 \times \$0.75 = \$1.50$.

7. C

$a = f$, since all the obtuse angles formed when two parallel lines are cut by a transversal are equal. f is an exterior angle of the small triangle containing angles c, d, and e, so it is equal to the sum of the two nonadjacent interior angles, c and d. Since $a = f$ and $f = c + d$, $a = c + d$, answer choice (C).

8. D

The first 3 minutes of the phone call cost 75 cents or 0.75 dollars. If the entire call lasted x minutes, the rest of the call lasted $x - 3$ minutes. Each minute after the first 3 cost 15 cents or \$0.15, so the rest of the call cost $\$0.15(x - 3)$. So the cost of the entire call is $0.75 + 0.15(x - 3)$ dollars.

If this isn't clear, pick numbers. Let $x = 5$. The first 3 minutes cost \$0.75 and the additional $5 - 3 = 2$ minutes are \$0.15 each. So the entire call costs $\$0.75 + 2(\$0.15) = \$1.05$. Plug 5 for x into all the answer choices to see which ones give you 1.05:

(A) $0.75(3) + 0.15x = 2.25 + 0.15(5) = 2.25 + 0.75 = 3.00$. Eliminate.

(B) $0.75(3) + 0.15(x + 3) = 2.25 + 0.15(5 + 3) = 2.25 + 1.20 = 3.45$. Eliminate.

(C) $0.75 + 0.15(3 - x) = 0.75 + 0.15(3 - 5) = 0.75 - 0.30 = 0.45$. Eliminate.

(D) $0.75 + 0.15(x - 3) = 0.75 + 0.15(5 - 3) = 0.75 + 0.30 = 1.05$. Works!

(E) $0.75 + 0.15(5) = 0.75 + 0.75 = 1.50$. Eliminate.

The only choice that yields the desired result is (D), so it must be correct.

9. B

Before you can find the area of the circle, you need to find the length of the wire. The wire is in the shape of a semicircle with diameter 12. Since circumference = πd, the length of a semicircle is half of that, $\frac{\pi d}{2}$. So the length of the wire is $\frac{\pi(12)}{2}$, or 6π. When this wire is bent to form a circle, the circumference of this circle will equal 6π. So the length of the circle's diameter must equal 6, and the radius must be 3. Now you can find the area of the circle:

$$\begin{aligned} \text{Area} &= \pi r^2 \\ &= \pi(3)^2 \\ &= 9\pi \end{aligned}$$

10. C

If $a^2 - a = 72$, then $a^2 - a - 72 = 0$. Factoring this quadratic equation: $(a - 9)(a + 8) = 0$. So $a - 9 = 0$ or $a + 8 = 0$, and $a = 9$ or $a = -8$. b to the nth power equals a, so b must be a root of either 9 or -8. Look through the answer choices to find the choice that is not a root of either 9 or -8:

(A) -8: $(-8)1 = -8$, so this can be a value for b.

(B) -2: $(-2)3 = -8$, so this can be a value for b.

(C) 2: $23 = 8$, *not* -8, so this *cannot* be a value for b.

(D) 3: $32 = 9$, so this can be a value for b.

(E) 9: $91 = 9$, so this can be a value for b.

So (C) is the only answer choice that cannot be a value for b.

ROUND 6

SAT Locker Room

A

Heavy Lifting: How to Learn New Words

You have to learn some new words. Raw talent isn't enough. We'll help you learn the plays. The Root List and Word Teams List you'll find in this section can boost your knowledge of SAT-level words, and that can help you get more questions right. No one can predict exactly which words will show up on your SAT test. But there are certain words that the test makers favor. The more of these you know, the better.

Knowing roots can help you in two ways. First, instead of learning one word at a time, you can learn a whole group of words that contain a certain root. They'll be related in meaning, so if you remember one, it will be easier for you to remember others. Second, roots can often help you decode an unknown SAT word. If you recognize a familiar root, you could get a good enough idea of the word to answer the question.

TIME CONSIDERATIONS

If you have less than a month to go before you take the SAT, your study time would be best spent learning the vocabulary strategies in chapter 3. If you have more than a month to go and you have at least two hours a week to devote to studying vocabulary, follow the plan of study outlined below. If you do learn a lot of SAT-type words, it can only help you on the test.

> **Two-Minute Drill**
>
> If you're short on time, you may want to just skim through these Vocabulary Study Aids to familiarize yourself with the types of words the SAT often tests.

MEMORIZING SAT WORDS

In general, the very best way to improve your vocabulary is to read. Choose challenging, college-level material. If you encounter an unknown word, put it on a flashcard or in your vocabulary notebook.

Here's a three-step method for learning new words:

1. Memorize ten new words and roots a day, using one or more of the techniques below.
2. Reinforce what you've learned. Periodically quiz yourself on all the words you've learned so far.
3. Two weeks before the test, stop learning new words. Spend a week reviewing the word list. Rest up during the last week.

Here are some techniques for memorizing words:

Q. In what sport is the term "foil" used?

1. Learn words in groups. You can group words by a common root they contain (see the Root List for examples of this), or you can group words together if they are related in meaning. If you memorize words in this way, it may help you to remember them.
2. Use flashcards. Write down new words or word groups and run through them when you have a few minutes to spare. Put one new word or word group on one side of a 3 × 5 card and put a short definition or definitions on the back.
3. Make a vocabulary notebook. List words in one column and their definitions in another. Test yourself. Cover up the meanings, and see which words you can define from memory. Make a sample sentence using each word in context.
4. Think of hooks that lodge a new word in your mind—create visual images of words.
5. Use rhymes, pictures, songs, and any other devices that help you remember words.

To get the most out of your remaining study time, use the techniques that work for you, and stick with them.

B

SAT Root List

root—a) to noisily encourage a team
b) the basis from which a word is derived

- ❑ A, AN—not, without
  amoral, atrophy, asymmetrical, anarchy, anesthetic, anonymity, anomaly
- ❑ AB, A—from, away, apart
  abnormal, abdicate, aberration, abhor, abject, abjure, ablution, abnegate, abortive, abrogate, abscond, absolve, abstemious, abstruse, annul, avert, aversion
- ❑ AC, ACR—sharp, sour
  acid, acerbic, exacerbate, acute, acuity, acumen, acrid, acrimony
- ❑ AD, A—to, towards
  adhere, adjacent, adjunct, admonish, adroit, adumbrate, advent, abeyance, abet, accede, accretion, acquiesce, affluent, aggrandize, aggregate, alleviate, alliteration, allude, allure, ascribe, aspersion, aspire, assail, assonance, attest
- ❑ ALI, ALTR—another
  alias, alienate, inalienable, altruism
- ❑ AM, AMI—love
  amorous, amicable, amiable, amity
- ❑ AMBI, AMPHI—both
  ambiguous, ambivalent, ambidextrous, amphibious
- ❑ AMBL, AMBUL—walk
  amble, ambulatory, perambulator, somnambulist
- ❑ ANIM—mind, spirit, breath
  animal, animosity, unanimous, magnanimous
- ❑ ANN, ENN—year
  annual, annuity, superannuated, biennial, perennial
- ❑ ANTE, ANT—before
  antecedent, antediluvian, antebellum, antepenultimate, anterior, antiquity, antiquated, anticipate

- ❑ ANTHROP—human
  anthropology, anthropomorphic, misanthrope, philanthropy
- ❑ ANTI, ANT—against, opposite
  antidote, antipathy, antithesis, antacid, antagonist, antonym
- ❑ AUD—hear
  audio, audience, audition, auditory, audible
- ❑ AUTO—self
  autobiography, autocrat, autonomous
- ❑ BELLI, BELL—war
  belligerent, bellicose, antebellum, rebellion
- ❑ BENE, BEN—good
  benevolent, benefactor, beneficent, benign
- ❑ BI—two
  bicycle, bisect, bilateral, bilingual, biped
- ❑ BIBLIO—book
  Bible, bibliography, bibliophile
- ❑ BIO—life
  biography, biology, amphibious, symbiotic, macrobiotics
- ❑ BURS—money, purse
  reimburse, disburse, bursar
- ❑ CAD, CAS, CID—happen, fall
  accident, cadence, cascade, deciduous
- ❑ CAP, CIP—head
  captain, decapitate, capitulate, precipitous, precipitate, recapitulate
- ❑ CARN—flesh
  carnal, carnage, carnival, carnivorous, incarnate
- ❑ CAP, CAPT, CEPT, CIP—take, hold, seize
  capable, capacious, captivate, deception, intercept, precept, inception, anticipate, emancipation, incipient, percipient

Q. In what sport did Vitaly Scherbo win an *unprecedented* six gold medals at the 1992 Olympics?

- ❑ CED, CESS—yield, go
  cease, cessation, incessant, cede, precede, accede, recede, antecedent, intercede, secede, cession
- ❑ CHROM—color
  chrome, chromatic, monochrome
- ❑ CHRON—time
  chronology, chronic, anachronism
- ❑ CIDE—murder
  suicide, homicide, regicide, patricide
- ❑ CIRCUM—around
  circumference, circumlocution, circumnavigate, circumscribe, circumspect, circumvent

- ❑ CLIN, CLIV—slope
  incline, declivity, proclivity
- ❑ CLUD, CLUS, CLAUS, CLOIS—shut, close
  conclude, reclusive, claustrophobia, cloister, preclude, occlude
- ❑ CO, COM, CON—with, together
  coeducation, coagulate, coalesce, coerce, cogent, cognate, collateral, colloquial, colloquy, commensurate, commodious, compassion, compatriot, complacent, compliant, complicity, compunction, concerto, conciliatory, concord, concur, condone, conflagration, congeal, congenial, congenital, conglomerate, conjugal, conjure, conscientious, consecrate, consensus, consonant, constrained, contentious, contrite, contusion, convalescence, convene, convivial, convoke, convoluted, congress
- ❑ COGN, GNO—know
  recognize, cognition, cognizance, incognito, diagnosis, agnostic, prognosis, gnostic, ignorant
- ❑ CONTRA—against
  controversy, incontrovertible, contravene
- ❑ CORP—body
  corpse, corporeal, corpulence
- ❑ COSMO, COSM—world
  cosmopolitan, cosmos, microcosm, macrocosm
- ❑ CRAC, CRAT—rule, power
  democracy, bureaucracy, theocracy, autocrat, aristocrat, technocrat
- ❑ CRED—trust, believe
  incredible, credulous, credence
- ❑ CRESC, CRET—grow
  crescent, crescendo, accretion
- ❑ CULP—blame, fault
  culprit, culpable, inculpate, exculpate
- ❑ CURR, CURS—run
  current, concur, cursory, precursor, incursion
- ❑ DE—down, out, apart
  depart, debase, debilitate, declivity, decry, deface, defamatory, defunct, delegate, demarcation, demean, demur, deplete, deplore, depravity, deprecate, deride, derivative, desist, detest, devoid
- ❑ DEC—ten, tenth
  decade, decimal, decathlon, decimate
- ❑ DEMO, DEM—people
  democrat, demographics, demagogue, epidemic, pandemic, endemic
- ❑ DI, DIURN—day
  diary, quotidian, diurnal
- ❑ DIA—across
  diagonal, diatribe, diaphanous
- ❑ DIC, DICT—speak
  abdicate, diction, interdict, predict, indict, verdict

- DIS, DIF, DI—not, apart, away
  disaffected, disband, disbar, disburse, discern, discordant, discredit, discursive, disheveled, disparage, disparate, dispassionate, dispirit, dissemble, disseminate, dissension, dissipate, dissonant, dissuade, distend, differentiate, diffidence, diffuse, digress, divert

- DOC, DOCT—teach
  docile, doctrine, doctrinaire

- DOL—pain
  condolence, doleful, dolorous, indolent

- DUC, DUCT—lead
  seduce, induce, conduct, viaduct, induct

- EGO—self
  ego, egoist, egocentric

- EN, EM—in, into
  enter, entice, encumber, endemic, ensconce, enthrall, entreat, embellish, embezzle, embroil, empathy

- ERR—wander
  erratic, aberration, errant

Q. Who could be *eulogized* as the first Negro Leagues player inducted into baseball's Hall of Fame?

- EU—well, good
  eulogy, euphemism, euphony, euphoria, eurythmics, euthanasia

- EX, E—out, out of
  exit, exacerbate, excerpt, excommunicate, exculpate, execrable, exhume, exonerate, exorbitant, exorcise, expatriate, expedient, expiate, expunge, expurgate, extenuate, extort, extremity, extricate, extrinsic, exult, evoke, evict, evince, elicit, egress, egregious

- FAC, FIC, FECT, FY, FEA—make, do
  factory, facility, benefactor, malefactor, fiction, fictive, beneficent, affect, confection, refectory, magnify, unify, rectify, vilify, feasible

- FAL, FALS—deceive
  infallible, fallacious, false

- FERV—boil
  fervent, fervid, effervescent

- FID—faith, trust
  confident, diffidence, perfidious, fidelity

- FLU, FLUX—flow
  fluent, affluent, confluence, effluvia, superfluous, flux

- FORE—before
  forecast, foreboding, forestall

- FRAG, FRAC—break
  fragment, fracture, diffract, fractious, refract

- FUS—pour
  profuse, infusion, effusive, diffuse

- ❑ GEN—birth, class, kin
generation, congenital, homogeneous, heterogeneous, ingenious, engender, progenitor, progeny

- ❑ GRAD, GRESS—step
graduate, gradual, retrograde, centigrade, degrade, gradation, gradient, progress, congress, digress, transgress, ingress, egress

- ❑ GRAPH, GRAM—writing
biography, bibliography, epigraph, grammar, epigram

- ❑ GRAT—pleasing
grateful, gratitude, gratis, ingrate, congratulate, gratuitous, gratuity

- ❑ GRAV, GRIEV—heavy
grave, gravity, aggravate, grieve, aggrieve, grievous

- ❑ GREG—crowd, flock
segregate, gregarious, egregious, congregate, aggregate

- ❑ HABIT, HIBIT—have, hold
habit, cohabit, habitat, inhibit

- ❑ HAP—by chance
happen, haphazard, hapless, mishap

- ❑ HELIO, HELI—sun
heliocentric, heliotrope, aphelion, perihelion, helium

- ❑ HETERO—other
heterosexual, heterogeneous, heterodox

- ❑ HOL—whole
holocaust, catholic, holistic

- ❑ HOMO—same
homosexual, homogenize, homogeneous, homonym

- ❑ HOMO—man
homo sapiens, homicide, bonhomie

- ❑ HYDR—water
hydrant, hydrate, dehydration

- ❑ HYPER—too much, excess
hyperactive, hyperbole, hyperventilate

- ❑ HYPO—too little, under
hypodermic, hypothermia, hypochondria, hypothesis, hypothetical

- ❑ IN, IG, IL, IM, IR—not
incorrigible, indefatigable, indelible, indubitable, inept, inert, inexorable, insatiable, insentient, insolvent, insomnia, interminable, intractable, incessant, inextricable, infallible, infamy, innumerable, inoperable, insipid, intemperate, intrepid, inviolable, ignorant, ignominious, ignoble, illicit, illimitable, immaculate, immutable, impasse, impeccable, impecunious, impertinent, implacable, impotent, impregnable, improvident, impassioned, impervious, irregular

Q. Who caught the "*immaculate* reception"?

Q. Who is the NFL's all-time *interceptions* leader?

- ❑ IN, IL, IM, IR—in, on, into
  invade, inaugurate, incandescent, incarcerate, incense, indenture, induct, ingratiate, introvert, incarnate, inception, incisive, infer, infusion, ingress, innate, inquest, inscribe, insinuate, inter, illustrate, imbue, immerse, implicate, irrigate, irritate
- ❑ INTER—between, among
  intercede, intercept, interdiction, interject, interlocutor, interloper, intermediary, intermittent, interpolate, interpose, interregnum, interrogate, intersect, intervene
- ❑ INTRA, INTR—within
  intrastate, intravenous, intramural, intrinsic
- ❑ IT, ITER—between, among
  transit, itinerant, transitory, reiterate
- ❑ JECT, JET—throw
  eject, interject, abject, trajectory, jettison
- ❑ JOUR—day
  journal, adjourn, sojourn
- ❑ JUD—judge
  judge, judicious, prejudice, adjudicate
- ❑ JUNCT, JUG—join
  junction, adjunct, injunction, conjugal, subjugate
- ❑ JUR—swear, law
  jury, abjure, adjure, conjure, perjure, jurisprudence
- ❑ LAT—side
  lateral, collateral, unilateral, bilateral, quadrilateral
- ❑ LAV, LAU, LU—wash
  lavatory, laundry, ablution, antediluvian
- ❑ LEG, LEC, LEX—read, speak
  legible, lecture, lexicon
- ❑ LEV—light
  elevate, levitate, levity, alleviate
- ❑ LIBER—free
  liberty, liberal, libertarian, libertine
- ❑ LIG, LECT—choose, gather
  eligible, elect, select
- ❑ LIG, LI, LY—bind
  ligament, oblige, religion, liable, liaison, lien, ally
- ❑ LING, LANG—tongue
  lingo, language, linguistics, bilingual
- ❑ LITER—letter
  literate, alliteration, literal
- ❑ LITH—stone
  monolith, lithograph, megalith

❑ LOQU, LOC, LOG—speech, thought
eloquent, loquacious, colloquial, colloquy, soliloquy, circumlocution, interlocutor, monologue, dialogue, eulogy, philology, neologism

❑ LUC, LUM—light
lucid, elucidate, pellucid, translucent, illuminate

❑ LUD, LUS—play
ludicrous, allude, delusion, allusion, illusory

❑ MACRO—great
macrocosm, macrobiotics

❑ MAG, MAJ, MAS, MAX—great
magnify, magnanimous, magnate, magnitude, majesty, master, maximum

❑ MAL—bad
malady, maladroit, malevolent, malodorous

❑ MAN—hand
manual, manuscript, emancipate, manifest, manumission

❑ MAR—sea
submarine, marine, maritime

❑ MATER, MATR—mother
maternal, matron, matrilineal

❑ MEDI—middle
intermediary, medieval, mediate

❑ MEGA—great
megaphone, megalomania, megaton, megalith

❑ MEM, MEN—remember
memory, memento, memorabilia, reminisce

❑ METER, METR, MENS—measure
meter, thermometer, perimeter, metronome, commensurate

❑ MICRO—small
microscope, microorganism, microcosm, microbe

❑ MIS—wrong, bad, hate
misunderstand, misanthrope, misapprehension, misconstrue, misnomer, mishap

❑ MIT, MISS—send
transmit, emit, missive

❑ MOLL—soft
mollify, emollient, mollusk

❑ MON, MONIT—warn
admonish, monitor, premonition

❑ MONO—one
monologue, monotonous, monogamy, monolith, monochrome

Q. Which Major League Baseball stadium was the last to install artificial *illumination*?

❑ MOR—custom, manner
moral, mores, morose

Q. Which World Series MVP is *immortalized* outside Pittsburgh's stadium?

❑ MOR, MORT—dead
morbid, moribund, mortal, amortize

❑ MORPH—shape
amorphous, anthropomorphic, metamorphosis, morphology

❑ MOV, MOT, MOB, MOM—move
remove, motion, mobile, momentum, momentous

❑ MUT—change
mutate, mutability, immutable, commute

❑ NAT, NASC—born
native, nativity, natal, neonate, innate, cognate, nascent, renascent, renaissance

❑ NAU, NAV—ship, sailor
nautical, nauseous, navy, circumnavigate

❑ NEG—not, deny
negative, abnegate, renege

❑ NEO—new
neoclassical, neophyte, neologism, neonate

❑ NIHIL—none, nothing
annihilation, nihilism

Q. Which sports legend's *cognomen* is the "Golden Bear"?

(A) Chicago Cub Sammy Sosa

(B) Football coach Bear Bryant

(C) Golfer Jack Nicklaus

❑ NOM, NYM—name
nominate, nomenclature, nominal, cognomen, misnomer, ignominious, antonym, homonym, pseudonym, synonym, anonymity

❑ NOX, NIC, NEC, NOC—harm
obnoxious, noxious, pernicious, internecine, innocuous

❑ NOV—new
novelty, innovation, novitiate

❑ NUMER—number
numeral, numerous, innumerable, enumerate

❑ OB—against
obstruct, obdurate, obfuscate, obnoxious, obsequious, obstinate, obstreperous, obtrusive

❑ OMNI—all
omnipresent, omnipotent, omniscient, omnivorous

❑ ONER—burden
onerous, exonerate

❑ OPER—work
operate, cooperate, inoperable

❑ PAC—peace
pacify, pacifist, pacific

❑ PALP—feel
palpable, palpitation

❑ PAN—all
panorama, panacea, panegyric, pandemic, panoply

❑ PATER, PATR—father
paternal, paternity, patriot, compatriot, expatriate, patrimony, patricide, patrician

❑ PATH, PASS—feel, suffer
sympathy, antipathy, empathy, apathy, pathos, impassioned

❑ PEC—money
pecuniary, impecunious, peculation

❑ PED, POD—foot
pedestrian, pediment, expedient, biped, quadruped, tripod

❑ PEL, PULS—drive
compel, compelling, expel, propel, compulsion

❑ PEN—almost
peninsula, penultimate, penumbra

❑ PEND, PENS—hang
pendant, pendulous, compendium, suspense, propensity

❑ PER—through, by, for, throughout
perambulator, percipient, perfunctory, permeable, perspicacious, pertinacious, perturbation, perusal, perennial, peregrinate

❑ PER—against, destruction
perfidious, pernicious, perjure

❑ PERI—around
perimeter, periphery, perihelion, peripatetic

❑ PET—seek, go towards
petition, impetus, impetuous, petulant, centripetal

❑ PHIL—love
philosopher, philanderer, philanthropy, bibliophile, philology

❑ PHOB—fear
phobia, claustrophobia, xenophobia

❑ PHON—sound
phonograph, megaphone, euphony, phonetics, phonics

❑ PLAC—calm, please
placate, implacable, placid, complacent

❑ PON, POS—put, place
postpone, proponent, exponent, preposition, posit, interpose, juxtaposition, depose

❑ PORT—carry
portable, deportment, rapport

Q. What is the *penultimate* leg of the Triple Crown in horse racing?

- ❑ POT—drink
  potion, potable
- ❑ POT—power
  potential, potent, impotent, potentate, omnipotence
- ❑ PRE—before
  precede, precipitate, preclude, precocious, precursor, predilection, predisposition, preponderance, prepossessing, presage, prescient, prejudice, predict, premonition, preposition
- ❑ PRIM, PRI—first
  prime, primary, primal, primeval, primordial, pristine

Q. Who is the *progenitor* of basketball?

- ❑ PRO—ahead, forth
  proceed, proclivity, procrastinator, profane, profuse, progenitor, progeny, prognosis, prologue, promontory, propel, proponent, propose, proscribe, protestation, provoke
- ❑ PROTO—first
  prototype, protagonist, protocol
- ❑ PROX, PROP—near
  approximate, propinquity, proximity
- ❑ PSEUDO—false
  pseudoscientific, pseudonym
- ❑ PYR—fire
  pyre, pyrotechnics, pyromania
- ❑ QUAD, QUAR, QUAT—four
  quadrilateral, quadrant, quadruped, quarter, quarantine, quaternary
- ❑ QUES, QUER, QUIS, QUIR—question
  quest, inquest, query, querulous, inquisitive, inquiry
- ❑ QUIE—quiet
  disquiet, acquiesce, quiescent, requiem
- ❑ QUINT, QUIN—five
  quintuplets, quintessence
- ❑ RADI, RAMI—branch
  radius, radiate, radiant, eradicate, ramification
- ❑ RECT, REG—straight, rule
  rectangle, rectitude, rectify, regular
- ❑ REG—king, rule
  regal, regent, interregnum
- ❑ RETRO—backward
  retrospective, retroactive, retrograde
- ❑ RID, RIS—laugh
  ridiculous, deride, derision
- ❑ ROG—ask
  interrogate, derogatory, abrogate, arrogate, arrogant

- ❑ RUD—rough, crude
  rude, erudite, rudimentary
- ❑ RUPT—break
  disrupt, interrupt, rupture
- ❑ SACR, SANCT—holy
  sacred, sacrilege, consecrate, sanctify, sanction, sacrosanct
- ❑ SCRIB, SCRIPT, SCRIV—write
  scribe, ascribe, circumscribe, inscribe, proscribe, script, manuscript, scrivener
- ❑ SE—apart, away
  separate, segregate, secede, sedition
- ❑ SEC, SECT, SEG—cut
  sector, dissect, bisect, intersect, segment, secant
- ❑ SED, SID—sit
  sedate, sedentary, supersede, reside, residence, assiduous, insidious
- ❑ SEM—seed, sow
  seminar, seminal, disseminate
- ❑ SEN—old
  senior, senile, senescent
- ❑ SENT, SENS—feel, think
  sentiment, nonsense, assent, sentient, consensus, sensual
- ❑ SEQU, SECU—follow
  sequence, sequel, subsequent, obsequious, obsequy, non sequitur, consecutive
- ❑ SIM, SEM—similar, same
  similar, verisimilitude, semblance, dissemble
- ❑ SIGN—mark, sign
  signal, designation, assignation
- ❑ SIN—curve
  sine curve, sinuous, insinuate
- ❑ SOL—sun
  solar, parasol, solarium, solstice
- ❑ SOL—alone
  solo, solitude, soliloquy, solipsism
- ❑ SOMN—sleep
  insomnia, somnolent, somnambulist
- ❑ SON—sound
  sonic, consonance, dissonance, assonance, sonorous, resonate
- ❑ SOPH—wisdom
  philosopher, sophistry, sophisticated, sophomoric
- ❑ SPEC, SPIC—see, look
  spectator, circumspect, retrospective, perspective, perspicacious, perspicuous

> Q. Who is the only golfer to win four *consecutive* majors?

- ❑ SPER—hope
  prosper, prosperous, despair, desperate
- ❑ SPERS, SPAR—scatter
  disperse, sparse, aspersion, disparate
- ❑ SPIR—breathe
  respire, inspire, spiritual, aspire, transpire
- ❑ STRICT, STRING—bind
  strict, stricture, constrict, stringent, astringent
- ❑ STRUCT, STRU—build
  structure, obstruct, construe
- ❑ SUB—under
  subconscious, subjugate, subliminal, subpoena, subsequent, subterranean, subvert

Q. Who were the first men to reach the *summit* of Mount Everest?

- ❑ SUMM—highest
  summit, summary, consummate
- ❑ SUPER, SUR—above
  supervise, supercilious, supersede, superannuated, superfluous, insurmountable, surfeit
- ❑ SURGE, SURRECT—rise
  surge, resurgent, insurgent, insurrection
- ❑ SYN, SYM—together
  synthesis, sympathy, synonym, syncopation, synopsis, symposium, symbiosis
- ❑ TACIT, TIC—silent
  tacit, taciturn, reticent
- ❑ TACT, TAG, TANG—touch
  tact, tactile, contagious, tangent, tangential, tangible
- ❑ TEN, TIN, TAIN—hold, twist
  detention, tenable, tenacious, pertinacious, retinue, retain
- ❑ TEND, TENS, TENT—stretch
  intend, distend, tension, tensile, ostensible, contentious
- ❑ TERM—end
  terminal, terminus, terminate, interminable
- ❑ TERR—earth, land
  terrain, terrestrial, extraterrestrial, subterranean
- ❑ TEST—witness
  testify, attest, testimonial, testament, detest, protestation
- ❑ THE—god
  atheist, theology, apotheosis, theocracy
- ❑ THERM—heat
  thermometer, thermal, thermonuclear, hypothermia

- ❑ TIM—fear, frightened
  timid, intimidate, timorous
- ❑ TOP—place
  topic, topography, utopia
- ❑ TORT—twist
  distort, extort, tortuous
- ❑ TORP—stiff, numb
  torpedo, torpid, torpor
- ❑ TOX—poison
  toxic, toxin, intoxication
- ❑ TRACT—draw
  tractor, intractable, protract
- ❑ TRANS—across, over, through, beyond
  transport, transgress, transient, transitory, translucent, transmutation
- ❑ TREM, TREP—shake
  tremble, tremor, tremulous, trepidation, intrepid
- ❑ TURB—shake
  disturb, turbulent, perturbation
- ❑ UMBR—shadow
  umbrella, umbrage, adumbrate, penumbra
- ❑ UNI, UN—one
  unify, unilateral, unanimous
- ❑ URB—city
  urban, suburban, urbane
- ❑ VAC—empty
  vacant, evacuate, vacuous
- ❑ VAL, VAIL—value, strength
  valid, valor, ambivalent, convalescence, avail, prevail, countervail
- ❑ VEN, VENT—come
  convene, contravene, intervene, venue, convention, circumvent, advent, adventitious
- ❑ VER—true
  verify, verity, verisimilitude, veracious, aver, verdict
- ❑ VERB—word
  verbal, verbose, verbiage, verbatim
- ❑ VERT, VERS—turn
  avert, convert, pervert, revert, incontrovertible, divert, subvert, versatile, aversion
- ❑ VICT, VINC—conquer
  victory, conviction, evict, evince, invincible
- ❑ VID, VIS—see
  evident, vision, visage, supervise

Q. Who broke Wilt Chamberlain's seemingly *invincible* NBA career scoring record?

- ❑ VIL—base, mean
  vile, vilify, revile
- ❑ VIV, VIT—life
  vivid, vital, convivial, vivacious
- ❑ VOC, VOK, VOW—call, voice
  vocal, equivocate, vociferous, convoke, evoke, invoke, avow
- ❑ VOL—wish
  voluntary, malevolent, benevolent, volition
- ❑ VOLV, VOLUT—turn, roll
  revolve, evolve, convoluted
- ❑ VOR—eat
  devour, carnivore, omnivorous, voracious

Q. Which *voracious* NCAA men's team is the only team to beat three No. 1 seeded teams in the tournament?

C

SAT Word Teams List

- **Talkative**
  - garrulous
  - glib
  - loquacious
  - raconteur
  - verbose
  - voluble

- **Secret/Hidden**
  - abscond
  - alias
  - arcane
  - clandestine
  - covert
  - cryptic
  - enigma
  - furtive
  - incognito
  - inconspicuous
  - lurk
  - obscure
  - skulk
  - subterranean
  - surreptitious

- **Not Talkative**
  - concise
  - curt
  - laconic
  - pithy
  - reticent
  - succinct
  - taciturn

- **Praise**
  - accolade
  - adulation
  - commend
  - eulogize
  - exalt
  - extol
  - laud
  - lionize
  - plaudit
  - revere

Q. Who is the *verbose* boxer who won the "Thriller in Manilla"?

❑ **Criticize/Scold**
admonish
berate
castigate
censure
chastise
defame
denigrate
disdain
disparage
excoriate
malign
obloquy
rail
rebuke
reproach
reprimand
reprove
revile
upbraid
vilify

Q. Who were the NBA's co-*Rookies* of the Year for the 1994–95 season?

❑ **Stubborn**
intractable
mulish
obdurate
obstinate
pertinacious
recalcitrant
refractory
tenacious

❑ **Lazy/Lacking Energy**
indolent
lackadaisical
laggard
languid
lassitude
lethargic
listless
loiter
phlegmatic
sluggard
somnolent
torpid

❑ **Cowardly**
craven
diffident
pusillanimous
timid
timorous

❑ **Inexperienced**
callow
fledgling
infantile
ingenuous
neophyte
novice
rookie
tyro

❑ **Obedient**
amenable
assent
compliant
deferential
docile
pliant
submissive
tractable

❑ **Haughty/Pretentious**
affected
aloof
bombastic
grandiloquent
grandiose
magniloquent
mannered
ostentatious
pontificate
supercilious

❑ **Friendly**
affable
amiable
amicable
bonhomie
convivial
gregarious

❑ **Lucky**
auspicious
fortuitous
opportune
serendipity
windfall

- ❑ **Soothe**
  allay
  alleviate
  anodyne
  assuage
  liniment
  mitigate
  mollify
  pacify
  palliate
  placate

- ❑ **Hostility/Hatred**
  abhor
  anathema
  animosity
  antagonism
  antipathy
  aversion
  contentious
  deplore
  odious
  rancor

- ❑ **Stupid**
  buffoon
  dolt
  dupe
  fatuous
  imbecile
  inane
  insipid
  obtuse
  simpleton
  vacuous
  vapid

- ❑ **Subservient**
  fawn
  grovel
  obsequious
  servile
  subjection
  sycophant
  toady

- ❑ **Argumentative**
  adversarial
  bellicose
  belligerent
  fractious
  irascible
  obstreperous
  pugnacious
  quibble

- ❑ **Cautious**
  chary
  circumspect
  discretion
  leery
  prudent
  wary

- ❑ **Impermanent**
  ephemeral
  evanescent
  fleeting
  transient
  transitory

- ❑ **Ability/Intelligence**
  acumen
  adept
  adroit
  agile
  astute
  cogent
  deft
  dexterous
  erudite
  literate
  lithe
  lucidity
  sagacious
  trenchant

- ❑ **Kind/Generous**
  altruistic
  beneficent
  benevolent
  bestow
  largess
  liberal
  magnanimous
  munificent
  philanthropic

Q. Which *adroit* Major League Baseball team averages better than one world championship every four years?

D

SAT Math Scouting Report

The math on the SAT covers a lot of ground—from arithmetic to algebra to geometry.

Don't let yourself be intimidated. We've highlighted the 100 most important concepts that you'll need for SAT Math and listed them in this chapter.

You've probably been taught most of these in school already, so this list is a great way to refresh your memory.

Two-Minute Dril

Even if you only have a week or two to prepare for the SAT, you should read through this entire chapter—it's essential and helpful to review the major math concepts.

A MATH STUDY PLAN

Use this list to remind yourself of the key areas you'll need to know. Do four concepts a day, and you'll be ready within a month. If a concept continually causes you trouble, circle it and refer back to it as you try to do the questions.

NUMBER PROPERTIES

1. Integer/Noninteger

Integers are **whole numbers**; they include negative whole numbers and zero.

2. Rational/Irrational Numbers

A rational number is a number that can be expressed as **a ratio of two integers. Irrational numbers** are real numbers—they have locations on the number line; they just **can't be expressed precisely as fractions or decimals**. For the purposes of the SAT, the most important **irrational numbers** are $\sqrt{2}$, $\sqrt{3}$, and π.

3. Adding/Subtracting Signed Numbers

To **add a positive and a negative**, first ignore the signs and find the positive difference between the number parts. Then attach the sign of the original number with the larger number part. For example, to add 23 and –34, first we ignore the minus sign and find the positive difference between 23 and 34—that's 11. Then we attach the sign of the number with the larger number part—in this case it's the minus sign from the –34. So, 23 + (–34) = –11.

Make **subtraction** situations simpler by turning them into addition. For example, think of –17 – (–21) as –17 + (+21).

To **add or subtract a string of positives and negatives**, first turn everything into addition. Then combine the positives and negatives so that the string is reduced to the sum of a single positive number and a single negative number.

4. Multiplying/Dividing Signed Numbers

To multiply and/or divide positives and negatives, treat the number parts as usual and **attach a minus sign if there were originally an odd number of negatives**. For example, to multiply –2, –3, and –5, first multiply the number parts: $2 \times 3 \times 5 = 30$. Then go back and note that there were three—an odd number—negatives, so the product is negative: $(-2) \times (-3) \times (-5) = -30$.

5. PEMDAS

When performing multiple operations, remember **PEMDAS**, which means **Parentheses** first, then **Exponents**, then **Multiplication and Division** (left to right), and lastly, **Addition and Subtraction** (left to right). In the expression $9 - 2 \times (5 - 3)^2 + 6 \div 3$, begin with the parentheses: $(5 - 3) = 2$. Then do the exponent: $2^2 = 4$. Now the expression is: $9 - 2 \times 4 + 6 \div 3$. Next do the multiplication and division to get: $9 - 8 + 2$, which equals 3. If you have difficulty remembering PEMDAS, use this sentence to recall it: **P**lease **E**xcuse **M**y **D**ear **A**unt **S**ally.

6. Counting Consecutive Integers

To count consecutive integers, **subtract the smallest from the largest and add 1**. To count the integers from 13 through 31, subtract: 31 – 13 = 18. Then add 1: 18 + 1 = 19.

DIVISIBILITY

7. Factor/Multiple

The factors of integer n are the positive integers that divide into n with no remainder. The multiples of n are the integers that n divides into with no remainder. For example, 6 is a factor of 12, and 24 is a multiple of 12. 12 is both a factor and a multiple of itself, since $12 \times 1 = 12$ and $12 \div 1 = 12$.

8. Prime Factorization

To find the prime factorization of an integer, just keep breaking it up into factors until **all the factors are prime**. To find the prime factorization of 36, for example, you could begin by breaking it into 4×9: $36 = 4 \times 9 = 2 \times 2 \times 3 \times 3$.

9. Relative Primes

Relative primes are integers that have no common factor other than 1. To determine whether two integers are relative primes, break them both down to their prime factorizations. For example: $35 = 5 \times 7$, and $54 = 2 \times 3 \times 3 \times 3$. They have **no prime factors in common**, so 35 and 54 are relative primes.

10. Common Multiple

A common multiple is a number that is a multiple of two or more integers. You can always get a common multiple of two integers by **multiplying** them, but, unless the two numbers are relative primes, the product will not be the *least* common multiple. For example, to find a common multiple for 12 and 15, you could just multiply: $12 \times 15 = 180$.

11. Least Common Multiple (LCM)

To find the least common multiple, check out the **multiples of the larger integer** until you find one that's **also a multiple of the smaller**. To find the LCM of 12 and 15, begin by taking the multiples of 15: 15 is not divisible by 12; 30 is not; nor is 45. But the next multiple of 15, 60, *is* divisible by 12, so it's the LCM.

12. Greatest Common Factor (GCF)

To find the greatest common factor, break down both integers into their prime factorizations and multiply **all the prime factors they have in common**. $36 = 2 \times 2 \times 3 \times 3$, and $48 = 2 \times 2 \times 2 \times 2 \times 3$. What they have in common is two 2s and one 3, so the GCF is $2 \times 2 \times 3 = 12$.

13. Even/Odd

To predict whether a sum, difference, or product will be even or odd, just **take simple numbers such as 1 and 2 and see what happens**. There are rules—"odd times even is even," for example—but there's no need to memorize them. What happens with one set of numbers generally happens with all similar sets.

14. Multiples of 2 and 4

An integer is divisible by 2 (which is even) if the **last digit is even**. An integer is divisible by 4 if the **last two digits form a multiple of 4**. The last digit of 562 is 2, which is even, so 562 is a multiple of 2. The last two digits form 62, which is *not* divisible by 4, so 562 is not a multiple of 4. The integer 512, however is divisible by four because the last two digits form 12, which is a multiple of 4.

15. Multiples of 3 and 9

An integer is divisible by 3 if the **sum of its digits is divisible by 3**. An integer is divisible by 9 if the **sum of its digits is divisible by 9**. The sum of the digits in 957 is 21, which is divisible by 3 but not by 9, so 957 is divisible by 3 but not by 9.

16. Multiples of 5 and 10

An integer is divisible by 5 if the **last digit is 5 or 0**. An integer is divisible by 10 if the **last digit is 0**. The last digit of 665 is 5, so 665 is a multiple of 5 but *not* a multiple of 10.

17. Remainders

The remainder is the **whole number left over after division**. 487 is 2 more than 485, which is a multiple of 5, so when 487 is divided by 5, the remainder will be 2.

Fractions and Decimals

18. Reducing Fractions

To reduce a fraction to lowest terms, **factor out and cancel** all factors the numerator and denominator have in common.

$$\frac{28}{36} = \frac{4 \times 7}{4 \times 9} = \frac{7}{9}$$

19. Adding/Subtracting Fractions

To add or subtract fractions, first find a **common denominator**, then add or subtract the numerators.

$$\frac{2}{15} + \frac{3}{10} = \frac{4}{30} + \frac{9}{30} = \frac{4+9}{30} = \frac{13}{30}$$

20. Multiplying Fractions

To multiply fractions, **multiply** the numerators and **multiply** the denominators.

$$\frac{5}{7} \times \frac{3}{4} = \frac{5 \times 3}{7 \times 4} = \frac{15}{28}$$

21. Dividing Fractions

To divide fractions, **invert** the second one and **multiply**.

$$\frac{1}{2} \div \frac{3}{5} = \frac{1}{2} \times \frac{5}{3} = \frac{1 \times 5}{2 \times 3} = \frac{5}{6}$$

22. Converting a Mixed Number to an Improper Fraction

To convert a mixed number to an improper fraction, **multiply** the whole number part by the denominator, then **add** the numerator. The result is the new numerator (over the same denominator). To convert $7\frac{1}{3}$, first multiply 7 by 3, then add 1, to get the new numerator of 22. Put that over the same denominator, 3, to get $\frac{22}{3}$.

23. Converting an Improper Fraction to a Mixed Number

To convert an improper fraction to a mixed number, divide the denominator into the numerator to get a **whole number quotient with a remainder**. The quotient becomes the whole number part of the mixed number, and the remainder becomes the new numerator—with the same denominator. For example, to convert $\frac{108}{5}$, first divide 5 into 108, which yields 21 with a remainder of 3. Therefore, $\frac{108}{5} = 21\frac{3}{5}$.

24. Reciprocal

To find the reciprocal of a fraction, **switch the numerator and the denominator**. The reciprocal of $\frac{3}{7}$ is $\frac{7}{3}$. The reciprocal of 5 is $\frac{1}{5}$. The product of reciprocals is 1.

25. Comparing Fractions

One way to compare fractions is to **re-express them with a common denominator**. $\frac{3}{4} = \frac{21}{28}$ and $\frac{5}{7} = \frac{20}{28}$. $\frac{21}{28}$ is greater than $\frac{20}{28}$, so $\frac{3}{4}$ is greater than $\frac{5}{7}$. Another way to compare fractions is to **convert them both to decimals**. $\frac{3}{4}$ converts to .75 , and $\frac{5}{7}$ converts to approximately .714.

26. Converting Fractions to Decimals

To convert a fraction to a decimal, **divide the bottom into the top**. To convert $\frac{5}{8}$, divide 8 into 5, yielding .625.

27. Converting Decimals to Fractions

To convert a decimal to a fraction, set the decimal over 1 and **multiply the numerator and denominator by ten raised to the number of digits to the right of the decimal point**. For instance, to convert .625 to a fraction, you would multiply $\frac{.625}{1}$ by $\frac{10^3}{10^3}$, or $\frac{1000}{1000}$. Then simplify: $\frac{625}{1000} = \frac{5 \times 125}{8 \times 125} = \frac{5}{8}$.

28. Repeating Decimal

To find a particular digit in a repeating decimal, note the **number of digits in the cluster that repeats**. If there are 2 digits in that cluster, then every second digit is the same. If there are three digits in that cluster, then every third digit is the same. And so on. For example, the decimal equivalent of $\frac{1}{27}$ is .037037037..., which is best written $.\overline{037}$. There are three digits in the repeating cluster, so every third digit is the same: 7. To find the 50th digit, look for the multiple of three just less than 50—that's 48. The 48th digit is 7, and with the 49th digit the pattern repeats with 0. The 50th digit is 3.

29. Identifying the Parts and the Whole

The key to solving most fractions and percents story problems is to identify the part and the whole. Usually you'll find the **part** associated with the verb ***is/are*** and the **whole** associated with the word ***of***. In the sentence, "Half of the boys are blonds," the whole is the boys ("of the boys"), and the part is the blonds ("are blonds").

PERCENTS

30. Percent Formula

Whether you need to find the part, the whole, or the percent, use the same formula:

Part = Percent × Whole

Example: What is 12% of 25?
Setup: Part = .12 × 25

Example: 15 is 3% of what number?
Setup: 15 = .03 × Whole

Example: 45 is what percent of 9?
Setup: 45 = Percent × 9

31. Percent Increase and Decrease

To increase a number by a percent, **add the percent to 100 percent**, convert to a decimal, and multiply. To increase 40 by 25 percent, add 25 percent to 100 percent, convert 125 percent to 1.25, and multiply by 40. 1.25 × 40 = 50.

32. Finding the Original Whole

To find the **original whole before a percent increase or decrease, set up an equation**. Think of the result of a 15 percent increase over x as $1.15x$.

Example: After a 5 percent increase, the population was 59,346. What was the population before the increase?
Setup: $1.05x = 59{,}346$

33. Combined Percent Increase and Decrease

To determine the combined effect of multiple percent increases and/or decreases, **start with 100 and see what happens**.

Example: A price went up 10 percent one year, and the new price went up 20 percent the next year. What was the combined percent increase?
Setup: First year: 100 + (10 percent of 100) = 110. Second year: 110 + (20 percent of 110) = 132. That's a combined 32 percent increase.

RATIOS, PROPORTIONS, AND RATES

34. Setting up a Ratio

To find a ratio, put the number associated with the word ***of*** **on top** and the quantity associated with the word ***to*** **on the bottom** and reduce. The ratio of 20 oranges to 12 apples is $\frac{20}{12}$, which reduces to $\frac{5}{3}$.

35. Part-to-Part Ratios and Part-to-Whole Ratios

If the parts add up to the whole, a part-to-part ratio can be turned into two part-to-whole ratios by putting **each number in the original ratio over the sum of the numbers.** If the ratio of males to females is 1 to 2, then the males-to-people ratio is $\frac{1}{1+2} = \frac{1}{3}$ and the females-to-people ratio is $\frac{2}{1+2} = \frac{2}{3}$. In other words, $\frac{2}{3}$ of all the people are female.

36. Solving a Proportion

To solve a proportion, **cross-multiply:**

$$\frac{x}{5} = \frac{3}{4}$$
$$4x = 3 \times 5$$
$$x = \frac{15}{4} = 3.75$$

37. Rate

To solve a rates problem, **use the units** to keep things straight.

Example: If snow is falling at the rate of one foot every four hours, how many inches of snow will fall in seven hours?

Setup:
$$\frac{1 \text{ foot}}{4 \text{ hours}} = \frac{x \text{ inches}}{7 \text{ hours}}$$
$$\frac{12 \text{ inches}}{4 \text{ hours}} = \frac{x \text{ inches}}{7 \text{ hours}}$$
$$4x = 12 \times 7$$
$$x = 21$$

38. Average Rate

Average rate is *not* simply the average of the rates.

$$\text{Average } A \text{ per } B = \frac{\text{Total } A}{\text{Total } B}$$

$$\text{Average Speed} = \frac{\text{Total distance}}{\text{Total time}}$$

To find the average speed for 120 miles at 40 mph and 120 miles at 60 mph, **don't just average the two speeds**. First figure out the total distance and the total time. The total distance is 120 + 120 = 240 miles. The times are two hours for the first leg and three hours for the second leg, or five hours total. The average speed, then, is $\frac{240}{5}$ = 48 miles per hour.

AVERAGES

39. Average Formula

To find the average of a set of numbers, **add them up and divide by the number of numbers**.

$$\textbf{Average} = \frac{\textbf{Sum of the terms}}{\textbf{Number of terms}}$$

To find the average of the five numbers 12, 15, 23, 40, and 40, first add them: 12 + 15 + 23 + 40 + 40 = 130. Then divide the sum by 5: 130 ÷ 5 = 26.

40. Average of Evenly Spaced Numbers

To find the average of evenly spaced numbers, just **average the smallest and the largest**. The average of all the integers from 13 through 77 is the same as the average of 13 and 77:

$$\frac{13 + 77}{2} = \frac{90}{2} = 45$$

41. Using the Average to Find the Sum

Sum = (Average) × (Number of terms)

If the average of ten numbers is 50, then they add up to 10 × 50, or 500.

42. Finding the Missing Number

To find a missing number when you're given the average, **use the sum**. If the average of four numbers is 7, then the sum of those four numbers is 4 × 7, or 28. Suppose that three of the numbers are 3, 5, and 8. These three numbers add up to 16 of that 28, which leaves 12 for the fourth number.

43. Median

The median of a set of numbers is the **value that falls in the middle of the set**. If you have five test scores, and they are 88, 86, 57, 94, and 73, you must first list the scores in increasing or decreasing order: 57, 73, 86, 88, 94.

The median is the middle number, or 86. If there is an even number of values in a set (six test scores, for instance), simply take the average of the two middle numbers.

44. Mode

The mode of a set of numbers is the **value that appears most often**. If your test scores were 88, 57, 68, 85, 99, 93, 93, 84, and 81, the mode of the scores would be 93 because it appears more often than any other score. If there is a tie for the most common value in a set, the set has more than one mode.

POSSIBILITIES AND PROBABILITY

45. Counting the Possibilities

The fundamental counting principle: If there are ***m*** **ways** one event can happen and ***n*** **ways** a second event can happen, then there are ***m*** **×** ***n*** **ways** for the two events to happen. For example, with five shirts and seven pairs of pants to choose from, you can put together 5 × 7 = 35 different outfits.

46. Probability

$$\textbf{Probability} = \frac{\textbf{Favorable outcomes}}{\textbf{Total possible outcomes}}$$

For example, if you have 12 shirts in a drawer and nine of them are white, the probability of picking a white shirt at random is $\frac{9}{12} = \frac{3}{4}$. This probability can also be expressed as .75 or 75 percent.

POWERS AND ROOTS

47. Multiplying and Dividing Powers

To multiply powers with the same base, **add the exponents and keep the same base:**

$$x^3 \times x^4 = x^{3+4} = x^7$$

To divide powers with the same base, **subtract the exponents and keep the same base:**

$$y^{13} \div y^8 = y^{13-8} = y^5$$

48. Raising Powers to Powers

To raise a power to a power, **multiply the exponents**:

$$(x^3)^4 = x^{3 \times 4} = x^{12}$$

49. Simplifying Square Roots

To simplify a square root, **factor out the perfect squares** under the radical, unsquare them and put the result in front.

$$\sqrt{12} = \sqrt{4 \times 3} = \sqrt{4} \times \sqrt{3} = 2\sqrt{3}$$

50. Adding and Subtracting Roots

You can add or subtract radical expressions **when the part under the radicals is the same:**

$$2\sqrt{3} + 3\sqrt{3} = 5\sqrt{3}$$

Don't try to add or subtract when the radical parts are different. There's not much you can do with an expression like:

$$3\sqrt{5} + 3\sqrt{7}$$

51. Multiplying and Dividing Roots

The product of square roots is equal to the **square root of the product:**

$$\sqrt{3} \times \sqrt{5} = \sqrt{3 \times 5} = \sqrt{15}$$

The quotient of square roots is equal to the **square root of the quotient:**

$$\frac{\sqrt{6}}{\sqrt{3}} = \sqrt{\frac{6}{3}} = \sqrt{2}$$

ALGEBRAIC EXPRESSIONS

52. Evaluating an Expression

To evaluate an algebraic expression, **plug in** the given values for the unknowns and calculate according to **PEMDAS**. To find the value of $x^2 + 5x - 6$ when $x = -2$, plug in -2 for x: $(-2)^2 + 5(-2) - 6 = 4 - 10 - 6 = -12$.

53. Adding and Subtracting Monomials

To combine like terms, **keep the variable part unchanged while adding or subtracting the coefficients:**

$$2a + 3a = (2 + 3)a = 5a$$

54. Adding and Subtracting Polynomials

To add or subtract polynomials, **combine like terms.**

$$(3x^2 + 5x - 7) - (x^2 + 12) =$$
$$(3x^2 - x^2) + 5x + (-7 - 12) =$$
$$2x^2 + 5x - 19$$

55. Multiplying Monomials

To multiply monomials, **multiply the coefficients and the variables separately:**

$$2a \times 3a = (2 \times 3)(a \times a) = 6a^2$$

56. Multiplying Binomials—FOIL

To multiply binomials, use **FOIL**. To multiply $(x + 3)$ by $(x + 4)$, first multiply the **F**irst terms: $x \times x = x^2$. Next the **O**uter terms: $x \times 4 = 4x$. Then the **I**nner terms: $3 \times x = 3x$. And finally the **L**ast terms: $3 \times 4 = 12$. Then add and combine like terms:

$$x^2 + 4x + 3x + 12 = x^2 + 7x + 12$$

57. Multiplying Other Polynomials

FOIL works only when you want to multiply two binomials. If you want to multiply polynomials with more than two terms, make sure you **multiply each term in the first polynomial by each term in the second.**

$$(x^2 + 3x + 4)(x + 5) =$$
$$x^2(x + 5) + 3x(x + 5) + 4(x + 5) =$$
$$x^3 + 5x^2 + 3x^2 + 15x + 4x + 20 =$$
$$x^3 + 8x^2 + 19x + 20$$

After multiplying two polynomials together, the number of terms in your expression before simplifying should equal the number of terms in one polynomial multiplied by the number of terms in the second. In the example above, you should have $3 \times 2 = 6$ terms in the product before you simplify like terms.

FACTORING ALGEBRAIC EXPRESSIONS

58. Factoring out a Common Divisor

A factor common to all terms of a polynomial can be **factored out**. Each of the three terms in the polynomial $3x^3 + 12x^2 - 6x$ contains a factor of $3x$. Pulling out the common factor yields $3x(x^2 + 4x - 2)$.

59. Factoring the Difference of Squares

One of the test maker's favorite factorables is the **difference of squares.**

$$a^2 - b^2 = (a - b)(a + b)$$

$x^2 - 9$, for example, factors to $(x - 3)(x + 3)$.

60. Factoring the Square of a Binomial

Learn to recognize polynomials that are squares of binomials:

$$a^2 + 2ab + b^2 = (a + b)^2$$
$$a^2 - 2ab + b^2 = (a - b)^2$$

For example, $4x^2 + 12x + 9$ factors to $(2x + 3)^2$, and $n^2 - 10n + 25$ factors to $(n - 5)^2$.

61. Factoring Other Polynomials—FOIL in Reverse

To factor a quadratic expression, **think about what binomials you could use FOIL on to get that quadratic expression**. To factor $x^2 - 5x + 6$, think about what **F**irst terms will produce x^2, what **L**ast terms will produce +6, and what **O**uter and **I**nner terms will produce $-5x$. Some common sense—and a little trial and error—lead you to $(x - 2)(x - 3)$.

62. Simplifying an Algebraic Fraction

Simplifying an algebraic fraction is a lot like simplifying a numerical fraction. The general idea is to **find factors common to the numerator and denominator and cancel them**. Thus, simplifying an algebraic fraction begins with factoring.

For example, to simplify $\frac{x^2 - x - 12}{x^2 - 9}$, first factor the numerator and denominator:

$$\frac{x^2 - x - 12}{x^2 - 9} = \frac{(x-4)(x+3)}{(x-3)(x+3)}$$

Canceling $x + 3$ from the numerator and denominator leaves you with $\frac{x-4}{x-3}$.

SOLVING EQUATIONS

63. Solving a Linear Equation

To solve an equation, do whatever is necessary to both sides to **isolate the variable**. To solve the equation $5x - 12 = -2x + 9$, first get all the xs on one side by adding $2x$ to both sides: $7x - 12 = 9$. Then add 12 to both sides: $7x = 21$. Then divide both sides by 7: $x = 3$.

64. Solving "in Terms of"

To solve an equation for one variable **in terms of** another means to **isolate the one variable on one side of the equation**, leaving an expression containing the other variable on the other side of the equation. To solve the equation $3x - 10y = -5x + 6y$ for x in terms of y, isolate x:

$$3x - 10y = -5x + 6y$$
$$3x + 5x = 6y + 10y$$
$$8x = 16y$$
$$x = 2y$$

65. Translating from English into Algebra

To translate from English into algebra, **look for the key words and systematically turn phrases into algebraic expressions and sentences into equations**. Be careful about order, especially when subtraction is called for.

Example: The charge for a phone call is r cents for the first three minutes and s cents for each minute thereafter. What is the cost, in cents, of a phone call lasting exactly t minutes? ($t > 3$)

Setup: The charge begins with r, and then something more is added, depending on the length of the call. The amount added is s times the number of minutes past three minutes. If the total number of minutes is t, then the number of minutes past three is $t - 3$. So the charge is $r + s(t - 3)$.

66. Solving a Quadratic Equation

To solve a quadratic equation, put it in the "$ax^2 + bx + c = 0$" form, **factor** the left side (if you can), and set each factor equal to 0 separately to get the two solutions. To solve $x^2 + 12 = 7x$, first rewrite it as $x^2 - 7x + 12 = 0$. Then factor the left side:

$$(x - 3)(x - 4) = 0$$
$$x - 3 = 0 \text{ or } x - 4 = 0$$
$$x = 3 \text{ or } 4$$

67. Solving a System of Equations

You can solve for two variables only if you have two distinct equations. Two forms of the same equation will not be adequate. **Combine the equations** in such a way that **one of the variables cancels out**. To solve the two equations $4x + 3y = 8$ and $x + y = 3$, multiply both sides of the second equation by -3 to get: $-3x - 3y = -9$. Now add the two equations; the $3y$ and the $-3y$ cancel out, leaving: $x = -1$. Plug that back into either one of the original equations and you'll find that $y = 4$.

68. Solving an Inequality

To solve an inequality, do whatever is necessary to both sides to **isolate the variable**. Just remember that when you **multiply or divide both sides by a negative number**, you must **reverse the sign**. To solve $-5x + 7 < -3$, subtract 7 from both sides to get: $-5x < -10$. Now divide both sides by -5, remembering to reverse the sign: $x > 2$.

COORDINATE GEOMETRY

69. Finding the Distance Between Two Points

To find the distance between points, use the **Pythagorean theorem or special right triangles**. The difference between the *x*s is one leg and the difference between the *y*s is the other.

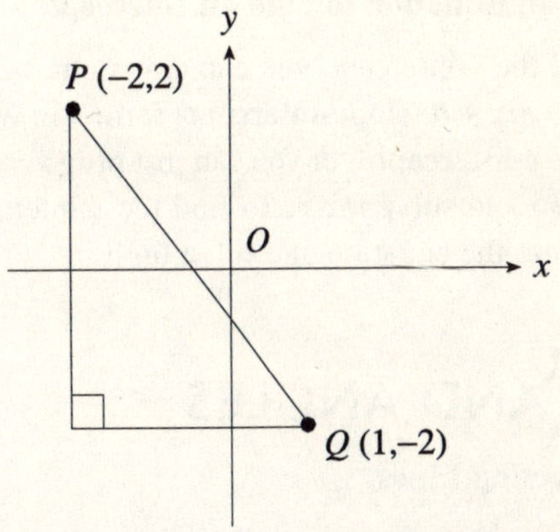

In the figure above, PQ is the hypotenuse of a 3-4-5 triangle, so $PQ = 5$.

You can also use the **distance formula**:

$$d = \sqrt{(x_1 - x_2)^2 + (y_1 - y_2)^2}$$

To find the distance between $R(3, 6)$ and $S(5, -2)$:

$$d = \sqrt{(3-5)^2 + [6-(-2)]^2}$$
$$= \sqrt{(-2)^2 + (8)^2}$$
$$= \sqrt{68} = 2\sqrt{17}$$

70. Using Two Points to Find the Slope

$$\textbf{Slope} = \frac{\textbf{Change in } y}{\textbf{Change in } x} = \frac{\textbf{Rise}}{\textbf{Run}}$$

The slope of the line that contains the points $A(2, 3)$ and $B(0, -1)$ is:

$$\frac{y_A - y_B}{x_A - x_B} = \frac{3-(-1)}{2-0} = \frac{4}{2} = 2$$

71. Using an Equation to Find the Slope

To find the slope of a line from an equation, put the equation into the **slope-intercept** form:

$$y = mx + b$$

The **slope is m**. To find the slope of the equation $3x + 2y = 4$, rearrange it:

$$3x + 2y = 4$$
$$2y = -3x + 4$$
$$y = -\frac{3}{2}x + 2$$

The slope is $-\frac{3}{2}$.

72. Using an Equation to Find an Intercept

To find the y-intercept, you can either put the equation into $y = mx + b$ **(slope-intercept)** form—in which case **b is the y-intercept**—or you can just **plug $x = 0$** into the equation and **solve for y**. To find the x-intercept, **plug $y = 0$** into the equation and **solve for x**.

LINES AND ANGLES

73. Intersecting Lines

When two lines intersect, **adjacent angles are supplementary and vertical angles are equal**.

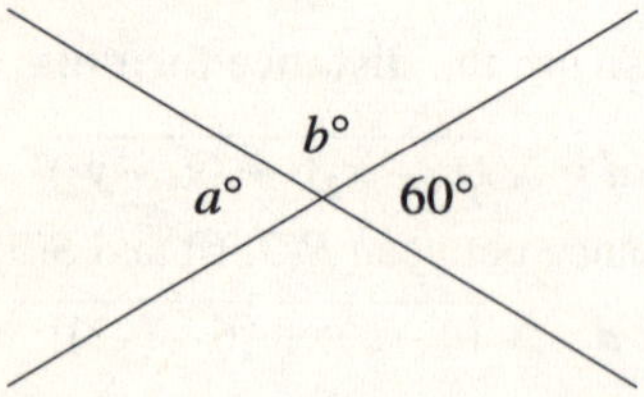

In the figure above, the angles marked $a°$ and $b°$ are adjacent and supplementary, so $a + b = 180$. Furthermore, the angles marked $a°$ and 60° are vertical and equal, so $a = 60$.

74. Parallel Lines and Transversals

A transversal across parallel lines forms **four equal acute angles and four equal obtuse angles**.

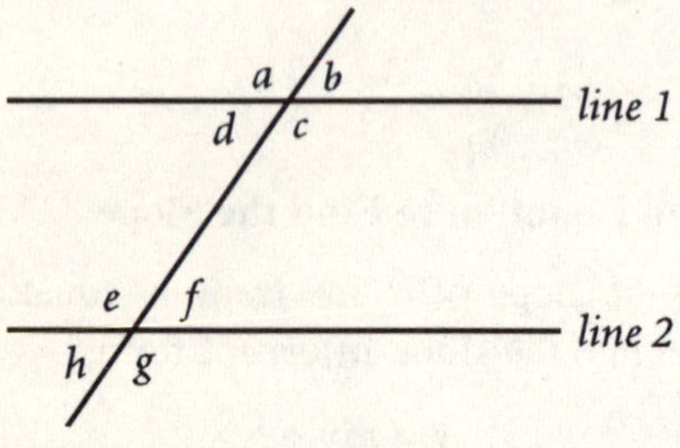

In the figure above, line 1 is parallel to line 2. Angles a, c, e, and g are obtuse, so they are all equal. Angles b, d, f, and h are acute, so they are all equal.

Furthermore, **any of the acute angles is supplementary to any of the obtuse angles**. Angles a and h are supplementary, as are b and e, c and f, and so on.

TRIANGLES—GENERAL

75. Interior Angles of a Triangle

The three angles of any triangle add up to 180°.

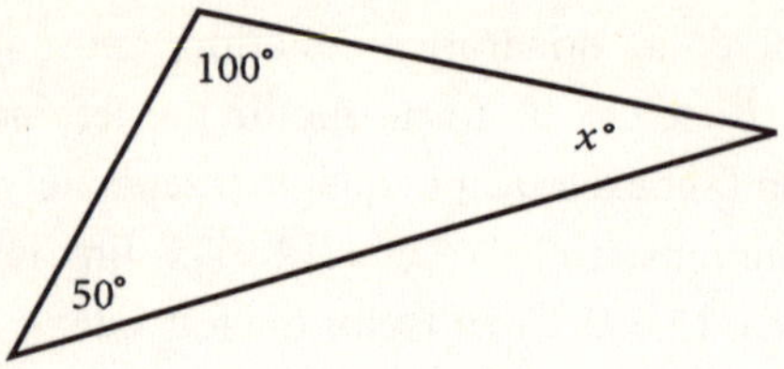

In the figure above, $x + 50 + 100 = 180$, so $x = 30$.

76. Exterior Angles of a Triangle

An exterior angle of a triangle is equal to the **sum of the remote interior angles.**

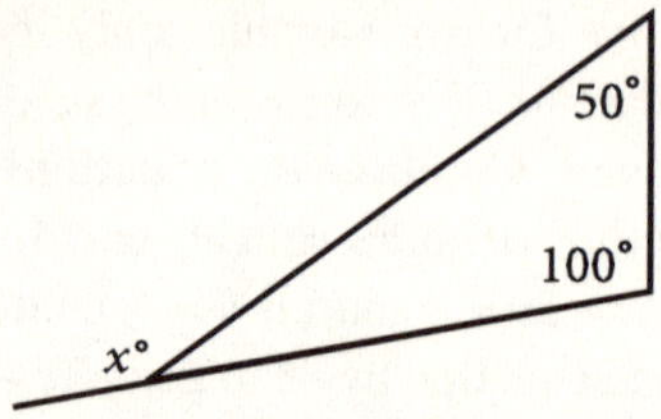

In the figure above, the exterior angle labeled $x°$ is equal to the sum of the remote angles: $x = 50 + 100 = 150$.

The three exterior angles of a triangle add up to 360°.

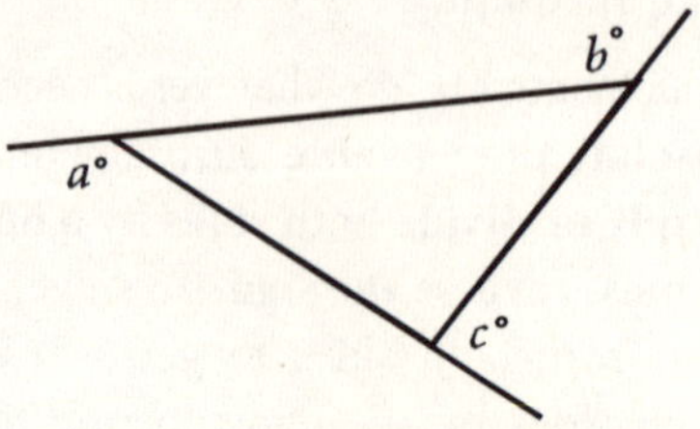

In the figure above, $a + b + c = 360$.

77. Similar Triangles

Similar triangles have the same shape; **corresponding angles are equal and corresponding sides are proportional.**

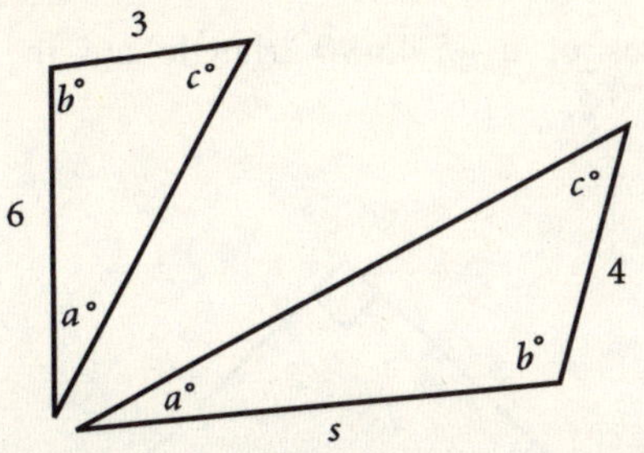

The triangles above are similar because they have the same angles. The 3 corresponds to the 4 and the 6 corresponds to the *s*.

$$\frac{3}{4} = \frac{6}{s}$$

$$3s = 24$$

$$s = 8$$

78. Area of a Triangle

Area of Triangle = $\frac{1}{2}$(base)(height)

The height is the perpendicular distance between the side that's chosen as the base and the opposite vertex.

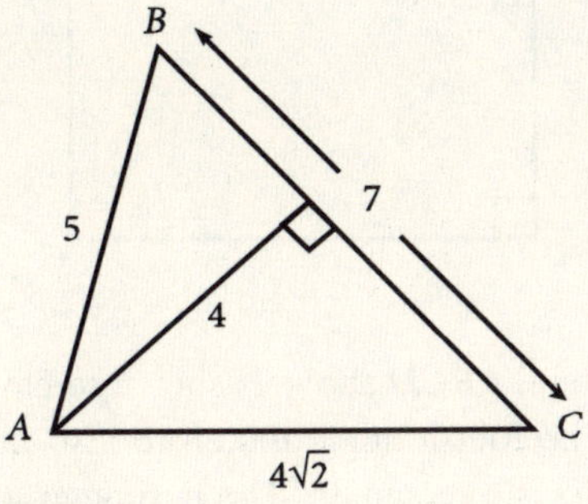

In the triangle above, 4 is the height when the 7 is chosen as the base.

$$\text{Area} = \frac{1}{2}bh = \frac{1}{2}(7)(4) = 14$$

79. Triangle Inequality Theorem

The length of one side of a triangle must be **greater than the difference and less than the sum** of the lengths of the other two sides. For example, if it is given that the length of one side is 3 and the length of another side is 7, then you know that the length of the third side must be greater than $7 - 3 = 4$ and less than $7 + 3 = 10$.

80. Isosceles Triangles

An isosceles triangle is a triangle that has **two equal sides**. Not only are two sides equal, but the angles opposite the equal sides, called base angles, are also equal.

81. Equilateral Triangles

Equilateral triangles are triangles in which **all three sides are equal**. Since all the sides are equal, all the angles are also equal. All three angles in an equilateral triangle measure 60 degrees, regardless of the lengths of sides.

RIGHT TRIANGLES

82. Pythagorean Theorem

For all right triangles:

$$(\text{leg}_1)^2 + (\text{leg}_2)^2 = (\text{hypotenuse})^2$$

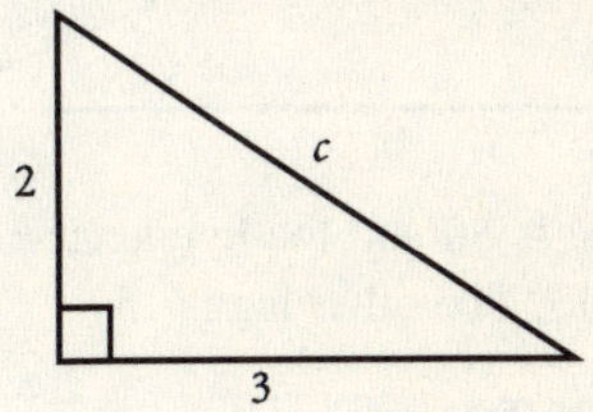

If one leg is 2 and the other leg is 3, then:

$$2^2 + 3^2 = c^2$$
$$c^2 = 4 + 9$$
$$c = \sqrt{13}$$

83. The 3-4-5 Triangle

If a right triangle's leg-to-leg ratio is 3:4, or if the leg-to-hypotenuse ratio is 3:5 or 4:5, it's a 3-4-5 triangle and you don't need to use the Pythagorean theorem to find the third side. Just figure out what multiple of 3-4-5 it is.

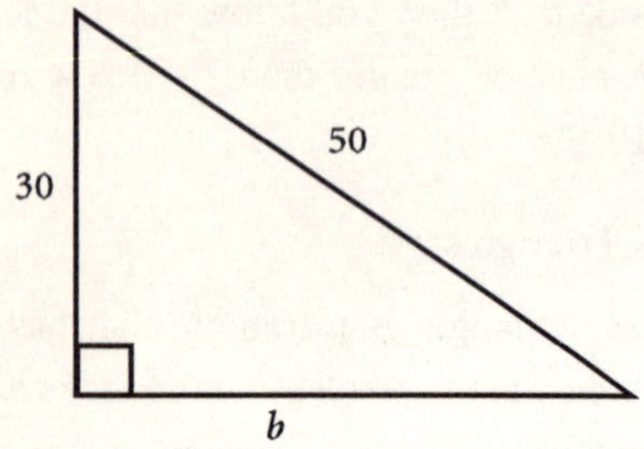

In the right triangle shown, one leg is 30 and the hypotenuse is 50. This is 10 times 3-4-5. The other leg is 40.

84. The 5-12-13 Triangle

If a right triangle's leg-to-leg ratio is 5:12, or if the leg-to-hypotenuse ratio is 5:13 or 12:13, then it's a 5-12-13 triangle. You don't need to use the Pythagorean theorem to find the third side. Just figure out what multiple of 5-12-13 it is.

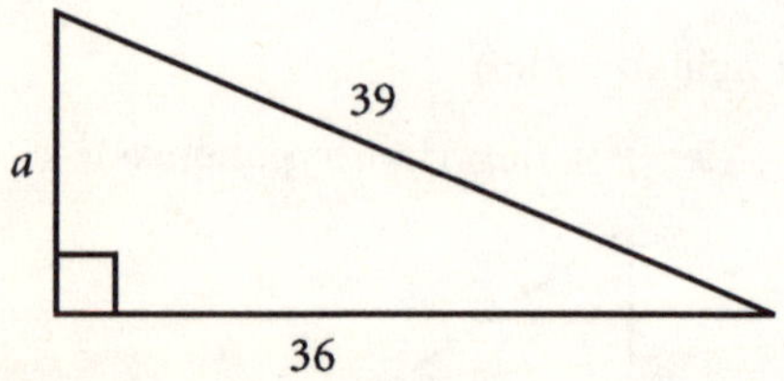

Here one leg is 36 and the hypotenuse is 39. This is 3 times 5-12-13. The other leg is 15.

85. The 30-60-90 Triangle

The sides of a 30-60-90 triangle are in a ratio of $x : x\sqrt{3} : 2x$; the Pythagorean theorem is not necessary.

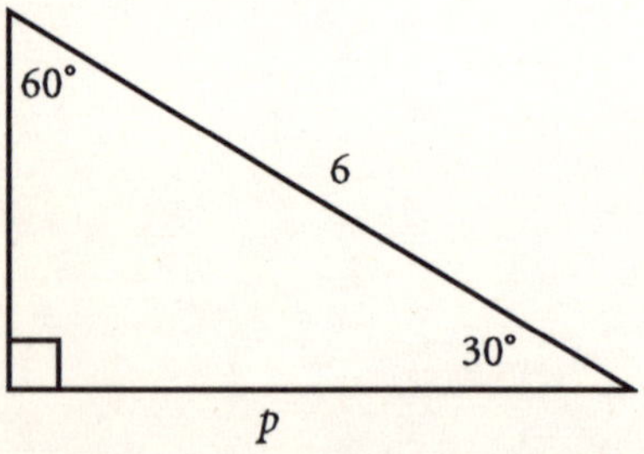

If the hypotenuse is 6, then the shorter leg is half that, or 3; and then the longer leg is equal to the short leg times $\sqrt{3}$, or $3\sqrt{3}$.

86. The 45-45-90 Triangle

The sides of a 45-45-90 triangle are in a ratio of $x : x : x\sqrt{2}$.

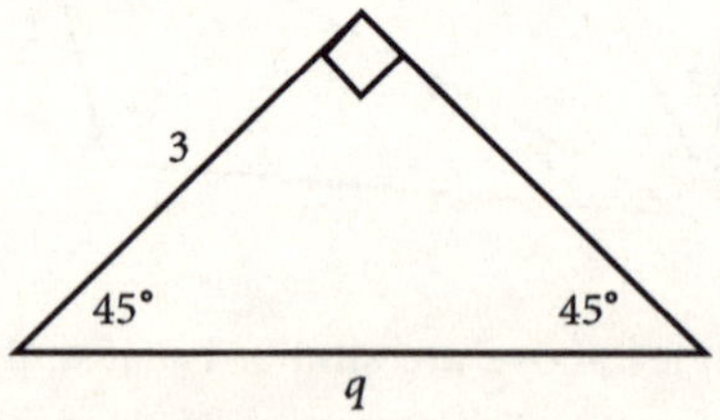

If one leg is 3, then the other leg is also 3, and the hypotenuse is equal to a leg times $\sqrt{2}$, or $3\sqrt{2}$.

OTHER POLYGONS

87. Characteristics of a Rectangle

A rectangle is a **four-sided figure with four right angles**. Opposite sides are equal. Diagonals are equal.

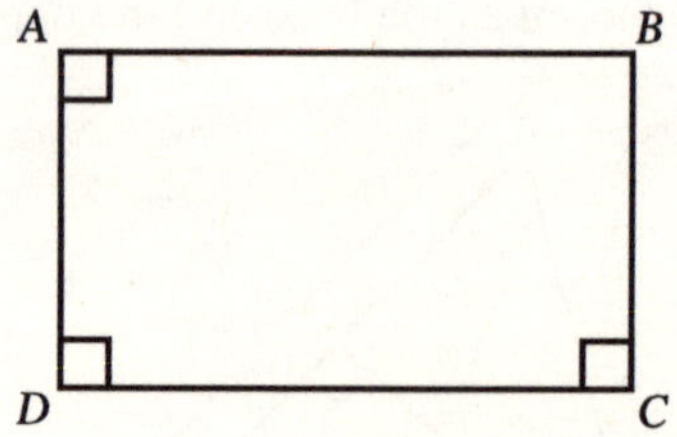

Quadrilateral *ABCD* above is shown to have three right angles. The fourth angle therefore also measures 90°, and *ABCD* is a rectangle. The perimeter of a rectangle is equal to the sum of the lengths of the four sides, which is equivalent to 2(length + width).

88. Area of a Rectangle

Area of Rectangle = Length × Width

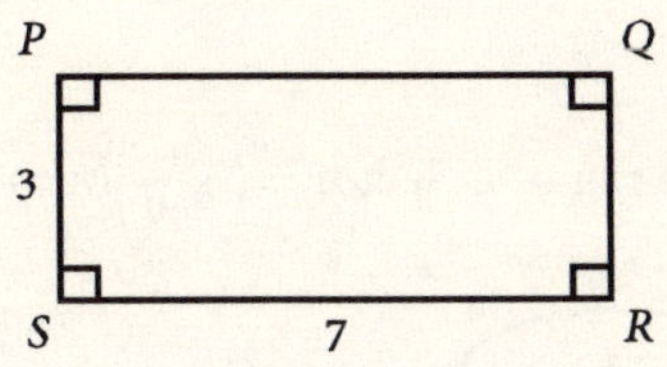

The area of a 7-by-3 rectangle is $7 \times 3 = 21$.

89. Characteristics of a Parallelogram

A parallelogram has **two pairs of parallel sides.** Opposite sides are equal. Opposite angles are equal. Consecutive angles add up to 180°.

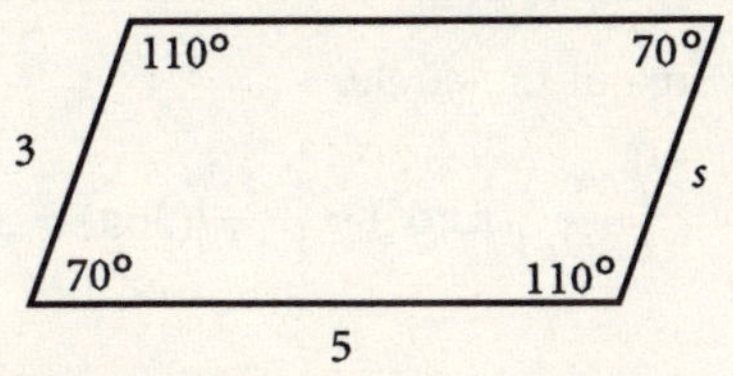

In the figure above, s is the length of the side opposite the 3, so $s = 3$.

90. Area of a Parallelogram

Area of Parallelogram = base × height

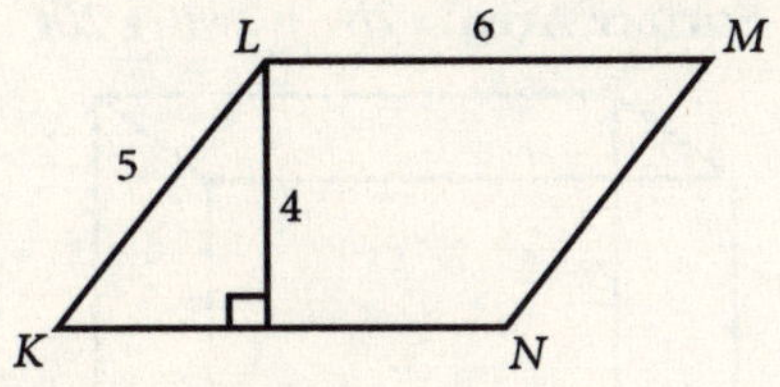

In parallelogram *KLMN* above, 4 is the height when *LM* or *KN* is used as the base. Base × height = $6 \times 4 = 24$.

91. Characteristics of a Square

A square is a **rectangle with four equal sides.**

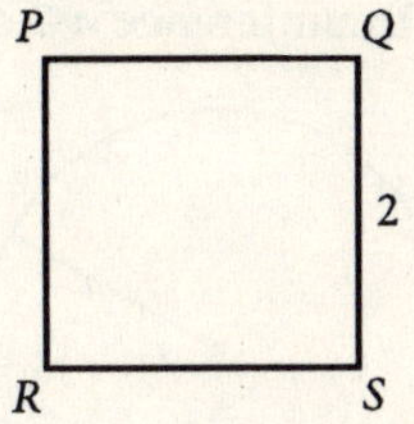

If *PQRS* is a square, all sides are the same length as *QR*. The perimeter of a square is equal to four times the length of one side.

92. Area of a Square

Area of Square = (Side)^2

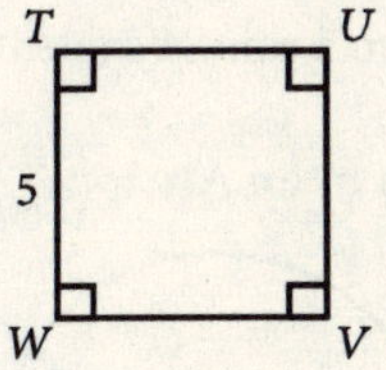

The square above, with sides of length 5, has an area of $5^2 = 25$.

93. Interior Angles of a Polygon

The **sum of the measures of the interior angles of a polygon = $(n - 2) \times 180$,** where n is the number of sides.

Sum of the Angles = $(n - 2) \times 180$

The eight angles of an octagon, for example, add up to $(8 - 2) \times 180 = 1{,}080$.

CIRCLES

94. Circumference of a Circle

Circumference = $2\pi r$

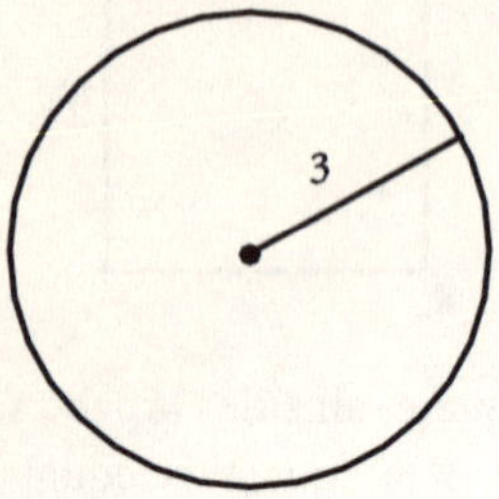

In the circle above, the radius is 3, and so the circumference is $2\pi(3) = 6\pi$.

95. Length of an Arc

An **arc** is a piece of the circumference. If n is the degree measure of the arc's central angle, then the formula is:

Length of an Arc = $\left(\frac{n}{360}\right)(2\pi r)$

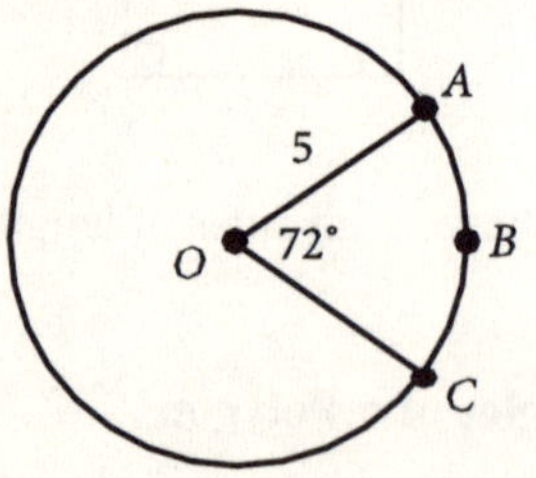

In the figure above, the radius is 5 and the measure of the central angle is 72°. The arc length is $\frac{72}{360}$ or $\frac{1}{5}$ of the circumference:

$$\left(\frac{72}{360}\right)(2\pi)(5) = \left(\frac{1}{5}\right)(10\pi) = 2\pi$$

96. Area of a Circle

Area of a Circle = πr^2

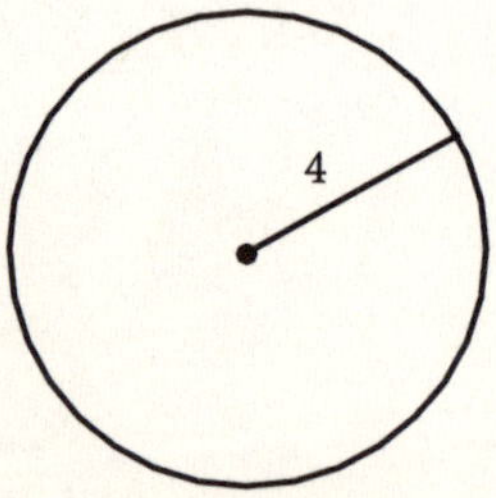

The area of the circle is $\pi(4)^2 = 16\pi$.

97. Area of a Sector

A **sector** is a piece of the area of a circle. If n is the degree measure of the sector's central angle, then the formula is:

Area of a Sector = $\left(\frac{n}{360}\right)(\pi r^2)$

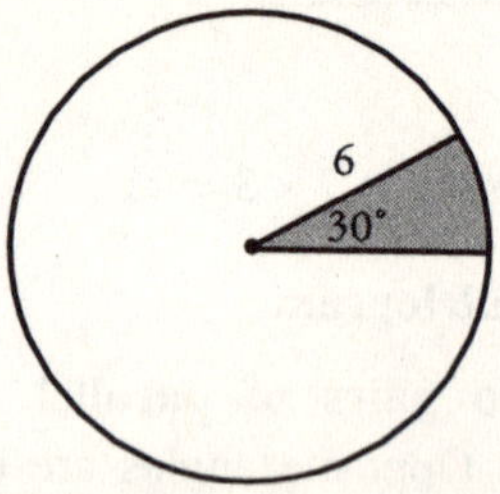

In the figure above, the radius is 6 and the measure of the sector's central angle is 30°. The sector has $\frac{30}{360}$ or $\frac{1}{12}$ of the area of the circle:

$$\left(\frac{3}{360}\right)(\pi)(6^2) = \left(\frac{1}{12}\right)(36\pi) = 3\pi$$

SOLIDS

98. Surface Area of a Rectangular Solid

The surface of a rectangular solid consists of three pairs of identical faces. To find the surface area, find the area of each face and add them up. If the length is l, the width is w, and the height is h, the formula is:

Surface Area = $2lw + 2wh + 2lh$

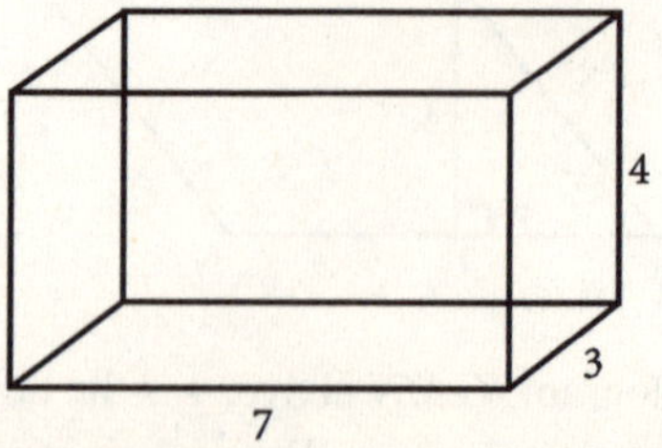

The surface area of the box above is: $2 \times 7 \times 3 + 2 \times 3 \times 4 + 2 \times 7 \times 4 = 42 + 24 + 56 = 122$

99. Volume of a Rectangular Solid

Volume of a Rectangular Solid = *lwh*

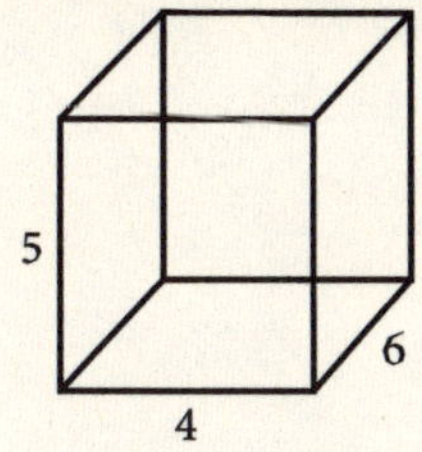

The volume of a 4-by-5-by-6 box is

$$4 \times 5 \times 6 = 120$$

A cube is a rectangular solid with length, width, and height all equal. If e is the length of an edge of a cube, the volume formula is:

Volume of a Cube = e^3

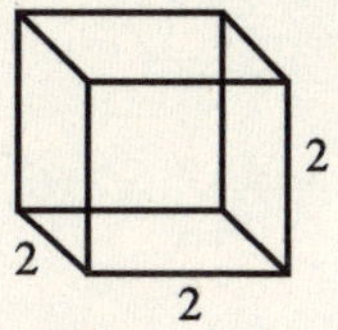

The volume of this cube is $2^3 = 8$.

100. Volume of a Cylinder

Volume of a Cylinder = $\pi r^2 h$

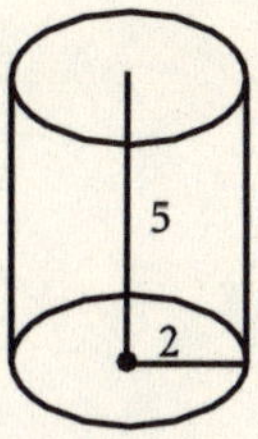

In the cylinder above, $r = 2$, $h = 5$, so:

$$\text{Volume} = \pi(2^2)(5) = 20\pi$$

ANSWERS TO THE ALL☆STAR TRIVIA QUESTIONS

page ix University of North Carolina; Geography

page xiii Martina Hingis (age 16 in 1997)

page 4 Football

page 6 24 seconds

page 7 Ted Williams (.406 in 1941)

page 8 (B) 400

page 10 Le Mans

page 15 Athens, Greece; Atlanta, Georgia

page 19 The Minnesota Vikings (*indomitable: fearless, unconquerable*)

page 21 Dunking (*eliminated: rid*)

page 23 George W. Bush (*malapropism: humorous misuse of words*)

page 24 Cycling (*velodrome:* from the French *velo* for bike)

page 29 Sailing (*tack (v.): to change the direction of a sailing ship; tack (n.): a sharp flat-headed nail*)

page 30 ELDEN Woods' nickname is TIGER.

page 33 Categories, Bridge Type #4 (A DOUBLE is a type of HIT.)

page 34 Deion Sanders

page 37 (B) baseball : glove (Only answer (B) has a strong bridge: A *glove* is a piece of equipment used in *baseball*. Using this same bridge, a CESTA, or basket, is a piece of equipment used in JAI ALAI. Correct!)

page 42 (C) fitting

page 44 (E) (Johnson's being stripped of a medal is a *stark*—meaning "firm," "sharp," or "bare"—example of the *pitfalls* of drugs. *Noisome* (A) means "stinking, putrid"; in (C), something *banal* is something trite.)

page 47 Dale Earnhardt

page 48 (D) unassisted

page 51 (B) (Here, you're looking for an answer that describes the poor performance of the 76ers, so you can immediately eliminate (D) and (E)—their 9-73 record was hardly *exemplary* or *outstanding*. In (A) *truculent* means "deadly" or "cruel," which doesn't quite fit, nor does (C)'s *querulous,* or "irritable." But an *anemic* (bloodless or lifeless) season would certainly describe an *egregious* (conspicuously bad) season.)

page 56 True

page 60 Lance Armstrong

page 61 Nine-iron

page 65 John Wooden (*inducted: placed ceremoniously*)

page 66 Wayne Gretzky

page 71 Carl Lewis (9 medals)

page 72 Brandi Chastain

page 76 Casey Stengel, Yogi Berra, Dallas Green, or Joe Torre

page 78 10

page 84 12

page 87 (C) 63 yards (The record was set by New Orleans Saints kicker Tom Dempsey in 1970, and tied by Denver Broncos kicker Jason Elam in 1998.)

page 88 Wrestling

page 92 (B) 70 (You could set up and solve the equation $x + (x - 4) = 136$, or you could try backsolving. You can eliminate (A), (D), and (E) immediately, and then plug in the choices for (B) and (C) to see which works. Either way, you get 70.)

page 95 200

page 97 Lou Gehrig (23 grand slams)

page 100 Hakeem Olajuwon

page 103 Detroit Red Wings

page 109 (A)

page 114 True

page 116 Rocky Marciano

page 119 Babe Ruth

page 124 Muggsy Bogues (5'3")

page 127 Carl Yastrzemski

page 129 Miami Dolphins

page 132 $6\frac{6}{7}$ mph. (Try picking numbers. Pick a number that is divisible by both rates of speed. Assume that the park is 24 miles from the jogger's home. (Okay, not realistic, but work with us—who says the SAT is realistic?) It will take her 3 hours to run to the park at 8 mph and 4 hours to run home at 6 mph. Therefore, she ran 48 miles (to the park and back) in 7 hours. The rate formula is $r \times t = d$ or $r = \frac{d}{t}$. So, $r = \frac{48}{7}$ or $6\frac{6}{7}$ mph.)

page 135 Arthur Ashe

page 137 63 (Wilt Chamberlain's record is 100 points, and when you plug that into the Percent formula, you get 63% × 100 (Chamberlain's record) = Michael Jordan's points scored, or 63.)

page 138 0.004 (That's about 1 in 2,500, so keep studying!)

page 141 Bo Jackson, in 1989

page 144 Cal Ripken, Jr.

page 147 Don Larsen

page 149 Skateboarding and snowboarding

page 151 1,080

page 153 $45\sqrt{2}$ (Draw the diagonals and use the Pythagorean theorem to get $x^2 + x^2 = 90^2$, where x is the distance between "third base" and the pitcher's mound as well as between the mound and home plate.)

page 155 Technical Knock-Out

page 161 Nancy Lopez

page 162 Archie Griffin, in 1974 and 1975

page 165 About \$17,000; \$24,000; \$28,000; \$43,000. (Those who earn a Master's, Ph.D., M.D., or J.D. earn \$65,000 and up.)

page 167 Walter Payton (275 yards)

page 168 $\frac{9}{8}\pi$ cubic inches (Use the Volume formula: $V = \pi r^2 h = \pi\left(\frac{3}{2}\right)^2 \frac{1}{2} = \frac{9}{8}\pi$)

page 170 Rebecca Lobo

page 172 Baseball

page 176 Pat Summitt (University of Tennessee Lady Vols)

page 177 The Banana Slugs

page 181 Notre Dame

page 182 10 feet

page 185 Sadaharu Oh (868 homers)

page 190 3

page 192 Dan O'Brien

page 194 True (He was a third-round draft choice.)

page 196 High jump

page 198 UCLA (88 games, 1970–1974)

page 200 Yogi Berra

page 266 Fencing (*foil (v.): to defeat, thwart, or frustrate; foil (n.): a light fencing sword*) page 268 Gymnastics (*unprecedented: novel, new, unexampled*)

page 270 Satchel Paige (*eulogized: praised highly in a public speech*)

page 271 Franco Harris (*immaculate: spotless, free from error*)

page 272 Paul Krause, with 81 (*intercept: to stop or interrupt the progress or course of*)

page 273 Wrigley Field (*illumination: lighting*)

page 274 Willy Stargell (*immortalize: to cause to live or exist forever*)

page 274 (C) Jack Nicklaus (*cognomen: nickname, family name*)

page 275 The Preakness (*penultimate: next to last*)

page 276 Dr. James Naismith (*progenitor: originator, forefather, ancestor in a direct line*)

page 277 Tiger Woods, 2000–2001 (*consecutive: successive, following after one another*)

page 278 Sir Edmund Hillary and Tenzing Norkay, in 1953 (*summit: top, peak*)

page 279 Kareem Abdul-Jabbar, with 38,387 career points (*invincible: unbeatable*)

page 280 Arizona, in 1997 (*voracious: having a huge appetite, eager*)

page 281 Muhammad Ali (*verbose: wordy*)

page 282 Grant Hill and Jason Ridd (*rookie: novice, beginner*)

page 283 New York Yankees (*adroit: skillful, accomplished, highly competent*)

How Did We Do? Grade Us.

Thank you for choosing a Kaplan book. Your comments and suggestions are very useful to us. Please answer the following questions to assist us in our continued development of high-quality resources to meet your needs.

The Kaplan book I read was: ______________________________

My name is: ______________________________

My address is: ______________________________

____

My e-mail address is: ______________________________

What overall grade would you give this book? (A) (B) (C) (D) (F)

How relevant was the information to your goals? (A) (B) (C) (D) (F)

How comprehensive was the information in this book? (A) (B) (C) (D) (F)

How accurate was the information in this book? (A) (B) (C) (D) (F)

How easy was the book to use? (A) (B) (C) (D) (F)

How appealing was the book's design? (A) (B) (C) (D) (F)

What were the book's strong points? ______________________________

How could this book be improved? ______________________________

Is there anything that we left out that you wanted to know more about?

Would you recommend this book to others? ☐ YES ☐ NO

Other comments: ______________________________

____

____

Do we have permission to quote you? ☐ YES ☐ NO

Thank you for your help. Please tear out this page and mail it to:

Dave Chipps, Managing Editor
Kaplan Educational Centers
888 Seventh Avenue
New York, NY 10106

Or, you can submit your comments electronically by using Kaplan's online feedback form at http://www.kaptest.com/customer-service/lvl5_comments.jhtml

Thanks!

SIXTY · YEARS · OF · BUILDING · FUTURES KAPLAN 60